A COGNITIVE THEORY OF LEARNING
Research on Hypothesis Testing

THE EXPERIMENTAL PSYCHOLOGY SERIES

Arthur W. Melton · Consulting Editor

MELTON AND MARTIN · *Coding Processes in Human Memory, 1972*

MCGUIGAN AND LUMSDEN · *Contemporary Approaches to Conditioning and Learning, 1973*

ANDERSON AND BOWER · *Human Associative Memory, 1973*

GARNER · *The Processing of Information and Structure, 1974*

MURDOCK · *Human Memory: Theory and Data, 1974*

KINTSCH · *The Representation of Meaning in Memory, 1974*

KANTOWITZ · *Human Information Processing: Tutorials in Performance and Cognition, 1974*

LEVINE · *A Cognitive Theory of Learning: Research on Hypothesis Testing, 1975*

A COGNITIVE THEORY OF LEARNING
Research on Hypothesis Testing

MARVIN LEVINE

*State University of New York
at Stony Brook*

 LAWRENCE ERLBAUM ASSOCIATES, PUBLISHERS

1975   Hillsdale, New Jersey

DISTRIBUTED BY THE HALSTED PRESS DIVISION OF

JOHN WILEY & SONS

New York   Toronto   London   Sydney

Lawrence Erlbaum Associates, Inc., Publishers
62 Maria Drive
Hillsdale, New Jersey 07642

Distributed solely by Halsted Press Division
John Wiley & Sons, Inc., New York

Library of Congress Cataloging in Publication Data

Levine, Marvin J   1928–
    Hypothesis testing: a cognitive theory of learning.

    Bibliography: p.
    Includes indexes.
    1. Discrimination learning.   I. Title.
LB1059.L46   153.1'528   75-5561
ISBN 0-470-53126-6

Printed in the United States of America

To

Tillie,
Laurie,
and Todd

CONTENTS

PREFACE

Originally, this book was to be a monograph describing my research of the past decade. I intended to bring together several scattered representations and experimental analyses of Hypothesis Theory. The plan was modified, however, by experiences with my graduate course on Human Learning. I found that the historical approach helped justify to the students the shift from a behavioral to a more cognitive formulation. Some of the seemingly peculiar restrictions in that formulation were better rationalized. The historical approach, furthermore, introduced students to the contributions of many of the major learning theorists, contributions seen in their proper context. Although this book has a narrower focus than that course—the emphasis here is not on the entire field of learning, but upon one sub-area—I nevertheless felt that the historical approach would provide an equally useful background for the review of my research.

The upshot is a book in two parts, a history and a monograph. Both parts have been written from a personal orientation. Indeed, I think of the result as a memoir. Even in the historical portion my aim was not to achieve impersonal thoroughness. Rather, I wanted to present the trends and events as I, an active researcher in the field, had experienced them. Thus, little is said here about the contributions to cognitive theorizing of the psycholinguists or the psychophysiologists, many and important though these contributions have been. It is simply that their influence upon the shape of the theory was not felt directly by me. Other authors, setting out to write the same sort of history, could describe, I am sure, a different panorama. I would submit, however, that the currents that moved me are not in a minor tributary. A glance at the list of reprint-authors will show that the contributors to this tradition constitute a veritable Who's Who of Learning Theory.

Nevertheless, the work is like a case history. As such, it contains more than a history and description of Hypothesis Theory. I have tried to include the background influences upon the research. These cover both the intellectual stimulation from colleagues and the homier events—a comment by a student, an incident with a subject—upon which inspiration occasionally depended.

Early in the project I decided that it would be foolish to rewrite all the articles. I have, instead, reprinted several, both to be sensible and to provide the reader with the authentic atmosphere of the original works. Each section, then, consists of an essay with illustrative reprints. A small amount of excerpting has been performed on these articles. Data analyses, digressions, and footnotes that have neither contemporary bearing nor relevance to the history have been deleted, as have sections redundant with earlier material. Care was always taken, of course, to maintain continuity within the article and to retain the author's primary ideas.

Many people deserve my gratitude. My students have contributed unstintingly their enthusiasm, ideas, and energy. My secretary, Mrs. M. Patricia Hallinan, kept me from falling too far behind schedule with the manuscript. I particularly wish to acknowledge the assistance from the National Institute of Mental Health. Their generosity, in the form of grant No. MH 11857, greatly facilitated my research and this book.

M. L.

A COGNITIVE THEORY OF LEARNING
Research on Hypothesis Testing

PART I
THE RISE AND FALL AND RISE OF HYPOTHESIS THEORY

The study of the learning process follows straightforward procedures: The scientist constructs a simple task, has Ss learn this task, and records aspects of the behavior that, he believes, reveal important details of the learning process. One large class of such tasks involves having S make one of a few (typically two) responses to a large variety of stimuli. The experimenter specifies the correct response to any one of the stimuli by some simple rule. Characteristic tasks within this class are discrimination learning and concept learning.

The theory to be presented in these pages will be of S's performance in these concept- and discrimination-learning tasks. Historically, there have been two major theories concerning the learning observed. One of these is a conditioning theory, which holds that something akin to instrumental conditioning and extinction accounts for the learning. The other is that Ss test hypotheses in this situation and learn by searching for and finding the correct rule. These theories clearly conflicted with each other, and each theory had its own eminent proponents. In recent years, the bulk of the research has been performed with the adult human as S. With this S hypothesis-testing theory (also referred to as Hypothesis Theory, or, more simply, as H theory) has come to predominate. Today, it is fair to say, H theory is preeminent in the field of adult human learning.

This section traces this history of H theory. It entails reviewing the confrontation with conditioning theory, since the debate is part of that history. The stress, however, will be on the emergence of H theory. The section begins with a comment published in 1929. Earlier work on the topic, especially that done with human Ss, never connected with the subsequent tradition. It never survived, so to speak, the behaviorist onslaught. The history, then, is unusual in that the origins of the present work are at a clear starting point.

1

1
THE BEGINNING

In the late 1920's Karl Lashley was investigating, by the method of ablation, brain functions in the learning processes of rats. One of the tasks presented was a simultaneous brightness discrimination in which the S faced two paths, one marked by a bright circle, the other by a dark circle. The two circles varied from path to path in the typical random manner from trial to trial, and the S had to learn that the path marked by the brighter circle consistently led to food. In the volume describing this research, Lashley (1929), as a casual aside, stated ". . . in the discrimination box, responses to position, to alternation, or to cues from the experimenter's movements usually precede the reactions to the light and represent attempted solutions which are within the rat's customary range of activity [p. 135]." He added, "The form of the learning curve is the more significant when considered in relation to such behavior. In many cases it strongly suggests that the actual association is formed very quickly and that both the practice preceding and the errors following are irrelevant to the actual formation of the association." After describing some of the effects of such "attempted solutions" upon the shape of the learning curve, he concluded "There is no present way to record such behavior [position or alternation habits] objectively, and I can present the description only as an impression from the training of several hundred animals in these problems. Nevertheless, I believe that the picture will be a familiar one to all who have had experience in training animals in the Yerkes box and that it justifies us in interpreting the discrimination habit as a simple association acquired only after a number of more familiar solutions have been tried unsuccessfully. [p. 136]."

An occasional musing of this sort hardly presages an important tradition, but Lashley's conclusion effectively piqued one young researcher. David Krech (né Krechevsky), a student at New York University, was inspired by Lashley's challenge. Krech has recently described the circumstances that led him to embrace this problem.* The description provides a clear instance of the interplay between

*Personal communication. From a manuscript prepared for a forthcoming volume of *The History of Psychology in Autobiography.*

the happenstance of daily life and scientific accomplishment. He tells us that during his senior year (1929–1930) at college he started running rats with the use of a four-unit discrimination apparatus. He then writes:

> During that winter I fell ill with the "flu," was paid a visit by "my girl" who came bearing a sick-bed gift, and I was then and there launched on my "hypothesis-in-rats" phase—a phase which was to last almost ten years. The gift which I received was Lashley's *Brain Mechanisms and Intelligence* which had just been published in 1929. Because the book had been given by "Her" and because, being in bed with the "flu," I could do nothing but read, I read Lashley most carefully—much more carefully than was (or is) my wont. I read the book so carefully that I found therein a crucial "incidental" passage, unnoticed by all reviewers, which almost got me out of bed shouting, Eureka!

Krech here refers to the first passage cited above from Lashley, that rats show systematic patterns that represent attempted solutions. After noting Lashley's further comment, that "there is no present way to record such behavior objectively," Krech writes:

> Well, I also had trained several animals in discrimination problems, and I experienced a delightful shock of recognition, for now that Lashley had expressed it that way, this was precisely my impression also! But—and this is what made me burn with something more than the "flu"—I thought I saw a clear and simple way "to record such behavior objectively." And, further, I thought I saw that if my hunch turned out to be correct, my data would necessitate a radical re-examination of some of the most firmly held notions and assumptions of contemporary (1930) learning theory. It was with difficult impatience that I waited out my "flu" to get to my box, my rats, my data. When I finally did, my hunch turned out to be bountifully correct.

One other detail from Krech's autobiography is of interest for the history of Hypothesis Theory. It reveals the christening of the movement. Krech had moved from N.Y.U. to Berkeley for further graduate work. He describes his first meeting with his new mentor:

> Tolman ushered me into his office and immediately imprinted me on him by asking me to tell him about my Master's research. I told him, but not at length, for I had no sooner given a bare outline of my findings when he caught fire and jumped out of his seat and practically shouted out "Hypothesis in rats!" And from then on we jabbered and talked and plotted experiments. Years later (perhaps twenty or more) when I reminded Tolman of this, he insisted that the word "hypothesis" was my own. I know full well it was his and I have my Master's Thesis as documentary evidence. In 101 pages there I write of "attempted solutions" and "position habits," but never of "hypotheses." It is quite true that I quickly accepted Tolman's 1931 suggestion and "Hypotheses in rats" soon did become my own.

Krech's work culminated in an early series of articles (Krechevsky, 1932a, 1933a, 1933b) of which Reading No. 1 is representative.

Reading No. 1

'HYPOTHESIS' VERSUS 'CHANCE' IN THE PRE-SOLUTION PERIOD IN SENSORY DISCRIMINATION LEARNING*

By I. Krechevsky

In a previous paper (Krechevsky, 1932a) it was pointed out that a re-examination of the data obtained from sensory discrimination experiments necessitates the adoption of a new description of learning. It was found that instead of considering the first part of 'learning' as consisting of random, haphazard behavior, we must recognize that the animal, during that period, is responding in an orderly, systematic manner. He is attempting various solutions and giving them up when they fail, until he hits finally upon the 'correct' one. The present paper presents part of the experimental evidence for such a thesis.

PROCEDURE

Apparatus

The apparatus used was a modification of Stone's (1928) multiple-unit discrimination box. The box consisted of four equal units, each unit presenting to the animal one discrimination and each unit continuous with the other.

Figure 1 shows the ground plan for the whole apparatus. The animal is started from a small 'home' cage just outside the entrance to the first box. The door, operated by a gravity-string arrangement, opens up into passageway x–y. $g1$ and $g2$ are metal guards serving to force the animal in a straight line toward the stimulus panel a–e. The mid-part of the box $(afle)$ contains the two stimulus chambers. Triangle po is a metal partition which not only serves to separate the two chambers, ab and ce, but is also so constructed as to prevent any light rays,

*Adapted from the *University of California Publications in Psychology*, 1932, **6**, 27-44. Originally published by the University of California Press; reprinted by permission of the author and of The Regents of the University of California.

5

FIG. 1

entering from the second unit through door *mn,* from reaching the animal in the vestibule *g1–g2.* It also serves to prevent the possibility of the animal's detecting the presence of the obstruction *(door d2)* in either of the two alleys.

Door *d2* swings on a pivot at *o,* so that, at the will of the experimenter, alley *ab* or *ce* can become the correct alley and the other, the cul-de-sac. In figure 1 the door is so arranged as to make *ab* the correct alley. When the animal enters the correct alley he is allowed to pass through pathway *mn* and into the next unit where he is presented with the very same situation as in the preceding unit. Immediately after entering the next alley, the door of the next box, corresponding to door *x–y,* is dropped so as to prevent any retracing.

For the most part the floor plan of this box is quite similar to Stone's apparatus except for a few insignificant differences in dimensions. In arranging the stimulus panel, however, a radical departure was made from Stone's apparatus. Figure 2 is a three-dimensional drawing of the stimulus chambers.[1]

In the hurdle discrimination set-up the only differentiating factor between both alleys was the presence of the hurdle. The animal actually had to climb this obstruction in order to gain entrance into the alley. The presence of the hurdle was meant to indicate the correct alley, i.e., the hurdle was the positive stimulus. While we are primarily interested here in the hurdle results, perhaps it would be appropriate to discuss this apparatus as used in setting up a brightness discrimination as well, since, in an experiment to be reported later and attacking the same general problem as here presented, brightness discrimination was used with this apparatus.

In making the correct choice (brightness discrimination) the animal is not only forced to go toward the light (as is the case in Stone's box) *but he is actually forced to go into and through the light as well.* This difference in procedure has some theoretical significance and one which, while it seems to be more and more recognized in actual practice, has not yet, by the very experimenters who make use of it, been explicitly acknowledged.

[1]The section labeled *abcd* is in the same position as the section similarly labeled in figure 1. In figure 2, *afgb* and *ckle* are the two tunnels through which the rat must run. These tunnels are divided into an upper and lower part by a plate of translucent glass at *fg* running parallel with the floor of the box. The upper part contains the electric lights and the lower is the tunnel through which the animal runs. The tops of the two stimulus boxes are covered. Most of the light is directed through the translucent frosted glass plates over the tunnels *afgb* or *ckle,* as the case may be; i.e., when the apparatus is used for setting up a brightness discrimination or else, through both tunnels as in the hurdle discrimination. At points *h2, 3, 4* and *1,* holes were bored which permitted the insertion of a hurdle at the entrance to either alley, as is indicated in figure 2.

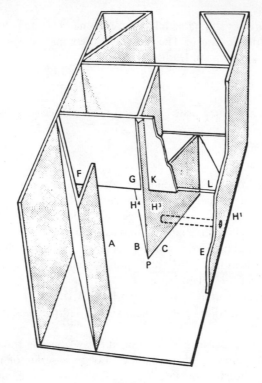

FIG. 2

The Gestaltists have been most forward with their criticisms of the usual experimental set-up used in studying animal learning on the ground that too often the animal is required to build up a wholly artificial connection between a given stimulus and a given response, with the result that the consequent performance does not give us a true picture of what the animal can do in a more 'natural' and reasonable problem situation. The stimulus, as in the case of the usual discrimination box and as is also the case in the Stone's box, is not something that is *intrinsically* connected with either the animal's response or his 'reward', it is merely something the experimenter brings *ab extra* and imposes, or wishes the animal to impose, upon the situation. In discussing this very point Köhler (1925) writes,

> The electric shock, for instance, applied to the legs, is not intimately connected to the task of getting a red spot as 'the negative stimulus'. There is only a very loose connection between them in space and time. If that spot *itself* would make a sudden movement against the animal and so frighten it . . . we should certainly have a situation much nearer the animal's learning in common life and a more efficient one.

It is apparent that in the hurdle discrimination set-up we have the same desirable situation. Here the animal must not only see the hurdle and travel toward it, but he must also actually *do* something with it. Hurdling the obstacle is an intrinsic and necessary part of the response. The set-up, in general, is one which should encourage rapid discrimination learning.

Animals

Forty previously untrained male albino rats, about three months of age, were used as subjects.

Method

No animal was used for experimental purposes until three weeks had elapsed from the time he had been received in the laboratory. Thus every animal was given a period in which to adapt himself to the general laboratory conditions. During these three weeks of acclimatization the animals were fed once a day, at about the same hour that their training series was to be run, in a special feeding cage. Their diet consisted of 'McCullum's Mixture' plus a semiweekly ration of lettuce. Fresh water was always available.

All runs were made at night. A night's work consisted of ten trials per animal. This program was adhered to until the animal satisfied the established norm for learning.

During the runs the experimenter was seated away from the apparatus and was able to observe the behavior of the animal through a series of mirrors which allowed a full view of the box and its contents from point of observation. The only light in the room, during experimentation, came from within the apparatus itself. Since the top of the apparatus was covered with a fine mesh wire, it would have been almost impossible for the animal to be able to see anything outside of the box. The mirror arrangement also obviated the necessity for the experimenter to move about during the run.

Special care was taken in drawing up the order of presentation of stimuli, to avoid introducing any but chance orders. It will be seen that the situation in this discrimination box is more complicated in this respect than it is in the single-unit discrimination box. In the latter case it is merely necessary that the positive stimulus be on the right as often as on the left, but in the present case it is not only necessary that the total number of stimuli be equated for their position, but also that each unit be equated for that factor. The order of presentation for ten trials is given below:

Trials	1	2	3	4	5	6	7	8	9	10
Unit 1	r	l	l	l	r	r	r	l	r	l
Unit 2	r	l	r	r	l	l	r	l	r	r
Unit 3	l	l	r	r	l	r	l	r	l	r
Unit 4	r	r	l	r	l	l	r	l	r	l

This order sufficed for ten trials or for one day's runs. Every day the same order was repeated. It is highly improbable that the rats learned this order, since the series contains 40 items and in no case was any rat presented with the series more than 12 times. Every rat was, of course, given the same series.

At the end of each trial the animal found in his food box a cube of milk-soaked bread. This cube was cut to a predetermined standard size which helped to equate somewhat the reward received by the different animals and the reward received by the same animal from trial to trial.

In keeping records of the performance, the following factors were considered: *(1)* ERRORS. An error was counted if the animal inserted his head into the wrong chamber. Complete entry was not necessary. *(2)* POSITION RESPONSES. Not only was a record made of the animal's response on the basis of the 'correct' stimulus, i.e., whether he entered a blind or a true alley, but the side of the box (left or right) was also noted. *(3)* NORM FOR LEARNING. The problem was considered mastered when the animal completed five errorless runs, that is, twenty consecutive errorless discriminations.

RESULTS AND DISCUSSION

In order to obtain significant data in attacking our problem, namely, the relation of the shape of the curve to the various 'interfering' position habits, we could not content ourselves with plotting the usual type of curve. The method we finally adopted, and the reasons therefore have been stated in detail in the previous paper (Krechevsky, 1932a), but for convenience we might briefly sum up the process here.

After the animals had mastered the discrimination problem the entire performance of each animal was individually analyzed, and the resulting learning curves were individually plotted. For each rat the following items were determined: *(1)* the number of 'errors' the animal made each day; *(2)* the number of turns to the left; *(3)* the number of turns to the right; *(4)* the number of turns which were in keeping with an 'alternating' scheme; and *(5)* the number of turns in keeping with a 'perseverance' scheme.

In considering the resulting curves one must be certain that the locus of any point on any one curve is a significant one. That is, since we are graphing almost every response of the animal it is imaginable that by a certain combination of circumstances some one curve will always appear to show systematic behavior yet actually be a chance fluctuation. To meet this criticism, the extreme limits beyond which chance alone would very rarely send any one curve were determined by the use of the formula $\sigma = \sqrt{PQ/N}$. That is, if chance were the sole determining influence for any one curve, that curve should never go beyond 50 per cent $\pm 3\sigma$. Doing this we find the σ for 40 chances (one day's work) to be 7.8 per cent, which would give, for the extreme limits of chance fluctuations 50 $\pm$ 21.4 per cent, or 28.6 and 71.4 per cent. The graphs have so been constructed as to concern only the upper limit, i.e., 71.4 per cent. This limit, to facilitate inspection of the curve, has been indicated by drawing a line at the proper point across each graph.

Now, if any of the resulting curves should go beyond this limit we can be fairly certain that such a change is owing to some systematic cause. If, therefore, any of the 'position' curves go beyond their chance zone limit, while the 'error' curve remains on the 50 per cent line we would be justified in saying that, during that period, the animal is responding to the situation in a *systematic spatial* manner; then, if that spatial curve goes back to the 50 per cent line and the 'hurdle' curve goes beyond the chance limit and finally reaches 100 per cent efficiency, we have a perfectly objective demonstration of Lashley's suggestion.

We are now ready for a discussion of the actual graphs. Out of the 40 graphs, figures 3 to 6 represent samples of the most clear-cut curves.

In figure 3 we find the rat, for perhaps the first five days, running according to 'chance', that is, his 'error' score remains well within the pure chance zone; then, during the sixth and seventh days he very rapidly brings his error score down, indicating complete mastery of the problem. A consideration of the broken-line curve, however (the curve representing the animal's turns to the right side of the box), shows that such a description is misleading and entirely untrue. The animal, during the first five days was *not* running by 'chance'; the animal, during that period was behaving in a definite, systematic manner, *but on a spatial basis*. During the so-called 'chance' period the animal adopted, brought to near-perfection, and then surrendered a perfectly legitimate and unified 'attempt at solution'. His choices on the basis of the presence or absence of the hurdle represent a second systematic series of responses, which was preceded by a different, but nevertheless just as unified series of responses.

In this specific case then, learning did not consist of haphazard chance responses which finally (through the action of the various Laws of Learning) became systematic, but learning consisted of one systematic series of responses followed by another.

Figure 4 represents the performance of another animal who also happened to show, as a previous 'attempt at solution', a right position habit. The implications here are also clear and need no further discussion.

In figures 5 and 6 the 'attempted' solutions are an 'alternating' and 'perseverance' habit respectively.[2]

A more detailed analysis of these curves strengthens the suggestion that the interpretation here proposed is a valid one.

A point that should be noticed in these curves is the close similarity between the

---

[2]The chance zone for these two habits will, of course, differ slightly from the chance zone for the left or right position habits, because that for the latter habits is based on 40 choices, and that for the former habits on but 30 choices, since the animal's first choice at every trial could neither be considered as 'alternating' nor 'perseverance'. Only the last three choices of each trial were therefore considered. This difference in number of choices gives, as the σ for the last two habits 9 per cent with the limit as 77 per cent instead of 7.14 per cent.

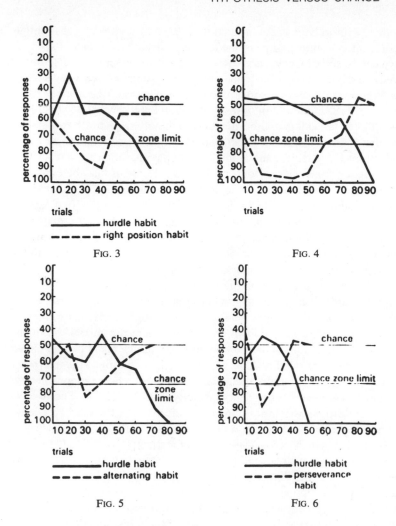

FIG. 3

FIG. 4

FIG. 5

FIG. 6

rapidity with which the animal builds up his position habit and that with which he builds up his hurdle habit. Thus in figure 3 it took the animal four days to bring his right position habit to the point of greatest efficiency, and it also took him four days to bring the hurdle habit to the same degree of efficiency. (It is obvious that this is so only when we consider the hurdle curve as beginning where the position curve leaves off.) The same is true for the other curves. This striking fact is a further substantiation of the assumption that the adoption of the various position habits is a real phenomenon of the learning act and not some 'chance' epi-phenomenon; as real, at any rate, as is the adoption of the hurdle discrimination by the rat, the same organism showing in either behavior the same characteristics of speed and efficiency.

Another point to be made is in relation to the 'difficulty' of a discrimination problem and the resulting shape of the learning curve. It may be pointed out that the 'typical' discrimination curve is obtained only where the discrimination involved is a more or less difficult one; where the problem is 'easy' no such curve results. We can see, from our proposed relationship between the shape of the curve and the animals' adoption of the various position habits, why one should expect that very thing. We call that discrimination problem 'easy' for the animal which requires but a few trials for its establishment. In order to establish any sensory discrimination habit rapidly the animal must 'pay attention to' ('react to') the correct stimulus from the very outset. That would mean that the experimental situations were of such nature as to make outstanding and most obvious the 'correct' stimulus. This would further mean that the animal's first 'attempted solution' was the correct one and therefore an analysis of his performance would reveal no other systematic 'attempted solutions', with the result that his 'error' curve would never remain on the 50 per cent line, but would show the same characteristics as the maze-learning curve, i.e. steady improvement.

Figure 7 shows a concrete example of the argument proposed above. Here the curve for the hurdle habit is atypical, it does not show the usual picture, but rather resembles more closely the curve obtained from the light-dark discrimination (see fig. 9), the 'easy' discrimination. It appears that here the animal 'hit upon' the correct stimulus from almost the very beginning with the result that he solved the problem with extreme rapidity. This would mean, according to the interpretation suggested above, that the animal did not at first attempt other 'wrong' solutions as, for example, spatial solutions. That is exactly what happened. The two curves representing the four possible position habits stay very close to the 50 per cent line, although they are not forced to do so by virtue of the locus of the hurdle curve. In other words it would have been possible, statistically considered, for the two position curves to go well beyond the 50 per cent line at the same time that the hurdle curve was at the 70 per cent line; nevertheless they failed to do so, the animal was not attempting a position solution.

It was remarked above, when introducing our curves, that we were reproducing only some of the most clear-cut ones. Not all of the remaining curves show quite the same things as those which we have reproduced. Out of the 40 curves, perhaps 15 are of the very same type as illustrated in figures 3 to 6 inclusive. The others are more confusing in implications. In figure 8 we have an example of a curve which does not fit in with our description of the others. While this curve is of the positively accelerated type, and in that respect shows a similarity to the others, nevertheless the curves representing the *position habits* for this animal do not show the same characteristics as the other curves; none of the four possible position habits going beyond a chance fluctuation. This curve, and it must be admitted there are a number of them, need not be interpreted however as contradictory to our general thesis. As a matter of fact, a close analysis of these very curves strengthens our hypothesis. Regarding figure 8 more closely it will be seen that while neither

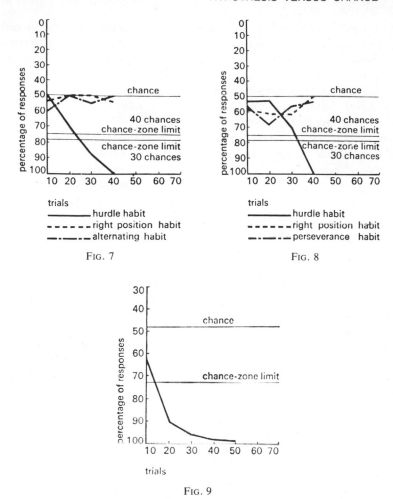

Fig. 7

Fig. 8

Fig. 9

the right position habit nor the perseverance habit ever get beyond the chance zone, the two curves do depart a little from the 50 per cent line, and depart from that line at the same time. On the second day both curves reach their maximum together. This suggests that at any one time (that is, over the space of one day's trials) the animal was responding not to one position habit, but to two, alternately. Further analysis proves this to be quite a tenable view. Upon inspecting the animal's individual responses more closely it was found that of *the ten responses* (on the second day) *which did not fit in with the perseverance scheme eight were choices to the right!* Every time the animal departed from his perservance scheme he went to the right side of the box. Only two times out of all 40 possibilities did he make a response which fitted in with neither 'hypothesis'.[3] This vacillation on the part of the rat, between a perseverance habit and a right position habit, would prevent the curve representing either habit from reaching a point outside the chance zone. Such behavior, however, is not different from the other behavior we have analyzed. In this case the animal, instead of making but one systematic attempt at solution before hitting upon the correct one, tries several, and each for a short period of time only. Even in these curves then, we fail to find room for haphazard and non-unified behavior patterns existing at many points of the learning process.

An analysis such as has just been made lays itself open to serious statistical criticisms. Essentially what we have done, the argument may be, is that by considering *every* response as part of some systematic form of behavior, we have of course eliminated, *ipso facto,* the possibility of finding any 'chance' responses. Such a criticism is difficult to meet here. All our learning curves are so short as to make it impossible to deal with our data in the statistical manner required in order to prove that our *combinations* of these various position habits do not lead to artifacts, but are statistically justified. In another experiment, the set-up was one which gave us longer learning curves and more data with the result that we were able to demonstrate quite definitely the validity of our method of combining the responses.

Throughout this paper we have been forced to present the data of individual animals only. Nowhere have we been able to call upon group results. The reason for this is obvious. An analysis such as we have made here would be impossible if we were to content ourselves with obtaining hypothetical averages of the hypothetical average rat and draw hypothetical learning curves. We feel that real and valid information in reference to the behavior of organisms can be obtained only by studying the actual individual *as* an individual. Such a method however has the obvious drawback of appearing non-quantitative in nature. We have attempted to devise some manner of presenting these results as group results. The value of such procedure is to suggest that the behavior, of which up to now we have merely given samples, is universal for the white rat.

The evidence is shown in table 1. This table was constructed in the following manner: The curve for each rat was surveyed, noting for each position habit the lowest point on the curve. (Thus for rat #810-C, figure 6, the lowest point for the perseverance habit would be 87 per cent; for the rat 51-D, figure 8, the lowest point for the right position habit would be 62 per cent and for the perseverance habit, 67 per cent, and so forth.) In table 1 are presented the frequency of occurrences of these points for the four possible position habits. Thus, five curves (from all 40) reached the 76-80 per cent line of efficiency for the right position habit, etc. *It will be seen that in all there are 36 cases of position-habit-curves going beyond the line allowed by chance (73 per cent);* twelve of these reaching an efficiency between 71

---

[3]For the use of the term 'hypothesis' to describe these various 'attempts at solution' see our introductory paper 'Hypotheses in Rats' (1932a).

TABLE 1

Percentages of Maximal Efficiency Reached by Animals in
Building Up Position Habits

Habit	71–75	76–80	81–85	86–90	91–95	95–100
Right	2	5	3	4	—	1
Left	3	1	1	—	—	—
Perseverative	4	2	—	1	—	—
Alternating	3	2	4	—	—	—
Total	12	10	8	5	—	1

and 75 per cent; ten, between 76 and 80; and 14 between 81 and 100 per cent. In other words, *the tendency to build up a systematic series of responses during the so-called period of chance is characteristic of most of the rats studied in this experiment.*

CONCLUSIONS

The characteristic form of the learning curve obtained in setting up discrimination problems was investigated in relation to the animal's tendency to form various position habits prior to mastery of the discrimination habit. Objective and quantitative evidence is presented of Lashley's (1929) suggestion that such position habits represent 'attempted solutions' on the part of the rat, and it is shown quite definitely that during that part of the learning performance, which is represented on the usual curve by an almost horizontal line at the 50 per cent point indicating no improvement, the animal is engaged in bringing to perfection various attempted solutions. After each 'wrong' solution is discarded in turn, the animal attempts another until he finally hits upon the 'correct' one. Four different such spatial 'attempts' at solution were isolated, a right-going habit, a left-going habit, a perseverance habit, and an alternating habit. The 40 animals used as subjects showed a total of 36 such habits before finally adopting the 'correct' response, a hurdle discrimination.

In the light of all the evidence presented here it is suggested that helter-skelter unorganized trial and error response as a description of the early part of the learning process is invalid, and that we must change our description of the learning process so as to recognize the existence of organized and systematic responses at *all* stages of the process.

2
THE REACTION

By the mid-1930's behaviorism was in bloom. Books by Pavlov, Watson, and Thorndike were already classics. The epoch-making work of Skinner and Hull was under way. It is not surprising, therefore, that Krechevsky's H theory, with its flagrant use of cognitive language, drew strong reaction. The most effective adversary was Kenneth W. Spence. He had just completed graduate training at Yale, where he was influenced by Hull. Spence accepted the fact that animals showed systematic patterns of responses but insisted that these patterns did not require a cognitive theory. He developed a quantitative model of discrimination learning based, instead, upon the processes of conditioning and extinction (Spence, 1936). According to the model, these processes could lead to sudden changes in systematic patters of responses. The following example schematizes Spence's model and illustrates in a simplified way the derivation of the response-pattern shifts.

Imagine a rat to be run in a T-maze in which each of the arms has a door near the choice point. The rat must push through one of the doors to reach the corresponding goal box. A discrimination problem will be presented, with Form as the solution dimension: One of the doors will have a circle on it, the other will have a triangle, with the locus of the forms varying from door to door, according to some irregular schedule. One of the forms (e.g., the circle) will always have food located in the goal box behind it. Food, then, is contingent upon response to the circle, but not to the triangle, and not to the two sides in any systematic way.

Assume the following: At the outset of the experiment the four stimulus components (left-side, right-side, triangle, circle) have some "strength," i.e., some tendency to evoke an approach response. Because of (unknown) events in the animal's history, left-side has a larger strength than the other components. Using an arbitrary numerical scale to represent the relative strengths of the components, let left-side have a strength of 20 and the other three components each have a strength of 15. Assume further that the component strengths add to each other. Thus, if on Trial 1 the circle is on the left side, then the strength of the

TABLE I

The Derivation of Response Patterns (cf. Columns D and E) from
Gradual Changes in Component Strength

	(A)			(B)	(C)		(D)	(E)
	Component strength			Location	Response strength		Response	Result
Trial	L	R	Circle	Triangle	of circle	Left	Right		
1	20	15	15	15	L	35	30	L	+
2	21	15	16	15	R	36	31	L	−
3	20	15	16	14	L	36	29	L	+
4	21	15	17	14	R	35	32	L	−
5	20	15	17	13	R	33	32	L	−
6	19	15	17	12	L	36	27	L	+
7	20	15	18	12	L	38	27	L	+
8	21	15	19	12	R	33	34	R	+
9	21	16	20	12	L	41	28	L	+
10	22	16	21	12	R	34	37	R	+
11	22	17	22	12	R	34	39	R	+

tendency to approach the left-hand door is $20+15=35$. Simultaneously, the comparable strength toward the right-hand door is $15+15=30$.

Assume, now, two rules, a Response Rule and a Conditioning Rule. The Response Rule is that the S approaches the side with the greater total strength. On Trial 1 of the present example, then, the S would turn left. The Conditioning Rule is in two parts (for conditioning and extinction): The Strength of each component responded to is changed by $+1$ when the response is rewarded, and by -1 when the response is not rewarded.

These are the essentials of the model. The numerical values are arbitrary, but it is clearly a system in which S-R strengths vary incrementally as a function of reward and nonreward. Table 1 illustrates how this system of gradual conditioning leads to a rapid shift in response patterning. The top row (Trial 1) of the table shows (A) the strengths of the four individual components, (B) that the circle is on the left-hand door, (C) the total strength for each response, (D) that, in accordance with the Response Rule, the S responds to the left side, and (E) that the response is rewarded ($+$). Applying the Conditioning Rule, i.e., adding $+1$ to the circle and left-side, yields the new component strengths, shown under column (A) in the next row. Following this routine through the series of trials yields the critical information in the Response (the next-to-last) column. It is seen there that the S will persist in running to the left side for the first seven trials. During these trials, however, the circle is gradually increasing in relative strength. By the sixth trial the circle has acquired enough strength to control responding, a condition that will continue for the remainder of the experiment (see the $+$'s in the last column). The conclusion is clear. Systematic response patterns, and an occasional, sudden change in these patterns, do not automatically invalidate a theory of gradual conditioning.

Spence's model was not only a brilliant *tour de force* but was the prototype of subsequent conditioning theories of discrimination learning. It is, therefore, worth stressing the chief characteristics of the model: *(a)* Discrimination learning arises from strengthening correct S-R relations and weakening incorrect S-R relations. *(b)* The changes in strength occur gradually with each trial. *(c) All* effective stimuli (in the present example, both the position and form components) at the time of the reinforcement are strengthened, i.e., there is no need for an attention concept. [Spence, acknowledged that Ss might make receptor adjustments that would improve reception of the stimuli. Thus, a dog might lift his ears, a rat might turn his head and fixate upon the stimulus, etc. These adjustments, or observing responses, are peripheral in nature, detectable in principle by suitable response measures, and involve no assumption about internal (neural or cognitive) selective states.] *(d)* There is no memory concept in the theory. Typically, conditioning theorists never assumed that S remembers anything from one trial to the next.*

These, then, are two reasons for the importance of Spence's article: It demonstrated that systematic patterns of responses were not damaging *per se* to conditioning models, and it embodied the essentials of conditioning models of discrimination learning. These features are inherent in the article itself. A third reason for its importance is historical: The theory influenced the nature of research during the next decade. According the Spence, the effects of reinforcement and extinction were the crucial processes. Systematic response patterns were uninteresting by-products of these processes. The clear implication was that the study of response patterns had low priority. They were, after all, merely the results of earlier unknown conditioning events. Even lower priority was explicitly produced by Spence's concluding assertion that the reversal-shift experiment was the proper task for investigation. This produced a series of such experiments in the attempt to prove that one theory or the other was wrong. This energetic dialogue, commonly called the Continuity-Noncontinuity Controversy, took the center stage. Lashley's and Krechevsky's original concern, the analysis of response patterns, was left waiting in the wings.

Many researchers contributed to this controversy with one or more reversal experiments. For each experiment performed by researchers of one theoretical persuasion, flaws were claimed by proponents of the other. In 1945 Spence, with an experiment (presented here as Reading No. 2) tailored to avoid what he felt were artifacts in previous experiments, demonstrated results consistent with the S-R position. That experiment, with one subsequently performed by his student (Ehrenfreund, 1948), effectively ended the controversy. The clarity of those experiments, and the fact that Hull's influence was then at its zenith, served to discourage interest in *H* theory. An occasional sporadic experiment was per-

---

*Lest this appear too ridiculous a generalization, it is worth noting that the term "memory" is not indexed in the major work of Hull (1943), or of Skinner (1938), or even in that more recent staple of conditioning theory, Kimble (1961).

formed, and Postman and Bruner (1948, 1952) were exploring an hypothesis theory of perception. Through the 1940's, however, when S-R theory was successful in its treatment of challenging data, and when S-R theorists dominated the field of learning, contributions to H theory went virtually unnoticed. Also, in these years the rat was the prototypic S, and the rat seemed to manifest S-R laws. An H theory of learning, therefore, went into a quiescent state.

Reading No. 2

AN EXPERIMENTAL TEST
OF THE CONTINUITY AND
NON-CONTINUITY THEORIES
OF DISCRIMINATION LEARNING*

By Kenneth W. Spence

I. INTRODUCTION

Beginning with the studies of Hamilton (1911) and Yerkes (1916), a number of investigations involving different types of situations and a variety of animal Ss have shown that the pre-solution period of learning is an organized, lawful, systematic process. Thus, in a series of experiments with rats involving soluble and unsoluble discrimination problems, Krechevsky (1932a, 1932b) demonstrated that this period was marked by the occurrence of systematic response tendencies or, as he termed them, hypotheses. These hypotheses, precisely defined by Krechevsky in statistical terms as responses which occurred within a block of trials with a frequency beyond the limits of chance expectancy, consisted in his experiments primarily of various types of spatial responses, e.g., left or right position habits, an alternating habit, etc. Employing the same statistical criterion, Spence found similar types of systematic response tendencies occurring among chimpanzees during the pre-solution period of multiple choice problems (Spence, 1939).

Contrary to the beliefs of certain recent writers (Kellogg & Wolf, 1940), then, there has been no disagreement concerning the behavioral facts. The pre-solution behavior of animals in such experimental situations as the multiple choice and discrimination problems is not a random, chance affair in the sense of being undetermined or unlawful. Instead it is to be described as consisting of systematic reactions or 'hypotheses,' if one defines this latter term in the statistical manner described above. Agreement ceases, however, over attempts at further interpretation of the phenomena.

*Adapted from the *Journal of Experimental Psychology*, 1945, **35**, 253-266. Copyright 1945 by the American Psychological Association. Reprinted by permission of the publisher.

From a suggestion originally made by Lashley (1929) has developed one theoretical interpretation of these phenomena which has come to be known as the non-continuity theory. Lashley's suggestion was that the systematic response tendencies, such as response to position in the discrimination situation, represent attempted solutions of the problem on the part of the animal. Furthermore, Lashley intimated that during the part of the practice (learning) period in which these attempts at solution were being made no association would be formed with respect to the cue stimuli. Krechevsky subsequently formulated this interpretation in the following manner:

"... Once an animal is immersed in a given problem-situation the animal selects out of the welter of possible stimuli certain sets of discriminanda to which he reacts. Each time (while 'paying attention to' this particular set of discriminanda) he makes what proves to be a 'correct' response, he learns (wrongly perhaps) something about the significance *of this particular stimulus;* each time he makes a 'wrong' response, he learns something else, *but he does not learn anything about the 'correctness' or 'wrongness' of the to-be-finally-learned set of discriminanda.* Eventually he gives up responding to his first set of discriminanda and responds to another set, and another set, etc., until he begins to respond to the relevant set. From then on, and from then only, is he learning anything about the discrimination involved, or, from then on only are his 'bonds' being strengthened, etc." (Krechevsky, 1938, p. 111).

As an alternative to this interpretation, the writer has proposed a theory based on conditioning or association principles (Spence 1936, 1937), which Krechevsky (1938) has included among the group which he has named the continuity theories in contrast to the non-continuity formulation. According to the writer's version of this type of continuity theory, discrimination learning is conceived of as a cumulative process of building up the excitatory tendency or association between the positive stimulus cue and the response of approaching it, as compared with the excitatory tendency of the negative stimulus cue, which receives only non-reinforcement, to evoke the response of approaching it. This process continues until the difference between the excitatory strengths of the two stimulus cues is sufficiently great to overshadow always any differences in excitatory strength that may exist between other aspects of the situation which happen on a particular trial to be allied in their response evoking action with one or the other of the cue stimuli. For example, the difference in the excitatory strengths of the cue stimuli to their responses must, for learning to be complete, become greater than the difference between the excitatory strengths of the position cues, e.g., the left and right alleys or food boxes.

As a critical test of this continuity theory and an alternative insight theory which was elaborated on the basis of Lashley's suggestion, the writer (Spence, 1936) proposed the following experiment. If, in a discrimination situation the significance of the stimulus cues is reversed, i.e., the positive stimulus made negative and vice versa, before the animal begins to show any learning whatever, the subsequent learning of the reversed problem would not, according to the non-continuity theory, be slowed up. The implication of the writer's continuity theory, on the other hand, was that the learning of the reversed group would be retarded when compared with a control group which did not have such initial reversed training.

The results of an already existent experiment on weight discrimination by McCulloch and Pratt (1934) were then cited by the writer as supporting the continuity type of theory and as opposed to the non-continuity theory. These investigators found that the group in which the cues were reversed subsequently required a longer time to learn than the control group. This result seemed to represent a clear cut refutation of the non-continuity type of hypothesis. But then the supporters of this viewpoint came to its defense with a variety of devices including new experimental data and restatements of the issue which completely departed from the original one (Haire, 1939d; Krechevsky, 1938).

First, Krechevsky (1937) called the McCulloch and Pratt data into question on the basis that their Ss might have been responding on the basis of two hypotheses, one of which was the weight cue. As McCulloch (1939a) was quick to point out, however, this was not possible for, with the exception of one case, their Ss did not respond more than 50 percent of the time to the positive stimulus before reversal. Obviously, then, they could not have been responding systematically to either one of the weight stimuli in combination with any other cue.

Next Krechevsky (1938) reported the results of a new experiment with visual discriminanda which were, in part, contrary to McCulloch and Pratt's findings. In a situation in which the stimulus cues were cards containing horizontal and vertical rows of black squares on a white background, an experimental group, in which the cues were reversed for 20 trials, showed no difference in speed of subsequent learning from the control group. A second experimental group given 40 trials before reversal, however, did show retardation in the subsequent learning of the reversal problem. Accepting the results of the first experimental group as supporting the non-continuity theory, Krechevsky attempted to explain away the embarrassing results of the 40-trial group on the basis of the assumption that the pre-solution period occupied less than 40 trials. Just why this assumption was made is difficult to understand. The different implicatons of the two opposing theories were originally based on the assumption that the reversal occurs "before the animal begins to show any learning *whatever* . . . ." (Spence, 1936, p. 444). All one had to do to verify the meeting of this condition was to ascertain whether the Ss had begun to respond more than chance to the positive stimulus. As both McCulloch (1939a) and Spence (1940) have pointed out, however, Krechevsky presented no evidence that his Ss were doing so. Moreover, McCulloch showed that the control group gave no evidence of responding above chance (50 percent) to the positive stimulus during trials 21-40, let alone responding systematically to it. It should be clear that the theoretical issue cannot be settled by such evasions. There is only one experimentally testable definition or criterion of the concept 'pre-solution period,' namely the occurrence of the correct systematic response tendency. The fact that the four-day group did not exhibit such a response tendency necessarily means that they were still in the pre-solution period. The results of this part of the experiment are thus seen to favor the continuity theory.

Turning now to the results of the 20-trial group, the writer has elsewhere (Spence, 1940) dealt at length with the fact that in visual situations involving form discrimination a new factor is introduced which is not present in the weight discrimination situation or in the case of brightness discrimination with the modern types of apparatus. Thus, when pulling in the differently weighted boxes, McCulloch and Pratt's Ss inevitably received discriminably different weight stimulations. Likewise, in brightness discrimination it is practically impossible for the S to respond and not receive discriminably different retinal stimulations from the two stimulus sources (assuming, of course, we have differences which are suprathreshold). In such an experiment as Krechevsky's, however, it is quite conceivable that his Ss did not receive discriminably different (proximal) visual stimulations from the two stimulus cards. Fixating the bottom portion of the stimulus cards, as the rat does at first in the Lashley jumping apparatus, the two stimulus patterns produced on its retina were very likely not discriminable. So long as the S continued this fixation, the retinal patterns of stimulation received from the two cards would not be distinguishable, and no differential learning with respect to the two cards would take place. In order for discrimination to develop in such a situation, it is necessary for the animal to learn first to make the appropriate receptor-orienting acts that will lead to the reception of the critical stimulus patterns or, to state it another way, that will lead to the reception of retinal stimulus patterns that are discriminable by the rat. Apparently in the Krechevsky experiment the Ss learned to make the appropriate receptor-orienting response sometime after the 20th trial and before the 40th.

It is obvious from the above discussion that our inability to specify the proximal retinal stimulus pattern in the case of form discrimination makes it impossible to employ this type of visual discrimination situation to settle the present theoretical issue. A more thorough analytical approach to the problem would have precluded its use in the first place. There is, nevertheless, a perfectly feasible way of testing the theoretical issue in a visual discrimination situation. It consists in the use of brightness cues rather than figure or pattern discrimination, for in the brightness problem there is no difficulty in arranging experimental conditions that will insure reception of the differential stimulus cues from the beginning of practice. Moreover, such an experiment provides a test of the theoretical issue in a learning situation in which the perceptual behavior is as simple as possible.

An investigation using brightness discrimination was recently carried out by Bollinger (1940) as a master's thesis under the writer's direction. This experiment compared the learning of a white (+) versus black (−) discrimination problem by albino rats following two different pre-learning conditions. The experimental group of Ss was trained during this period for 30 trials on the reverse problem (black positive), while the control group was run for 30 trials with 50 percent reinforcement on black and 50 percent reinforcement on white.[1] Only Ss that exhibited chance responses during this pre-learning period were run in the subsequent learning problem. The results of this experiment were in complete agreement with those of McCulloch and Pratt. Both errors and trials were greater for the experimental group than the control group. The differences were significant beyond the one percent level as shown by the values of the t statistic.

Bollinger also ran a second experiment in which the experimental group was given only 20 trials in the pre-reversal training. Again the results were contrary to the implication of the non-continuity theory, for the experimental group required a significantly greater number of trials and errors than its control group. The t statistic for errors was again significant at the one percent level while that for trials was significant at the five percent level.

II. STATEMENT OF THE PRESENT PROBLEM

In the experiment of Bollinger it was found that not all Ss exhibited a definite systematic response tendency or hypothesis during the 20 (30) trial pre-learning period. While no differences appeared in the subsequent learning of those Ss that did exhibit such hypotheses and those that did not, it was decided to conduct a further investigation to ascertain whether, in a brightness discrimination situation, any association would be set up between the color cue and the reinforced response to it during a period in which the S was exhibiting a definite hypotheses with respect to some other cue, e.g., a dominant reaction to position. In other words, if an S has a systematic position preference, does consistent differential training to the color cues (e.g., reinforcement on black, non-reinforcement on white) have any subsequent effect so far as learning to respond to these cues is concerned? Examination of the formulation of Krechevsky quoted above will be seen (1) to emphasize the presence of such hypotheses and (2) the fact that the S does not, while so responding, learn "anything about the 'correctness' or 'wrongness' of the to-be-finally-learned set of discriminanda" (Krechevsky, 1938, p. 111).

The problem was investigated by first establishing a position habit in the Ss, and then for a 20-trial period reinforcing one group of Ss (experimental) consistently on one of the color cues, while a second group (control) was not reinforced differentially, but only 50 percent of the time on *each* of the color cues. The presence of a difference in the subsequent learning of the brightness discrimination by the experimental and control groups would suggest that an association was developed between the response and the color cue during the dominance of reaction to the spatial position. Absence of such a difference would be an indication that a spatial 'hypothesis' prevents the association of the simultaneously

[1] The purpose of the preliminary training with the control group will be discussed in the theoretical interpretation of the present experiment.

acting color cues with the response. The latter finding would lend support to the non-continuity type of theory, the former result to the continuity theory, as the writer understands these theories.

III. EXPERIMENTAL PROCEDURE

A. Subjects

In all, 44 albino rats, bred in the laboratory of the psychology department of the University of Iowa, were employed. The ages of the Ss at the beginning of the experiment ranged from 75 to 90 days. Half of the Ss were males and half females. They were distributed equally between the experimental and control groups. Four Ss were discarded from the experiment because of brightness preferences as will be described later in the discussion of results.

B. Apparatus

The apparatus differed somewhat from previous types employed with white rats. It was designed (1) to eliminate the necessity of handling the rats except at the beginning of each day's trials, (2) to insure the reception of the stimulus cues by the S, and (3) to give immediate reward or non-reinforcement upon response.

The principal parts of the apparatus are shown in the ground plan of Fig. 1. A turntable divided into two portions, A_1 and A_2, by means of partitions, stood four feet above the floor and moved on a pivot made by two iron pipes. The smaller pipe, which was fastened to the table, fitted inside a larger one, which was based on the floor. The fit of the pipes was sufficiently close so that there was practically no play in the table, and yet it could be easily rotated by means of a stock attached to one of its sides. A one-foot alley (B), two in. in width, connected the two open sides of the table. A vertically sliding door in the middle of this alley permitted the E to allow the S to pass from one side of the apparatus to the other.

The second main part of the apparatus consisted of a stand which provided a one-way screen (C) behind which E was situated and which supported two elevated runways (D_1, D_2) 3½ × 10 in. The latter were interchangeable; one was painted white and the other black. The food box (F_1, F_2) consisted of a hole ¾ in. in diameter, drilled in a block of wood (2 × 3½ × 4 in.) placed at the end of the elevated runway. Immediately behind this block a vertical piece of plywood (6 × 6 in.) was fastened. The runways were fitted into grooves which permitted them to be moved back a few inches and thus permit the rotation of the apparatus between trials. A distance of 10 in. separated the two runways.

In addition to the white and black runways, two duplicate runways painted an intermediate grey were provided. These were used in the preliminary training and in certain other parts of the experiment as will be described in the next section.

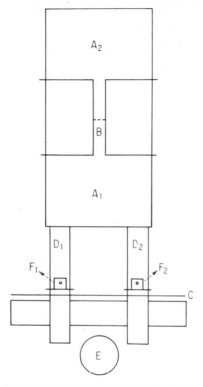

FIG. 1. Diagram of the apparatus.

C. Procedure

The experiment may be divided into five periods: (1) preliminary training, (2) position habit training, (3) pre-solution training, (4) position reversal training, and (5) the learning problem.

Before the preliminary training was begun the subjects were placed on the turntable in groups of two to four in order to familiarize them with it. The *preliminary training* involved two days. On day 1 with the grey runways in place each *S* was placed on the left (or right) runway and permitted to eat food. On day 2 the animal was placed on the side of the platform away from the food runways and trained to run through alley *B* to the food boxes upon the raising of the door.

Each *S* was next given three days of *position habit training*. Employing the grey runways, 10 trials were given each day with food being available on only one side. Half of the *S*s were trained to the left and half to the right position.

The *pre-solution training* employed the white and black runways. It differed in procedure for the experimental and control group *S*s. The former were reinforced (i.e., received food) only when they chose the black pathway (half of the group

TABLE I

Showing Development of Position Responses

| | Percent Responses to Preferred Side | |
Day	Experimental Group	Control Group
1	86.0	85.0
2	91.5	90.0
3	94.5	94.5
4	78.0	82.0
5	78.0	86.0

were reinforced only on white). This meant that an *S* which persisted in its position habit was reinforced 50 percent of the time as the white and black runways were presented equally often on the left and right side. Twenty trials in all (two days) were given during this period. The control-group *S*s were not reinforced consistently on either the white or black pathways during this period, but instead were reinforced 50 percent of the time on black and 50 percent on the white. As in the case of the experimental group, the white and black runways appeared equally often in each spatial position. A pre-arranged position of the white and black cues was followed in which each was reinforced equally often on each side in the 20 trials. In all periods of training no correction of an erroneous response was ever permitted. Instead the turntable was rotated and after the usual period of time between trials (approximately 30 sec.) the next trial was given.

Position reversal was carried out on the following day. With the grey runways present, food was placed on the side opposite to that on which the original position habit was established. Training was continued until the *S* chose the newly rewarded position for three successive trials, or for four out of five trials.

In the *learning period* both groups of *S*s learned to respond to one of the color cues, white or black. In the case of the control group half of the *S*s were trained to white and half to black. In the case of the experimental group, those rewarded on the black runway during the pre-solution period were trained on the white path during the learning period, while those rewarded on the white during the pre-solution period were required subsequently to learn to go to the black. Ten trials were given daily and training was continued until the criterion of 90 percent correct in 20 trials was attained.

IV. RESULTS

The development of the position habit in both groups of *S*s, experimental and control, during the initial three day period is shown by the data in Table I. It will be seen that the mean strength of the preference was approximately the same for the two groups during the first three days. Days 4 and 5 in this table represent the position responses of the pre-solution period. Although both groups of Ss continued to respond to their preferred position during the 20 trials of this period, there was a noticeable decrease in the percentage of such responses, particularly in the case of the experimental group. The relation of the maintenance of the position hypothesis during this period to the subsequent learning of the discrimination problem will be discussed later.

During the pre-solution period none of the Ss responded more than 65 percent of the trials to either the black or white stimulus. As was indicated in the description of the Ss, four animals were discarded from the experiment at this point because they exhibited a preference greater than this amount for either the black or white stimulus. Two of these were trained under the control condition in the pre-solution period and two under the experimental condition.

The data on the learning of the discrimination problem in terms of errors and trials are presented in Table II. It will be observed in the case of both measures that contrary to the non-continuity theory the experimental group was considerably retarded in its learning when compared with the control group. That the differences are statistically significant is shown by the t-values of 3.72 obtained for errors and 3.36 for trials. A t-value of approximately 3.5 is at the one tenth of one percent level of significance with this number of degrees of freedom.

Figure 2 presents a further comparison of the learning of the experimental and control groups. This graph shows the percent of correct responses in the learning of the discrimination problem *by the two sub-groups which had the white stimulus positive*. One of the most interesting aspects of this graph is the effect of the elimination of the position habit on the experimental group. During the pre-learning period while these Ss were responding predominantly to a position cue (approximately 80 percent of trials) they chose the white stimulus 51 and 56 percent in the successive 10-trial blocks. They were, of course, reinforced during this period every time they responded to the black card. Following the elimination of the position preference, these same Ss responded correctly (i.e., to the white stimulus) 37, 46, 46, and 42 percent of the time, on the first four successive 10-trial periods. This result would suggest that during the pre-solution period there was some kind of learning or association formed with respect to the black stimulus,

TABLE II
Data on Learning of Discrimination Problem

Group	Errors		Trials	
	Mean	σM	Mean	σM
Experimental	41.00	3.11	95.00	5.60
Control	26.05	2.55	70.50	4.66
Difference	14.95		24.50	
	3.72		3.36	

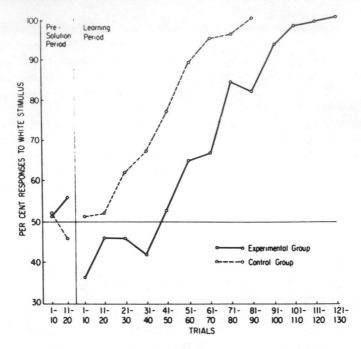

Fig. 2. Pre-learning and learning data for Ss trained to the white stimulus.

and then when the masking position preference was eliminated it was able to exhibit itself. Comparison of the two curves of learning suggests, furthermore, that the experimental group takes longer because it starts from a lower value. From the 50 percent point on, the two curves pretty well parallel each other.

One final point with respect to the experimental data: Examination of the responses made during the pre-solution period with the brightness stimuli revealed the fact that not all Ss maintained the position habit throughout the 20 trials. The question immediately arises as to whether there is any difference in the learning of the subsequent discrimination problem between those Ss of the experimental group that did maintain their position hypothesis and those that did not. Analysis of the data revealed that 10 of the 20 Ss maintained a position preference, averaging (as a group) 92 percent of their responses to the preferred side in their last five trials. These 10 Ss averaged 41.4 errors and 98 trials, which values, it will be seen by comparison with Table I, differ little from the means for all experimental Ss. Furthermore, it was found that seven Ss of this experimental group that did not maintain their position habit throughout the 20 trials (in fact, they responded only 52 percent of the last five trials to the favored side) made about the same learning record in the subsequent discrimination problem. These seven Ss had a mean of 43 errors and required an average of 100 trials to learn. It should be obvious from this that the presence or absence of a position habit during this period made no difference whatsoever in the learning of the subsequent discrimination problem.

V. DISCUSSION OF RESULTS

The issue between the continuity and non-continuity theories, stated in the form of a question, is as follows. Does the animal before it learns a discrimination problem, i.e., before it responds systematically to the positive stimulus cue and while it may be responding systematically to other stimulus cues, learn anything about (form any associations with) the positive stimulus cue? The non-continuity theory, building on the suggestion of Lashley, answers the question in the negative. During this pre-solution period, it holds, the animal may be responding systematically to other cues, e.g., position, and thus learning about them, but it does not learn anything about the 'to-be-finally-learned set of discriminanda.' Not until the S begins to respond to the relevant set of discriminanda, says Krechevsky, does it learn anything about the discrimination involved or "from then on only are his 'bonds' being strengthened, etc." (Krechevsky, 1938, p. 112). On the other hand, the continuity formulation, holding that the formation of associations is a continuous process, would insist that so long as the animal received discriminably different stimulation from the stimulus objects, differential associative tendencies would be developed with respect to them.

Consider, now, the results of the present experiment. The question of whether any associations were formed between the positive stimulus of the pre-learning period in the case of the experimental group can be answered in two ways: first, by the occurrence of any tendency to prefer this stimulus following the removal of the masking position habit and, secondly, by the slower learning of the discrimination problem on the part of the experimental group as compared with the control group. Both of these experimental implications were borne out by the present data as Table I and Fig. 2 show. This evidence points to the interpretation that in the experimental group the consistent reinforcement of one of the stimulus cues had a definite effect. Contrary to the suggestion of Lashley, associations apparently were being formed with the relevant stimulus cue even though the Ss were responding on the basis of some other hypothesis.

3

THE TRANSITION:
CONDITIONING THEORY
IN THE FIFTIES

During the decade of the 1950's the theory of discrimination learning followed two important lines. Conditioning theory was refined, and H theory was revived. This and the following chapter will deal with each of these developments, respectively.

Conditioning theory was streamlined and polished by mathematical theorists, notably Estes, Burke, Bush, Mosteller, and Restle (for a survey of this development see Estes, 1959). Not only did this work set high standards of precision for learning theorists, but most important for present concerns, the adult human became the S to whom the theory was applied. The applicability of conditioning theory to both rat and man appeared self-evident, and the shift to the human was casually made. Thus, in an early theoretical article, Estes and Burke (1953) drew upon animal and human data for confirmation of the theorems. Restle's initial article (1955) contained applications to both humans and rats.

These theorists, after developing the theory for the simplest conditioning situations, extended it to the discrimination-learning situation. As one goes from the operant-conditioning to the discrimination-learning task the changes are so structurally simple that, it seems obvious, simple corresponding adjustments will convert the theory of conditioning to a theory of discrimination learning. A review, therefore, of the basic conditioning ideas held by Estes and Burke will clarify their analysis of discrimination learning in Reading No. 3. Estes had previously applied the theory to the adult human in a simple learning task. The essentials of the experimental procedure were as follows: The S faced a board on which were a large central light, serving as a ready-signal that the trial was beginning, two smaller bulbs, one to the right and one to the left, and two response keys, one below each bulb. A few seconds after the ready-signal appeared, one of the two bulbs would light up. The S had been instructed to "predict," upon appearance of the ready-signal, which of the two bulbs would light. He was to indicate his prediction by pressing the corresponding key. The S, then, received a series of trials, each of which consisted of the sequence: ready-signal, button-press response, outcome (i.e., bulb illumination) indicating the correctness of the response. Typically, one of the two outcome events was more frequent than the other. In simple conditioning, for example, one bulb would always light up; the other would always stay dark. The two possible events were symbolized by E_1 and E_2, E_1 referring to the more frequent event. The corresponding responses were abbreviated A_1 and A_2.

Estes conceived of the stimulus situation at the time of the ready-signal as a universe of a large number of elements. These elements may be thought of as all the discriminable features of the situation: details of the board, the walls of the room, the ready-signal, kinesthetic cues, etc. Each element, it was assumed, was conditioned in an all-or-none way to either one response or the other. It was further assumed that at the outset of the experiment half of the elements were conditioned to evoke A_1, half to evoke A_2. At the start of each trial S took a random sample of these elements. This sample was particularly important in two ways. First, it determined S's response: The probability of the A_1 response was equal to the proportion of elements in the sample that were conditioned to A_1. Second, the conditioning produced by the reinforcement applied only to the sample: All the elements in the sample became conditioned to the "correct" response, i.e., to the response corresponding to the outcome event that had just occurred. For example, suppose on trial 1 S took a random sample of 10 elements, 5 of which were conditioned to A_1 and 5 to A_2. The probability that S would make the A_1 response on that trial would be 0.5. Suppose also that (regardless of which response S actually made) E_1 occurred. This would cause the 5 A_2-conditioned elements in the sample to change their state, i.e., to become conditioned to A_1. At the end of this trial, then, all the elements in this sample would be conditioned to A_1.

At the outset of the next trial, this sample is returned to the universe of elements and a new random sample is taken. If E_1 occurred on every trial, then, it is obvious, more and more elements would become conditioned to A_1 as the experiment progressed, and the probability of the A_1 response would approach 1.0. It is equally obvious that if E_1 appeared half the time on some random schedule, with E_2 appearing on the remaining trials, the proportion of elements conditioned to A_1 (hence, the probability of A_1) would fluctuate around .5 throughout the experiment. These expectations were contained in a general theorem derived by Estes. The theorem, dubbed the Matching Law, states that the probability of A_1 will approach the relative frequency of E_1. To take one more example, suppose E_1 were to appear randomly on 70% of the trials, with E_2 on the remaining 30%. According to the Matching Law, as the experiment progressed the number of elements in the universe conditioned to A_1 would stabilize at about 70%, and the probability of A_1 would tend toward an asymptote of .7.

Estes and Burke modified these conceptions for the discrimination-learning situation in the most straightforward way. Consider, first, how the task is changed to a discrimination task. Suppose the ready-signal light can be one of two colors, red or green.* The red signal is always followed by E_1, and the green signal by E_2. This defines a simple successive discrimination. Consider now the stimulus-element conception. To a red ready-signal, the universe of elements consists of all those elements mentioned earlier plus the elements corresponding to redness. To a green ready-signal the universe is similar, differing only in the elements corresponding to the color. The two universes, then, have many elements in common, but also unique elements. In this discrimination situation, learning occurs because more and more of the unique elements (i.e., those associated with each color) become conditioned to the corresponding response. In the example above, red is always followed by E_1 so that all the "redness elements" eventually become conditioned to A_1. Similarly, the elements corresponding to green become conditioned to A_2.

In Reading No. 3, Estes and Burke employ a variant of this simple task. Following one signal (called S_1) E_1 always appears, but following the other signal (S_2) E_2 appears randomly, half the time. Since S_1 and S_2 appear equally often, E_1 appears on 75% of the trials and E_2 on 25% of the trials. The authors derived and confirmed surprising predictions for this situation: Despite the perfect contingency between S_1 and E_1, the A_1 response will occur on less than 100% of the S_1 trials; despite the random relation between S_2 and E_2, the A_2 response will occur on more than half the S_2 trials. As will be seen in Reading No. 3, the data matched these derivations.

Confirmation of this counterintuitive prediction is a compelling sign of the validity of the conception. Nevertheless, the theory contained a fundamental problem. For the standard simple-discrimination task described above, where red and green are always followed by E_1 and E_2, respectively, the theory predicted only imperfect learning. It is true that the elements from each color will all become conditioned to the appropriate responses. All the other stimuli in the room, however (the so-called background stimuli), contribute the same elements when either the red signal or the green signal is presented. These background elements, therefore, are sometimes conditioned to A_1 and sometimes to A_2, with no systematic change in their status throughout the experiment: About half are always conditioned to each response. Consider an S late in the simple-discrimination experiment, at the start of a red-signal trial. The theory states that S takes a *random* sample of elements from the universe. That is, his sample contains not only red elements (virtually all of which will by now be conditioned to A_1) but also elements from the background stimuli (half of which will be conditioned to A_1, the other half to A_2). Since the probability of A_1 is the proportion of elements

---

*The signals are described as red or green lights to give concrete embodiment to the procedure. Various experiments used different sorts of signals. In Reading No. 3, for example, different clusters of lights were used.

in the sample that are conditioned to A_1, this probability will be less than 1.0. According to this theory, the S, college student though he may be, will never perform perfectly in this simplest of discriminations. Since many experiments showed the contrary, this limitation existed as a clear problem within the theory.

It is possible to modify the theory in a number of ways to solve this problem. Obviously, one wants the background stimuli to become less and less important as the experiment progresses. Intuitively, one expects that Ss will become less likely to sample background elements and more likely to sample the relevant signal elements. Restle's form of the theory of discrimination learning incorporates this idea (Restle, 1955, see Reading No. 4). For Restle the universe contains two distinct subsets of cues (Restle's term for elements): the relevant cues (those associated with the colors, to continue with our example) and the irrelevant or background cues. At the outset of the experiment S takes a random sample from the entire universe, but two processes are presumed to occur as a result of successive trials. The first process applies to the relevant cues. These are conditioned in a manner analogous to the elements in Estes's and Burke's theory. Restle describes this process by stipulating that the probability that a particular relevant cue (e.g., the kth cue) is conditioned to the correct response at the $(n + 1)$th trial [this probability is symbolized as $c(k,n+1)$] is greater than the corresponding probability at the nth trial, $c(k,n)$, by a fixed amount. This increment is a constant proportion, θ, of those relevant cues not yet conditioned to the correct response. This relation may be stated as a simple equation,

$$c(k,\, n\, +\, 1)\, =\, c(k,\, n)\, +\, \theta\big[\,1{-}c(k,\, n)\big]$$

The second process applies to the irrelevant cues. During the course of the experiment these become *adapted*, where an adapted cue is one that S no longer samples. Irrelevant cues become adapted in the same manner in which relevant cues become conditioned, so that the probability that irrelevant cue k' is adapted at the outset of trial $n + 1$ (symbolized as $a(k',\, n + 1)$ is given by

$$a(k',\, n\, +\, 1)\, =\, a(k',\, n)\, +\, \theta\big[\,1{-}a(k',\, n)\big]$$

Restle assumes that at the outset of the experiment (a) none of the relevant cues are conditioned to the *correct* response, i.e., they are unconditioned, contributing equally to each response, and (b) none of the irrelevant cues are adapted. That is, $c(k,1) = a(k',1) = 0$. Since θ is presumed constant throughout the experiment, one may start at the first trial and derive the state of the cues (conditioned, unconditioned, and adapted) at each trial of the experiment. This in turn leads to the derivation of the learning curve. An introduction to Restle's theory will be found in Reading No. 4.

Mathematical conditioning theory was elaborated not only for simple discrimination learning but for a range of situations as varied as avoidance conditioning and rote learning. From the present perspective the most important application of the theory was to concept-identification (or complex discrimination) studies. At the end of the decade Bourne and Restle (1959) extended the latter's conditioning-and-adaptation model to treat various complex tasks performed by the adult human. A summary of the accomplishments will indicate the reach of the theory.

This achievement will be better understood if the concept-identification task, as it was becoming standardized during the 1950's, is first described. The stimuli consisted of a set of cards or slides, each of which contained one of two forms, e.g., a circle or a triangle. Each of these two forms could vary along several attributes, or *dimensions,* typically taking on one of two values, or *levels,* of these dimensions. Thus, the forms might vary both along the size dimension, being either large (e.g., 3 inches) or small (1 inch) and along the color dimension (red or green). Since the forms also took on one of two values (circle or triangle) there was said to be a form dimension.

The above, then, describes three-dimensional bilevel stimuli. The *S* would see a large red circle, or a small red triangle, or a small green circle, etc. Typically, the *S* made one of two responses to each of the stimuli, and *E* provided feedback, i.e., said "right" or "wrong," according to some preselected rule. For present purposes, the *simple rules* are of interest: One response had to be made to one level of one dimension; the other response, to the other level of that dimension. If, for example, the responses were the words "positive" and "negative," "positive" might be correct for any red stimulus (regardless of its form or size) and "negative" for any green stimulus. In this example, color is said to be the *relevant dimension*; the other two dimensions are *irrelevant*. The *E* obviously can vary the number of dimensions in the task. To the three already mentioned he might add a border dimension (the border of the form could be solid or dashed), a position dimension (the form could be at the top or the bottom of the card), etc. He would have, then, an *n*-dimensional task with, if the simple rule were applied, one relevant and $n-1$ irrelevant bivalued dimensions.

One variation of this task is of further interest here. Dimensions could be confounded. The *E* could use a subset of the stimuli such that, for example, triangles are always red and circles are always green. In this case the color and form dimensions are said to be *redundant*. If *E* selects the redundant dimensions as the basis for correct responding, then there would be two redundant relevant dimensions and $n-2$ irrelevant dimensions.

Now, let us return to Bourne and Restle (1959) and to the extensions of mathematical conditioning theory. Bourne and Haygood (1959) had performed an experiment varying both the number of redundant, relevant dimensions and the number of irrelevant dimensions. Bourne and Restle specified a single set of parameters that permitted the theory to account for the results in each condition. Figure 1 shows the match between data and theory, and it is typical of the predictive success throughout their essay.

The problems referred to in Figure 1 used the standard two-response task. Bourne and Haygood also provided data from problems that were similar but required four responses. The authors, having inferred the necessary parameters from the two-response problems, used these to account nicely for the four-response data.

Bourne (1957) had demonstrated that for a fixed interstimulus interval (the time between the onset of each trial was constant), delay of feedback impaired performance. Bourne and Restle expressed quantitatively the idea that S's sample would tend to diminish over the delay period. This supplement to the theory permitted them to derive, with the usual precision, the learning impairment with longer delays.* This additional assumption also permitted them to account for the impairment produced when the feedback was omitted occasionally.

This impressive application to concept identification climaxed the mathematical-model developments during the decade. The pertinent features of these developments may be characterized as follows: (1) The theory was applied to the adult human. (2) The data to be accounted for were choice responses by the S. Even though you now had an S who could speak and who, perhaps, could provide some description of the internal processes by which he learned, such speech was neither required of the S nor considered. Verbal reports of any sort were assumed to have no bearing on the validity of the theory, which was testable only by the match between the theorems and the corresponding choice-response data. (3) The theory was applied to complex forms of discrimination learning. (4) Despite application to adult humans in complex tasks, the basic tenets of the theory continued to be that (a) the learning evolved from reinforcement and extinction effects and (b) the learning was incremental, i.e., each reinforcement increased the probability of the correct response by a small amount. (5) The theory was mathematically cast. The formulation was unambiguous, and the implications were always clear. Future theories of learning would be challenged by this demanding standard.

During the 1950's, incidentally, it was not only the mathematical learning theorists who extended conditioning principles to the human. Greenspoon (1955), a graduate student at Indiana during Skinner's tenure as chairman, performed his classic experiment, which in turn provided the impetus for several dozen studies (see Kanfer, 1968; Krasner, 1958). As is well known, Greenspoon demonstrated operant conditioning of verbal responses (uttering plural nouns in a quasi-free-association situation) by a fairly subtle social reinforcer (E would say "mm-hmm" after each plural noun spoken). Researchers employed this technique, called "verbal conditioning," to demonstrate not only operant conditioning, but discrimination learning and assorted complex processes. Commenting on

---

*This might seem like an inherently plausible supplement to the theory, that forgetting of the stimulus would occur with longer delays of feedback and that this forgetting could be expressed as a diminution in the size of the effective sample. Bourne and Bunderson (1963), however, showed this interpretation of Bourne's (1957) earlier study to be incorrect.

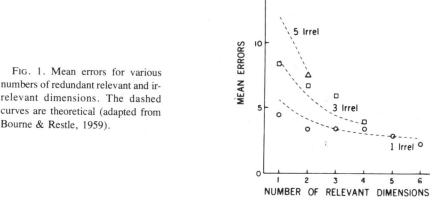

FIG. 1. Mean errors for various numbers of redundant relevant and irrelevant dimensions. The dashed curves are theoretical (adapted from Bourne & Restle, 1959).

Greenspoon's study, Dollard and Miller (1950) said that it "clearly demonstrates that the effects of a reinforcement can be entirely unconscious and automatic [p. 44]." This view, held by many of the verbal-conditioning researchers in the '50's, paralleled the assumption in the aforementioned discrimination-learning models, that the S-R-reinforcement contingency operates relentlessly to produce the learning.

Skinner was particularly vigorous at this time in extrapolating conditioning principles to complex human behavior. The extensions were to be found in his book on verbal behavior (1957), in his promotion of the teaching machine (1958), and in his general orientation to society (1953).

The 1950's, then, saw conditioning theory come to fruition in three ways. It became more rigorous and, hence, clearer; it was applied to the adult human; it was extended to a variety of tasks, many of which could be characterized as complex discrimination learning.

Reading No. 3
APPLICATION OF A STATISTICAL MODEL TO SIMPLE DISCRIMINATION LEARNING IN HUMAN SUBJECTS[*]

By William K. Estes
 Cletus J. Burke

It is assumed by all S-R reinforcement theories that discrimination learning is compounded in a simple way from cumulative effects of reinforcement and nonreinforcement. If so, then whenever explicit laws of acquisition and extinction have been formulated for a given situation, the main facts of discrimination learning should be predictable from these laws without the addition of special hypotheses. In the present study we have tried to evaluate this assumption in a situation where the necessary preliminary analysis of elementary learning has been carried far enough to permit explicit predictions.

A series of recent experiments on simple human learning under random reinforcement (Burke, Estes, and Hellyer, 1954; Estes and Straughan, 1954; Neimark, 1953; Straughan, 1953) have been interpreted with considerable success in terms of a theory which incorporates a statistical model of the stimulus situation and contiguity assumptions concerning the learning process. In these experiments S's task is to learn to predict which of a designated set of uncertain events will occur following a signal. In the experimental situation used for this type of study in our laboratory, the ready signal which begins each trial is a pattern of lights on a panel. Following the signal, S predicts by operating one of a pair of telegraph keys, A_1 or A_2, which of a pair of "reinforcing" lights, E_1 or E_2, he expects to follow. Actually E_1 and E_2 appear in accordance with a predetermined random schedule independently of the nature of the signal pattern and of S's behavior. The main findings predicted successfully by the theory are: (a) the exponential form of the learning curve, plotted in terms of proportion of A_1 responses per trial block; (b) the asymptote of the learning curve, with mean response probability equal to the

[*]Adapted from the *Journal of Experimental Psychology*, 1955, **50**, 81-88. Copyright 1955 by the American Psychological Association. Reprinted by permission of the publisher and the senior author.

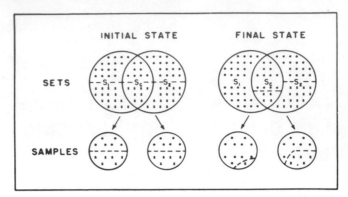

FIG. 1. Schematic representation of discrimination learning. Response A_1 is reinforced with probability 1.0 on trials when S_1 is presented and with probability .50 when S_2 is presented. The large circles represent the stimulus sets to be discriminated, some elements being common to the two sets. Stimulus elements conditioned to response. A_1 are represented by dots, elements conditioned to A_2 by x's. The small circles represent samples of stimulus elements which are drawn on individual S_1 and S_2 trials.

probability of reinforcement; and (c) the inverse relation between rate of learning and variability of the signal pattern.

Now let us see how the theoretical treatment can be extended to situations in which probability of reinforcement does depend on the nature of the signal, i.e., situations involving discrimination learning. The principal assumptions that we will be concerned with are, in brief: (a) An experimentally reproducible stimulus situation, e.g., the signal pattern in a prediction experiment, determines a population of cues, or more formally, stimulus elements, which is sampled by S on each trial. (b) A reinforcing event determines whether the response that terminates a trial is compatible or incompatible with the response being learned. In a prediction experiment we assume that reinforcing light E_1 evokes a response compatible with that of predicting E_1 and E_2 evokes a response compatible with that of predicting E_2. (c) The response that terminates a trial is conditioned to the cues sampled on the trial. (d) Probability of a response in the presence of a given stimulus population is directly related to (under the simplifying conditions of the present study, equal to) the proportion of elements conditioned to the response.

To convert the learning situation described above into a discrimination problem we need only use two different signal patterns and arrange experimental contingencies so that probability of reinforcement of a given response depends upon which signal pattern is present. Suppose that the set of lights on the signal panel is divided into two nonoverlapping subsets (call them S_1 and S_2) which are presented in a random order with S_1 being followed by reinforcing event E_1 100% of the time and S_2 being followed by E_1 only 50% of the time. How should we expect learning to proceed under these conditions?

If there were no stimuli in the situation at the beginning of a trial except the signal lights, then over a series of trials all of the stimulus elements in S_1 would become conditioned to response A_1, while elements in S_2 would be equally likely to become conditioned to either response. Thus the curve of responding in S_1 would go to 100% A_1 responding and the curve in S_2 would fluctuate around the 50% level.

It is not quite true, however, that the lights are the only stimuli in the situation. There must also be some background cues and some response-produced stimuli from preceding trials, and these will be common to S_1 and S_2 trials. Conditioning to the common elements should be expected to proceed as on a random reinforcement schedule; in the present instance, response A_1 will be reinforced, on the average, 75% of the time in the presence of the common elements, and therefore the proportion of these elements conditioned to the response should tend to .75 as an asymptote. As illustrated in Fig. 1, S will sample some common elements and some elements from S_1 or S_2 on each trial. Therefore the effect of the common elements will be to draw the probability of an A_1 response in S_1 somewhat below and the probability in S_2 somewhat above the values of 1.0 and .50, respectively, that they would otherwise have.

Under these conditions, effects of stimulus variability should be the same as those found previously (Burke, *et al*., 1954) in the simple random reinforcement situation with a single stimulus set. The greater the size of the trial sample relative to the size of the total stimulus set (see Fig. 1) the faster will be the predicted rate of learning.

To test the adequacy of this analysis, we have carried out a study of discrimination learning in human Ss which differs from previous investigations in three salient respects: (*a*) the simplicity of the experimental conditions, an obvious prerequisite for quantitative analysis; (*b*) the use of partial reinforcement rather than uniform nonreinforcement on the "negative" stimulus; and (*c*) the inclusion of stimulus variability as an experimental parameter.

METHOD

Apparatus.   The apparatus has been described in detail elsewhere (Estes & Straughan, 1954). The experimental room was dark except for light coming from the apparatus, and contained four booths and a signal panel. On the signal panel were mounted 12 12-V,·.25-amp light bulbs, evenly spaced around a circle of 9-in. radius. The booths were placed so that all Ss would have a clear view of the signal panel at a distance of approximately 7 ft. Within each booth was a pair of telegraph keys, each key directly beneath a reinforcing light. The presentations of the signal and of the reinforcing stimuli were controlled by an automatic programming device and the responses of Ss were recorded automatically.

Subjects.   The Ss were 128 students obtained from beginning courses in psychology during the academic year 1952-53. They were scheduled in subgroups

TABLE I
Probability of Reinforcement By The
E_1 Light Following Stimulation
From The S_1 or S_2 Signal
Sets*

Part	Set	Trials 1–120	Trials 121–240
I	S_1	1.0	0
	S_2	.5	.5
II	S_1	1.0	1.0
	S_2	.5	.5

* Design applies to both the Constant stimulus group and the Variable stimulus group.

of four for the experimental sessions. Within each part of the experiment, each group of four was assigned randomly to a treatment group, with the restriction that there be an equal number of Ss under each treatment.

Design.   Four groups of Ss were run for 240 trials in the experimental situation described above. For each S the 12 lights on the signal panel were divided into two subsets, S_1 and S_2. For all groups S_2 was followed by each reinforcing light with a .50 probability throughout the series. For two of the groups, constituting Part I of the experiment, S_1 was always followed by reinforcing light E_1 during the first half of the series and always by E_2 during the second half. Since we will measure learning in terms of changes in probability of response A_1, we will refer to the first half of the S_1 trials as conditioning and the second half as extinction. For the other two groups constituting Part II of the experiment, S_1 was uniformly followed by E_1 throughout the entire series.

Part I was the originally planned experiment. After Part I was completed, it was decided to run Part II in order to check on the failure of the conditioning and extinction curves to approach asymptotes of unity or zero, respectively. Although the observed terminal levels of response probability in Part I were in good agreement with predictions from the formal theory, they were nonetheless rather surprising from a common-sense standpoint, and further investigation seemed desirable.

Within each part of the experiment, 32 Ss were assigned to the Constant stimulus group and 32 to the Variable stimulus group. For the Constant groups all six of the S_1 lights appeared on each S_1 trial and all six of the S_2 lights on each S_2 trial. For the Variable groups, a randomly selected sample of three lights from S_1 appeared on any S_1 trial and a randomly selected sample of three lights from S_2 on any S_2 trial.

For each subgroup of four Ss, either the six signal lights on the left half of the panel or the six on the right half were designated as S_1 and the other six as S_2. Random sequences of S_1 and S_2 trials were generated for the subgroups, with the restrictions that S_1 and S_2 must each be used 120 times in the total series of 240 trials for each subgroup, and that each sequence drawn for a subgroup of the Constant group should be used also for a matched subgroup of the Variable group.

For each S, one of the reinforcing lights was designated E_1 and the other E_2. Either E_1 or E_2 appeared following the signal on each trial. The side of the E_1 light was counterbalanced within each subgroup of four Ss and the side of the S_1 set within each treatment group. Conditions of reinforcement obtaining in all parts of the experiment are summarized in Table 1 in terms of the probability of E_1 after stimulation by S_1 or S_2.

Procedure.   When Ss had been seated in the booths, they were read instructions, similar in detail to a set reported elsewhere (Estes and Straughan, 1954), to the effect that they were to respond to the signal pattern on each trial by operating the telegraph key corresponding to the reinforcing light that they expected to follow. Then the recorder was started and the 240 experimental trials were run off in continuous sequence. Temporal relations within the series were as follows: signal duration, 2 sec; interval from cessation of signal to onset of reinforcing light, 1 sec; duration of reinforcing light, .8 sec; intertrial interval, .4 sec.

RESULTS AND DISCUSSION

In Fig. 2 are presented empirical curves for all groups, plotted in terms of mean proportion of A_1 responses (i.e., depressions of the key below reinforcing light E_1) per block of 10 trials in the presence of either stimulus. Over-all trends seem generally in accord with the assumption that discrimination learning in this situation is a simple resultant of the effects of reinforcement and nonreinforcement. It will be noted that curves of responding under uniform reinforcement or nonreinforcement in S_1 and curves of responding under partial reinforcement in S_2 are similar in most respects to the acquisition and extinction curves reported by previous investigators (Grant, Hake, and Hornseth, 1951; Humphreys, 1939; Neimark, 1953) who have studied simple, nondiscriminative learning under similar reinforcement schedules.

Considering the Constant vs. Variable comparison, the rate of conditioning is slightly but insignificantly faster for the Constant group in both parts of the experiment, while rate of extinction in Part I shows a large and significant difference in favor of the Constant group. Analyses of variance using the variance estimate from within-sequence subgroups as the error term show no differences significant at the 5% level during conditioning; during extinction, frequency of A_1 responding during the first 20 trials is significant (F of 6.43, with 1, 48 df), while differences during the latter half of extinction are not significant (F of 3.96, with 1, 48 df). Response frequencies in S_2 do not differ significantly for the Constant and Variable groups in either part of the experiment.

As anticipated on the assumption of common stimulus elements, curves of responding in S_1 level off somewhat below 1.0 during conditioning and above zero

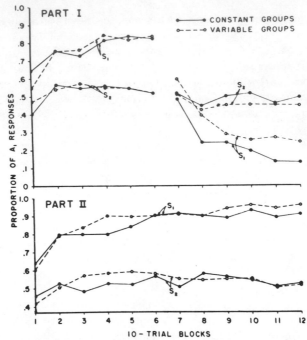

FIG. 2. Obtained data for all groups in terms of mean proportion of A_1 responses per block of 10 trials in the presence of stimulus set S_1 or S_2 as indicated.

during extinction, while curves in S_2 run somewhat above .5 during conditioning and somewhat below during extinction.

For each of the groups in Part I considered separately, rates of conditioning and extinction are approximately equal. The very rapid extinction following 100% reinforcement found uniformly by previous investigators does not appear; possibly the procedure of interspersing the S_1 trials with the partially reinforced trials in S_2 has produced this result by reducing both the homogeneity of the stimulating situation and the opportunities for effective verbalization that usually characterize 100% series with human Ss.

The fact that the curves of responding in S_2 start out below .5 in all cases was not anticipated on theoretical grounds. It is possible that this effect is a manifestation of the same initial "alternation tendency" that has been observed in two-choice situations with random reinforcement (Estes and Straughan, 1954; Jarvik, 1951).

In order to facilitate detailed comparisons of the data with predictions from the statistical model, the theoretical curves shown in Fig. 3 have been computed from a mathematical formulation of the model schematized in Fig. 1. The derivations are too lengthy to be included here, but will be made available elsewhere.[1]

[1]An article entitled "A model for stimulus variables in discrimination learning" by W.K. Estes and C.J. Burke is in preparation. The mathematical methods needed for the derivations can be found in the recent treatises on stochastic models by Bush and Mosteller (1955).

Since values of the free parameters in the curves of Fig. 3 have been taken from the data of a preceding experiment on simple random reinforcement (Burke et al., 1954), certain absolute predictions can be considered as well as the relative predictions discussed above. We shall confine our attention to the curves in S_1, which are sufficiently orderly to be compared in some detail with the corresponding theoretical curves. Comparing Fig. 2 and 3, it will be seen that the slopes and terminal levels of both conditioning and extinction curves are surprisingly close to expectation, considering that the predictions are entirely a priori and that no adjustments have been made for observed initial levels. It is the disparities between predicted and observed patterns that are of most interest, however, since these may be expected to provide indications as to the behavioral complications that are associated with the procedural change from simple random reinforcement to a combination of differential and random reinforcement.

The fact that the observed asymptotes appear to be slightly closer to 1.0 and zero during conditioning and extinction, respectively, than the theoretical asymptotes, suggests that the stimulus sets associated with the signal lights may have a greater weight, relative to the set associated with background and response-produced cues, in the discrimination experiment than in the simple random reinforcement experiment. The presence, although not the amount, of this effect could probably have been anticipated in advance, since trials of a given type, say those on which

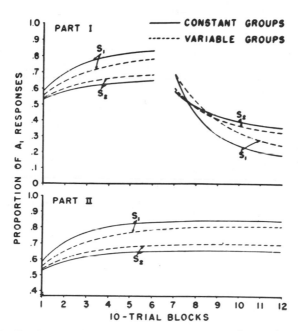

FIG. 3. Predicted curves of discrimination learning in terms of proportion of A_1 responses per block of 10 trials in the presence of stimulus set S_1 or S_2 as indicated.

S_1 is used, are spaced out by a longer average inter-trial interval in the discrimination experiment, and we would assume that under nearly all circumstances, the relative weight of the common stimulus set should be a decreasing function of intertrial interval.

A second set of disparities which may have a common theoretical interpretation should be mentioned. In the empirical curves for Part II it will be observed that the curves in both S_1 and S_2 appear to level off by the end of the first 50 trials; then the curves in S_2 begin to drift back toward .50, while the curves in S_1 drift on upward toward 1.0. In Part I also, the curves in S_2 have clearly begun to drop back toward .50 before the end of the conditioning series. These observations, together with the smaller than expected differences in learning rate between Constant and Variable groups during conditioning, would be accounted for if there were a progressive reduction in the set of common elements during the course of the experiment. This reduction might occur if, for example, a set of stimulus elements attributable to the giving of instructions and to initial postural and verbal adjustments to the situation on the part of the Ss were present on the early trials but tended to drop out during the experiment, leaving the signal lights as the principal source of stimulation on later trials. An independent check on this hypothesis will, of course, have to wait upon further experimentation.

In conclusion, it appears that the principal trends in the data of this two-stimulus learning experiment are predictable from the theory developed in connection with simpler experiments. It seems clear, however, that further simplification of the two-stimulus situation, including adequate spacing of trials and minimization of background cues, will be necessary before a reasonably full quantitative account of the course of discrimination learning will be possible.

Reading No. 4

A THEORY OF DISCRIMINATION LEARNING*

By Frank Restle

This paper presents a theory of two-choice discrimination learning. Though similar in form to earlier theories of simple learning by Estes (1950) and Bush and Mosteller (1951), this system introduces a powerful new assumption which makes definite quantitative predictions easier to obtain and test. Several such predictions dealing with learning and transfer are derived from the theory and tested against empirical data.

The stimulus situation facing a subject in a trial of discrimination learning is thought of as a set of cues. A subset of these cues may correspond to anything—concrete or abstract, present, past, or future, of any description—to which the subject can learn to make a differential response. In this definition it does not matter whether the subject actually makes a differential response to the set of cues as long as he has the capacity to learn one. An individual cue is thought of as "indivisible" in the sense that different responses cannot be learned to different parts of it. Informally, the term "cue" will occasionally be used to refer to any set of cues, all of which are manipulated in the same way during a whole experiment.

In problems to be analyzed by this theory, every individual cue is either "relevant" or "irrelevant." A cue is relevant if it can be used by the subject to predict where or how reward is to be obtained. For example, if food is always found behind a black card in a rat experiment, then cues aroused by the black card are relevant. A cue aroused by an object uncorrelated with reward is "irrelevant." For example, if the reward is always behind the black card but the black card is randomly moved from left to right, then "position" cues are irrelevant. These concepts are discussed by Lawrence (1950).

In experiments to be considered, the subject has just two choice responses. No other activities are considered in testing the theory. Any consistent method of

*Adapted from *Psychological Review*, 1955, **62**, 11-19. Copyright 1955 by the American Psychological Association. Reprinted by permission of the publisher and the author.

describing these two responses which can be applied throughout a complete experiment is acceptable in using this theory.

THEORY

In solving a two-choice discrimination problem the subject learns to relate his responses correctly to the relevant cues. At the same time his responses become independent of the irrelevant cues. These two aspects of discrimination learning are represented by two hypothesized processes, "conditioning" and "adaptation."

Intuitively, a conditioned cue is one which the subject knows how to use in getting reward. If k is a relevant cue and $c(k,n)$ is the probability that k has been conditioned at the beginning of the nth trial, then

$$c(k,n+1) = c(k,n) + \theta [1-c(k,n)] \qquad [1]$$

is the probability that it will be conditioned by the beginning of the next trial. On each trial of a given problem a constant proportion, θ, of unconditioned relevant cues becomes conditioned.

To the extent that a conditioned cue affects performance, it contributes to a correct response only, whereas an unconditioned relevant cue contributes equally to a correct and to an incorrect response.

Intuitively, an adapted cue is one which the subject does not consider in deciding upon his choice response. If a cue is thought of as a "possible solution" to the problem, an adapted cue is a possible solution which the subject rejects or ignores. If $a(k,n)$ is the probability that irrelevant cue k has been adapted at the beginning of the nth trial, then

$$a(k,n+1) = a(k,n) + \theta [1-a(k,n)] \qquad [2]$$

is the probability that it will be adapted by the beginning of the next trial. On each trial of a given problem a constant proportion of unadapted irrelevant cues becomes adapted. An adapted cue is nonfunctional in the sense that it contributes neither to a correct nor to an incorrect response.

It will be noticed that the same constant θ appears in both equations 1 and 2. The *fundamental simplifying assumption* of this theory deals with θ. This assumption is that

$$\theta = \frac{r}{r+i} \qquad [3]$$

where r is the number of relevant cues in the problem and i is the number of irrelevant cues. Thus, θ is the proportion of relevant cues in the problem. This proportion is the same as the fraction of unconditioned cues conditioned on each trial, and the fraction of unadapted cues adapted on each trial.

The performance function $p(n)$, representing the probability of a correct response on the nth trial, is in accord with the definitions of conditioning and adapting given above. The function is in the form of a ratio, with the total number of unadapted cues in the denominator and the number of conditioned cues plus one-half times the number of other cues in the numerator. Thus conditioned cues contribute their whole effect toward a correct response, adapted cues contribute nothing toward either response, and other cues contribute their effect equally toward correct and incorrect responses. Formally,

$$p(n) = \frac{\Sigma^r c(k,n) + \frac{1}{2} \Sigma^r [1 - c(k,n)] + \frac{1}{2} \Sigma^i [1 - a(k,n)]}{r + \Sigma^i [1 - a(k,n)]} \qquad [4]$$

Here Σ is the sum taken over the r relevant cues and Σ is the sum taken over the i irrelevant cues.

SOME CONSEQUENCES REGARDING SIMPLE LEARNING

If the subject is naive at the beginning of training, so that for any relevant cue k, $c(k,1) = 0$, and for any irrelevant cue k, $a(k,1) = 0$, and if he receives n trials on a given problem, then by mathematical induction it can be shown that if k is relevant,

$$c(k, n + 1) = 1 - (1 - 0)^n \qquad [5]$$

and if k is irrelevant,

$$a(k, n + 1) = 1 - (1 - \theta)^n. \qquad [6]$$

Under these circumstances we can substitute equations 5 and 6 into equation 4 and, taking advantage of the simplifying effects of equation 3, we have

$$p(n) = 1 - \frac{1}{2} \frac{(1 - \theta)^{n-1}}{\theta + (1 - \theta)^n}. \qquad [7]$$

Plotting equation 7 shows that p is an S-shaped function of n with an asymptote (for $\theta > 0$) at 1.00. Also, $p(1) = \frac{1}{2}$. Since $p(n)$ is a monotonic increasing function of θ we can estimate θ from observations of performance. If we want to know the theoretical proportion of relevant cues in a problem for a particular subject, we have the subject work on the problem, record his performance curve, and solve equation 7 for θ. This result depends directly upon the simplifying assumption of equation 3.

Since the instability of individual learning curves makes it difficult to fit curves to them, it is fortunate that θ can be determined in a different way. Suppose a subject makes E errors in the course of solving the problem to a very rigorous criterion and it is assumed for practical purposes that he has made all the errors he is going to make. Theoretically, the total number of errors made on a problem can be written

$$E = \sum_{n-1}^{\infty} [1 - p(n)].$$

Under the conditions satisfying equation 7, this can be evaluated approximately by using the continuous time variable t in place of the discrete trial variable n, and integrating. The result of this integration is that

$$E \simeq \tfrac{1}{2} + \tfrac{1}{2}\, \frac{\log \theta}{(1 - \theta) \log (1 - \theta)}. \qquad [8]$$

By equation 8, which relates the total number of errors made on a problem to θ, it is possible to make relatively stable estimates of θ.

AN EMPIRICAL TEST OF THE SIMPLE LEARNING THEORY—COMBINATION OF CUES

Consider three problems, s_1, s_2, and s_3, all of which involve the same irrelevant cues. Two of the problems, s_1 and s_2, have entirely separate and different relevant cues, while in problem s_3 all the relevant cues of s_1 and s_2 are present and relevant. That is, $r_3 = r_1 + r_2$ and $i_1 = i_2 = i_3$. If we know θ_1 and θ_2 we can compute θ_3, since by equation 3

$$\theta_1 = r_1 /(r_1 + i)$$
$$\theta_2 = r_2 /(r_2 + i)$$
$$\theta_3 = (r_1 + r_2)/(r_1 + r_1 + r_2 + i).$$

Solving these equations for θ_3 in terms of θ_1 and θ_2 we get

$$\theta_3 = (1 - \theta_1)(1 - \theta_2)/(1 - \theta_1\theta_2) \qquad [9]$$

This theorem answers the following question: Suppose we know how many errors are made in learning to use differential cue X and how many are used to learn cue Y, then how many errors will be made in learning a problem in which either X or Y can be used (if X and Y are entirely discrete)?

Eninger (1952) has run an experiment which tests equation 9. Three groups of white rats were run in a T maze on successive discrimination problems. The first group learned a visual discrimination, *black-white*, the second group learned an auditory discrimination, *tone-no-tone*, and the third group had both cues available and relevant.

Since each group was run to a rigorous criterion, total error scores are used to estimate θ_1 and θ_2 by equation 8.[1] The values estimated are $\theta_1 = .020$, based on an estimated average of 98.5 errors made on the auditory-cue problem, and $\theta_2 = .029$, based on an estimated average of 64.5 errors on the visual-cue problem. Putting these two values into equation 9 we get

$$\theta_3 = .029 + .020 + 2(.020)(.029)/1 - (.020)(.029) = .049.$$

This value of θ_3 substituted into equation 8 leads to the expectation of about 33 total errors on the combined cues problem. In fact, an average of 26 errors was made by the four subjects on this problem. The prediction is not very accurate. However, only 14 animals were employed in the entire experiment, in groups of five, five, and four. Individual differences among animals within groups were considerable. If account is taken of sampling variability of the two single-cue groups and of the combined-cue group of subjects, the prediction is not significantly wrong. Further experimentation is needed to determine whether the proposed law is tenable.

It is easily seen that θ_3 will always be larger than θ_1 or θ_2 if all three problems are solved. Learning will always be faster in the combined-cues problem. Eninger in his paper points out that this qualitative statement is a consequence of Spence's theory of discrimination. However, Spence's theory gives no quantitative law.

[1] Total error scores do not appear in Eninger's original publication and are no longer known. However, trials-to-criterion scores were reported. Total error scores were estimated from trials-to-criterion scores by using other, comparable data collected by Amsel (1952). Dr. Amsel provided detailed results in a personal communication.

4
THE TRANSITION: FORESHADOWINGS IN THE FIFTIES

During the 1950's, programs of importance for the development of H theory were begun in a few laboratories. These works were somewhat obscured at the time because of the dazzling success of the conditioning theorists. Their impact, however, was widely felt in the 1960's.

BRUNER, GOODNOW, AND AUSTIN

Starting in the late 1940's, Bruner was one of the isolated spokesmen for H theory. His most important contribution in those years was in the area of perception where he argued that perception was a classification process, and that a person achieved a stable perception by testing hypotheses, i.e., by searching for a classification consistent with all the cues. Needless to say, this work was rarely referenced by conditioning theorists. In 1956, however, he, with his associates Jacqueline Goodnow and George A. Austin, published a monograph on concept learning by humans. The authors simply assumed without polemics that adult humans tested hypotheses. They further assumed that one could ascertain S's hypotheses (Hs) in standard concept studies by having him state or write them. They then investigated concept learning in terms of the Hs stated by the S. The nature of their procedure is worth reviewing and distinguishing both from the pre-behaviorist introspective procedures (cf. Fisher, 1917; Heidbreder, 1924) and from the behaviorist traditions.

Within the early introspectionist tradition it was also taken as valid that Ss tested Hs and that one need only ask S to speak during these problems to determine the dynamics of the learning process. The problems, however, were quite complex in structure and were not susceptible to analysis. The Ss received little instruction about the possible range of solutions. Anything S said, therefore, might be relevant. In this circumstance, Ss tended to give long utterances containing all the ambiguities of ordinary English. The H had to be inferred from this material.

A critique of these early concept-identification problems was made by Hovland (1952). Starting with a mathematical theory of information then in vogue among students of language, Hovland argued that it was impossible to assess, in these early studies, the amount of information provided by each of the stimuli. He showed that greater simplicity and more precise control are achieved if stimuli are specified in terms of dimensions and values.*

Bruner et al. followed Hovland's suggestions, thereby simplifying the situation confronting S. They not only employed stimuli analyzable into dimensions and values, but they also informed S about the characteristics of these stimuli and specified that the solution to the problem would be a function of these. They further restricted S's output not to ordinary speech but to marking a symbol corresponding to his H. Thus, although S was technically "introspecting," i.e., directly revealing his inner state, methodologically the procedure was neat: The stimuli were organized into dimensions and values, S knew that the solution would be based upon these, and, with a set of symbols unambiguously representing these values, S described (presumably) his H.

Although Bruner et al. vastly improved upon the earlier introspective methodology, they still did not fulfill the behaviorists' requirements. The latter had rejected introspection partly because it contained ambiguities but also because it was based upon a viewpoint unique in the sciences. One had to assume processes hidden from all but one individual. Bruner et al., by having S describe his H, tacitly made this assumption. Probably because of this, they had no perceptible impact on contemporaneous conditioning theorists. Thus, Bourne and Restle, who consider virtually the identical tasks as Bruner et al., make no mention of their work.

Bruner et al. analyzed a large variety of concept-learning procedures. The most germane of these, which they call the *reception* task, is presented in Reading No. 5. This is the ordinary concept-identification task, in which stimuli are presented in sequence to the S.† The authors, however, incorporate into the task some variations not previously described in this history. In all the experiments reviewed above, the S made one of two responses (e.g., said "positive" or "negative") and E provided feedback (e.g., said, "right" or "wrong"). In the present experiment this procedure was short-circuited: The S did not make a choice response; the E, for each stimulus, simply indicated that it was "positive" or "negative." The S was required only to indicate his H about the rule defining the positive instances. Another procedural variation concerned the nature of this rule. Previously, we considered simple rules, e.g., all red stimuli are positive. Bruner et al. also employed *conjunctive rules*. With this type of rule, a stimulus must have values from two (or more) dimensions in order to be properly called "positive." For example, the E might hold the rule that any card containing a red triangle is positive;

*The stimuli were thus specified above, in connection with the work of Bourne, who was influenced by Hovland's arguments.

†The authors contrast this with the *selection* task, in which the S is free to choose the stimulus about which he wishes to receive feedback.

all other cards (containing green triangles, red circles, etc.) are negative. In this example, there are two relevant dimensions. There could be, of course, more than two relevant dimensions, as well as several irrelevant dimensions.

The value of the new procedures is seen in Reading No. 5. The *H* statements in this crisp context led to a clear delineation of different strategies employed by different individuals. Also, the influence of task demands upon *S*'s mode of problem solving could be detected. Mainline learning theorists were not prepared to accept verbal reports as data. As we will see, however, the rich picture of human functioning that the technique revealed was hard to ignore.

THE KENDLERS

Howard and Tracy Kendler (see Reading No. 6; also, Kendler & D'Amato, 1955), following a demonstration by Buss (1953), explored a discrimination-learning task in which adult humans differed both from subhuman animals and from theoretical (i.e., simple conditioning) expectations. For a review of their experimental paradigm consider the following task. The *S* receives a *simultaneous discrimination* problem, i.e., a discrimination of the Lashley-Krech type, in which *S* must choose between two complementary stimulus configurations. Thus, on a given trial *S* might be faced by a choice between a large white triangle and a small black circle. The stimuli vary along several (at least two) dimensions. One dimension, e.g., size, is relevant, *S* being correct only when he chooses the large stimulus.

The Kendlers, who had been students of Spence, were concerned with the appropriateness of Spence's theory of discrimination learning (see pp. 17–19) for the adult human. According to this theory, "largeness" (in the example just cited) comes to evoke the response most strongly, "smallness" loses control over responding, and the stimulus properties of the irrelevant dimensions acquire intermediate strength. This theoretical description may be tested by transferring the *S* to one of two second problems. For half the *S*s the second problem has the solution reversed: Choice of the small stimulus would be correct (the reversal-shift condition). For the other half, the new solution would come from one of the other dimensions: Choice of, e.g., the *white* stimulus would be correct (the nonreversal-shift condition). Spence's theory, in effect, predicts that the reversal-shift group should do worse. This, indeed, was the case with rats (Kelleher, 1956). For adult humans, however, the opposite held. They learned reversal shifts faster than nonreversal shifts.

The Kendlers suggested that the human performance is attributable to a covert process, that the *S* learns to make an internal response appropriate to the relevant dimension (e.g., he says "size is correct") during the first problem. This mediating response is still appropriate and, hence, facilitative during the reversal shift. With the nonreversal shift, on the other hand, the mediating response must be extinguished first, with a consequent delay in relearning.

It is both this postulation of a mediating response in discrimination learning and the presentation of convincing data that make the Kendler's work important in the present context. Although they chose to incorporate the mediating-response concept into the conditioning framework (assuming, particularly, the incremental effect of reinforcement upon the strength of the mediating response), the concept was compatible with an H-theoretic orientation in two details. First, the response was covert—it was necessary to consider the state of the S; second, it was selective—S was, so to speak, attending to one dimension and not to the others. This enlargement of conditioning theory helped prepare the way for acceptance of still more cognitive formulations.

THE SUBHUMAN PRIMATE TRADITION

Who, during this decade, was interested in the analysis of response patterns during discrimination learning? Krech himself was moving to physiological psychology. The occasional use he made of his multi-choice hypothesis box served to elucidate the relation between brain chemistry and behavior. Goodnow and several coworkers (Goodnow & Pettigrew, 1955; Goodnow & Postman, 1955; Goodnow, Shanks, Rubinstein & Lubin, 1951), working with adult human Ss, described patterns like win-stay-lose-shift. Coming in the heyday of conditioning theory, this work had limited influence. There was, however, one further contributor whose work started a tradition. On the threshold of the '50's Harry Harlow (1949) published his demonstration of learning set by monkeys. While the research was acclaimed for its theoretical challenge, Harlow saw in it another, seemingly more pedestrian, virtue. Each S, over a period of many months, learned several hundred discrimination problems. If one *were* interested in response patterns, this study provided him with enormous amounts of response sequences, conveniently subdivided into a large number of natural units, the problems.

Harlow became interested in response patterns almost because of the experimental arrangements of the Wisconsin General Test Apparatus. It is not automatic. The E, who must run each trial, can observe the monkey through a one-way screen—and there is little else for him to do. Under such conditions of watchfulness, systematic response patterns leap out even to an untutored E. A monkey, for example, might respond to one position for dozens of consecutive trials, or he might persist in selecting the incorrect object for as long as it is presented. Harlow surmised that the apparent gradualness in learning may be due not to the difficulty of the material to be learned, but to the interference of these response tendencies with performance of the correct response. These interfering response tendencies, or "error factors" as he called them, masked the learning process. It was important, he concluded, to describe these error factors, to chart their time course, and, eventually, to incorporate this information within a general theory of learning. These ideas were first presented in the article reproduced here (Reading No. 7). The analysis was of the data described in the original learning-set article.

In the next few years several of Harlow's students and other primate researchers performed error-factor analyses of their data. Perhaps the most obvious feature of this budding tradition was that no two articles contained the same analyses. The use of an oddity task, for example, called for special factors, as did delayed response, etc. Furthermore, the method of measurement of each factor tended to be improvised. Even the four factors in Reading No. 7 are unrelated to each other. This small domain, therefore, quickly developed a chaotic appearance.

In 1956 I became a graduate student in Harlow's laboratory, where I undertook, almost as a hobby, the task of systematizing error-factor analysis. I thought of this task as having two general goals: defining error factors in such a way as to permit a standard mode of measurement, and finding a theoretical (hopefully, mathematical) framework from which the measurement was a natural consequence. It was almost two years before both of these goals were attained. In this time I made a number of small changes in the treatment of error-factors. First, problem length was standardized. I continued with Harlow's idea that the "problem" was the natural unit for specifying a particular response pattern. Thus, for any particular problem, I wanted to look at the responses and to conclude that this problem reflected stimulus preference, or position alternation, etc. How long should this problem-unit be? Learning-set experiments had been done with as few as two trials per problem and as many as 12 trials per problem. What number of trials would be ideal for the proposed analysis? On the one hand, the problems shouldn't be too short. The number of trials had to be long enough to disentangle the various possible patterns. Consider, for example, a two-trial-per-problem experiment. On half the problems the two objects would occupy the same positions for the two trials. A monkey who chose the same object on both trials might be manifesting a position preference, a stimulus preference, or any one of half a dozen systematic patterns that come to mind. Thus, this problem could not be readily categorized.* On the other hand, if long (e.g., six-trial) problems were used, then the S might change his H within the problem. The S might begin, for example, with a stimulus preference and then shift to some other pattern at trial 4. In this case, no single systematic effect would be seen throughout the problem. The number of trials per problem, then, had to be long enough to permit unambiguous specification of a reasonably large number of factors and short enough to warrant the assumption that a single error factor held throughout the response sequence. A three-trial unit was finally chosen.

Second, I enlarged the class of response patterns to be considered and, in the interests of standardization, redefined the error factors that previous researchers had employed. For example, Harlow's "Differential Cue" factor became "Win-Stay-Lose-Shift with respect to Position." Also, Harlow's "response-shift" factor was dropped both because it was difficult to define a three-trial manifestation of this factor and because I found its appearance to be weak and infrequent in ordinary learning-set data.

Third, correct responding was specified as a pattern along with the other (error factor) patterns. Harlow's error factor "differential-cue responding" was man-

*Reading No. 12 contains an analysis of two-trial-per-problem experiments and shows the limitations of this procedure.

ifested when S responded to the position rewarded on the previous trial. One might add an analogous pattern in which S went to the *object* rewarded on the previous trial. This pattern, however, yields perfect performance in the standard learning-set experiment. Just as differential-cue responding was renamed "win-stay-lose-shift with respect to position," correct responding was labeled "win-stay-lose-shift with respect to the object." Correct responding, then, could be treated simply as another systematic response pattern. The rubric "error-factor" was no longer appropriate for the class of all possible response patterns. I substituted Krech's term, "hypothesis," (abbreviating it immediately to H).

These changes facilitated solving the general problem, i.e., that of formulating a mathematical system for inferring from data the various H strengths (defined as the probability of each of the various systematic response patterns). I had been toying with probability equations for several months when, suddenly, the system leading to the sets of simultaneous equations emerged for me. This solution occurred about six weeks before I was scheduled to take my "prelims" (the final pre-thesis exams). The immediate impact of the solution was that I suddenly had the rudiments of a Ph.D. dissertation. Longer range effects will be seen throughout the remainder of this book. Reading No. 8 is based upon part of that dissertation.

The three lines of research described in this chapter proved to be influential throughout the following decade. They do not exhaust, however, all the experiments in the '50's compatible with or pointing toward an H theory of complex discrimination learning. Thus, as noted above, Goodnow was analyzing two-choice response patterns as strategies. Hovland, who had analyzed the concept-identification situation in terms of stimulus information (he spoke of the number of given "hypotheses" defined for a given situation, and of the number logically eliminated by each stimulus), performed a series of experiments in which the amount of information was manipulated. Greenspoon's experiment and the conclusion favoring automatic conditioning were reacted against by cognitive theorists who argued that S must become aware of the contingencies (or that S must discover the correct hypothesis) before correct responding would increase. Also, major trends in other research areas were creating an atmosphere favorable to cognitive theorizing. In Britain, research was proceeding on attention in humans (Broadbent, 1958). Physiologists, who seemed to be unencumbered by the behavioristic superego, used cognitive concepts and S's introspections with apparent success. Thus, Hernandez-Peon, Scherrer, and Jouvet (1956) described physiological evidence for an attention mechanism; Penfield (1959) showed cortical points which, when stimulated, evoked (descriptions of) specific experiences and memories. Finally, computer theorists spoke freely of the memory of computers, and of the strategies they employed.

In retrospect, one can see a changing ambiance during the 1950's. At the time, however, a rigorous form of conditioning theory, developed systemically by such notables as Bush, Mosteller, Estes, Burke, and Restle, dominated the field of complex discrimination learning.

Reading No. 5

RECEPTION STRATEGIES IN CONCEPT ATTAINMENT*

By Jerome S. Bruner
    Jacqueline J. Goodnow
    George A. Austin

Let us begin at the beginning of modern neurology by taking Paul Broca as our subject: a gifted neurologist of the mid-19th century.† He has a chance to carry out an autopsy on an aphasic patient. He finds massive damage in that portion of the brain at the base of the third frontal convolution (since named, in his honor, Broca's area), "the speech center." But this describes only part of the properties of the "instance." For Broca's exact description of the patient's lesion shows a softening of the brain in the left hemisphere all the way from the frontal lobe dorsally to the parieto-occipital junction, extending downward as far as the superior portion of the temporal lobe. One can sum this up more simply by saying that there is much more destroyed than Broca's area alone. It is at this point that Broca is able to exercise his major freedom: the freedom to formulate an hypothesis. He could attribute the aphasia to *all* of the destroyed areas or to any part thereof. He takes his option and proposes that aphasia is caused by damage to a speech center: the famous "Broca area." Perhaps there is reason in the fact that this is the area of most concentrated degeneration. Nonetheless, the die is cast. The neural defining attribute of aphasia is this particular "speech center."

At the other extreme we have Flourens, who adopts another option. No *specific* lesion is taken as a defining attribute of aphasia. If the aphasic's brain shows specific damage, it is the interaction of the damaged areas and the intact areas together that create the final common path of aphasia.

What is of great interest about these two innovators is that each has a line of

---

†In the interest of exposition, we shall take certain liberties with the history of this complex field. If the reader finds that our historical license leads us to over-exaggeration, he will, we hope, forgive us and treat our examples as fictional rather than real figures.

descendants, call them the localists and the totalists. The former seek always a specific area where possible: some set of limited defining attributes, adding new attributes only when forced by the burden of much evidence. The list of localists, requiring oversimplification in its compiling, includes such names as Fritsch, Hitzig, Bianchi, Flechsig, and Adrian. The totalists have wanted to stay as close as possible to the whole cortex as an explanation, and it is only with the greatest reluctance that they will subtract any of its attributes as irrelevant. Here too we find a distinguished list: Goltz, Munk, Hughlings Jackson, Head, Goldstein, Lashley. The interesting thing about each group is not only that they attempt to proceed as they do but that they urge the absurdity of proceeding in any other way.

In point of fact, one could begin either way—adopting either a part or a whole hypothesis—and arrive at the same conclusion provided one did not become rigidified before the process of proof was completed. Here we must leave real neurology, for the issues are too tangled. But if one works with the kind of schematization used in the last chapter, it is possible that, when one encounters an aphasic, one may base an hypothesis on the state of *all* areas or upon the state of *one* particular area. What is even more important than the starting hypothesis is what one does with it when one encounters new instances that differ from it. For an hypothesis is not a final declaration so much as it is something to be tried out and altered. We shall be considering in this chapter the manner in which, in the kinds of problems we have been discussing, hypotheses are changed to conform to the arbitrary stream of events to which they are exposed.

The first and obvious thing about an hypothesis is that it can have any one of four fates when exposed to a new event to which it is relevant. Let us bring Paul Broca back on the scene. He has declared his hypothesis on the relevance of the speech center. Each new patient he sees can have his speech center intact or destroyed. Again, each patient he sees must either have the symptoms of aphasia or not have them. Broca's world, then, is made up of four contingencies.

	Speech Area	Symptomatology
1.	Destroyed	Aphasia
2.	Intact	Aphasia
3.	Intact	No aphasia
4.	Destroyed	No aphasia

It is apparent that two of the contingencies confirm, or at least fail to infirm, Broca's hypothesis. A patient with the speech center destroyed and the symptoms of aphasia confirms it. One with the center intact and without aphasia at least fails to infirm his hypothesis. Two of the outcomes are damaging to Broca's hypothesis. A patient with speech center intact and aphasia is as infirming as one whose speech center is destroyed but who shows no sign of aphasia. Let us adopt the language of medicine, for the moment, and speak of any case as positive which shows the signs of illness we are investigating; its absence negative. Whether it is positive or negative, a case can confirm or infirm the hypothesis in force. In this fashion of speaking, then, the four contingencies that Broca can meet are:

1. Positive confirming: Aphasic with speech center destroyed.
2. Positive infirming: Aphasic with speech center intact.
3. Negative confirming: Nonaphasic with speech center intact.
4. Negative infirming: Nonaphasic with speech center destroyed.

A good reception strategy consists in being able to alter hypotheses appropriately in the face of each of these contingencies. At an even more primitive level, obviously, it consists in being able to recognize their existence and to formulate hypotheses in such a way that, whatever the contingency met, one will know how and whether to change one's hypothesis.

A PARADIGM AND TWO STRATEGIES

Three things are required to reproduce in the laboratory a task comparable to the examples we have given. *First,* one must construct an array of instances that are alike in some respects and different in others, so that there are multiple ways in which the instances in the array may be grouped. *Second,* instances must be encountered by the person in an order over which he has no control. *Third,* the subject must know whether each instance is positive or negative in the sense of exemplifying or not exemplifying a concept. *Fourth,* the subject must be given freedom to formulate and reformulate hypotheses on each encounter with an instance. Given these requisites, a task is easily set. A grouping or a concept to be attained is chosen, and the subject is shown in succession exemplars and nonexemplars of this conept. His objective is to formulate an hypothesis that will distinguish an exemplar from a nonexemplar among the instances he encounters.

We begin with instances composed of the combinations of three values of each of four attributes—cards each showing four properties, such as "two red squares and three borders" or "one black cross and two borders." We decide upon a "concept:" say "all black figures." We present one instance at a time to the subject, telling him whether or not it exemplifies the concept, whether it is positive or negative. After each card, the subject is asked to indicate his best hypothesis concerning the nature of the correct concept. Thus, following the presentation of any given card, he offers an hypothesis. The experimenter makes no comment. The next card the subject encounters must perforce represent one of the four possible contingencies. It may be *positive* or it may be *negative*. Whether it is one or the other, it also has the property that it *confirms* or *infirms* the subject's previously held hypothesis about the nature of the correct concept.

Before examining the behavior of subjects dealing with such problems, it is perhaps well to consider the ideal strategies that are applicable. First, there is a focussing strategy which is useful both for maximizing information yield and for reducing the strain on inference and memory. The surprisingly simple rules for the alteration of hypotheses with this strategy are best presented with the aid of an illustration.

The clinician begins, let us say, with an aphasic showing a badly damaged brain—Areas I to VI destroyed. He takes as his first hypothesis that destruction in *all* six areas must be responsible for aphasia. If he should encounter a positive-confirming instance (another aphasic with like destruction), he maintains the hypothesis in force. If he should meet a negative-confirming instance (a nonaphasic with some or all of the areas intact), he still maintains his hypothesis. The only time he changes is when he meets a positive-infirming instance. An example of one such would be an aphasic with Areas I to III intact, and Areas IV to VI destroyed. Under these circumstances, he alters his hypothesis by *taking the intersect between his old hypothesis and the new instance:* those features common to the two. The features common to the old hypothesis and the new positive instance can be readily seen:

Old hypothesis: Areas I, II, III, IV, V, VI destroyed produce aphasic.

New positive instance: Aphasic with Areas I, II, III, intact; IV, V, Vi destroyed.

Thus the clinician chooses as his new hypothesis: ''Areas IV, V, and VI destroyed produce aphasia.''

Now consider the rules in their barest form. The first one is of central importance. *Take the first positive instance and make it* in toto *one's initial hypothesis.* From here on, the rules can be simply described. They are:

	Positive Instance	Negative Instance
Confirming	Maintain the hypothesis now in force	Maintain the hypothesis now in force
Infirming	Take as the next hypothesis what the old hypothesis and the present instance have in common	Impossible unless one has misreckoned. If one has misreckoned, correct from memory of past instances and present hypothesis

By following this procedure, the subject will arrive at the correct concept on the basis of a minimum number of events encountered. The strategy has only two rules in addition to the initial rule that one begin with a positive instance *in toto* as one's hypothesis. These two rules are:

1.   Consider what is common to your hypothesis and any *positive-infirming* instance you may encounter.

2.   Ignore everything else.

It is apparent, of course, that focussing in the present case is analogous to the focussing strategy under conditions where the subject chooses the order of the instances that he will consider. In both types of problems, the first positive card encountered is used *in toto* as a guide, in the reception case as the basis for all subsequent hypotheses, and in the selection case as the point of departure for all subsequent choices of instances whose positive or negative character will systematically delimit the concept. In focussing where one chooses instances, the problem-solver tests attribute values of the focus card one at a time as a means of seeing which features of the initial focus card are relevant to the concept. In the reception case, one embodies this focus card in one's initial hypothesis and then evaluates its attribute values in the light of subsequent instances encountered.

In the interest of brief nomenclature, we shall refer to the ideal strategy just described as the *wholist strategy* since it consists in the adoption of a first hypothesis that is based on the whole instance initially encountered, followed by an adherence to the rules of focussing just described. From time to time, we shall also use the expression *focussing* to describe the strategy.

As in the selection case, scanning strategies are also possible here. Again, they may take one of two forms. The first is the simultaneous process where a person attempts to use each instance to make all possible inferences about the correct concept. A first positive card "eliminates these 240, and renders possible these 15 hypotheses," etc. This is the "simultaneous" form of the scanning strategy, so called because all alternative possible hypotheses are entertained simultaneously. It is of little interest to us primarily because we find no behavior conforming to it. Nor, for that matter, did we observe the kind of "lazy" successive scanning that can be described in ideal terms as formulating one hypothesis at a time and holding on to it so long as confirming instances are encountered, changing only when an infirming instance is encountered to an hypothesis not yet tested. Then one starts afresh to test the new hypothesis with no reference to instances used for the test of prior hypotheses. This of course is successive scanning in its pure, discontinuous form.

The type of scanning strategy that best describes the behavior of our subjects is, as before, a compromise between these two forms. It is a strategy that begins with *the choice of an hypothesis about part of the initial exemplar encountered. When this hypothesis fails to be confirmed by some subsequent instance, the person seeks to change it by referring back to all instances previously met and making modifications accordingly.* That is to say, he bets on *some* feature of the exemplar, choosing it as his hypothesis about why the instance is an exemplar of the category—why it is correct. So long as the next exemplars also exhibit this feature, the hypothesis is retained. Or if nonexemplars do not show it, it is also retained. But as soon as an instance infirms the hypothesis, the hypothesis is changed. The change is made with as much reference as possible to what has gone before. He now seeks to formulate an hypothesis that will be consistent with all instances thus far encountered. To do so requires either a system of note-taking or a reliance on memory. Let us look more specifically at the way contingencies are handled.

Confirming contingencies are handled as in the ideal wholist strategy. The subject maintains the hypothesis in force. The two infirming contingencies present a challenge to the strategy in that both of them require him to go back in his memory over past instances encountered.

To sum up, the rules of the scanning strategy are as follows. Begin with *part* of the first positive instance as an hypothesis. The remaining rules can be put in the familiar fourfold table:

	Positive Instance	Negative Instance
Confirming	Maintain hypothesis now in force	Maintain hypothesis now in force
Infirming	Change hypothesis to make it consistent with past instances; i.e., choose an hypothesis not previously infirmed	Change hypothesis to make it consistent with past instances; i.e., choose hypothesis not previously infirmed

For describing this procedure we shall use the expression *part-scanning strategy or,* on occasion, *part strategy*.

Let us now briefly sum up the differences between the two strategies:

1. Part-scanning obviously makes more demands on memory and inference than does the focussing strategy. The wholist's hypothesis is modified at each step to incorporate the information gained from the instances he has encountered. He need never recall either his past hypotheses or the relation between these. *For his present hypothesis is a current summary of all these*. Only when he must recover from an error is recourse to memory necessary. The part-scanner must fall back on memory or the record every time he encounters an infirming instance.

2. The scope of one's initial hypothesis—whether a part or a whole hypothesis—will alter the probability of encountering the four different contingencies. This is a straightforward matter of arithmetic that will be made clear later in the chapter. The most dramatic feature of this "arithmetical fate" of the two strategies is that a wholist who follows all the rules of his strategy will *never* encounter the most psychologically disrupting of the contingencies: the negative-infirming case.

3. To succeed, the scanner must remain alert to all the characteristics of the instances he is encountering, for he may have to revise his hypothesis in the light of these. Such a degree of alertness and spread of attention is not required of the focusser. If he stays with the rules of focussing, he need pay no heed to the characteristics of the instances encountered after he has used them to correct his hypothesis. If you will, the scanner must keep a continuing interest in nature; the focusser need only be preoccupied with his hypothesis.

So much, then, for the ideal strategies. Specifically, we have three objectives in the research to which we now turn.

1. The first is to examine the degree to which performance corresponds to the ideal strategies, the degree to which one acts like a Broca or a Flourens from problem to problem and from contingency to contingency.

2. The second is to examine change in performance over a long series of problems varying in the cognitive strain they impose.

3. Finally, we wish to raise some questions about the effectiveness of the two strategies under varying work conditions. We know, for example, that scanning is more dependent upon memory and inference that is focussing. What difference does this make for success and failure in attaining concepts?

AN EXPERIMENTAL DESIGN

Our experimental operations can be sketched rapidly so that the present design may be contrasted with some of the classical studies. At the outset the nature of the task is fully described for the subject. As noted earlier, an array of instances is constructed. The subject is presented instances from this array one at a time, and each is designated as either positive or negative. The first instance presented is always positive. The subject is asked after each instance to state his hypothesis concerning the correct concept: what it is that the first positive card exemplifies. Instances are presented until the subject has had at least as many instances as would be required logically to eliminate all hypotheses save the correct one. At no time does he have more than one instance before him, and should he ask about instances previously encountered, the experimenter demurs. No such aids as paper and pencil are permitted him. Moreover, it is explained at the outset just what it is about the instances that need be considered: the shape of the figure they contain, the color of these figures, their number, etc.*

For the reader not well acquainted with the literature on concept attainment, we should like to point out here several crucial differences between the conduct of this experiment and of classical experiments in this field which have also used arbitrary sequences. First no effort was made to conceal the nature of the subject's task. He knew that his job was to find out the ''correct concept.'' He knew what a concept was: a grouping of instances in terms of common properties. He knew what properties of instances were worth considering. And he knew, finally, that what he was seeking was a conjunctive concept, and that only one concept was to be attained in each problem.

Details of Procedure

The instances were cards containing various shapes, colors, and numbers of figures; and various kinds, colors, and numbers of borders. The six attributes and their values comprising the problems were:

---

*We are particularly indebted to Mrs. Mary Crawford Potter for aid in designing and executing this experiment as well as devising techniques of analysis for it.

Number of figures: one, two, or three.
Kind of figures: square, circle, or cross.
Color of figures: red, blue, or green.

Number of borders: one, two, or three.
Kind of borders: solid, dotted, or wavy.
Color of borders: red, blue, or green.

Subjects were run in groups of about ten. They were first shown a sample of several stimulus cards and the experimenter points out how the cards vary in their attribute values. It was then carefully explained to the subject that a concept is a combination of attribute values, e.g., "all cards containing crosses," or "all cards containing one green figure." Thus, the experimenter points out, certain cards represent positive instances of the concept. For example, the card containing "one green circle with three borders" (1GO3b) is a positive instance of the concept "cards containing one green figure." By the same token, the subject was informed about the meaning of a negative instance as a card not exemplifying the concept.

We then said: "I will now show you a sequence of cards and tell you whether each is a positive or a negative instance of the concept I have in mind. *After each card, please write down your best guess of the concept.*" Each subject was provided with a response sheet. Each problem was done on a single sheet, the last entry on the sheet being the subject's final answer. If the final answer corresponded to the correct concept, the subject was considered to have attained the concept. Cards were presented one at a time for only ten seconds. No hints were given and once a card had been shown and removed, the subject was not reminded of what it had been. The subjects were instructed to write down on their score sheets only their hypotheses and nothing else. It was not possible for them to refer back to previous hypotheses since the subjects were asked to cover them, as soon as they are written down, by a card. This covering card was also a "code card" containing abbreviations for the subjects to use in writing their response.

Sampling of Subjects and Problems

The subjects, 46 Harvard and Wellesley undergraduates, were given 14 problems to solve. The problems varied in the number of possibly relevant attributes with which the subject had to deal and in the number of attributes that defined the concept. The number of possibly relevant attributes that actually defined the correct concepts varied from one to five.

The attributes used for any given problem were chosen at random, with the restriction that all six attributes were used equally often in the 14 problems. When, for example, a problem involved the use of three attributes, subjects were told what these were and the other attributes were kept at a constant value so as not to distract subjects from their task. The attributes that defined a concept were similarly chosen at random, with the same restriction as mentioned before.

TABLE 1
The 14 Problems Given Subjects in One Subgroup

	Problems													
	1	2	3	4	5	6	7	8	9	10	11	12	13	14
Attr. values of concept	1	2	1	2	3	3	1	2	3	4	1	2	3	4
Total attributes in array	3	3	4	4	4	4	5	5	5	5	6	6	6	6
Informative pos. instances*	3	2	3	3	2	2	3	3	3	2	3	3	3	3
Redundant pos. instances	0	1	0	0	0	1	0	0	0	1	0	0	0	0
Informative neg. instances	1	2	2	2	3	3	2	2	3	4	1	2	3	4
Redundant neg. instances	2	1	1	1	0	0	1	1	0	0	2	1	0	0
Total instances presented	6	6	6	6	5	6	6	6	6	7	6	6	6	7

*This includes the positive instance, i.e., the initial card presented.

The instances used for each problem were such as to approximate as closely as possible the following desiderata. *First*, that just enough instances be given so that the subject have sufficient information for attaining the concept with no redundant instances included in the series. *Second*, that the total number of instances presented for each problem be the same. *Third*, that the ratio of positive to negative instances presented in the various problems be the same. *Fourth*, that each problem occur equally often in the first, second, third, or fourth quarter of the series of problems. While we were able to come close to these prescriptions, it was combinatorially impossible to realize them completely. Subjects had to be divided into four subgroups and given slightly different sets of problems. The nature of the instances presented in the set of problems given to one subgroup is set forth in Table 1.

But the fit to our prescription was not bad at that. All but three of the problems in this set contained six instances, and these three were only one away from this number. Four of the problems involved instances comprising exactly one full informational cycle with no redundant instances; the others contained one positive redundant instance, and sometimes one or two negative redundant instances. The balance of positive and negative instances was practically constant throughout. Finally, nearly all the possible combinations of ratios of defining to total attributes were represented all the way from one defining attribute value for a three-attribute array to four defining attribute values for a six-attribute array.

ADHERENCE TO STRATEGY

Two ideal strategies have been described in terms of a set of rules for constructing a first hypothesis and for changing it upon encountering various contingencies. The general question we wish to ask is whether, on the whole, subjects adhere consistently to the rules of these strategies or whether, if you will, their behavior is random. The question is reminiscent of one asked years ago by Krechevsky

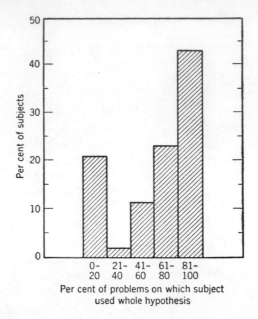

FIG. 1. The percentage distribution of subjects with respect to the relative frequency with which they used initial whole hypotheses in dealing with problems.

(1932a) about maze-learning in the rat: is it a chance performance or systematic, this process of finding the way to a correct solution?

Three concrete questions can be put. Problems are begun with either the "part" hypothesis of the scanner or the "whole" hypothesis of the focusser. Are subjects consistent from problem to problem in using a whole or a part initial hypothesis? Given an initial hypothesis of one or the other type, to what extent do subjects follow the remaining rules of the ideal strategy that would permit them to reach a correct solution with minimum information? Where does a subject's performance diverge from the ideal strategy?

Regarding consistency in the utilization of part and whole hypotheses on a series of problems done by a single subject, there is a very marked tendency for the subject to use one or the other approach consistently. In this type of problem, at least, people are either consistently like Broca or like Flourens. The relevant data are presented in Figure 1.

We also see in this figure that it is the exception for subjects to use the two forms of initial hypothesis with equal frequency. It is rather interesting, too, that the whole hypothesis is preferred to the part hypothesis.* In fact, about 62% of the problems were begun with whole hypotheses. A word must be said about the strength of this preference.

Upon being shown an instance exhibiting, say, four attribute values, there are

*In a partial replication of this experiment, with subjects run individually and with no time pressure, the same preference for whole hypotheses was found.

TABLE 2
Percentage of Problems Begun with Whole
Hypotheses and Percentage Expected by Chance

Number of Attributes in Array	Percentage Begun with Whole Hypothesis	Percentage Expected by Chance
3	70	12
4	65	7
5	59	3
6	70	2

15 opening hypotheses possible. Of these, one contains all four attribute values, and 14 contain fewer than all four of these. The larger the number of attributes in an instance, the greater the number of alternative hypotheses possible. But always, there is only one of these alternatives that contains all the attribute values on the instance—the so-called whole hypothesis. Thus, the probability of choosing a whole hypothesis by chance alone diminishes as the number of attributes used increases. The best way of showing the strength of our subjects' preference for whole hypotheses is to consider the proportion of whole hypotheses actually used and the number expected by chance.

The first question posed was whether subjects are consistent from problem to problem in their preference for either part or whole hypotheses. The answer can be given in three parts: *a*. They are consistent from problem to problem. *b*. There is a preference for whole hypotheses far in excess of chance. *c*. Both the consistency and the preference hold for problems of varying complexity.

Why this preference for whole hypotheses? Two explanations suggest themselves. The first is that when the number of attributes to be dealt with is relatively limited, a person may be willing to deal with them all at once. Perhaps had we gone well above the subjects' immediate memory-and-attention span, there might have been a tendency to break the task down by dealing with packets of attributes. A second explanation takes us back to the preceding chapter where the role of verisimilitude was discussed. In the kind of abstract material used here, it is not likely that subjects will have any strong preferences about the relevance of particular attributes in the array. They have no favorites to ride. In consequence, there is no preformed tendency to concentrate upon any particular attribute.

[Omitted here is a section describing the various contingencies (positive-confirming, etc.) and their influence upon *S*'s performance.   M.L.]

THE EFFECTIVENESS OF THE TWO STRATEGIES

Which strategy leads more often and more efficiently to success? Complete adherence to the ideal rules of either, of course, leads with inevitability to success. But there are deviations from the ideal rules: all wholists do not always adhere to the rules of focussing, nor partists to scanning.

If one can compare the success of partists and wholists, taking their strategic behavior as we find it, the advantage lies with the wholists. But the real question is: *which strategy is the more effective under what conditions?* Does the effectiveness of each strategy vary with the over-all difficulty of the problem to which it is applied, and is there a difference between the two in this effectiveness? Recall that the problems given to subjects varied in difficulty: difficulty depending upon the number of attributes to which one had to attend. For the larger the number of attributes represented by instances to be dealt with, the larger the number of hypothetical concepts in terms of which the instances may be grouped. If A attribute values are present in a first positive instance presented, the number of possible hypotheses about the correct concept will equal the sum of A values taken one at a time (for one-value hypotheses), taken two at a time (for two-value hypotheses), up to A at a time (for A-value hypotheses). The number of possible concepts for each case used, then, is*:

> Three-attribute problems = 7 possible concepts.
> Four-attribute problems = 15 possible concepts.
> Five-attribute problems = 31 possible concepts.
> Six-attribute problems = 63 possible concepts.

It is quite evident that the task of keeping track of possible hypotheses increases considerably in difficulty with an increase in the number of attributes in the array.

Figure 2 indicates that the number of attributes in a problem is indeed a source of increasingly difficulty. It is not surprising that the wholists were more effective with problems at *all* levels of difficulty. The fact of the matter is that it is easier for a subject to follow all the rules of focusing, and the superiority of the wholist does indeed derive from this kind of total adherence. For all levels of difficulty, there were more people who seemed able to adhere to all the rules of focussing than those able to follow through with memory-bound scanning. The only explanation we can give as to why the partists who relied on scanning did not "fall apart" faster when problems grew more difficult than did wholist focussers was that the pace of the experiment was too fast. With an increased number of attributes in the instances, and with instances coming one after the other at a rapid rate, the focusser was as likely to get confused in remembering his hypothesis as the scanner was in recalling past instances. We have no direct evidence in support of the explanation, but it seems reasonable.

*The formula for the number of hypotheses after a first positive instance is

$$H = \sum_{i=1}^{A} \binom{A}{i},$$

where H is the number of hypothetical concepts possible after a first positive instance and A is the number of attributes in the array.

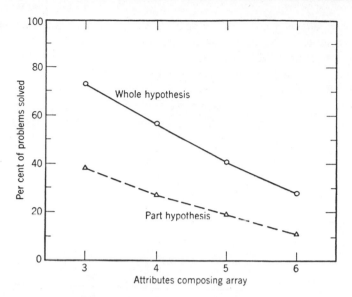

FIG. 2. The percentage of problems begun with whole and with part hypotheses that are solved as a function of the number of attributes represented in the problem.

Under what conditions would one expect wholist focussing to show marked superiority to partist scanning? The results thus far presented indicate a general superiority of the former over the latter. It seems reasonable, does it not, that the more difficult one made the task of remembering instances, the more marked would this superiority be. Take, for example, the "time strain" imposed by the ten-second presentations used in the experiment just described. What if the subjects had been run individually and had been allowed to get instances for testing at their own pace and with as much time registering on instances as they wished? An exploratory study of just this kind has been done (Austin, Bruner, and Seymour, 1953). The same strategies emerge, the same proportion of wholists and partists, although the degree of adherence to ideal strategy is greater under these relaxed conditions. It is interesting to compare the behavior of subjects in this experiment with that of the time-pressured subjects with whose behavior we have been principally concerned in this chapter. Consider the effectiveness of wholists and partists on comparable three- and four-attribute problems. *Without time pressure and proceeding at their own pace, wholists and partists do equally well:* 80% of problems done by wholists were solved correctly; 79% done by partists. But *with time pressure*, 63% of problems done by wholists were solved; 31% done by partists. In short, time pressure has a relatively small deleterious effect on the success of focussing, but a major effect on the success of scanning—literally halving its effectiveness.

The reasonable conclusion, akin to the conclusion of the preceding chapter, is that the more a task increases the strain inherent in a strategy, the more hazardous will such a strategy become. If one increases the number of alternatives to be kept in mind (e.g., Bruner, Miller, and Zimmerman, 1955), or cuts down redundancy, or increases stress and time pressures, it seems reasonable to expect that a strategy requiring feats of memory and inference will suffer more than one not requiring such feats.

Reading No. 6
LEARNING, DEVELOPMENT, AND THINKING[*]

By Tracy S. Kendler

Behavioristic learning theory is committed to studying the processes that relate the organism to its environment through its past history. It has produced a growing, vigorous science that studies the effect of experimental manipulations of three classes of variables on behavior: motivation, reinforcement, and stimulation. There is an implicit assumption common to all learning psychologists that the processes uncovered by experimental investigations are common to all organisms. It is presumed that there is a generality to the laws that relate the organism to his environment that spreads across phylogenetic and ontogenetic divisions and that there is a commonality to the learning process from its simplest to its most complex manifestations.

Learning psychologists are thus freed to study one convenient laboratory organism, primarily the rat or the pigeon, bolstered by the assumption that their findings are not limited to the species studied. The emphasis is on generating laws of behavior. Phylogenetic and ontogenetic comparisons are considered mildly interesting but not basic. Where human beings serve as subjects, the emphasis is on demonstrating the universality of the behavioral laws derived from animal experiments. The similarities are more important than the differences.

As long as behaviorists deal with simple processes, concentration on one organism like the pigeon, in one kind of experimental situation like the Skinner box, has immense advantages. It provides a stable methodology, reduces problems of communication between experimenters, and increases experimental control. However, when we become concerned with "thinking" we find we must leave these safe shores and grapple with the complexities presented by differences between species and differences between age levels.

*Excerpted from the *Annals of the New York Academy of Sciences*, 1960, **91**, 52-63. Copyright 1960 by the New York Academy of Sciences. Reprinted by permission of the publisher and the author.

FIRST DISCRIMINATION

SECOND DISCRIMINATION

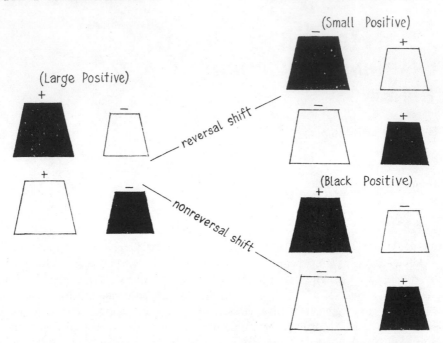

FIG. 1. A paradigm of the successive discriminations in reversal and nonreversal shifts.

Does this departure imply a break with the assumption of generality? Not necessarily. It could strengthen the position with empirical demonstration. For the past several years Howard H. Kendler and our associates and I have been engaged in research that applies a comparative-developmental approach to the study of concept-formation. We have been as much, or perhaps more, interested in the differences between species and age levels as in the similarities. Nevertheless our theorizing has been, to date, entirely within the S-R behaviorist tradition.

The program began with an experiment on concept-formation in college students (Kendler and D'Amato, 1955) that used a technique that was later adapted to each of the experiments I will describe today. Since the procedure is complex and each study involved a minor modification, it will be easier to explain and to understand if I present a paradigm of the technique at the outset. I say paradigm because it is not actually identical to any of the procedures but conveys the essence of all of them.

The procedure that is illustrated in Figure 1 consists essentially of two successive discriminations between pairs of stimuli. The first discrimination differs simultaneously on two dimensions; size and brightness. S is rewarded for responses to one dimension; the other dimension is irrelevant. For example, S has to learn to choose the large cup, regardless of brightness. After reaching criterion

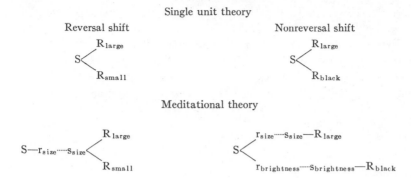

Fig. 2. A diagram of the competition between the habits during reversal and nonreversal shift according to the single unit and mediational theories.

he is shifted, without warning, to a new pattern of reinforcement. If he is a reversal shift S, he is required to respond to the same dimension on which he was originally trained, but his overt choice has to be reversed, for example, he has to shift from a large cup to a small one. For a nonreversal shift S, the previously irrelevant dimension becomes relevant, for example he has to shift from large to black.

Comparison between these two types of shifts is of particular interest because analyses of the acquisition process based on mediated and unmediated S-R connections yield different and easily tested predictions about their relative efficiency. Figure 2 presents a schematic diagram of both types of connections.

The single unit formulation would predict that reversal shift would be learned more slowly than the nonreversal shift. This would follow because, at the time of the shift, the difference between the strength of the dominant incorrect habit and the to-be-correct habit is much greater for the reversal than for the nonreversal shift. It should therefore be more difficult to learn to respond to the previously relevant stimuli in an opposite manner than to respond to a stimulus that was previously irrelevant.

To check the prediction, Kelleher (1956) applied the reversal-nonreversal shift technique to rats. His results confirmed the single unit theory. For rats, a reversal shift was more difficult than a nonreversal shift.

First Buss (1953) and a little later Kendler and D'Amato (1955) used college students as subjects in a more complex, concept-formation variation of the reversal and nonreversal shifts. Both investigations reported that, unlike the rats, the students performed the reversal shift more rapidly than the nonreversal shift.*

* Buss (1953) initially attributed the slowness of the nonreversal shift to the fortuitous intermittent reinforcement of the previously correct concept under this condition. All of the research comparing these two types of shifts cited in this paper, with the exception of the 1953 Buss study, used procedures that eliminated such intermittent reinforcement. In 1956 Buss compared reversal and nonreversal shift with this factor eliminated. Under these conditions he also found that for college students reversal shift occurred more readily than nonreversal shift.

It may be unexpected to the reader, but the difference between rats and students was no surprise even to behavior theorists. As early as 1930 Hull had pointed the way for behavior theory to extend its range by introducing the concept of the pure stimulus act. This "act" or, as it is more frequently called, cue-producing response may be overt or it may be covert. Either way is is assumed to give rise to stimuli that can, like an environmental stimulus, become associated with an overt response thus enabling an organism to generate his own cues. These cues, in turn, serve to guide his behavior.

Kendler and D'Amato applied a mediational analysis to predict that reversal shift would be relatively easy for college students. As illustrated in the bottom half of Figure 2, reversal shift requires S to utilize the same mediated response that he has previously employed with success. Only the overt response must be changed. A nonreversal shift, on the other hand, requires the acquisition of a new mediated response, the cues of which must become attached to a new overt response. Consequently the reversal shift, which requires a change in only the last link, should yield faster learning than the nonreversal shift.

Reading No. 7
ANALYSIS OF DISCRIMINATION LEARNING BY MONKEYS[*]

By Harry F. Harlow

PURPOSE AND INTRODUCTION

The purpose of the present experiment is to analyze various factors which operate to produce errors in discrimination learning of monkeys.

Discrimination learning has been demonstrated in many animals; the learning curves have been plotted and the characteristics of these curves have been expressed in mathematical form. Theoretical articles have been written concerning the factors operating in error production, but no one has made any direct analysis of error-producing factors or their relative roles in discrimination learning. Until the nature of error factors can be experimentally demonstrated, there is little hope for the formulation of an adequate discrimination learning theory.

The great variability in rate of discrimination learning commonly encountered from subject to subject, from problem to problem, and from trial to trial has rendered analysis of error-producing factors difficult. The present study was so designed as to keep variability of performance at a minimum. Control over test variables was obtained by using a highly standardized test situation and by using stimuli whose differences could readily, and probably immediately, be perceived by the subjects. These stimuli, stimulus-objects differing in multiple dimensions, have been described in an earlier paper (1949). The use of such stimuli makes possible rapid and consistent discrimination learning in monkeys and offers the further advantage of providing numerous stimuli from which long series of discrimination problems of equated difficulty can be arranged without duplication of any of the objects.

SUBJECTS

Subjects in this investigation were 10 rhesus monkeys, Numbers 90, 92, 94, 101, 102, 104, 105, 106, 107, 108, and one mangabey, Number 109. Their

*Adapted from the *Journal of Experimental Psychology*, 1950, **40**, 26-39. Copyright 1950 by the American Psychological Association. Reprinted by permission of the publisher and the author.

weights ranged from 6 to 10 pounds. These subjects had been tamed and adapted to the test situation for a period of two to three months, following which they received their first laboratory problem, a series of 32 preliminary discriminations of 50 trials each. The animals were then given a series of 200 six-trial discriminations, the data from which form the basis of the discrimination analysis part of this paper. Eight of these monkeys, Numbers 101 to 109 inclusive, were then tested on a series of 112 discrimination reversal problems. Only data obtained on these eight animals were used in the analysis of the formation of learning sets.

APPARATUS AND METHOD

The apparatus was the same as that standard at the Wisconsin Laboratory and described previously (Harlow, 1949). Each trial was run by lowering the forward opaque screen, baiting the correct food-well in the stimulus tray, and covering the two food-wells with the stimulus-objects to be discriminated. The stimulus tray was pushed forward so that the stimuli were just within reach of the subject. The one-way vision screen was then lowered and the forward opaque screen raised. The animal was allowed to displace one stimulus, after which the stimulus tray was retracted a few inches. The one-way vision screen was raised and after a pause of about two sec., the monkey was given a piece of food. This is referred to as inter-trial reward and was given whether or not the discrimination choice had been correct. The purpose was to keep frustration at a minimum.

Succeeding trials were run in the same manner, with no opportunity allowed the subjects to correct errors. An interval of approximately 15 sec. intervened between trials.

The specific procedures for discrimination analysis were as follows. Each animal was given the series of 200 object-quality discriminations. A different pair of stimulus-objects was, of course, used for each discrimination. Ten six-trial discriminations were run each day, making a total of 60 trials per day. So far as possible, the animals were run on consecutive days. There was a pause of about 30 sec. between successive discrimination problems, during which time the subject was fed several pieces of food.

A set of 10 different positional sequences was employed. The entire set was used daily, but the order in which the sequences appeared was varied. Running each subject on a large number of varied positional sequences using different stimulus pairs of approximately equal difficulty, adds greatly to the possibilities offered for analysis of the factors producing errors in discrimination learning.

Table I presents the 10 positional sequences. The letters R (right) and L (left) indicate the position of the correct member of each stimulus pair in the series of six trials.

This block of 10 positional sequences was balanced to provide reward of the right and left positions an equal number of times on each of the six trials. There were included four sequences in which the position of the correct stimulus shifted

TABLE I

Positional Sequences

Trial	Sequence Number									
	A	B	C	D	E	F	G	H	I	J
1	R	R	R	R	R	L	L	L	L	L
2	L	L	R	R	R	R	R	L	L	L
3	R	L	L	L	R	L	R	R	R	L
4	L	R	L	R	L	R	L	R	L	R
5	R	L	R	L	L	L	R	L	R	R
6	L	R	L	L	R	R	L	R	R	L

on the second trial, and six sequences in which the first-trial position of the stimuli remained constant on the second trial. On two of the 10 sequences, the position of the positive stimulus remained constant through the first three trials.

The data for analysis of the formation of learning sets include those obtained on (1) the 200 object-quality discriminations just described, (2) the first six trials of each of the 32 preliminary discriminations, and (3) the first six trials of each of an additional 112 discriminations (Discriminations 201-312) that comprise the discrimination portion of the series of discrimination-reversal problems. Both the Preliminary series and the Discrimination series 201-312 were balanced for left-right position on all trials. The latter series contained 14 positional sequences in which the position of the correct stimulus changed on the second trial in six, on the third trial in four, on the fourth trial in two, and on the fifth trial in two. Fuller details will be given in a later publication on analysis of discrimination-reversal learning.

RESULTS

Learning Curves for Discriminations 1-200

Discrimination learning curves showing the mean percent errors made by the 11 monkeys on each of the six trials for Discriminations 1-100 and Discriminations 101-200 are presented in Fig. 1. These curves show that learning was extremely rapid. On Trial 2 of the first and second hundred discriminations 82 and 87 percent correct responses were made, respectively. Improvement in performance continued in the remaining trials, although the rate of improvement on these trials is significantly less than would be predicted from Hull's postulated general learning curve based on a constant increment of growth (1943, p. 114). Chi-square tests of goodness of fit (with Yates' correction) of the obtained errors and theoretical errors as predicted from Hull's formula, yield *P*-values of .001 at all measured points (i.e., Trials 3, 4, 5, and 6 for Discriminations 1-100 and 101-200).

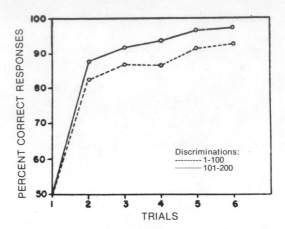

FIG. 1. Discrimination learning curves.

Analysis of Error Factors: Stimulus Perseveration Errors

Stimulus perseveration errors are defined as the excess of consecutive errors following a first trial error beyond those which would be predicted from the obtained frequencies of all errors. Though errors of this type appeared to result from preference for, or avoidance of, particular stimulus-objects, this error factor is defined independently of underlying causes.

The theoretical probability of consecutive errors through any given trial is computed for that trial by taking the product of the obtained percentage of errors on that and all preceding trials. For example, the probability that consecutive errors will have continued through Trial 4 of a discrimination representative of Discriminations 1-100, is the product of .5, .175, .130 and .135. (See Fig. 1.)

The theoretical number of consecutive errors on any of the six trials for any group of discriminations is the product of the theoretical probability of consecutive errors through that trial, and the total number of responses of all the subjects on that trial, and the total number of responses of all the subjects on that trial on all the discriminations in the group. The data of Table II give the theoretical and obtained number of consecutive errors for the first and second hundred discrimination problems, based in each case on 1100 responses.

The number of stimulus perseveration errors was found by subtracting the theoretical consecutive errors from the obtained consecutive errors, the excess of the obtained over the theoretical errors for any one trial being, by definition, stimulus perseveration errors. In Table III are given the number of stimulus perseveration errors and the percent total errors made on a particular trial that may be attributed to stimulus perseveration.

Analysis of Error Factors: Differential Cue Errors

The trial on which the stimulus-object first changes position is of particular significance in learning theory. Prior to this trial, a correct choice leads to reward

TABLE II
Theoretical and Obtained Numbers
of Consecutive Errors

Discrimi-nations	Theoretical Errors Trial					Obtained Errors Trial				
	2	3	4	5	6	2	3	4	5	6
1–100	96	11	1	0	0	129	42	22	10	7
101–200	69	6	0	0	0	67	12	1	0	0

of the *multiple cues* which the positive stimulus offers, including its position and its physical characteristics independent of position. Likewise, an incorrect response on a trial preceding the shift of position is followed by failure of reward of the *multiple cues* offered by the incorrect stimulus. This situation is referred to by Spence (1936) as 'ambiguous reinforcement,' since the position and object-qualities of the chosen stimulus are simultaneously rewarded or unrewarded. On the first trial in which the positions of the stimuli change, the subject must make a response in terms of *differential cues*—he must respond either to the *positional* or *object-quality* cues which have previously been confounded. The term differential cue trial is used to designate this first trial involving change of position of the stimuli.

In the present experiment there are four positional sequences in which the initial differential cue responses occur on the second trial, four in which initial differential cue responses occur on the third trial, and two in which the fourth trial is critical. For any of the first four trials (e.g., Trial 2) we can compare the percentage of errors made on those particular sequences which offer differential cues for the first time (sequences AFBG) with the percentage of errors made on those positional sequences in which the cues remain multiple (CHDIEJ). The difference is a measure of the role of shift from multiple to differential cues in the production of errors.

Table IV presents a comparison of the errors made on differential cue and on multiple cue trials for Trial 2 and 3. The significance of the differences between the errors on the differential cue and multiple cue trials, and the comparable-trial

TABLE III
Number and Percentage of Stimulus
Perseveration Errors

Discrim-inations	No. Perseveration Errors Trial					Percent Persevera-tion Errors Trial				
	2	3	4	5	6	2	3	4	5	6
1–100	33	31	21	10	7	17	22	14	12	9
101–200	−2	6	1	0	0	−1	6	2	0	0

TABLE IV

Comparison of Errors Made on Comparable Multiple Cue
and Differential Cue Trials

MC = multiple cue, DC = differential cue

Positional Sequences	Nature Trial	Total Responses	Total Errors	Percent Errors	x^2	P	CTE Error Ratio
Discriminations 1-100 Trial 2							
CHDIEJ AFBG	MC DC	660 440	103 89	16 20	3.91	.05	1.25
Discriminations 1-100 Trial 3							
EJ CHDI	MC DC	220 440	18 72	8 16	8.33	.01	2.00
Discriminations 101-200 Trial 2							
CHDIEJ AFBG	MC DC	660 440	68 71	10 16	11.20	.01	1.60
Discriminations 101-200 Trial 3							
EJ CHDI	MC DC	220 440	14 50	6 11	4.18	.05	1.45

error ratios are also presented. The comparable-trial error ratio (C.T.E. ratio) is obtained for any trial by dividing the percentage of errors made on those positional sequences in which the response is to differential cues, by the percentage of errors made on those positional sequences in which the response is to multiple cues.

The data of Table IV show that a higher percentage of errors is always made on the first differential cue trial than on comparable multiple cue trials, and that the ratio of errors between these two cue-type trials ranges from 1.25 to 2.00. The confidence level for the significance of the differences in errors as measured by chi-square ranges from .01 to .05.

Figure 2 presents graphically the percentage of correct responses made on the second and third trials for both the multiple and differential cue trials. These data can be analyzed in terms of the percentage of total errors on the differential cue trial attributable to the shift from multiple cue trials. The difference between the percentage of total errors made on the differential cue trial and the comparable multiple cue trial for any particular trial (Trial 2 or Trial 3) is divided by the percentage of total errors made on the same differential cue trial. The resulting quotients are presented in Table V.

These data show that the percentage of errors attributable to shift from multiple to differential cues is greater on Trial 3 than on Trial 2. It is also seen that the percentage of errors attributable to shift from multiple to differential cues remains almost constant in the first and second 100 discriminations, indicating that this

TABLE V

Percentage of Errors on the Differential
Cue Trials Attributable to Shift from
Multiple to Differential Cues

Discriminations	Trial 2	Trial 3
1–100	29	50
101–200	31	45

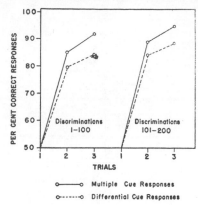

FIG. 2. Correct responses on multiple
cue and differential cue trials.

shift is a much more persistent error-producing factor in the series of problems than is stimulus perseveration.

Analysis of Error Factors: Response Shift Errors

A consistent tendency for monkeys to make more errors following a correct response than following an incorrect response in discrimination training situations has been reported (Harlow & Poch, 1945; Moss & Harlow, 1947). This behavior could be thought of as a tendency to 'try out' or 'explore' both stimuli in a discrimination problem. In this paper it is called *response shift*.

Response shift errors are seriously confounded with other errors, particularly in the early trials where stimulus perseveration errors and differential cue errors are frequent. Indications of the presence of response shift are obtainable, however, especially on the later trials. The two measures used here to separate out response shift errors were selected so as to include as few extraneous errors as possible. In so doing, we are no doubt excluding many errors which stem from the tendency to shift response. The measures here presented are regarded as minimal indicators of response shift tendencies, rather than accurate measures of the percentage of response shift errors.

Two measures of response shift errors have been calculated: (1) The difference has been found between the percentage of errors on Trials 4, 5, and 6 when all previous responses have been correct, and percentage of errors on the corresponding trials when the first trial was incorrect and the intervening trials were correct. (2) The difference has been computed between the percentage of errors on the trial immediately following a sequence of two, three or four correct responses when Trial 1 was correct and therefore included in the sequence, and the percentage of errors when Trial 1 was incorrect and therefore excluded from the sequence. Thus, this second measure compares error frequencies after equal numbers of correct responses and thereby utilizes noncomparable trials, whereas the first measure compares corresponding trials following unequal sequences of correct responses.

TABLE VI

Response Shift Errors on Comparable Trials

Trial	Trial 1 Correct			Trial 1 Incorrect			Percent Response Shift Error Responses	x^2 Number of Errors	P
	Number Responses	Number Errors	Percent Errors	Number Responses	Number Errors	Percent Errors			
4	770	85	11.0	784	55	7.1	3.9	6.83	.01
5	737	33	4.5	761	23	3.0	1.5	2.20	.20
6	699	38	5.4	743	18	2.4	3.0	6.29	.02
Total	2206	156	7.1	2288	96	4.2	2.9	17.78	.001

In view of the small number of total errors on Trials 3-6, the data of Discriminations 1-200 were grouped for the response shift error analysis.

Table VI presents data on the percentage of response shift errors computed by the first method—comparable trial analysis. It is seen that a total of 156 errors in 2206 responses was made on the trial following a series of three, four or five successive correct responses, whereas only 96 errors in 2288 responses were made on the trials following two, three or four successive correct responses preceded by the incorrect Trial 1 response. The P-value for difference in number of errors on Trials 4-6, as measured by chi-square, is .001. Comparable chi-square tests on individual trials yield P-values of .20 to .01. The percentages of responses on Trials 4-6 which can be regarded as response shift errors are seen to range from 1.5 to 3.9. Response shift errors comprise 41 percent of all errors on Trials 4-6 of those sequences in which all preceding responses were correct. This is obtained by dividing the percentage of response shift error responses (2.9) by the percentage of all erroneous responses on these trials (7.1).

Parallel data for response shift errors on trials following equal sequences of correct responses are given in Table VII. It is found that the percentage of responses on Trials 3-5 which can be regarded as response shift errors is greater than that obtained on Trials 4-6 by the first method (see Table VI). It is to be noted, also, that the P-values for chi-square tests of differences in errors following equal sequences of correct responses range from .05 to .001 for individual trial comparisons. Fifty-seven percent of all errors may be considered response shift errors on Trials 3-5 for those sequences meeting the criterion of no preceding errors. This compares with 41 percent response shift errors analyzed by the first method on Trials 4-6.

Phenomena similar to these reported here have been mentioned by previous workers. Tolman (1925) and Hunter (1920) have described spontaneous alternation of responses in rats, and Dennis (1939) has presented quantitative data to confirm the phenomenon. The operation of Hull's construct, reactive inhibition (1943), might produce errors of the type described.

Analysis of Error Factors: Position Habit Errors

The right-position errors and the left-position errors were computed for each of the monkeys, and the significance of the differences was determined by chi-square

TABLE VII

Response Shift Errors Following Series of Equal
Numbers of Successive Correct Responses

Trial	Trial 1 Correct				Trial 1 Incorrect			Percent Response Shift Error Responses	χ^2 Number of Errors	P
	Number Responses	Number Errors	Percent Errors	Trial	Number Responses	Number Errors	Percent Errors			
3	819	110	13.4	4	784	55	7.1	6.3	16.9	.001
4	770	85	11.0	5	761	23	3.0	8.0	37.5	.001
5	737	33	4.5	6	743	18	2.4	2.1	4.67	.05
Total	2316	228	9.8		2288	96	4.2	5.6	102.21	.001

tests. No difference beyond the 10 percent confidence level was found for any animal for Discriminations 1-100. For Discriminations 101-200, three subjects—90, 104, and 108— showed tendencies toward left position errors significant at or beyond the one percent confidence level. These data show that position preferences operated as error producing factors in some subjects after very extensive discrimination training.

DISCUSSION

It has been customary to present the data of learning experiments in the form of learning curves and, frequently, to express the characteristics of these curves by mathematical equations. Such curves are obviously the resultants of complex processes neither defined nor delimited by the individual curve or its equation. To differentiate and identify the underlying processes, it is essential to go beyond the individual curve and to compare multiple curves obtained by systematic manipulation of independent variables in the learning situation. Such manipulation and comparison has revealed, as we showed in the preceding pages, the presence of certain underlying partially separable processes which we have called error-producing factors.

Reading No. 8
A MODEL OF HYPOTHESIS BEHAVIOR IN DISCRIMINATION LEARNING SET[*]

By Marvin Levine

In discrimination learning, or learning-set experiments, one typically measures the percentage of correct responses on a given trial (or block of trials, or, in learning set, on a block of problems) and ignores the changes in other systematic response patterns. An alternative approach was taken by Krechevsky (1932a) who first measured position preferences, position alternation, and light-going tendencies in the white rat in a discrimination problem. He described each tendency as a "hypothesis" (H), which may be defined as a specifiable pattern of response to a selected stimulus set. Harlow (1950) demonstrated other Hs by the monkey in the discrimination learning-set experiment, and Goodnow and several co-workers (Goodnow & Pettigrew, 1955; Goodnow & Postman, 1955; Goodnow, Shanks, Rubinstein, & Lubin, 1957) demonstrated patterns of response in humans.

While these researchers have found that such analyses provide useful insights into the nature of the learning process, the methods of measurement were selected for the specific demonstration at hand. No comprehensive picture of H behavior was available to suggest the total set of Hs which existed, to insure a lack of confounding in the measurement of various Hs, and to show the proportion of behavior under the control of each H. The purpose of this paper is to provide such a picture, to describe a mathematical model of H behavior which permits an analysis having the following characteristics: (*a*) The operation of a large number of Hs can be analyzed simultaneously. As many as nine will be so analyzed, although this number is by no means an upper limit. (*b*) The relative strength of each H, i.e., the proportion of responses controlled by each H, can be demonstrated at successive stages of the experiment. (*c*) The measure of a given H is uninfluenced by the presence of other Hs. (*d*) The analysis is independent of the particular reward and stimulus sequences employed. For example, the correct stimulus may be permit-

*Adapted from *Psychological Review*, 1959, **66**, 353-366. Copyright 1959 by the American Psychological Association. Reprinted by permission of the publisher.

ted to perseverate on one side for three consecutive trials, or not, or may alternate from side to side as frequently as it perseverates, or may not, etc.

This model will be applied to the behavior of the rhesus monkey in a discrimination learning-set experiment in which each problem is presented for only three trials. The stimuli in this experiment consist of two objects per problem, response to one object producing a reward (a raisin or peanut), response to the other going unrewarded. Every three trials the problem is changed by introducing two new objects, and several hundred problems are typically presented in this manner. A more detailed description of the learning-set procedure is given by Harlow (1949).

No analysis will be made in this paper of data beyond the third trial of any problem. The analysis may be applied to learning-set experiments utilizing longer problems simply by ignoring all trials past the third trial. The description of the behavior in such cases applies only to the first-three-trial sets. Attempts are currently being made to generalize the model in a more satisfactory way. Work is now in progress, for example, extending the model to oddity learning-set data in which each problem is presented for 12 trials and to single discrimination problems several hundred trials in length.

ASSUMPTIONS AND DEFINITIONS

The first assumption is that if an H is appearing, its occurrence will be manifested over all three trials of a given problem. Suppose, for example, that an S has a position preference on one problem. The only acceptable manifestation of this preference will be response to one position for the three trials. Response to this position for two out of the three trials will not serve as an instance of this H.

The second assumption is that the stimuli determining a response go no further back than the immediately preceding trial. A double-alternation H, for example, will not be considered, since the response on Trial n requires residual stimulation from the response on Trial $n - 2$.

Given these two restrictions, the definition of a few symbols will provide sufficient background for describing the set of Hs which are considered in this paper. In any learning-set experiment the E decides in advance the sequence of positions which the reward (and rewarded object) will take. The reward sequence may go LLR on the first problem, RRR on the second problem, etc. He records the outcome for the three trials as $+ + -$, $- + -$, etc., and from the combination of L, R, and $+$, $-$ sequences can deduce the S's responses. There are then three sets of symbols that are necessary: The reward sequences, the response sequences, and the outcome sequences. For any three-trial problem there are eight possible reward sequences. These may be paired into symmetrical pairs of (LLL, RRR), (LLR, RRL), (LRL, RLR), and (LRR, RLL). From the standpoint of the subsequent analysis the pairs may be combined. That is, the important property is how the reward varies rather than the particular side on which it appears on a given trial. If the sequence goes LLL, the important fact is that the food was on one side for three trials. The additional fact that it was the left side is here irrelevant. This considera-tion reduces the reward sequences to four: *AAA*, *AAB*, *ABA*, and *ABB*, where *A* is defined as the location of the reward on the first trial, and *B* is defined as the other position. A similar combining applies to the *S*'s responses. The four resulting response sequences will be symbolized by *III*, *IIO*, *IOI*, *IOO*, where *I* is the position responded to on the first trial, and *O* is the other position. Whereas the reward and response sequences reduce to four, the +, − outcome sequences will not be combined so that all eight of these will be used.

The manifestation of the Hs considered in this paper may now be specified. These Hs, their general definition, and rationale for selection are listed below. In parentheses, following the definition, is the manifestation of the H as it appears in the raw data.

1. Position Preference: consistent response to one position. This H has been frequently observed in monkey and in rat behavior (*III*).

2. Position Alternation: alternating between positions from trial to trial. While this H has been noted only rarely in the monkey, Gellermann (1933) felt that it might occur in sufficient degree to control for it. It is a common phenomenon in rats (*IOI*).

3. Stimulus Preference: consistent response to one of the stimulus objects irrespective of reinforcement. This too has been commonly found in the primate and other orders (+ + + or − − −).

4. Stimulus Alternation: alternating between stimuli from trial to trial. This, like its position analogue, is uncommon in the monkey, It has, however, been shown to occur in other orders (+ − + or − + −).

5. Win-stay-Lose shift (with respect to position): repetition of a response to a position which has just been rewarded and alternating away from a position not rewarded. This type of H has been noted in human behavior by Goodnow and Pettigrew (1955), and in monkey behavior by Harlow (1950) in a slightly different form under the name "differential cue" (*I + I* or *I − O*).

6. Lose-stay-Win-shift (with respect to position): repetition of a response to a position not rewarded on the preceding trial, and alternation away from a position just rewarded. This is the reverse of the H above, and would not be expected to occur except in *S*s with special experimental histories. It was included in order to provide an H which one would expect to have zero strength (*I − I* or *I + O*).

7. (Problem-solution behavior)₂ or Win-stay-Lose-shift (with respect to the object): repetition of a response to an object which has just been rewarded, and alternation away from an object not rewarded. This H yields maximum reward in the learning-set situation, since correct responding begins on the second trial of the problem (+ + +, or − + +).

8. (Problem-solution behavior)₃: manifestation of the correct response on the third trial although not on the second trial. This H is required by the well-known fact that the correct response may suddenly appear on later trials (+ − + or − − +).

9. Random Responding: this H, while it has a single form of manifestation, may be produced in any one of three ways: (*a*) The determinants of a response may fluctuate nonsystematically from trial to trial, in which case all sequences would be expected to occur with approximately the same frequency. (*b*) The *S* may be systematically responding to stimulus changes which are unrecorded and which are randomly related to the position sequence of the rewarded object. In this case, again, all response sequences would have equal expected frequencies. (*c*) Under certain special conditions Hs which have been ignored will contribute to this Random Responding H without affecting the estimation of any other H. These conditions are described elsewhere (Levine, 1959a). For now it is

TABLE 1
DEFINITION OF THE IIs EVALUATED IN THE PRESENT PAPER

H	Definition	Manifestation	Prob-ability Symbol
Position Preference	Sequence of response to one side	*III*	a
Position Alternation	Alternating between positions on consecutive trials	*IOI*	b
Stimulus Preference	Sequence of responses to one of the relevant stimuli	+++ or ---	c
Stimulus Alternation	Alternating between the relevant stimuli on consecutive trials	+-+ or -+-	d
Win-stay-Lose-shift (pos.)	Response to the position rewarded on the preceding trial	*I+I+I* or *I+I-O* or *I-O+O* or *I-O-I*	a
Lose-stay-Win-shift (pos.)	Response to the position not rewarded on the preceding trial	*I+O+I* or *I+O-O* or *I-I+O* or *I-I-I*	v
(Problem-solution)$_2$ or Win-stay-Lose-shift (obj.)	Learning manifested on the second trial of a problem	+++ or -++	p_2
(Problem-solution)$_3$	Learning first manifested on the third trial of a problem	+-+ or --+	p_3
Random Responding	Responses uncorrelated with recorded stimulus changes	All sequences	R

sufficient to note that the Random Responding measure is conceptualized as an estimate of both nonsystematic responding and residual sequence strength. (This H is manifested in all sequences.)

These nine Hs, their definitions, and manifestations are summarized in Table I. In the last column of this table are the symbols which will be used to represent the probability of occurrence of an H or the proportion of problems showing the H in a set of data. For example, the result $a = 0.5$ means that Ss show Position Preference on 50% of the problems. The first goal of this paper is to demonstrate a technique for evaluating these probabilities.

Two further assumptions will be useful in attaining this goal. The first is that the Hs are mutually exclusive. The occurrence on a single problem of the sequence +++ may mean, among other possibilities, that either Stimulus Preference or (Problem-solution)₂ has taken place, not both. In general, if a sequence may be attributed to two or more Hs and several instances of the sequence have occurred, different Hs may have been operating on different problems, but two Hs never combine on the same problem. The second assumption is that the above set of Hs includes all Hs whose probability is greater than zero. These two assumptions permit the following statement:

$$a + b + c + d + u + v + p_2 + p_3 + R = 1.00$$

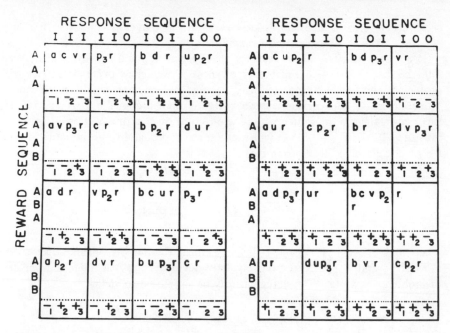

FIG. 1. Thirty-two cells representing the 32 possible sequences which can occur in a three-trial problem. The symbols in each cell represent the Hs which can produce the associated response sequence.

THE EVALUATION OF THE H STRENGTHS

The assumptions outlined above determine the relationship between a set of data and the probabilities of the Hs. Figure 1 shows a set of 32 cells, each one of which represents one of the 32 possible sequences which can occur in a three-trial problem. The 32 cells are organized into two blocks of 16 each, the block on the left containing those sequences with a first trial minus, the other containing those sequences with a first trial plus. The rewarded position sequences are on the rows and the response sequences are on the columns.

Any one sequence may be a manifestation of some Hs and not of others. For example, $A - {}_1A - {}_2A - {}_3$ may be interpreted as Position Preference, Stimulus Preference, Lose-stay-Win-shift (with respect to position), or Random Responding, but not as any of the other five Hs. If, when E presents AAA, any of the other five Hs should be occurring, then $-{}_1-{}_2-{}_3$ cannot occur. In the $A - {}_1A - {}_2A - {}_3$ cell are listed the probability symbols associated with the four possible Hs. In general, each cell contains the symbols for the Hs which may produce the indicated sequence. The only new symbol is r. This is used here instead of R to represent Random Responding, and is defined by $r = R/4$. The justification for this change of variable is that the Random Responding H enters into four times as many cells as any of the other Hs. If $a = 1$, for example, a's influence is felt in only eight cells whereas if $R = 1$ its influence is distributed over 32 cells. Its effect on any one cell would be ¼ the corresponding effect of any of the other Hs.

In a three-trial-per-problem learning-set experiment the data may be analyzed into the frequencies with which each of these 32 sequences occurs in a block of problems, and these frequencies may be used to estimate certain conditional probabilities. In particular, the probability of the outcomes on trials two and three given the reward sequence and the outcome on trial one may be estimated. For the $A -_1 A -_2 A -_3$ sequence, such a probability is symbolized as $P(-_2 -_3 | A -_1 AA)$. In this example,

$$P(-_2 -_3 | A -_1 AA) = \frac{P(A -_1 A -_2 A -_3)}{P(A -_1 AA)} = \frac{\dfrac{n(A -_1 A -_2 A -_3)}{N}}{\dfrac{n(A -_1 AA)}{N}},$$

where $n(A -_1 A -_2 A -_3)$ and $n(A -_1 AA)$ mean the number of times that $A -_1 A -_2 A -_3$ and $A -_1 AA$, respectively, have occurred, and N is the total number of problems presented. The statement may be simplified to yield

$$P(-_2 -_3 | A -_1 AA) = \frac{n(A -_1 A -_2 A -_3)}{n(A -_1 AA)} \qquad [2]$$

From the assumptions, it follows that on a certain proportion of the problems Position Preference may occur, producing $(-_2 -_3 | A -_1 AA)$, on a certain proportion of the problems Stimulus Preference may occur, producing the same sequence; and so on, for the four Hs which can produce this sequence. Because the Hs are mutually exclusive the $P(-_2 -_3 | A -_1 AA)$ is equal to the sum of the probabilities of each of the associated Hs, i.e.,

$$P(-_2 -_3 | A -_1 AA) = a + c + v + r \qquad [3]$$

From Equations [2] and [3] it follows that

$$a + c + v + r = \frac{n(A -_1 A -_2 A -_3)}{n(A -_1 AA)} \qquad [4]$$

Now, $n(A -_1 A -_2 A -_3)$ is the frequency with which $A -_1 A -_2 A -_3$ has occurred in the experiment and $n(A -_1 AA)$ may be obtained from the left-hand matrix of Fig. 1 as the row total of the row containing $n(A -_1 A -_2 A -_3)$. That is,

$$n(A -_1 AA) = n(A -_1 A -_2 A -_3) + n(A -_1 A -_2 A +_3)$$
$$+ n(A -_1 A +_2 A -_3) + n(A -_1 A +_2 A +_3)$$

The right side of $\lfloor 4 \rfloor$ is, therefore, a number obtainable from the data, and Equation $\lfloor 4 \rfloor$ is an equation in four unknowns.

With nine unknowns to be evaluated, nine such equations are required for simultaneous solution. These equations may be obtained from any nine cells yielding nonparallel equations. If the assumption is made that a given H has the same strength no matter in which cell it appears, then the solutions from the nine equations will give estimates of the nine H strengths for the block of problems considered. The first problem, then, that of evaluating the strengths of the various Hs, has been solved. In general, the solution may be summarized by the following:

> Theorem: The probabilities associated with a set of m independently specifiable Hs may be obtained from the solution of m equations of the form
>
> $$(j+k+\cdots)_i = \frac{\text{(frequency of the } i\text{th sequence)}}{\text{(frequency of the corresponding row total)}}$$
>
> where $(j+k+\ldots)_i$ represents the sum of the probabilities of the Hs which may produce the ith sequence.

A TEST OF THE MODEL

It is now possible to apply the analysis to data from a learning-set experiment and to determine, for each block of problems, the relative strength of the Hs. Using the technique outlined above, one could solve three sets of nine equations based on 27 different sequences and obtain three estimates of each H. If the 27 sequences were carefully selected, the remaining five sequences could contribute another estimate of five of the Hs. Averaging the estimates for each H would yield a mean estimate of each of the H probabilities based on all the data. There is, however, one important objection to this procedure: application of the method without some prior testing of the model would leave the validity of the estimates in question. Some indication is first required that the estimates are a product of the behavior, and not simply of the mathematical machinery.

The present section deals with such validation. The test consists in estimating the probabilities from some of the sequences and then in predicting, on the basis of these estimates, the frequencies with which each of the remaining sequences should occur. These frequencies may be predicted from Equation 4 once the H probabilities are known. This frequency prediction was applied to four sets of data, with a slightly different treatment for each. Each of these sets will be discussed in turn.

The first application was to the first block of three-trial-per-problem data from Levine, Levinson, and Harlow (1959). Eighteen sequences were selected in order to have two estimates of each H. The criterion for selection of each sequence was that it be based on no more than three Hs. Both sequences based only on Random Responding (i.e., $A+_1A+_2A-_3$ and $A+_1B+_2A-_3$), all eight sequences based only on two Hs, and eight of the sequences based on three Hs were selected. Averaging the solutions from the two sets of nine equations yielded:

$$a = 0.08, \qquad b = 0.03, \qquad c = 0.16,$$
$$d = 0.02, \qquad u = -0.02, \qquad v = -0.01,$$
$$p_2 = 0.20, \qquad p_3 = 0.07, \qquad R = 0.44$$

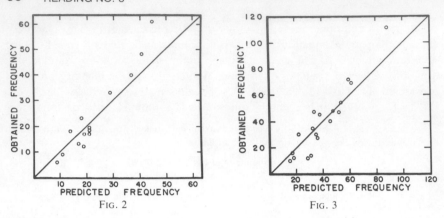

FIG. 2. Sequence frequencies from Block I (Problems 1-96) of the Levine et al. experiment.
FIG. 3. Sequence frequencies from Block I (Problems 1-100) of the Harlow et al. experiment.

A few interesting aspects of these results may be noted. First, the Lose-stay-Win-shift H was included with the Prediction that $v = 0$ and a close estimate of zero was obtained. Second, b, d, u, and v all appear to be estimates of zero. This finding is not of special significance here, but will be referred to later because of its consistent emergence. Third, Equation 1 was not used in obtaining these estimates and may serve as a prediction. The sum of the obtained estimates is 0.97.

The values for these nine Hs were substituted into the equations for each of the remaining 14 sequences, and the predicted frequency for each sequence was obtained. The observed and predicted frequencies are plotted in Fig. 2 with each axis in the same units, so that perfect prediction would yield 14 points lying along the 45 line. It will be seen that the points distribute themselves in reasonable fashion along this line.

In order to quantitatively describe the accuracy of prediction, a statistic describing the proportion of variance explained (PVE) by the predicted frequencies was devised. This is given by

$$\text{PVE} = 1 - \frac{\sigma_{o.p}^2}{\sigma_o^2} \qquad [5]$$

where σ_o^2 is the variance of the observed values, and $\sigma_{o.p}^2$ is the variance around the 45 line, i.e.,

$$\sigma_{o,p}^2 = \Sigma^n (o - p)^2 / n.$$

The symbols o and p represent the observed and predicted frequencies, respectively, and n represents the number of points. For these data, PVE = 0.85.

The second set of data to which this test was applied was from the first 100 problems of a learning-set study by Harlow, Harlow, Rueping, and Mason (1960). A new criterion was used in selecting the sequences for solution. The H

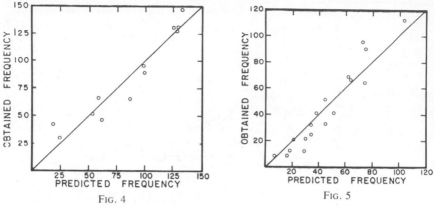

FIG. 4

FIG. 4. Sequence frequencies from Block I (Problems 1-80) of Schrier's experiment.

FIG. 5. Sequence frequencies from Block VI (Problems 501-600) of the Harlow et al. experiment.

probabilities were obtained primarily from sequences with a third trial minus, and predictions were made primarily for the sequences ending in third trial plus. To accomplish this, it was convenient to use eight Hs, and so here it was assumed that $v = 0$. Twelve sequences ending in a third-trial minus, and two sequences with a third-trial plus (the two based only on p_3 and r) were selected to solve for all Hs but p_2. This H was then obtained from Equation 1. As a result, predictions could be made for 14 third-trial-plus sequences, and four third-trial-minus sequences. These 18 points are plotted in Fig. 3, where the PVE = 0.84. The specific probability values are

$$a = 0.13, \qquad b = 0.00, \qquad c = 0.19, \qquad d = -0.03,$$
$$u = 0.02, \qquad p_2 = 0.13, \qquad p_3 = 0.12, \qquad R = 0.44$$

Again b, d, and u appear to be estimates of zero. This finding, along with the assumption that $v = 0$, repeats the earlier finding.

The test was next applied to the first block of problems from a study by Schrier (1958). The same method of selection used in the preceding study was employed here in determining the sequences for solution, i.e., as many third-trial-minus sequences as necessary, two third-trial-plus sequences and Equation 1 were used. There was one minor difference, however. Schrier did not permit the reward to perseverate on one side for three consecutive trials. In this experiment, therefore, the top row of eight cells (see Fig. 1) does not exist, leaving only 24 sequences. In order to increase the number of sequences for which predictions could be made, it was assumed that $b = 0$, $v = 0$. This permits prediction for 12 sequences: 10 third-trial-plus and 2 third-trial-minus sequences. The results are shown in Fig. 4. Here the PVE = 0.91. The specific H probabilities are: $a = 0.13, c = 0.07, d = 0.00, u = -0.01, p_2 = 0.32, p_3 = 0.14, R = 0.36$. Again, d and u are estimates of

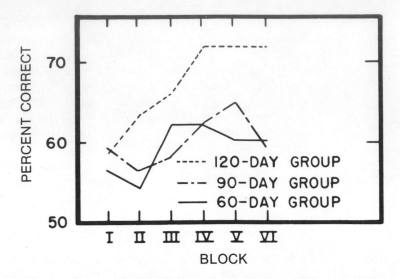

FIG. 6. Performance of the three groups in the Harlow et al. experiment as measured by the percentage of correct responses on Trial 2 for each 100-problem block.

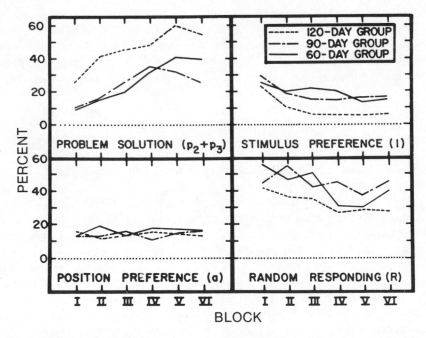

FIG. 7. Analysis of the three Harlow et al. groups. Each quadrant shows the percentage of problems in which the behavior was determined by the indicated H.

zero, and the assumption that $b = 0$, $v = 0$, did not serve to reduce the PVE.

The PVE, in fact, is somewhat larger in this study than in the preceding two sets of data. The difference is not so great as to warrant extensive speculation, but it was also noted that in the Schrier data R was lower than in the preceding sets. A check on whether variance and Random Responding were related entailed applying the analysis to another block of data, the last 100 problems of the learning-set study described above by Harlow et al. This block of problems was selected because it became known in subsequent work that its R value was 0.20. Precisely the same analysis was applied as with the first 100 problems for this group. The results are shown in Fig. 5. The resulting PVE was 0.91 which bears out the possibility of the relationship. More relevant to the present topic, it provides another confirmation of the applicability of the model by this test, and suggests, along with the finding that R decreases throughout an experiment (to be described in the next section), that the PVEs would have been even higher had the test been applied to last blocks rather than first blocks of problems.

AN ANALYSIS OF LEARNING-SET FUNCTIONS INTO H COMPONENTS

Now that the model has been described and its correspondence to behavior has been indicated the analysis may be applied to demonstrate its value in describing behavioral processes. Harlow, Harlow, Rueping, and Mason (1960) have performed a learning-set experiment with young rhesus monkeys in which they compared the effects of age upon the acquisition of learning set. Three groups of 10 Ss each received 600 problems starting at 60, 90, or 120 days. The learning set functions showing percentage correct on Trial 2 for blocks of 100 problems are plotted in Fig. 6. By t test, the 60- and 90-day groups are not significantly different but the 120-day group is significantly different from both of these.

The H analysis was applied to each block for each of the three groups, producing 18 separate analyses. Each analysis was based on all the nine Hs listed in Table I. A detailed description of the analysis is given elsewhere by the author (Levine, 1959a).

In the preceding section it was found either empirically or by assumption that b, d, u, and v could consistently be regarded as having zero strength. It might be predicted that in the 18 blocks of problems considered here these four Hs would yield 72 estimates of zero. These 72 estimates ranged from -0.05 to $+0.05$. The mean was at -0.002 with $\sigma=0.02$. This finding further validates the model by confirming an expected finding, and simplifies the Harlow et al. data by eliminating four of the Hs from consideration.

The remaining Hs are plotted in Fig. 7. The p_2 and p_3 values have been added together to depict the number of problems manifesting a learning H, and are plotted in the upper left-hand quadrant. The differences here reflect the differences seen in Fig. 6, that the 120-day group shows more problem-solution behavior throughout than the 60- and 90-day groups.

Consideration of the remaining three Hs suggests some of the sources of these differences. The Position Preference H, plotted in the lower left-hand quadrant, is striking in that this H has the same strength for the three groups. Thus, the difference in over-all performance between the 120-day and the 60- and 90-day groups is not attributable to this H. The basis for the difference between the learning-set functions may be seen in the right-hand side of Fig. 7. This difference is attributable specifically to the differences in Stimulus Preference and Random Responding.

In addition to providing more detail about the differences among the three groups, Fig. 7 shows the various behavioral processes which underlie the learning-set functions. Position Preference is again unique in that it does not decrease but has a constant strength at about 0.18. A comparison of this H with the other two nonsolution Hs shows that Hs do not extinguish simultaneously or at the same rate. Also, the $p_2 + p_3$ plot shows the progress of learning "purified" of the other behavior patterns. It may well be, although this is clearly conjecture at present, that the formulas describing these elementary processes will have greater simplicity and universality than the formulations of what is here seen as a complex, composite function: *the* learning curve.

DISCUSSION

The model presented here has a few useful features. Primarily, it provides a technique for evaluating the strengths of a variety of Hs. This method follows directly from certain relatively simple assumptions concerning the appearance of response patterns. Secondly, almost all of the variance of the frequencies of response sequences occurring in a block of problems may be explained by the model (Figs. 2-5). Then, evaluation of H strengths at successive stages of learning shows that Hs follow regular functions (Fig. 7).

While the data are, for the most part, in accord with predictions from the model, an intriguing systematic discrepancy is to be noted. This is illustrated in Figs. 2-5 where the points typically organize themselves around a line whose slope is slightly larger than the 45 line. Although insufficient analysis has been performed to determine the source of this discrepancy a promising lead is that the sequences $-+-$ and $++-$ are occurring somewhat more frequently than would be predicted by the model. It may be shown that the discrepancy would appear if this were the case.

Assuming that the model in its current form is approximately correct, it provides interesting implications for some current psychological problems. The central property of the model is that it takes as the dependent variable unit the H, defined as a pattern of responses to selected stimuli. The specification of a behavior pattern means that this pattern as a whole is susceptible to the traditional effects of reinforcement operations, i.e., it is possible to reinforce some Hs and extinguish others. Thus, one may reinforce Position Alternation, Stimulus Alternation, or various kinds of stay-shift combinations. This idea of the reinforcement of a response pattern has specific relevance for understanding the phenomenon of learning-to-learn as seen in the discrimination learning-set situation. Since Harlow's (1949) demonstration that Ss show progressive improvement on Trial-2 performance in successive problems the question of the nature of this improvement has provided a challenge to theory.

The explanation of learning-set development suggested here results from assuming that the S is capable of responding in terms of Hs, and that Hs may be reinforced. One of the Hs, Win-stay-Lose-shift (with respect to the object), is the H which the E chooses to reinforce. There is nothing unique about this H. It has the same formal status as responses to one position or any of the other Hs. Learning-set development then is the gradual strengthening, via 100% reinforcement, of this H, and the gradual extinction, because of 50% reinforcement, of the other Hs. Thus, this example of learning-to-learn is amenable to treatment by any conventional reinforcement theory, so long as a *pattern* of response is taken as the dependent variable.

The model provides description not only of the H which is reinforced but also of other Hs. An important empirical finding presented in this paper is that these Hs may not all extinguish at the same rate. This finding creates a problem for current learning theories, which make no provision for several extinction processes. It is, of course, too soon to know how many different extinction processes must be postulated and to develop theories about the nature of the differences. The analysis described herein should make a contribution toward solving these problems.

5
THE RENAISSANCE: MATHEMATICAL LEARNING THEORISTS IN THE EARLY SIXTIES

In the next decade, the first events of note in the development of H theory were produced by conditioning theorists. Estes and Restle independently announced a major shift in their views. When respected leaders veer, disciples follow. These first events, then, were important sociologically as well as intellectually.

ESTES

A few years earlier, Rock (1957) had published a study that challenged the assumption that verbal learning was incremental. Rock compared two groups, both of which learned a list of eight nonsense-syllable pairs. The Control Group went through this list on successive trials until S could give the correct response word to each stimulus word. The Experimental Group began with the same list. However, each time S made an incorrect response, unknown to him that syllable pair was eliminated and a new one substituted for the next trial. The Experimental S, therefore, had to learn a few new pairs on each repetition of the list. If S learned each pair by a process of gradual (incremental) strengthening, then responses that had received some strengthening (but not enough to produce the correct response at every trial) were being eliminated and brand new responses were being conditioned. It would follow that the Control Group should reach the criterion of one perfect pass through the list faster than the Experimental Group. Rock, however, found no appreciable difference between these two groups. He argued that a "failed" item meant that the response had a strength no greater than that of a brand new item. Prior to responding correctly, the strenth of the response was always zero. Learning, in short, was all-or-none.

Estes was puzzled by, and took seriously, Rock's result. He was also puzzling over the problem with his theory (discussed above, p. 35 ff), that the stimulus-sampling model predicted less than perfect performance in simple discrimination situations. Rock's result, this problem, and some research of his own led Estes to the notion that response strengthening in many learning tasks might be all-or-none. In 1960 he published the article announcing and buttressing this view (see Reading No. 9). His shift had strong impact. This article was republished five times; several younger mathematical psychologists subsequently developed models incorporating an all-or-none assumption.*

Although the shift from an incremental to an all-or-none assumption is not synonymous with adopting an H theory, it is certainly consonant with such a theory. One feature of *H* theory, it will be recalled from the Krechevsky-Spence exchanges, is that discriminations are presumably learned on an all-or-none basis. As the label indicates, the Continuity-Noncontinuity Controversy centered around this facet of H theory. Estes, then, while not explicitly promoting H theory, nevertheless indirectly contributed to its reemergence.

RESTLE

Restle's influence was direct. In a series of three articles (1960, 1961, 1962—the last is presented as Reading No. 10) he proclaimed a mathematical theory of discrimination learning based upon the assumption of *H* (Restle initially used the term "strategy") testing. The work was seminal. Much of the subsequent *H* theorizing and experimenting took this model as the point of departure.

The model had three forms. The first contained the following assumptions. (1) At the outset of a discrimination-learning task the *S* has a universe of *H*s from which he samples one. The sampled *H* dictates *S*'s response. (2) If his response is called "right," *S* keeps his *H* for the next trial. (3) If his response is called "wrong," he returns this *H* to the universe and randomly resamples for the next trial. According to this last assumption, the *S* may resample the *H* he has just rejected. More specifically, if there are *N H*s in the universe he will resample the just-rejected *H* with probability $1/N$. Because this assumption implies that *S* has forgotten the *H* he has just rejected, it came to be characterized as a *zero-memory* assumption.

In the other two forms of this model the first assumption was slightly modified. In one, the *S* starts the problem by sampling all the *H*s in the universe; in the other, he samples some intermediate number of *H*s. In both of these variants a "right" causes *S* to retain from the sample only those *H*s that were just confirmed; a "wrong" causes him to return the entire sample to the universe and to resample. This last assumption, which means that *S* starts the problem anew after each "wrong," is again the zero-memory assumption. These variants may, for the present, be ignored. Restle demonstrated that the three models led to the same

---

*The all-or-none developments within verbal learning are introduced here because of their relation to the revival of *H* theory. The reader should not be left with the impression, however, that Rock's experiment and Estes's theory went unchallenged. For a review of some of the succeeding developments within verbal learning see Restle (1965).

basic theorems. Partly for this reason, and partly because of the simplicity of the assumption that S tests one H at a time, the first version was employed during the next few years.

The zero-memory assumption is clearly counterintuitive (and in subsequent years was criticized and modified, even by Restle—see Restle & Emmerich, 1966). Despite this flaw, the model proved to be important. One can adduce several reasons for its influence. First, it was the work of a major figure in an important theoretical tradition. Many workers in that tradition accorded the model the serious study that any work by Restle deserves. Second, as we have seen, theorists were becoming receptive to a cognitive formulation of human learning. Third, the theory was mathematically cast. Restle demonstrated that a cognitive theory could meet as high a standard of rigor as (mathematical) conditioning theory. Accusations about unclear implications, a charge directed against earlier cognitive formulations, were now not applicable. Fourth, the implications of the theory were not about inner processes or about statements S might make to describe those processes, but about choice responses. The predictions, that is, were about data that met behavioristic requirements.

From the outset, then, this model seemed likely to have an impact. One is nevertheless, puzzled at the appearance of this model so soon after the Bourne and Restle (1959) article. The latter, as we saw, contained a sophisticated application of Restle's conditioning theory. Earlier applications, to learning-set data (1958) and to maze-learning by rats (1957), were also successful. In spite of this, we see Restle abruptly turn from this theory to formulate a new statement. Restle has recently provided some information on this transition.* These comments, which follow here, help fill the gap in the story:

> It is true that the earlier cue-adaptation theory was quite successful in calculations of many experimental results. What does not come out of that statement is the additional fact that the calculations were rather laborious; furthermore, they did not simplify. The equations of that earlier theory are almost entirely intractable, and it was very difficult to obtain even an approximate expression for the total errors made to solution, let alone anything fancier. In the years from 1953 to about 1958, I became incredibly quick at reading tables of logarithms, including reading complements, and at fingering Monroe calculators. By about 1957 I was thoroughly tired of so gluey a theory.
>
> In 1957 I made a desperate attempt to revise this theory with a complicated process, long happily forgotten, by which subjects compared one cue or dimension with another and decided which, if either, should be deleted. This was presented to a summer meeting of mathematical psychologists at Stanford. At the end of my talk, Professor W. K. Estes gently inquired if I was trying for the prize for most complicated model of the year. This remark, though justified, was sharp enough to redirect my thinking toward a simplified model.
>
> Remember that 1957 was the year of Irvin Rock's 'all-or-none'' paper, which was followed up closely by Estes' replications. At the same time, Bob Bush had worked out statistics for several learning models, including what he called a ''Krechevsky'' model which was simple all-or-none learning—Bush showed correctly that such a model would

*Personal communication.

not fit some avoidance learning data. However, in 1957 the general concept of all-or-none learning was in the air all over, and since I was fortunately within the inner circle of mathematical psychologists, I received preprints and letters about all the new discoveries as soon as they were made. I am sure I heard of Gordon Bower's work with paired-associates very early—he also had been at the Stanford conference. In that same year, Tom Trabasso showed up as a graduate student at Michigan State, and we soon got together.

The idea of the hypothesis-sampling process was not terribly difficult to think of. However, I saw two apparently fatal objections to it. First, it seemed to say that the organism responded to only one cue at a time, ignoring all others. Therefore, a learner would learn only a single cue. This seemed to me to conflict with what I knew of rats in mazes, as well as some other data and all personal experiences. Second, the theory did not produce a nice smooth learning curve, but a jumble of results, with one subject varying widely from another for no good reason at all.

As Trabasso and I began to collect and study concept-learning data in our own laboratory, we found rather large individual differences. I can recall our drafting out but never publishing a calculation, using my earlier discrimination-learning model, in which the model predicted very little variance, and the data showed so much that one had to assume that individual differences were enormous. This pointed directly toward the all-or-none model. I found that one of my objections was erroneous—the data did actually look exactly like the widely-variable jumble that would result from hypothesis sampling.

But my main objection still held—not even rats, and certainly not human subjects, would be satisfied to take only one cue per trial. I began wondering what would happen with a model in which the subject took two hypotheses at a time. There followed several weeks of fumbling with algebra again and again reformulating ways in which the subject could try to work with two hypotheses at a time. Then, suddenly, I noticed that under certain natural conditions, two hypotheses acted just like one!

The point is not easy to make in an informal way, but the result is two-fold and lovely. If a subject takes two hypotheses at the same time, this is not necessarily more efficient than taking one at a time. When taking two at a time the subject has a higher probability of taking the correct hypothesis, but he gets it mixed with wrong ideas and then must sort out which is correct. In that process, he can very easily take a wrong step and lose his correct hypothesis, and have to start over. The finding is that these probabilities exactly balance, so that the subject does not do better when taking two than one hypothesis, and in fact he can take any number, N, of hypotheses in his sample and still not profit. Furthermore (and here the analysis was somewhat deeper), he would appear to learn all-or-none, even though in truth he would be going through a complex and more-or-less graded process of sorting hypotheses.

These mathematical results, obtained partly from Feller's 1950 book and partly from hard work, removed my last objection to the hypothesis-sampling, all-or-none model. I was soon able to see that the learning curves I had been seeking were, in fact, mere averages and not true facts about individual subjects. I studied the statistics of learning models better than I had, and found that this particular all-or-none model was the easiest of all to handle.

* * *

The influence of the theoretical shift by Estes and Restle may be seen in the next development. Gordon Bower, whose previous experiments on human learning served to support the all-or-none assumption in verbal learning (Bower, 1962), and Tom Trabasso, Restle's above-mentioned graduate student, teamed up at Stanford to refine and to test Restle's model. They employed the simplest variant of that model, that Ss sample and test one H at a time, and applied it to adult human performance in multidimensional concept-identification problems.

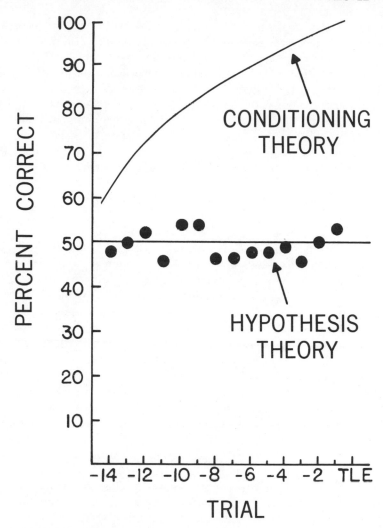

FIG. 2. The points show the percentage of correct responses at each trial before the trial of last error (TLE). The curves are theoretical.

The first test concerned responses before the criterion, defined as a long run (e.g., 15) of consecutive correct responses. According to the Restle-Bower-Trabasso view, when, following some error, S samples the correct H, he responds correctly, keeps the H, responds correctly to the next trial, etc., producing the criterion run. In this model, S cannot make an error once he samples the correct H. Any observed error, therefore, implies that up until that trial S has always sampled Hs other than the correct H. In particular, the final error in a protocol, that error which just precedes the criterion run, is pivotal (and is important enough to have its own name—the TLE, for Trial of Last Error). Before the TLE S has sampled only incorrect Hs; following it S must be holding the correct H. Since an incorrect H will lead to a correct response only by chance, before the TLE S should, in a two-response task, make the correct response with probability = ½.* Furthermore, this value should hold for each trial before the TLE. Obtaining from all the protocols, combined, the proportion of correct responses at one trial before the TLE, at two trials before, at three trials before, etc., one should obtain a flat, or stationary, backwards learning curve. The series of proportions should fluctuate around 0.5. A typical result, adapted from Trabasso (1963), is shown in Fig. 2. This result has since been replicated many times (Bower & Trabasso, 1964; Erickson, Zajkowski, & Ehmann, 1966; Wickens & Millward, 1971; see also Reading No. 15).

Another set of predictions concerned the sequence of correct (+) and incorrect (−) responses prior to the TLE. In this presolution state S randomly samples incorrect Hs. Since any irrelevant H is liable to lead to a correct response with probability = ½, the sequences of + and − should show properties of events randomly distributed. For example, after any error (before the TLE) the probability that there will be an error on the very next trial is, according to the model, ½; the probability that the next error will come two trials later (i.e., that the sequence + − will occur) is $(½)^2$. In general, after some error trial the probability that the next error will occur K trials later is $(½)K$. Bower and Trabasso (1964) tabulated the distribution of run-lengths between errors and showed that the obtained proportions fitted the predicted probabilities almost exactly. A variety of other tests all confirmed the prediction that before criterion + and − appeared in random sequence.

A third set of predictions concerned the effect of changing solutions during the precriterion phase of the problem. According to the model, immediately following an error the S faces the full universe of Hs and is about to resample randomly. The E can continue with the solution that has been in force up until that trial or he can unobtrusively switch to a new solution. It should take the S just as long to solve the problem no matter which procedure was followed. This, of course, is the same argument that led to the Continuity-Noncontinuity experiment two decades earlier (see Reading No. 2). Now, however, the theory was precise and stipulated comparable precision in the experimental test. In the earlier research E had to go to some trouble to show that S manifested no learning—no hint of having sampled the correct H—at the time of the solution shift. Spence, for example, trained his E in a position preference that had to be maintained throughout the initial discrimination phase. In the present version of the theory, *any* error is a signal that S has not yet sampled the correct H. The solution, therefore, may be changed at any error trial without, according to the theory, impairing the learning. Bower and Trabasso tested this implication for a variety of solution shifts. The results are described in Reading No. 11.

---

*The exact value depends upon the task and some subsidiary assumptions. In general, the probability should be constant.

Reading No. 9
LEARNING THEORY AND THE NEW "MENTAL CHEMISTRY" *

By W. K. Estes

The basic concepts and assumptions of learning theory are universally supposed to refer to states and processes of the individual organism. Yet the existing evidence for the assumption that associative strength is an increasing function of number of reinforcements comes from performance curves representing average response measures over groups of learners, or from measures of resistance to extinction or retention scores averaged over groups of learners having different values of the independent variable. Even the few bits of negative evidence are indirect, depending on performance curves obtained under deviations from the usual experimental paradigms but still representing changes in average scores over series of trials for groups of subjects (Ss). It would seem that if our basic conceptions are sound, it should be possible to cut through the web of group performance curves and obtain more direct and compelling evidence for the existence of the assumed states and processes in individual organisms. This, in any event, is what I set out to accomplish for the concept of associative strength in a series of experiments now to be reported.

ON THE DEFINITIONS OF "REINFORCEMENT," "TEST TRIAL," AND "LEARNING"

In standard human learning situations, "learning" is almost universally defined and measured in terms of a change in the probability, or frequency, with which a given stimulating situation evokes a response (or instances of a response class) that has been designated as "correct" by the experimenter. With one reservation, to be

*Adapted from *Psychological Review*, 1960, **67**, 207-223. Copyright 1960 by the American Psychological Association. Reprinted by permission of the publisher and the author.

noted below, I shall follow this usage. But the situation is quite different with "reinforcement," the same term being used in at least two quite different senses by different investigators and thus promoting no end of confusion. My own habitual usage is the "neutral definition" (Hilgard, 1956, p. 409) which identifies reinforcement empirically with the operation that is supplied by the experimenter in order to produce learning, as defined above, in any given situation. In a paired-associate situation, the reinforcing operation is the paired presentation of the stimulus and response members of an item; in classical conditioning it is the paired presentation of CS and US; in verbal conditioning, the reinforcing operation for a given predictive response (e.g., predicting that the left light will appear) is the occurrence of the corresponding event (appearance of the left light)—in each case without regard to whether the S correctly anticipated the response member of the paired-associate item, gave a CR prior to occurrence of the US, or correctly predicted the event on the trial in question. The only property that different types of reinforcing operations are assumed to share is their common quantitative effect on the conditional probabilities of the possible alternative responses to the stimulating situation in which reinforcement occurs.

A narrower definition, favored especially by writers associated with a drive-reduction interpretation of reinforcement, would limit the term reinforcement to an operation that follows and is contingent upon the occurrence of the reinforced response on any trial. In this usage, reinforcement in paired-associate learning occurs only when the S has made a correct response in anticipation of the paired stimulus-response presentation, and reinforcement in verbal conditioning occurs only on trials when the S correctly predicts the trial outcome. Whether, according to this view, reinforcement occurs on only those trials of a classical conditioning experiment on which a CR occurs prior to the US depends upon theoretical decisions as to whether the CR and UR are "the same response" and whether reinforcement occurs at the onset or the termination of the US.

The primary advantage I see in the "neutral definition" is that it can be applied in an objective and consistent manner independently of one's position of systematic or theoretical issues. Learning certainly may occur prior to the first correct anticipation in a paired-associate experiment, prior to the first correct prediction in verbal conditioning, prior to the first CR in classical conditioning. The present usage permits us to speak, for example, about changes in probability of a response as a function of reinforcements on trials preceding its first occurrence, on the one hand, and changes as a function of reinforcements on trials including and following its first occurrence, on the other, without changing our definition of reinforcement.

It should be emphasized that the neutral definition does not beg such questions as whether presentation of a US following a CR constitutes the same reinforcing operation as presentation of a US on a trial when the CR did not occur; these two procedures represent instances of the same reinforcing operation if and only if they produce the same change in the probability of evocation of the CR by the CS. However, it seems strategic to avoid issues of this sort when, as in the present investigation, we are concerned with the nature of the changes in response tendencies during learning rather than with the conditions giving rise to these changes. Consequently, in the experiments to be reported, we have attempted so far as possible to avoid the customary confounding of reinforcement with antecedent response. In paired-associate situations, for example, we have deviated from the usual anticipation procedure by separating the reinforcement (paired-presentation of stimulus and response members of an item) from the test for learning (presentation of the stimulus member alone) so that an item may receive more than one reinforcement before the first test trial or may receive repeated test trials without intervening reinforcement.

For purposes of measuring retention, it would be ideal if one could give test trials on which no learning at all occurred. Indeed, so long as "learning" is conceived solely in terms of the definition given above (increase in probability of the "correct" response to a given stimulus), this goal is not too difficult to approximate. It seems intuitively clear, and can be demonstrated empirically (Estes, Hopkins, & Crothers, 1960), that no systematic increase in probability of correct responses to, say, paired-associate items will occur over a series of trials on which the stimulus members are presented alone and the S's responses receive no reward or informational feedback from the experimenter. We cannot, however, rule out the possibility that on these trials there might be learning in the sense of an increase in probability of whatever responses, correct or incorrect, actually occur. In fact, there is evidence that such learning does occur, but at a relatively low rate compared to the learning that occurs on reinforced trials (Estes et al., 1960). Consequently, in the analyses to follow, I shall assume that unreinforced trials can be treated, without serious error, simply as "neutral" test trials when primary interest is in measuring the effects of preceding reinforced trials.

Suppose we ask what is the minimum set of operations and observations actually needed in order to demonstrate learning. Normally there must be a pretest in order to determine the initial probability of the to-be-learned behavior in the test situation; in practice the experimenter often has a priori information about initial response probabilities which makes the pretest dispensable. There must be a presentation of some reinforcing operation, and afterward a test to assess the change in performance produced by the reinforcement. If the function of response occurrences and nonoccurrences is to be determined, there will have to be a second test trial. And there we have it. Controlled comparisons relative to effects of the principal events occurring during an acquisition series can, in principle, be accomplished in an experiment running to about a trial and a half. By usual standards, this constitutes what can only be called a "miniature experiment." However, miniature experiments appeared to be what the tactical situation called for, and therefore miniature experiments are what we set out to run.

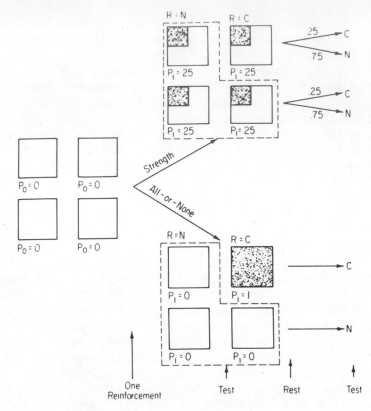

FIG. 1. Schema representing effects of a single reinforcement according to incremental (upper branch) vs. all or none (lower branch) theories. Squares represent Ss, with the proportion of darkened area in each indicating the probability of the correct response (C) for the given individual.

CONCEPTIONS OF THE ACQUISITION PROCESS: ASSOCIATIVE STRENGTH VS. ALL-OR-NONE MODELS

In the first of these experiments,[1] we used a paired-associate situation with consonant syllables as stimuli and numbers as responses. Forty-eight Ss were run with an eight-item list, yielding 384 observations on the first test trial. The principal portion of the experiment consisted simply in presenting each S once with each stimulus-response pair and then testing with each stimulus alone (in a new random order). Before proceeding to the results, let us examine the outcome expected on the basis of the notion of learning as a change in associative strength. In Figure 1 the situation is schematized in terms of a single item. The four squares at the left represent four hypothetical Ss, the emptiness of the squares indicating that all start the experiment with zero probabilities of making the correct response. Now we give a single reinforcement (paired presentation of the stimulus and

[1] This experiment was conducted at Indiana University with the assistance of B. L. Hopkins; for a full report of the method and results see Estes et al. (1960).

correct response), the result of which is to raise the probability of the correct response (C) to, say, .25. The upper arrow leads to the theoretical state of affairs after this reinforcement, according to an interpretation based on the conception of associative strength. The strength of the association is increased for all of the Ss; and, neglecting for the moment possible individual differences, the probability of the correct response is now .25 for each individual, the one at the upper right who happened to make a correct response on the test, and the three who did not.

Suppose now that the interpretation based on the concept of strength were completely wrong and that stimulus-response associations really formed on an all-or-none basis. Then the state of affairs after the reinforcement should be as shown in the lower part of the figure. Again the probability of a correct response increases from zero to .25, but the .25 now refers only to the group, not to any individual S. One S has formed the association (darkened square), and three have been unaffected by the reinforcement (empty squares).

To distinguish empirically between these two logically possible outcomes, we need only add the remaining half-trial to our trial-and-a-half, i.e., give another test without intervening reinforcement. Now, if the upper branch of the diagram is essentially correct, all Ss should have equal probabilities of making the correct response on the second test trial, regardless of what they did on the first test. But if the lower branch is correct, correct responses on the second test should come only from Ss who made correct responses on the first test. None should come from Ss who made incorrect responses (N) on the first test, for these Ss would not have profited at all from the learning trial.

There might be some attenuation of the expected proportions of correct responses on Test 2 by Ss making correct responses on Test 1 if there is any forgetting in this situation, but the proportions of correct following incorrect provide a critical comparison. If the all-or-none view is correct, then this proportion should be zero, or at least no greater than could be achieved by sheer guessing. But if any version of the strength conception is correct, then the proportion of correct following incorrect responses should be greater than chance. In order to make the outcomes that can be tolerated by the two interpretations sharply different, we need only choose our experimental materials and conditions so that the overall proportions correct on both first and second tests are well above chance. It can be seen in Figure 2 that this has been achieved, for approximately 50% of the items were correct on the first test and nearly 40% on the second. Considering the critical lower branch of the diagram, leading from an incorrect response on the first test to a correct response on the second, we see that the results lean strongly in the direction prescribed by an all-or-none conception, for the 9% of correct following incorrect responses is less than the 12½% that could be achieved even by rather unintelligent guessing with an eight item list if the reinforcement had no effect at all on these items. The difference between this value and the 71% of correct following correct responses is so large that a statistical test would be an empty formality.

A possible defense that might be advanced by a "strength theorist" is the

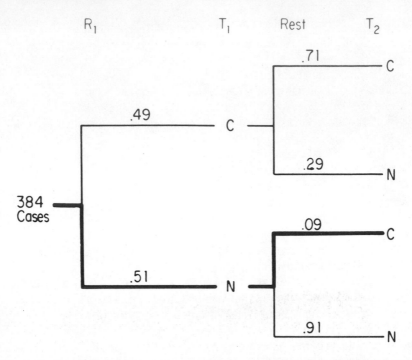

FIG. 2. Results of miniature experiment on acquisition of paired-associates. Empirical values are proportions of instance in which correct (C) and incorrect (N) responses on first test trial after a single reinforcement (paired presentation of stimulus and response members) were followed by C and N responses on a second test trial.

hypothesis that the 51% of cases with incorrect responses on the first test simply represent preponderantly slower learners or more difficult items than the 49% of cases with correct responses. If so, then a control condition in which a second reinforcement is given between the first and second tests should yield a percentage of correct responses on Test 2 following incorrect on Test 1 that is much smaller than the percentage correct on Test 1. This control was run (with the same 48 Ss but different items), and the result is shown in Figure 3. The effect of the first reinforcement on the full set of Ss and items was to raise the probability of a correct response from near zero to .40; the effect of the second reinforcement on cases having incorrect responses on the first test was to raise the probability of a correct response from near zero to .46. Thus there seems to be no support forthcoming for the hypothesis of a large difference in learning rate between cases which did and cases which did not have correct responses on the first test.

Although it would be nice to claim credit for rare prescience in predicting the outcome of this little experiment, the fact is that the result came as a distinct jar to my preconceptions. In designing the study, our idea was not to undermine the strongly entrenched concept of associative strength, but to support it by showing that the results of Rock's experiments, apparently calling for an all-or-none interpretation, must be attributed to some artifact concealed in his ingenious but somewhat complex procedures. Thus when Hopkins and I examined the data from our initial group of 24 Ss and found the pattern shown in Figures 2 and 3, our first reaction was to replicate the whole thing with another group. But when the two replications turned out to agree in every essential respect, we were left with no obvious course but to begin digesting an unanticipated and not entirely palatable conclusion. The most cleanly controlled comparisons we had managed to devise yielded no evidence that repeated reinforcements in this situation have any function other than to give repeated opportunities for the discontinuous formation of a learned association between observed stimuli and responses.

Still, it is well known that theoretical doctrines do not yield readily to negative evidence. One whose theories are based on a concept of strength will lose little ground if he can make a stand on the claim that all-or-none acquisition is simply a perculiarity of the paired-associate experiment and not characteristic of human learning in general. To evaluate this possible defense of the strength concept, we clearly shall have to turn to some different situation that is quite different in the response mechanism and reinforcing operations from paired-associate learning. Eyelid conditioning meets these specifications, and it is convenient for our purposes since a colleague, I. Gormezano, has kindly made available his data from

$$R_1 \qquad T_1 \qquad R_2 \qquad T_2$$

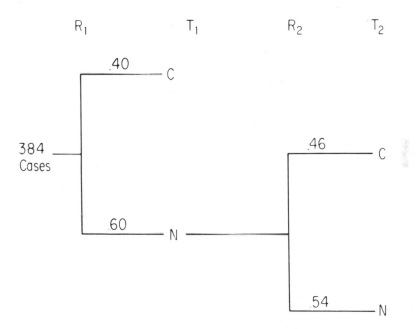

FIG. 3. Proportion correct on test after a second reinforcement for cases not having correct responses on first test compared with proportion correct on first test for the full set of Ss and items. The Ss and situation are the same as those represented in Fig. 2.

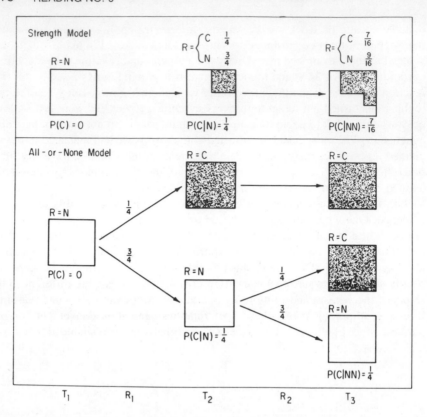

Fig. 4. Schema for first two trials of eyelid conditioning experiment showing changes in CR probability (proportion of darkened area in squares representing Ss) prescribed by incremental vs. all-or-none theories.

an intensive period of data collecting in the Wisconsin conditioning laboratory. Gormezano trained a sufficiently large group, approximately 170 Ss, under identical conditions so that the first few acquisition trials can be treated as one of our miniature experiments and analyzed in much the same way as the paired-associate study.

The situation obtaining over the first couple of trials is schematized in Figure 4. In the diagram, T_1 is the first CS presentation, prior to the first reinforcement, and we shall consider only Ss who made no CR on this test. Thus the initial probability of a CR is taken to be zero. Suppose now that the effect of the first reinforcement is to raise the probability of a CR to .25. According to the strength conception, shown in the upper panel, each S has his strength of conditioning increased by the same amount by this reinforcement and now has probability .25 of making a CR. Then the second reinforcement increases the conditioned strength for each S again; and, regardless of whether or not a particular S happened to make a CR on T_2, he now has a higher probability ($7/16$ if we apply the linear function mentioned

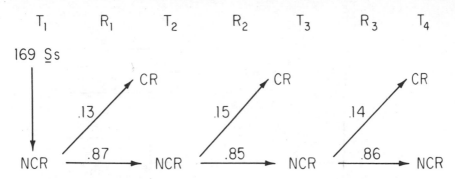

FIG. 5. Trial-by-trial acquisition data from Gormezano's study of eyelid conditioning. Values of particular interest are the proportions of CRs following 1, 2, or 3 consecutive non-CRs.

earlier).[2] According to an all-or-none conception, the situation after the first reinforcement, shown in the lower panel, is that for ¼ of the Ss the CR has become associated with the CS and for the remaining ¾ of the Ss no conditioning has occurred. The effect of the second reinforcement is to give the unconditioned Ss another chance, and ¼ of these now become conditioned. The differential prediction, then, concerns the probability of a CR on the third test for Ss who made no CR on the second test (and similarly the probability of a CR on the fourth test for Ss who made none on any previous test, and so on). The strength conception requires this conditional probability to increase, whereas the all-or-none conception requires it to remain constant. The test seems quite sharp, for even with allowance for variation in conditioning rates among Ss, a model which assumes that associative strength increases with reinforcements cannot stand constancy of this probability unless its assumptions are so restricted that it reduces to an all-or-none model.

The pertinent results of Gormezano's study are shown in Figure 5, carried through the first four trials, beyond which the number of cases begins to drop off too much for comfort. Inspecting the sequence of probabilities of CR's after 1, 2, or 3 consecutive NCRs—.13, .15, .14—we find the hypothesis of constancy appearing rather more attractive than the progressively increasing trend required by the strength interpretation. (According to a linear model, for example, the value .15 for a CR after an NCR should have been .24, and the .14 for a CR after two NCRs should have been .34.)

The consistency of these conditioning data with those of the paired-associate situation is almost too good to be true. In psychology we are not used to having quantitative tests of alternative theoretical notions yield such apparently decisive

---

[2]For this example, the parameter θ in the function $\Delta p = \theta(1 - p)$ is equal to ¼ and after the first experiment p is also equal to ¼. Therefore we have
$$\Delta p = \frac{1}{4}(1 - \frac{1}{4}) = \frac{3}{16}$$
and for the new probability after the second reinforcement.
$$p + \Delta p = \frac{1}{4} + \frac{3}{16} = \frac{7}{16}.$$

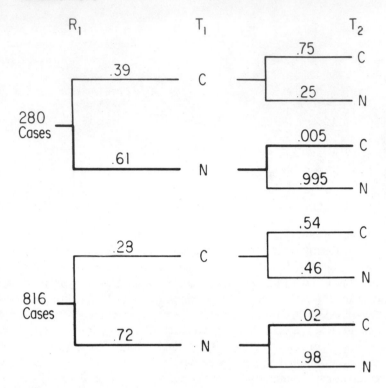

FIG. 6. Results of two miniature experiments on free verbal recall, showing near-zero proportions of correct responses on a second test trial for cases which did not have correct responses on the first test after a single reinforcement.

outcomes. Consequently, and considering the importance of the theoretical issue, perhaps we will not yet be accused of beating a dead hypothesis if we look for one more test with experimental arrangements differing from both of those preceding. We would like a situation similar to paired-associate learning in that unreinforced test trials can readily be given without disturbing the learners but one which eliminates the possibility of achieving substantial proportions of correct responses by guessing. A situation which meets these desiderata is the free verbal recall experiment used by Bruner, Miller, and Zimmerman (1955). For our present purposes the minimal experiment will consist of a single reinforcement followed by two recall tests. The reinforcement involves merely the experimenter's reading a list of words aloud to S. On a recall test, S is asked to write down as many words as he can remember (in any order). Then after an interval during which no additional reinforcement is given, S is (unexpectedly) tested again.

Results of two experiments of this sort are shown in Figure 6. The upper tree represents an experiment with 35 Ss, each given a list of eight words at R_1. On the first test, T_1, 61% of the 280 opportunities for correct responses (C) yielded either incorrect responses or omissions (N), and of these less than 1% were followed by correct responses on the second test, T_2. In a replication conducted with some minor variations in procedure, 102 Ss were presented with eight words each on the reinforced trial. This time (lower tree in Figure 6) there were 72% N responses on the first test and less than 2% of these were followed by C responses on the second test. Clearly, if a word is not given correctly on the first test by a particular S, the chances are virtually *nil* that it will be correct on a second test.

This result does not, of course, *prove* that reinforcement has exerted no strengthening effect on the associations in the cases when the correct response failed to occur on the first test. But one whose theory requires him to assume that such strengthenings occur has a taxing assignment in producing a case for the existence of factors or processes which appear in just sufficient force to cancel out the hypothesized increments in response strength under each set of experimental procedures we have examined. Explanations depending on such factors as individual differences are not very prepossessing in the light of control comparisons of the type exhibited in Figure 3 (a similar control, with similar result, was used for the free-verbal-recall situation). One might appeal to the effects of learning which occurs on the first test trial itself arguing that an incorrect response which occurs on the first test receives a large increment in associative strength (from sheer contiguity or perhaps from some unspecified source of reinforcement) and therefore recurs with high probability on the next test. One important difficulty with this hypothesis is that the data do not support it. In the paired-associate study cited above, for example, the observed relative frequency with which an incorrect response occurring on the first test was repeated on the second test was only .24. Interpretations which preserve the incremental conception of associative learning should certainly be sought with all vigor; at the time of writing, however, none has come to my attention that seems at all plausible.

Reading No. 10
THE SELECTION OF STRATEGIES IN CUE LEARNING[*]

By Frank Restle

In a cue learning problem (discrimination learning, concept formation, and maze learning) the subject chooses one of two or more responses on each trial. The correctness of the response depends on some aspect of the situation at the time of response.

In this paper it is assumed that subjects have difficulty with cue learning problems to the degree that they tend to use strategies (habits, patterns of response) which conflict with the strategy intended by the experimenter. It is often assumed that the subject must also associate correct responses with cues in the situation. However, in most cue learning experiments the subject is instructed or pretrained to make the desired responses before the cue learning process begins. Further more, the experimental situation constrains the subject to make exactly one of the available responses per trial. It seems reasonable to assume that cue learning is not so much a matter of the formation as of the selection of responses. The present theorectical discussion begins with a set of strategies and is concerned with the mechanisms by which the subject might select out those strategies intended, and consistently rewarded, by the experimenter.

The term "strategy" is employed in a sense related to the more common terms, "habit" and "hypothesis," to designate a particular pattern of responses to stimuli. Consider, for example, a rat being trained to jump to the larger of two white circles in a Lashley Jumping Stand. Some possible strategies include; jumping to the left side, jumping to the right side, jumping alternately left and right, jumping always to the side last reinforced, jumping to the side which last was punished, jumping in the direction the rat was placed down on the stand, jumping toward the circle with less (or more) acute curvature, jumping toward the side with more white area, jumping toward the side which reflects more total light,

*Adapted from *Psychological Review*, 1962, **69,** 329-343. Copyright 1962 by the American Psychological Association. Reprinted by permission of the publisher and the author.

and so forth. Each such pattern of behavior, if it occurs in isolation for a sufficiently long sequence of trials, can be identified by the experimenter. It will be seen that there are ordinarily a large number and variety of possible strategies in a cue learning problem, and that a number of strategies may be perfectly confounded. In the example above, jumping to the circle with less acute curvature will always lead to the same result as jumping to the side which reflects more light, since these will both be jumps to the larger circle.

The general idea developed here is that the problem gives rise to a set of strategies. The subject uses these various strategies, which at first are selected at random, and attempts to select strategies which will consistently lead to correct responses. For simplicity the discussion is limited to problems in which there are at least some strategies which are always correct.

Let H be the set of strategies available to the subject at the beginning of the problem. Suppose that some subset C of these strategies are always correct, another subset W are always wrong, and the remainder, I, are sometimes correct and sometimes wrong. For simplicity of presentation, begin with a problem in which the strategies of I are correct and wrong, on successive trials, with independent probabilities all of which are ½, and restrict attention to the two-choice problem.

Presentation of the theory of this conventional discrimination learning problem will begin with a special case in which one strategy is used on each trial. Then an alternative theory will be proposed, in which the subject uses all strategies at once and attempts to narrow down to the correct one. Third, a model will be proposed in which the subject chooses a random sample of all strategies and attempts to narrow down to the correct strategies within his sample. These three models will be shown to be essentially equivalent, in a theorem which may be called the "indifference to sample size" theorem. Following proof of that theorem, some empirical implications of the theory will be derived and compared with relevant data.

One Strategy at a Time

On the first trial of the experiment, the subject selects a certain single strategy from H at random and makes the indicated response. If the response is correct, the same strategy is used on Trial 2. If it is again correct, it is used again on Trial 3, and so forth. If, on any trial, the response is incorrect, the subject returns his strategy to the set H and then chooses a strategy again at random. It is considered possible that the same strategy may be resampled, so that the sampling process is with replacement. Imagine that an error occurs on Trial 2. Then a new strategy is chosen and this strategy is used on Trial 3. If it is correct it is used again on Trial 4. If the response on Trial 3 is wrong, the subject again chooses an hypothesis at random for Trial 4.

Notice that if the subject chooses a correct strategy, he will make no more errors. The correct strategy leads to correct responses, and when the response is correct the subject does not change strategy. Thus, the learning process is terminated by the choice of a correct strategy.

Since sampling is with replacement, the probabilities of choosing a correct, a wrong, or an irrelevant strategy are constant from trial to trial. Let these three probabilities be c, w, and $i = 1 - c - w$.

At the beginning of training the subject chooses a strategy of one of the three types, which have probabilities c, w, and i. After each error he also chooses a strategy, with probabilities c, w, and i. Thus an error is an event which returns the subject to exactly the same condition (in terms of the probabilities of future events) with which he started—it resets the process and makes it begin over. Such an event is called a "recurrent event" (Feller, 1950). Since our experimental interest centers around errors and correct responses, we can limit attention to errors and thus to the theory of recurrent events.

Imagine that at some Trial n the subject makes an error. There is a certain probability f_1 that the next error occurs at Trial $n + 1$, a probability f_2 that the next error occurs at Trial $n + 2$, and in general a probability distribution f_j that the next error after Trial n occurs at Trial $n + j$. In a model of recurrent events like the present one, the distribution f_j is the same for all Trials n on which an error occurs, and is the same as the distribution of probabilities that the first error occurs on Trial 1, 2, etc.

The random process and all of its properties are specified by the distribution f_j. However, the analysis of the process from the distribution f_j will be postponed until two steps have been completed; first, calculation of the distribution f_j for the one-strategy-at-a-time model, and second, the formulation of two other models, very different in assumptions, which also lead to systems of recurrent events with the same distribution. When these steps are completed, the generality of the f distribution will be apparent, and derivations of properties of the process will be justified.

First, f_1 is the probability of an error immediately following another error. The second error can occur because a wrong strategy was chosen (with probability w) or because an irrelevant strategy was chosen and turned out to be wrong (with probability $i/2$). These are mutually exclusive events and exhaust the possibilities, so that

$$f_1 = w + \frac{1}{2}i.$$

An error occuring on the second trial after the last one, with a correct response intervening, cannot result from the selection of a wrong strategy for the wrong strategy would not lead to an intervening correct response. If the error does occur on the second trial we know that the strategy chosen was not correct. Hence it must be an irrelevant one which led first to a correct and then to a wrong response. In simple discrimination learning, the probability that an irrelevant strategy would lead to a correct and then a wrong response is $\frac{1}{2} \cdot \frac{1}{2} = (\frac{1}{2})^2$. The probability of choosing an irrelevant strategy which gives this sequence, correct-wrong, is therefore

$$f_2 = i(\tfrac{1}{2})^2$$

By the same reasoning, any value of f_j, $j > 2$, implies that an irrelevant strategy was chosen and then led to $j - 1$ correct responses followed by a wrong response. The probability of a string of exactly $j - 1$ correct responses each with probability ½, followed by an error with probability ½, is (½) . Hence, for $j \geqslant 2$

$$f_j = i(\tfrac{1}{2})^j$$

Summarizing the results we have the distribution

$$f_1 = w + \tfrac{1}{2}i$$
$$f_j = i(\tfrac{1}{2})^j$$

for all $j \geqslant 2$. The distribution f is not a proper probability function because it does not sum to unity. Notice that

$$\sum_{j=1}^{\infty} (f_j) = w + i \sum_{j=1}^{\infty} (\tfrac{1}{2})^j = w + i = 1 - c$$

In Feller's terms this means that errors are *uncertain* recurrent events, for with probability c the subject chooses a correct strategy and never makes another error. Some of the probability of the f distribution is located at the (improper) point ∞, and the proportion so located is c. This merely reflects the fact that learning occurs in the present model and the subject can eliminate errors. The fact that f_j is not a probability function does not place any serious difficulties in the way of analysis.

[Omitted here is a description of two variants of the model just presented. In one S samples all strategies at once; in the other he takes a random sample of strategies. These are shown to lead "to the same system of recurrent events" as the first (see text, p.).   M. L.]

STATISTICAL PROPERTIES OF THE RAW DATA

The discussion above has been restricted to the distribution f_j, the probability that an error follows the last error by exactly j trials. The f distribution can be estimated directly from raw data, but this is neither a conventional nor a very interesting way of describing the data of cue learning. In this section the data generated by this model are analyzed in several of the ways commonly employed by experimenters. Details are given in Restle (1961).

Learning Curve(s)

Consider three versions of the learning curve. One is the succession of correct and wrong responses by an individual subject. A second is the average learning curve of a group of subjects. The third is a corrected or idealized form of the learning curve computed by adjusting a group learning curve (Vincentizing) or by averaging the data of subjects who are selected after the fact for similarity of over-all performance (Spence, 1956).

According to the present theory, the individual data are composed of a sequence of correct and wrong responses in irregular order, followed by an infinite sequence of correct responses. If $w > 0$, there will be somewhat more errors than correct responses on the presolution trials, and there will be a tendency for errors to follow other errors more often than errors follow correct responses. The probability of an error following an error will be $(w + i/2)/(w + i)$ whereas the probability of an error following a correct response is $\frac{1}{2}$. An individual subject will produce such below-chance behavior for some block of trials and then abruptly, after some error, will either happen on a correct strategy (in the one-strategy-at-a-time model) or will begin a process c᾿ elimination which ends up with all correct strategies. This is an extreme form of the "discontinuous" or insightful learning curve. Unfortunately it is difficult to decide whether any individual subject does or does not exhibit this pattern, so data are usually combined.

The group learning curve is merely the average of a set of (theoretically) discontinuous individual curves. If all subjects have the same parameters $c, w,$ and $i,$ they will nevertheless happen to master the problem at different trials, so that the average learning curve is gradual. Its mathematical form is complex but in general appearance, the group learning from this theory resembles the common "growth" curve (Restle, in 1961).

If one selects, from a larger group of subjects, those who make the same number of total errors, or those who reach criterion at the same time, and averages their learning curves; or if one rescales learning trials as by the Vincent-curve method, the resulting curve will usually be S shaped. The writer has investigated this question by generating data which arise directly from the assumptions of the present model, by use of tables of random numbers. When, from a large set of such data, one selects a subgroup of "subjects" who all make the same number of errors, or who reach criterion at about the same trial, and average the performance within such a subgroup, the result is an S shaped curve. Exact Vincentizing produces a flat (stationary) learning curve before criterion.

The reason for the S shaped curves is not difficult to find; the above methods of selecting or rearranging the data tend to put the (theoretically random) times of solution close together. If the times of solution are put exactly together a step-function should result, but if the times of solution are only grouped close to one another, the step is blurred and an S shaped curve results (Spence, 1956).

Summary Statistics of the Data

In the present theory the actual trial on which learning takes place is not in any way fixed, but depends upon the random outcome of the process of selecting strategies. The result is large intrinsic variance in the acquisition phase, which can most conveniently be described in terms of the total errors made by each subject. If each subject is trained until a long sequence of consecutive correct responses has been obtained, one is reasonably sure that the number of errors made approximates the theoretical total errors.

On the first trial or after any error the subject may either make another error, sometime later, or he may make no more errors. The probability that the subject will make at least one more error, the first one in exactly j trials, is f_j. Thus the total probability of at least one more error is

$$\sum_{j=1}^{\infty} (f_j) = 1 - c$$

With probability c the subject never makes another error at all. From this it is not difficult to show that the probability of exactly k errors is $(1 - c)^k c$. This is the geometric distribution which has mean

$$E(k) = (1 - c)/c$$

and variance

$$\text{Var}(k) = (1 - c)/c^2.$$

The standard deviation of the distribution of error scores should be nearly equal to its mean, according to the theory, and the distribution should show an extreme positive skewness.

Provided that irrelevant strategies are correct just half the time at random, trials-to-criterion behaves very much like total errors.

Methods of Estimating the Parameters *w* and *c*

An important step in any mathematical development of a learning theory is the estimation of parameters. Fortunately, in the present model quite simple and efficient estimates are available. A maximum-likelihood estimator of c is given by

$$\hat{c} = 1/(\bar{T} + 1)$$

where T is the mean total error score of a group of subjects. The variance of this estimate, with N subjects in the group, is

$$\text{Var}(c) = c^2(1 - c)/N$$

It is also possible to estimate w by the maximum-likelihood method. As was mentioned earlier, a high frequency of consecutive errors in the presolution phase is an indication of a relatively large proportion of wrong strategies, whereas a chance frequency of consecutive errors is an indication that there are relatively few wrong strategies; provided that the irrelevant strategies are correct and wrong strictly at random. The method is to count "Trial 0," an imaginary trial before training begins, as an error. Then for each subject divide this expanded set of errors into M_0 errors which are followed by correct responses and M_1 errors which are followed by errors. Then computing the means of these statistics one has

$$\hat{w} = \frac{\bar{M}_1 - \bar{M}_0 + 1}{\bar{M}_0 + \bar{M}_1}$$

as a maximum-likelihood estimator of w (Restle, 1961).

ADDITIVITY OF CUES

In several papers regarding another theory the writer has discussed the additivity of cues (Restle, 1955, 1957, 1958, 1959a; see also Bourne & Restle, 1959, and Trabasso, 1960). In simple terms the experiment involves three groups; one learns a problem based on a set A of cues, the second learns a problem based on the set B of cues, and the third learns a problem which can be solved using either A or B cues disjunctively. If the sets A and B are separate then the third set $A \cup B$ should have measure $m(A \cup B) = m(A) + m(B)$, (see Trabasso, 1960). Experimental results have been reconciled with an S-R theory involving adaptation of irrelevant cues (Restle, 1955).

Generally speaking, the calculations from the present model are in good numerical agreement with those from the "adaptation" model. Reanalysis of three of the most satisfactory sets of data used before, and one set not previously used, are reported here. The other data previously discussed are so fragmentary that analysis will hardly be fruitful; and Trabasso (1960) used such difficult problems that many of his subjects failed to learn at all on the more difficult problems, making analysis by the present model unsatisfactory. In general, the estimates reported below are not the maximum-likelihood estimates because the subjects were not run to a strong criterion. However, since learning was nearly complete, the approximate estimates are adequate.

Scharlock (1955; see also Restle, 1957) ran a place-versus-response experiment with rats in which the relative weight of correct place (extra-maze) and correct response (intra-maze) strategies can be estimated. He also ran one group with both place and response strategies correct, and a group with response strategies correct and no place cues present. In the calculations below it is assumed that the number of wrong strategies of a given type (place or response) equals the number of correct strategies. This is a symmetry assumption which, while not strictly appropriate for Scharlock's experiment, is needed to permit prediction, since separate estimates of wrong strategies cannot be made on the available data.

Rats learned to go to the same place (using extra-maze cues), with response cues irrelevant, making an average of 9.7 errors. Using the estimate $\hat{c} = 1/(1 + \bar{T})$, one estimates that the correct place strategies make up $1/10.7 = .093$ of the total set of strategies. Other rats learned to make a constant response to different places, averaging 6.7 errors. We estimate that correct response strategies constitute $1/7.7 = .130$ of the total set.

The simplest interpretation of the experiment is that when both place and response strategies would work, the proportion of correct strategies would be the sum of the proportions of place and response strategies, since the same total set of strategies is available. One predicts that with place-plus-response learning, $\hat{c} = .093 + .130 = .223$. We have the formula that the expected errors to solution is $(1-c)/c$. Hence the expected mean errors is $.777/.223 = 3.4$; the obtained mean was 4.0, which is adequately close. The discrepancy can partly be explained by the fact that the place-learning and response-learning groups were not run to a high criterion and probably would have made more errors if tested longer. The fast-learning place-plus-response group would likely not have made more errors, since their performance was excellent at the end of the training given.

Another group learned a fixed response in the absence of any good place cues. We assume that this group simply had neither correct nor incorrect place strategies. Its predicted proportion of correct strategies is $.130/1 - 2(.093) = .130/.814 = .160$. The expected errors is $.840/.160 = 5.25$; the observed mean was 5.0. Both predictions are close to the obtained results, well within sampling deviations.

Warren (1959) has reported data on monkeys in an experiment analogous to Scharlock's study of rats. Warren's monkeys had to learn position habits in some problems and object-discriminations in other problems. Warren also used a response-plus-object problem (object discrimination with the objects left in the same place each trial) and a pure response problem (e.g., choose the left one of two indistinguishable objects.) Predictions followed the same formulas as above, and were extremely accurate: the proportions of object and response strategies were estimated from behavior on object (position-varied) and position (object-varied) problems. When these values were added to predict object-plus-position, the prediction was a mean of 0.67 errors, whereas Warren observed 0.63. For pure response learning, the model predicted 3.25 mean errors and the observed value was 3.04. These agreements between theory and data are well within the range of probable sampling error.

Similar results were obtained by analyzing Warren's experiment on the additivity of color, form, and size cues (Warren, 1953). The analysis is substantially the same as that given in a previous paper (Restle, 1958). Learning data are collected on problems involving only color, only form, or only size differences between the objects. These data are used to calculate the proportional weights of the three sources of strategies, and the resulting values are recombined to compute predicted learning rates for problems involving two or more dimensions; for example, discrimination of a red triangle from a green circle involves color plus form cues. In each calculation account is taken of the greater total number of strategies involved in problems with added cues, and it is assumed that whenever a set of correct strategies is introduced by adding cues, an equally large set of wrong strategies also enter the situation.

Calculations on Warren's (1953) data afforded four predictions of total errors to solution. The four predictions were wrong by -17, 0, 5 and 10 percent respectively, and all of the errors can reasonably be attributed to sampling variations.

The hypothesis of additivity of cues has also been applied to human learning (Restle, 1959a) in an experiment which required subjects to learn differential verbal responses to consonant syllables. The procedure was simple concept formation with individual letters of the syllables used as cues, and the same sort of additivity of cues as above. The adaptation model gave quite accurate predictions and the present model is, if anything, slightly more accurate; it predicts (given data on the two cues separately) that the added-cue group should make an average of 5.26 errors, whereas the observed mean was 5.25. Considering the variability of the data, the extreme closeness is coincidental.

COMPARISON WITH OTHER THEORIES

The three models of the selection of strategies are conceptually similar to the writer's adaptation theory of discrimination learning (Restle, 1955). The "strategies" of the present model resemble the "cues" of the earlier theory. The strategy-selection model has, as a theorem, that the rate of learning depends upon the proportion of correct strategies. A similar idea is expressed in the adaptation model in which it was assumed that the rate of learning (θ) would depend upon the proportion of relevant cues.

Several of the serious faults of the adaptation theory are corrected in the theory of strategy-selection. First, in the adaptation theory the subject was supposed to begin conditioning relevant cues and adapting irrelevant cues, with a rate θ equal to the proportion of relevant cues, right from the first trial of training. Of course, at that first trial the subject has no possible way of knowing which cues will turn out to be relevant—it would be possible for the experimenter to change his mind after the first trial is complete. Hence, the adaptation theory could apply only to a prescient subject. The selection-of-strategies theory does not have the subject treat different strategies differently except on the basis of trials already completed, hence avoids the absurdity. Second, the idea that the structure of the problem (proportion of relevant cues or correct strategies) controls the rate of learning was only a simplifying assumption, with no justification, in the adaptation model; but is an inescapable theorem of strategy-selection. Third, the adaptation theory yielded a determinate learning curve in the sense that $p(n)$ was exactly specified for a given θ and $p(1)$. The variance of typical data was in large part left unexplained by the adaptation model and had to be attributed to individual differences, even though it is notoriously difficult to find any strong predictor of such learning. In the strategy-selection model learning itself is a random event and the model generates variability comparable with that obtained in the data.

Despite these important differences, the present theory is close enough to the adaptation theory to make it possible to carry over many of the theoretical insights, though in modified form. The one type of prediction discussed in this paper was additivity of cues, but other ideas such as the proposed basis of learning sets (Restle, 1958) and various quantitative relationships in concept identification (Bourne & Restle, 1959) can be recast in the mold of the selection of strategies. The many similarities and few differences in predictions must be studied in detail and cannot be discussed here, except to mention that most of the results of the Bourne and Restle paper can be reproduced using the strategy-selection model.

In more general terms, it may be remarked that the strategy-selection model is similar to the ideas of Lashley (1928) and Krechevsky (1932a) in general intent. In comparison with stimulus-sampling theories (Restle, 1959b) the strategy-selection model is like theories of the observing response (Atkinson, 1959a, 1959b; Wyckoff, 1952), except that in the strategy-selection model there is no conditioning, only observing (selecting). The mathematical structure of the model is very close to that of Bower's (1960) one-element association model.

Reading No. 11
REVERSALS PRIOR TO SOLUTION IN CONCEPT IDENTIFICATION[*]

By Gordon Bower
Thomas Trabasso

In the typical two-category concept identification experiment, S is shown a series of complex patterns which vary in several, binary attributes. As each pattern is presented, S attempts to anticipate the correct classification; following his response, he is informed of the correct response. The patterns are divided into two mutually exclusive classes, R_1 and R_2. If, say, color (red or blue) is the relevant attribute, then red objects might be assigned to Response Class R_1 and blue objects to Class R_2. We will refer to this rule as a particular S-R assignment.

In recent studies (Bower & Trabasso, 1964; Trabasso, 1963) of this situation with college students, Ss appeared to learn suddenly. Backward learning curves were horizontal at the chance level of 50% correct classifications over all trials until S's last error before solving. The performance of an S might be characterized by saying that on any given trial he is either in the presolution state or in the solution state, with corresponding probabilities of .50 or 1.00 of correctly classifying the stimuli. According to this two-state description of the performance, learning would be identified as a discrete, one-trial transition from the initial, presolution state into the terminal, solution state.

The theories of cue-selection learning proposed by Restle (1962) and Bower and Trabasso (1964) imply this two-state description of individual performance. These theories assume that S is selectively attending to or sampling cues from the stimulus display and that he is testing hypotheses regarding the relevance of these cues to the correct solution. If S's response is correct, it is supposed that he continues to use the same hypothesis; if his response is incorrect, he resamples at random from the set of possible hypotheses. Assume further that the proportion of correct hypotheses is c whereas the remaining proportion $1 - c$ is irrelevant hypotheses which lead to correct and incorrect responses half the time. By these

*Adapted from the *Journal of Experimental Psychology*, 1963, **66,** 409-418. Copyright 1963 by the American Psychological Association. Reprinted by permission of the publisher and the senior author.

assumptions, the probability that S solves the problem after any given error is a fixed constant, c. This elementary theory has been used successfully in predicting quantitative details of several sets of data (Bower & Trabasso, 1964).

The present studies investigate whether S acquires partial knowledge about the solution to the problem. The all-or-nothing theory supposes that he does not. Specifically, it says that when S makes an error, he has not yet learned anything of relevance regarding the correct concept. Three experiments were performed to provide tests of this assumption; the first two are described now.

EXPERIMENTS I AND II

Experiments I and II are identical in design; Exp. II was a replication of Exp. I with an easier problem and different stimulus materials. The design resembles that used in several animal experiments conducted on the continuity-noncontinuity issue in discrimination learning theory (e.g., Krechevsky, 1938; McCulloch & Pratt, 1934). Control Ss in Group C learned a problem with the same S-R assignments throughout (Cue A-R_1, Cue B-R_2). Two other groups worked on different S-R assignments initially and then were transferred to the assignments of the control group. This transfer occurred immediately after S made an error following a critical trial of the initial series. Group R, a reversal group, was trained initially with the opposite assignments, A-R_2 and B-R_1. Group NR, a nonreversal-shift group, was trained initially with Cues A and B present but irrelevant while another set of cues was relevant (C-R_1, D-R_2).

The question of interest is whether the initial wrong-way training retards performance of Ss in Groups R and NR who are shifted to the final, transfer problem before solving their initial problem. If Ss partially learn responses to the initially relevant cues before the shift, then such partial learning should induce negative transfer on the final problem. However, if S's error initiating the shift indicates that nothing of importance has yet been learned, then the performance on the final problem should be the same for the three groups, independent of the initial S-R assignments.

Method

Experimental design.   A schematic outline of the design is presented in Table 1. Only two of the several stimulus attributes are represented in the left columns of Table 1. The rows give the combinations of stimulus values in the patterns and the correct responses to each pattern are listed under each condition. The Control and Reversal groups had Cues A and B relevant but they had opposite response assignments during initial training (10 trials in Exp. I and 5 trials in Exp. II). The Nonreversal group had one of the other dimensions (Cues C and D) relevant during initial training.

The Ss who made an error on Trial 10 in Exp. I or Trial 5 in Exp. II or soon

TABLE 1
Design for Exp. I and II

Patterns		Response Assignments			
		Initial Trials			Final Problem
Dimension 1	Dimension 2	Control	Reversal	Nonreversal	
A	C	R_1	R_2	R_1	R_1
A	D	R_1	R_2	R_2	R_1
B	C	R_2	R_1	R_1	R_2
B	D	R_2	R_1	R_2	R_2

thereafter were immediately shifted to the final problem listed in the right hand column of Table 1. We wished to compare on this final problem only those Ss who had not yet learned their initial problem by Trial 10 (or 5 in Exp. II). Consequently, if an S in any group began a criterion run of 16 consecutive correct responses on or before the critical trial (10 or 5), he was not shifted but was, as a result, excluded from the critical comparison between those Ss who did get put into the final problem. According to the theory, these latter Ss were equalized at the start of the final problem since each S made an error before the shift was effected.

Procedure.   The same instructions were read to all Ss. The S was to classify a set of patterns into two classes. In Exp. I, the classificatory responses were MIB and CEJ; in Exp. II, the numerals 1 and 2. The S was told that the patterns could be classified by a simple principle.

Patterns were presented one at a time on a card holder. The S paced his verbal responses and E then stated the correct classification. The S was allowed 4 sec. to view the pattern after reinforcement. A different order was presented each S by shuffling the cards before the session. Cards were reshuffled at the end of every 64 trials if S had not yet reached the learning criterion of 16 successive correct responses.

Stimulus materials.   For Exp. I, patterns were constructed by sampling a single letter from each of four pairs of letters, (V or W), (F or G), (X or Y), (Q or R). Thus, VFYQ was a pattern, WVXR was not. The four letters were printed in a diamond shape on a 3 × 5 in. card. The letters appeared fixed in the order given above, but their locations at the four diamond corners rotated randomly from trial to trial. Location was an irrelevant cue. For Groups C and R, the letter pair (V, W) was relevant; the classification depended on which one of the letters was present on the card. One of the other letter pairs was selected randomly to be initially relevant for each S in Group NR, whereas (V, W) was irrelevant. The final problem was with (V, W) as the relevant cues with response assignments V-MIB and W-CEJ.

For Exp. II, the stimuli were geometric figures drawn in crayon pencil from templates on white 3 × 5 in. file cards. There were six binary dimensions: color (red or blue); size (large or small); shape (square or hexagon); number (three or four figures); position (figures arranged along right or left diagonal); and colored

TABLE 2
Mean Errors and Trial of Last Error, *SD*s, and *c* Estimates for the Final Problem

Group	N	c	Mean Errors	*SD*	Mean Trial of Last Error	*SD*
Exp. I						
Control	18	.052	19.11	19.01	38.33	32.50
Reversal	18	.052	19.11	16.42	39.56	32.27
Nonreversal	18	.055	18.28	19.28	36.94	38.23
Exp. II						
Control	10	.078	12.90	8.42	28.60	20.82
Reversal	10	.067	14.90	9.77	29.00	19.71
Nonreversal	10	.071	14.00	14.15	26.90	26.45

area within each figure (upper-right and lower-left or upper-left and lower-right quadrants). There was one relevant dimension and five irrelevant dimensions for each group. Color was relevant for Groups C and R. One of the other five dimensions was randomly selected and made relevant during initial training for each *S* in Group NR.

Subjects.   For Exp. I, the *S*s were 65 students in the introductory psychology course at Stanford University. Eleven *S*s began a criterion run on or before Trial 10; there were 4, 3, and 4 *S*s in Groups C, R, and NR, respectively. These *S*s do not enter into the comparison on the final problem since they were not transferred. Setting aside these *S*s, 18 *S*s (13 males and 5 females) remained in each group.

For Exp. II, the *S*s were 46 students in the introductory psychology course at Stanford University. Since the problem was easier, a larger proportion of *S*s was expected to solve within a few trials. Hence, fewer initial training trials (five) were used so that the majority of *S*s would not have to be set aside. Sixteen *S*s, 5 in Group C, 4 in Group R, and 7 in Group NR, began a criterion run on or before Trial 5. These *S*s were excluded from comparisons on the final problem. There remained 10 *S*s (6 males and 4 females) in each group for comparison on the final problem.

Results

In Exp. I, one *S* in Group C and one in Group NR failed to reach criterion within 140 trials on the final problem; all other *S*s solved within 140 trials. In Exp. II, all *S*s solved the final problem. Comparisons among groups on final-problem performance refer to trials following the error trial that initiated the shift to the final problem for a given *S*. Average errors and trial of last error are shown in Table 2 for the three conditions in both experiments.

The group differences on mean errors and mean trial of last error on the final

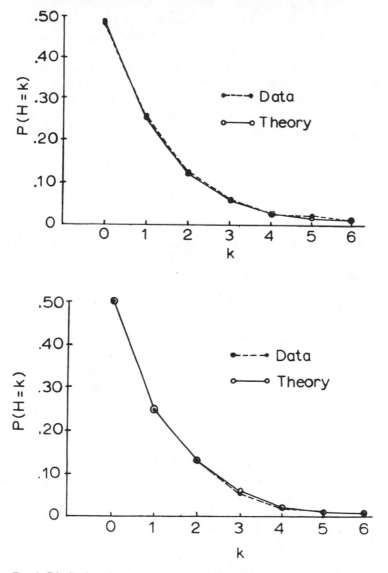

FIG. 1. Distribution of numbers of successes intervening between two adjacent errors.

problem were negligible in both experiments. The learning-parameter estimates (reciprocal of mean errors) are shown in Table 2; a likelihood ratio test for equality of c's was nonsignificant in both experiments. Further, a likelihood ratio test that each S's learning parameter, c_i, was equal to a common c was tested for all 65 Ss in Exp. I and for all 45 Ss in Exp. II. In each case, the null hypothesis could not be rejected—for Exp. I, $x^2 (64) = 53.3, p > .05$; for Exp. II, $x^2 (45) = 42.4, p > .05$.

Thus, the data were consistent with the hypothesis of a common c for Ss in each experiment; the differences among Ss' error scores could be attributed to the variability inherent in the theoretical process.

The lack of group differences indicates that performance on the final problem was unrelated to the response assignments reinforced during the initial series. Correspondingly, there was no evidence for partial learning of the relevant cues or partial elimination of irrelevant cues (cf. Group NR). Effectively, we may rely upon a single error by S to indicate that he is "naive" about the correct solution. An error in this situation has the properties of an uncertain recurrent event (Restle, 1962); when S commits an error, we may, so to speak, reset him back to the starting point from which he began working on the problem. It should be noted that the null effects of reversal and nonreversal shifts before solution differ from the effects of such shifts after initial solution has occurred (Kendler & Kendler, 1962). What differs in the two cases is that after solution, S has a strong bias to attend to the formerly relevant cue, whereas before solution he is sampling cues at random to test (Kendler, Glucksberg, & Keston, 1961).

Presolution analyses.   The data prior to the last error of each S were analyzed according to the expectations of the all-or-none theory. In theory, the presolution responses of S may be represented as a stationary and independent binomial process. To test for a constant probability of success prior to the last error, backward learning curves (Hayes, 1953) were constructed. These were stationary near .50 in each experiment. Pooling the two experiments, the probabilities of a correct classification on Trials -1, $-2 \cdots -8$ backwards from the last error were .50, .50, .52, .53, .54, .49, .51, and .50. Furthermore, the curve was flat when analyzed in two-trial blocks for 40 trials backwards from criterion, χ^2 $(19) = 19.31$, $p > .05$.

Successive correct or incorrect responses prior to the last error were also statistically independent. For Exp. I, the conditional probability of a success was .52 following a success and .53 following an error; in Exp. II, the conditional probabilities were .50 and .52, respectively. Neither set of data permits rejection of the hypothesis of independence.

If presolution responses approximate a binomial series, then the number of successes between two successive errors should be geometrically distributed as qp^n, where p is the probability of a success and $q = 1 - p$. Figure 1 shows that this random variable has a geometric distribution in the data of the two experiments.

A number of numerical predictions has been made accurately for these data, and they are reported elsewhere (Bower & Trabasso, 1964). The distribution of total errors should be geometric, i.e., $\Pr\{T=k\}=c(1-c)^{k-1}$, and this was observed in both experiments. The geometric distribution implies that the SD will be large but slightly less than the mean. Pooling all Ss in Exp. I from Trial 1, the mean errors were 20.85; the observed σ was 18.49 with 20.30 predicted. Pooling all Ss in Exp. II from Trial 1, the mean errors were 11.45; the observed σ was 11.02 with 10.96 predicted.

TABLE 3

Correct (C) and Error (E) Responses of a Hypothetical S in the Reversal Group

Alternating S-R Assignments	Trials													
	1	2	3	4	5	6	7	8	9	10	11	12	13	14
Red-VEK Blue-CEJ	C	E	C	E↓			C↑	E	E↓			C↑	E	
Blue-VEK Red-CEJ					C	C	E	C	E		C	E	C	E

A criticism that might be made is that the theory asserts the null hypothesis, and what has been shown is that our experiments had inadequate power to reject the null hypothesis. The methodological status of such matters has been discussed elsewhere (Binder, 1963; Grant, 1962). Our opinion is that if the partial learning is of such small magnitude that it does not appear with a combined total of 28 Ss in each condition, then indeed it may be considered a negligible effect. To provide a more severe test of the theory, Exp. III was conducted by extending the presolution reversal design. In Exp. III, the S-R assignments were reversed after every second error that S made. Thus, as S proceeded along through his series of trials, the S-R assignments were switching repeatedly back and forth.

EXPERIMENT III

The procedure will be illustrated briefly in order to make the theoretical predictions meaningful. Table 3 shows the first 14 trials for a hypothetical S. The stimulus patterns vary in five binary dimensions. Color is the relevant attribute and this S begins with the assignments "Red in Class VEK, Blue in Class CEJ." Suppose that his responses to the patterns on Trials 1 and 3 are correct according to these assignments, whereas his responses to the patterns on Trials 2 and 4 are wrong. The second error, occurring on Trial 4, initiates an immediate reversal of the S-R assignments, and S is told "Correct" for his response on Trial 4. According to the reversed assignments, the responses on Trials 4, 5, and 7 are correct whereas those on Trials 6 and 8 are errors. The second error of this subseries, occurring on Trial 8, initiates another immediate reversal back to the original S-R assignments, and the response on Trial 8 is called "Correct." The series of reversals on every second error continues in this fashion until S produces a string of 10 consecutive correct responses since his last reversal. A second group of control Ss was never reversed; they simply learned a fixed set of S-R assignments by the conventional training procedure in which they were informed of every error.

The prediction from the theory is that the number of *informed* errors (those not arrowed in Table 3) before learning for the Reversal Ss will be equal to the number of informed errors before learning made by the Control Ss. That is, no interference should result from the multiple reversals that occur during training. This predic-

tion follows from the assumptions that learning occurs in one trial, that opportunities for giving up an irrelevant hypothesis, and hence learning, occur only after
informed errors, and that the probability of learning following an informed error is
not affected by the past S-R assignments for the relevant cues. The point of the last
statement might be phrased in terms of the cues to which S is attending; if S is
selectively attending to irrelevant cues and is not "noticing" the color, then his
behavior when he starts noticing color is unaffected by the past history of changing
correlations between the reinforced responses and the unnoticed color values. In
contrast to the equality prediction above, if any one of the three assumptions is
wrong, the Reversal Ss should make more informed errors than do the Control Ss.

Method

Subjects.   The Ss were 33 paid volunteers from elementary history and
psychology classes at Foothill Junior College who were randomly assigned to two
groups (10 or 11 males and 6 females each).

Procedure.   The instructions were the same as those used in Exp. I and II.
The classificatory responses were VEK and CEJ. The learning criterion was 10
successive correct responses.

Stimuli.   The patterns were identical to those used in Exp. II with the exception that the area which was colored within each figure was kept constant. Thus,
there were one relevant and four irrelevant binary dimensions. Color was the
relevant dimension for both groups.

Design.   The Control group of 16 Ss learned a problem with fixed S-R
assignments throughout. For 8 of these Ss, the assignments were Red-VEK and
Blue-CEJ; the other 8 Ss had the opposite pairings. The Reversal group of 17 Ss
learned the same color-relevant problem but the response assignments were
reversed on every second error that each S committed. On alternate errors, S's
response was confirmed (called "Correct") in accord with the instantaneous
reversal of the assignments which E made as soon as S's second error of a subseries
occurred. The procedure was discussed above in connection with Table 3. By this
procedure, it would not be feasible to reverse S on every error since he would
always be told "Correct" and E would forfeit any control over what S learns.

Results

All but two Ss, one in each group, met the learning criterion. The two nonsol-
vers arrived late for their experimental session and had less time than the other Ss to
complete the problem; therefore, they are excluded from the following analyses.
Since both Ss made about the same number of errors, their exclusion does not
affect the comparisons.

The remaining 16 Ss in the Reversal group averaged 7.00 reversal shifts before
meeting criterion. The average numbers of informed errors were nearly equal for
the two groups. For the Reversal group, the average number of informed errors

was 7.81; for the Control group, it was 8.00. The *SD* of errors for the Control group was 8.22. Thus, the difference of .19 informed errors is not significant.

Two *S*s in each group learned after only one error. As a result, two *S*s in the Reversal condition were never reversed because they learned their initial response assignments. Removing these two *S*s from each group, the mean number of reversals was 8.00; the mean number of informed errors was 8.79 for the Reversal group and 9.08 for the Control group, a nonsignificant difference.

On those trials where a reversal occurred, *S* was told "Correct" when in fact he made an error. Such a procedure should serve to maintain an irrelevant hypothesis for at least one more trial. The net effect of this procedure would be to produce more "correct" responses before the last error for the Reversal *S*s than for the Controls. The mean numbers of correct responses prior to criterion for the Reversal and Control groups were 21.1 and 9.6, respectively, $t(29) = 1.99$, $p = .05$.

The mean trial of last error can be predicted for both groups once the mean errors for the Control group are known. These predictions are made to rule out the possibility that (*a*) length of success runs increased over trials in the Control group and (*b*) successive reversals tended to become more spaced out in the Reversal group over trials. For both predictions, the probability of a success prior to the last error is assumed to be constant and the a priori one-half. Let T_c be the total errors made by an *S* in the Control group; then his expected trial of last error is $2T_c$. The predicted mean trial of last error for the Control group was 16.00; the observed was 17.60. The difference was not significant by a matched *t* test, $t(14) = 1.75$, $p > .05$.

For the Reversal group, let T_r be the number of informed errors and r be the number of reversals before learning. Then the average trial of last error, n', for the Reversal group should be

$$n' = T_r + r + 1 + 2(T_r - 1). \qquad [1]$$

The first two terms, T_r and r, in Equation 1 count the number of informed error trials plus the reversal trials. The additional terms $1 + 2(T_r - 1)$ are the expected number of correct responses for an *S* who makes T_r informed errors in the Reversal group. The T_r informed errors partition the successes as follows: there is an average of one success before the first error, and an average of two successes between each of the $T_r - 1$ remaining informed errors. By hypothesis, the informed errors should be the same for both groups, so that $T_c = T_r$. Secondly, r is related to T_r, for if *S* makes T_r informed errors, then his number of reversals should be $T_r - 1$, assuming that he makes one more error after his rth and final reversal. (Note that the average number of reversals was 7, or exactly $T_c - 1$.) Substituting into Equation 1 the relations $r = T_r - 1$ and $T_c = T_r$, the following relation is obtained between T_c and the average trial of last error for the Reversal group:

$$n' = 4T_c - 2. \qquad [2]$$

Substituting the observed $T_c = 8.00$ into Equation 2, the predicted mean trial of last error (n') is 30.00. For the 16 solvers in the Reversal group, the observed value was 28.81; the SD was 26.09. The prediction is thus not significantly discrepant from the data.

The results of Exp. III favor a one-step, all-or-none interpretation of two-category concept identification in adult Ss. In addition, the results indicate that the effective information promoting learning in these problems occurs on informed error trials. Finally, the results are consistent with the notion that S's probability of solving after any given informed error is unaffected by the past history of inconsistent reinforcements to the relevant cue on which he solves.

Again the criticism may be lodged that our experiment had inadequate power to reject the null hypothesis. To provide further power for the test, we presently are running the design of Exp. III with larger groups of Ss, a different problem, and more explicit instructions to S regarding the dimensions of the stimuli, the form of the solution, etc. To date, with 24 Ss in each condition, the mean numbers of informed errors in the Control and Multiple Reversal groups are 8.22 and 7.94, respectively. Thus, the qualitative results of Exp. III are being replicated.

DISCUSSION

The Reversal and Control conditions in Exp. I and II resemble the standard ones used with this design on the continuity-noncontinuity issue. Judging from the review by Blum and Blum (1949), nearly all of the previous studies involved rats learning simultaneous discriminations with a small number of cues. On balance, that evidence favored a continuity position supplemented by constructs such as receptor orienting acts (e.g., Ehrenfreund, 1948). Whether such results should have a crucial bearing on a situational theory of adult human concept identification is a moot question. Writing for the continuity position, Spence (1940) pointed out early that the results from the animal studies may not be directly relevant to adult human learning mediated by complex symbolic mechanisms. Such mechanisms evidently are used by adults in solving concept problems, and current theorizing emphasizes such mechanisms (e.g., Bower & Trabasso, 1964; Hunt, 1962; Kendler & Kendler, 1962; Underwood & Richardson, 1956). Our working hypothesis is that the extent to which an S's discrimination learning fits the all-or-none as opposed to the incremental description depends on the extent to which symbolic mediating responses are available to S.

It would appear that one reason why the all-or-nothing model predicts accurately in these experiments is that the conditions promote "focus sampling" (Bruner, Goodnow, & Austin, 1956) because the memory load on S is otherwise overwhelming. The random-cue selection postulate implies that S's selection following an error of a new focus sample of cues to test is not affected by the past history of response assignments for the various cues. Such random selection of a sample focus is reasonable only if S's memory of specific past information is in some way impoverished. The experimental conditions presumably responsible for such poor memory include (a) the complexity of the stimuli, here 5 or 6 bits plus the 1-bit response, (*b*) the relatively rapid rate of presentation of this information (average time viewing each card was approximately 6 sec), and (*c*) S has a specific set to identify the relevant cue, not to memorize and later recall the information he is seeing. In other experiments by us, direct tests of recall of specific information under these conditions showed the memory for six-card series to be very poor. Judging from the limited capacity of Ss for quickly processing and storing such large amounts of information, it is not surprising to find that they resort to focus sampling of specific cues to test.

The present results extend previous findings (Trabasso, 1963) that single-cue concept problems can be characterized as a one-step learning process. However, it is clear that not all varieties of concept learning can be so simply described. Our aim was to explore initially the most elementary form of concept learning, in a situation similar to a conventional discrimination learning procedure. Obviously, the simple all-or-nothing model must be elaborated and extended before it will account for learning of compounds of simpler concepts (e.g., conjunctions or disjunctions of several cues). Such extensions are currently under investigation (Trabasso & Bower, 1966).

PART II
VISIT TO A SMALL LABORATORY

The remainder of the book describes my work of the past decade. I have continued the historical pattern, permitting the theory and experiments to appear as they emerged over time, rather than placing everything into some latter-day, up-to-the-minute theoretical formulation. Nevertheless, the result is not disorganized, since the outcome of one experiment typically led to the next theoretical development or experiment.

Part 2 also has the same plan as the preceding section, i.e., it is an essay with illustrative readings. Descriptions of my research have been scattered throughout the literature. For this reason and to better reveal the above-mentioned pattern, I have brought many of these together. In keeping with the case-history character, the essay material provides glimpses behind-the-scenes. Here will be found events and observations that motivated my thinking and that, in retrospect, still seem crucial and dramatic. Thus, an experience while running an S, some comment by an assistant, etc., are included. These are the sorts of events that are typically significant in the *psychology* of the scientist, but rarely appear in any formal scientific statement. These details, if of no other interest, provide some of the links between the experiments.

6

THE ANALYSIS OF RESPONSE PATTERNS
BY HUMAN ADULTS

The contemporary pool of H theory and research has been formed from two sources. One wellspring was the mathematical theory described in the last chapter. As we saw there, H testing was assumed and the implications were explored. The focus, however, was not upon the detailed dynamics of H testing, but rather upon such relatively peripheral effects as the learning curve, the number of trials to reach criterion, and transfer phenomena. The other source was my own attempt to detect Hs directly, by studying response patterns. The next series of chapters will describe the course that this work followed.

It is self-evident that H theory could be more easily developed if one could detect S's H during a problem. It would, that is, be useful to have some probe that permitted E to know S's H at any point in a problem. My thinking and research in the early '60's were guided by this conviction. Success with the analysis of the monkey's learning-set data (Reading No. 8) encouraged me to look for the needed probe in short patterns of responses.

In the late 1950's, while dealing with the monkey results, I chanced to read an article by Bendig (1951) concerning performance by the adult human. Bendig compared two large groups of college students who were asked to guess three coin tosses. One group was run in the standard fashion. That is, each S wrote his first guess, the coin was tossed, and the result announced. Then he wrote his second guess, and so on for the three guesses. The other group was run without feedback until all responding was finished. That is, each S wrote three guesses and then E tossed the coin three times. Thus, in one group "reinforcement" (to use Bendig's term) followed each response and could influence succeeding responses; in the other group nothing followed the individual response. Bendig investigated the relationship between the distribution of response patterns in the two groups. True to the custom of his day, he applied Hullian theory to these data. The analysis failed and the treatise was published as a minor disconfirmation of Hull's theory of response inhibition. The major virtue of the article was the presentation of the response-pattern distribution from the two groups.

I read Bendig's article shortly after completing the learning-set H model and, like Bendig, became intrigued about the relationship between the two groups. Since response sequences were being compared, my conviction was that a response-pattern analysis, similar to the one performed on the monkeys' data, would prove fruitful. I speculated that the human had some "set" (expectancy, prediction, or *hypothesis)* at the start of the experiment about how the three tosses would fall. An S in the group receiving no feedback would manifest his prediction directly. For example, the S in this group who expects that the three coin tosses will fall the same would write either Heads, Heads, Heads, or Tails, Tails, Tails. An S in the feedback group, on the other hand, would adjust his responses according to each outcome. The S in this latter group who expects that the three tosses would fall the same might respond Heads for the first toss. Should a "Tail" be announced as the first outcome he would then respond Tails for the second toss (he is, remember, predicting that the three outcomes will be the same).

One can see from this example that the two distributions of response patterns will not be identical, but that they will undoubtedly be related. These ideas permitted the derivation of one of these distributions from knowledge of the other (Chapter 6 in Levine, 1959a). The details of the analysis are not important here. They were generally similar to those for the learning-set model. What is important is the shift that occurred in the use of the term "hypothesis." In treating the monkey's responses an H was a preference, or habit, or *Response-set* (e.g., a position preference). In dealing with the human, however, an H could also be a *Prediction* about nature, and S was assumed to respond in the way that would maximize his rewards if his Prediction were correct.* Response-sets were conceived of as automatic and rigid, the response pattern appearing regardless of the feedback. Predictions manifested a more flexible system, with the Prediction and its concomitant responses sensitively contingent upon feedback. Specifically, a "wrong" outcome would have no effect upon Response-sets but would modify Predictions.

Armed with this distinction, challenged by the relationship between outcome and nonoutcome problems (respectively, problems with and without feedback after each response), and successful in the treatment of Bendig's data, I approached the domain of adult human discrimination learning. Along the way, new experiments were devised which permitted easier application and broader exploration of the (now enlarged) H model. It is fair to say that the resulting achievements (Levine, 1963b; see Reading No. 12) had little impact upon other researchers. The work is important, however, in the evolution of my own research program. Experiment I and the analysis thereof were tightly tied to the procedures of the learning-set model already described. As in my Ph.D. thesis, Hs were detected

*To follow an earlier usage (Levine, 1963b; see Reading No. 12), Predictions by the S are capitalized to distinguish them from predictions by the E.

indirectly by mathematical analysis. The results, however, led in a natural way to Experiment II, which introduced the use of four consecutive blank (i.e., nonout-come) trials. It was demonstrated that such a series of trials serves as a probe for S's H. This diagnostic technique became important in much of my subsequent research. Thus, Reading No. 12 provides for a continuity between the mathematical analysis of my early work and the later experimental analyses.

This article also contains a few other features that assume importance in later research. First, as already noted, the distinction was made between Response-set Hs (position preference, stimulus preferences—the sort of hypotheses to which Krech and Harlow referred) and Prediction Hs (S's expectancy about the contingencies). Response-set Hs were described as insensitive to feedback: S manifests a given response pattern whether his responses are called "right" or "wrong." Prediction Hs, on the other hand, were assumed to change when responses are called "wrong." Employment of this distinction yielded the discovery that college students never manifested Response-set Hs. This datum, which was clearly confirmed in later research (see, especially, Gholson, Levine, & Phillips, 1972—Reading No. 18), simplified the task of probing for Hs.

Second, the relationship between response patterns with and without feedback was demonstrated. I had assumed that S (the adult human) retained his H under two conditions: when he was told "right" and when he was told nothing. Only a disconfirmation would cause S to change his (Prediction) H. This implies that during a series of blank trials S would respond as though E were saying "right" after each response. The corollary is that the distribution of response patterns obtained from a group of Ss during a series of blank trials would be the same as the distribution obtained if E said "right" after each of those trials. This relationship was labeled the Blank-Trials Law and was validated in a series of Experiments (Levine, Leitenberg, & Richter, 1964; see Reading No. 13). The relationship was proclaimed (a bit grandly) a law because it held with a variety of procedures. Subsequent work (Moore & Halpern, 1967; Richter & Levine, 1965; Spence, 1970) further attests to its generality.*

---

*An occasional contradiction appears (see e.g., Cairns, 1967). The relationship should hold if blank trials are presented as test trials or as otherwise neutral. If, because of instructions or experience (Buchwald, 1959a), S learns that the absence of feedback signifies an error, different results will, of course, be obtained.

READING NO. 12
MEDIATING PROCESSES IN HUMANS AT THE OUTSET OF DISCRIMINATION LEARNING *

By Marvin Levine

The conception central to the model to be delineated has been suggested in a wide variety of sources (Bruner, 1951; Hovland, 1952; Kendler & Kendler, 1962; Restle, 1962—to name but a few recent ones). The conception is that the adult human starts a problem with a mediating process ("prediction," "hypothesis," "expectancy," "set" are alternative terms which have been employed) and that this mediating process affects the overt behavior in specifiable ways. The model will describe the set of such processes available at the outset of short discrimination problems, will lead to techniques for evaluating their frequency, and will permit the deduction of novel theorems about behavior. Later sections of this paper will present experimental tests of these theorems.

The present formulation is a development from a model (Levine, 1959b) of the behavior of monkeys engaged in a series of three-trial discrimination problems. The fundamental assumption in that model was that there is a set of Hs (short for hypotheses, after Krechevsky, 1932b), defined as systematic response patterns, one of which is chosen by the subject on each problem. Examples of Hs are "Position Preference" (defined as repeated response to one position), "Stimulus Preference" (defined as repeated response to one stimulus), and "Win-stay-Lose-shift with respect to the stimulus" (defined as response to the stimulus correct on the preceding trial). That model yielded a method of analysis for determining the frequency of occurrence of the various Hs. It became possible to conclude, for example, that Position Preference occurred on 18% of the problems and to decompose the learning-set function into the underlying set of H functions.

The same assumption, that there is a set of Hs among which the subject chooses, and the same general method of analysis will be applied to adult human behavior over a series of discrimination learning problems. The hypothesis then, will

*Adapted from *Psychological Review*, 1963, **70**, 254-276. Copyright 1963 by the American Psychological Association. Reprinted by permission of the publisher.

continue to be the basic dependent variable, and will continue to be symbolized by H. There will be, however, a shift in the definition of this symbol. Whereas it had been previously defined as a response pattern, it will here after be defined as the *determinant* of a response pattern, as a mediating process which results in the particular response pattern. The rationale for such a change will become clear as the model is presented and will be discussed following the presentation of the experiments.

The human experimental situation to which the analysis will be applied incorporates the general procedures of the learning-set experiment (Harlow, 1949). In the most usual form of that experiment two stimulus objects are presented simultaneously for a few trials. Typically, the stimuli are relevant (response to one of them is consistently rewarded) for these few trials; their positions, which reverse on 50% of the trials, are irrelevant. A series of problems are presented, new stimuli being used for each problem.

The present experiments will differ from the previous experiments in one important detail: the experimenter will have two procedures instead of one. In the typical discrimination learning experiments with monkeys the experimenter uses a single procedure: one of the two responses is always rewarded, the other not. The analogous procedure with humans is that one of the responses is followed by the word "right," the other by the word "wrong." With humans, the experimenter may have a second procedure: "blank" trials may be presented, i.e., during some problems the experimenter may say nothing.

There are then two types of problems: Outcome problems (the experimenter says "right" or "wrong" after each response) and Nonoutcome problems (the experimenter says nothing after each response). The subject will have been instructed that both types of problems would occur and that he is to try to obtain 100% correct in either case. A major aim of the model will be the prediction of behavior during Nonoutcome problems from behavior during Outcome problems, and vice versa.

The model will be developed to specify the Hs with which the subjects start any problem. The description of subsequent Hs involves arbitrary assumptions about resampling of Hs and will not be considered here. As a result, behavioral data only through the first two trials of Outcome problems will be considered. The initial experiment to which the model will be applied will consist of precisely two-trial problems. The Hs at the outset of longer problems will be considered in the second experiment.

A two-trial problem, the subject's behavior, and the experimenter's behavior will be summarized by a few symbols. If the two stimuli maintain the same positions on Trials 1 and 2 the problem type will be described as "A"; if they reverse positions from Trials 1 to 2 the problem type will be described as "B." The response sequence will be described as I_s, if the subject chooses the *identical stimulus* on Trial 2 to the one chosen on Trial 1. Choice of one then the *other stimulus* will be described as O_s . From knowledge of the problem type (A or B) and of the subject's sequence of stimulus selection (I_s or O_s) one may deduce his sequence of position selections. Nevertheless, it will be useful to symbolize also the sequence of position responses. Response to the same position for the two trials will be described as I_p; response to one then the other position will be described as O_p. The symbols $+_1$, and $-_1$, will be used to denote that the experimenter said "right" or "wrong," respectively, following the response on Trial 1. The symbol pair $+_1 I_s$ means that the subject chose a stimulus on Trial 1, the experimenter said "right" and the subject chose the same stimulus on Trial 2. The symbol pairs $+_1 O_s$, $-_1 I_s$, and $-_1 O_s$ are analogously defined.

The problem type (A or B) and these four symbol pairs describe all possible relevant outcome-response sequences for a single Outcome problem. On a single Nonoutcome problem the problem type and the symbols I_s and O_s describe all possible response sequences.

DISCRIMINATION MODEL

As already indicated, the basic conception will be that during any one problem the behavior of a subject is determined by an H, defined as a determinant of systematic responding, and to be interpreted as a prediction by the subject or his set. The Hs available to a subject in a two-trial simultaneous discrimination problem will now be considered. In this situation Hs have three characteristics. The first is that an H may be contingent either on the stimuli or on the positions. For example, a subject may Predict that one of the two stimuli is always correct (the subject Predicts that one of the *stimuli* is correct and will repeat) or that one of the two positions is always correct (the subject Predicts that one of the *positions* is correct and will repeat).[1] There are then two classes of Hs, half directed toward stimuli, half toward positions. The second feature of Hs is that they are sequence oriented. For example, a subject may Predict that one of the two stimuli is always correct (the subject Predicts that one of the stimuli is correct and will *repeat)* or that the correct stimulus changes from Trial 1 to Trial 2 (the subject Predicts that the correct stimulus will *alternate).*

The stimulus-position breakdown combined with the repeat-alternate breakdown yields four Hs. Consideration of the third feature of Hs will increase the number to eight. In all the examples just given it was assumed that the subject *Predicts* an event sequence for the first two trials. It is unrealistic to assume that this process is the only source of systematic behavior. It is conceivable that systematic response to a position or a stimulus may occur in other ways. Consider the following examples: The subject does not care about this experiment and wants to get out as fast as he can. He decides to choose always the stimulus on the left side; one of the two stimuli is repulsive to the subject and he will always choose the other even though the experimenter always says "wrong"; the subject decides to alternate stimuli (or positions) for want of anything better to do.

It is clear that these sets will yield systematic behavior, but it is equally clear that

---

[1]The word "predict" will have two usages: as subject's mediating process, or as the usual outcome of theoretical analysis. To help distinguish the two usages, the former will be capitalized.

these processes are different from Predictions about correct events. One may also surmise that the resulting response patterns should be different from the patterns produced by Predictions. The distinction will be made, therefore, between *Prediction H*s and *Response-set H*s, the latter term referring to *H*s of the sort described in the last three examples.

The three two-way classifications (stimulus, position; perseveration, alternation; Prediction, Response-set) lead to eight *H*s, each of which may now be described. In order, however, to relate each *H* to behavior it is necessary to introduce two postulates, one describing behavior if a Prediction *H* exists, one if a Response-set *H* exists.

Prediction postulate: If a subject Predicts how a series of rewards will occur he behaves so that if the Prediction were correct rewards would be maximized.

Suppose, for example, that a subject Predicts that one of the stimuli is correct and repeats, i.e., will be correct on both trials of the problem. If his Prediction is correct he can insure a "right" on Trial 2 of an Outcome Problem by following this rule: If the experimenter says "right" after Trial 1 choose the same stimulus on Trial 2; if the experimenter says "wrong" after Trial 1 choose the other stimulus on Trial 2. Thus, on Outcome Problems the Prediction that one of the stimuli is correct and repeats will lead to the behavior pattern formerly described (Levine, 1959b) as "Win-stay-Lose-shift with respect to the stimulus."

On a Nonoutcome problem the Prediction postulate means simply that the subject strives to obtain 100% correct. A subject with the Prediction that one of the stimuli is correct and repeats would choose the same stimulus for all trials of the problem. No other behavior pattern can, if this Prediction is correct, yield 100% correct.

The four Prediction *H*s are described below. The behavior manifestations are given for Outcome problems and for Nonoutcome problems, followed by the summary form in parenthesis:

Hypothesis a (H_a): *The subject Predicts that one of the stimuli is correct and will repeat.* Outcome-problem behavior: The subject shows "Win-stay-Lose-shift with respect to the stimulus" ($+ _1I_s$ or $- _1O_s$). Nonoutcome-problem behavior: The subject chooses the same stimulus on Trials 1 and 2 (I_s).

Hypothesis a' (H_a'): *The subject Predicts that the correct stimulus will alternate.* Outcome-problem behavior: The subject shows "Win-shift-Lose-stay with respect to the stimulus" ($+_1O_s$ or $-_1I_s$). Nonoutcome-problem behavior: The subject chooses one stimulus on Trial 1 and the other stimulus on Trial 2 (O_s).

Hypothesis b (H_b (: *The subject Predicts that one of the positions is correct and will repeat.* Outcome-problem behavior: The subject shows "Win-stay-Lose-shift with respect to position" ($+_1I_p$ or $-_1O_p$). Nonoutcome-problem behavior: The subject chooses the same position on Trials 1 and 2 (I_p).

Hypothesis b' (H_b'): *The subject Predicts that the correct position will alternate.* Outcome-problem behavior: The subject shows "Win-shift-Lose-stay with respect to position" ($+_1O_p$ or $-_1I_p$). Nonoutcome-problem behavior: The subject chooses one position on Trial 1 and the other position on Trial 2 (O_p).

Response-set postulate: If a subject has a Response-set H the behavior has the pattern described by that H and is independent of outcomes.

Suppose, for example, that the subject has the set that he will always choose the stimulus on the left. He will manifest a sequence of responses to the left side, no matter what kind of outcomes the experimenter presents.

The four Response-set Hs are described below. The behavior manifestation, which is the same for both Outcome and Nonoutcome problems, is given for each H, followed by the summary form in parenthesis.

Hypothesis x (H_x): *The subject has a Response-set to repeat the same stimulus.* Behavior: Stimulus Preference, i.e., the subject chooses the same stimulus on Trials 1 and 2 (I_s).

Hypothesis x' ($H_{x'}$): *The subject has a Response-set to alternate stimuli.* Behavior: The subject chooses one stimulus on Trial 1 and the other stimulus on Trial 2 (O_s).

Hypothesis y (H_y): *The subject has a Response-set to repeat the same position.* Behavior: Position Preference, i.e. the subject chooses the same position on Trials 1 and 2 (I_p).

Hypothesis y' ($H_{y'}$): *The subject has a Response-set to alternate positions.* Behavior: The subject chooses one position on Trial 1 and the other position on Trial 2 (O_p).

A detail to note is that the Hs have been paired off according to the words "repeat" and "alternate." Any such pair will be described as complementary, because both members of the pair dovetail in their manifestations, yielding all possible behavior patterns. This relation is denoted by employing for a given pair the same subscript letter and distinguishing the two by primes (for example, H_a and H_a'). The effect of complementarity will become explicit when the evaluation of the H strengths is discussed.

EVALUATION OF THE H PROBABILITIES

Corresponding to each H will be a probability denoting the theoretical proportion of times that the H is selected. The subscript letter will be employed to represent the probability, i.e., $P(H_a) = a$, $P(H_a') = a'$, etc.

The assumption will be made that the Hs are mutually exclusive and exhaustive, i.e., that only one of the Hs occurs to a given subject on a given problem. This assumption permits the following statement:

$$a + a' + b + b' + x + x' + y + y' = 1.00. \qquad [1]$$

Given this additional assumption, a techniques is available (Levine, 1959a) for evaluating H probabilities from Outcome problem data. A set of equations is derived in which these probabilities are expressed as functions of the obtained frequencies of the outcome-response sequences. Appendix A presents this technique, in more general form than previously, as part of the attempt to solve for a, a',

$b, \ldots, y'.$[2] It is shown there that in the present case a complete solution is not possible, that there is available only a relative solution which describes by how much one of a complementary pair of Hs exceeds the other. That is, one may solve only for

$$D_a = a - a'; \quad D_b = b - b'; \quad D_x = x - x'; \quad D_y = y - y'.$$

Any of the D_i may range from -1.0 (if only one H involving alternation is employed) to $+1.0$ (if only one H involving perseveration is employed). For example, $D_a = +1.0$ means that, for the block of problems considered, the subjects always have H_a, the Prediction that the correct stimulus perseverates. $D_a = 0$ means that $a = a'$. They may both be 0 or as much as .5.

PREDICTION OF RESPONSE PATTERNS

Appendix A shows that the D_i are obtained as numerical values from the Outcome problem data. It is possible to employ these values to predict the behavior of the subjects during the Nonoutcome problems. The theory may be developed to predict NI_s, the number of times that the subject chooses the same stimulus for both trials of a problem in a block of Nonoutcome problems.

Appendix B presents this development of the theory for the condition when the number of A and B Nonoutcome problems are the same.[2] It is shown there that

$$NI_s = (T/2)[D_a + D_x + 1], \tag{2}$$

where T represents the total number of Nonoutcomes problems under consideration, D_a reflects the degree to which the subject Predicts stimulus repetition (if D_a is positive) or alternation (if D_a is negative), and D_x reflects the degree to which the subject has a Response-set to repeat or alternate stimuli (if D_x is positive or negative, respectively).

Embodied in Equation 2 is the strategy for testing the model. It is worth, therefore, repeating that D_a and D_x are numbers obtained from the Outcome problems and NI_b is the theoretical number of repeated stimulus selections in a block of Nonoutcome problems. The test consists in comparing this theoretical number with the obtained number.

EXPERIMENT I

Method

Subjects. Eighty students from the introductory psychology courses at Indiana University served as subjects.

Apparatus. The stimuli were 180 different three-letter nonsense syllables selected from Glaze's (1928) lists. Pairs of syllables were randomly selected to

---

[2]The Appendices may be found in Levine (1963b).

form the stimulus objects for a given trial, and were typed .5 inch apart on a 3 × 5 inch card. The same two syllables on a pair of cards constituted the materials for a problem, and a deck of 90 such pairs of cards constituted the materials for the experiment.

Design. A learning-set experiment consisting of 90 two-trial problems was presented under four experimental conditions to four groups of 20 subjects. The four conditions differed along a continuum defined by the experimenter's manner of reinforcement. At one end of this continuum is the standard learning-set procedure in which the experimenter selects the stimulus to be correct, and reinforces responses only to it on each trial of the problem. This procedure holds for every problem in the experiment. That is, the correct stimulus is the same for both trials on 100% of the problems. The group receiving this condition will be referred to as G-100. At the other end of the continuum is a procedure in which the stimulus designated as correct by the experimenter alternates from Trial 1 to Trial 2, a procedure first utilized by Behar (1961) and designated as an Alternation Learning-Set. The correct stimulus is never the same for the two trials of any problem, or, conversely, is the same for 0% of the problems. The group receiving this condition will be referred to as G-O. In between the two extremes the experimenter may follow one procedure or the other for as many problems as he wishes. For the two remaining conditions the correct stimulus was the same during 80% of the problems, changing during the remainder (G-80), and the correct stimulus was the same during 20% of the problems, changing during the remainder (G-20). The four groups, then, were G-100, G-80, G-20, and G-0, where the number describes the percentage of problems on which the experimenter caused the correct stimulus to perseverate.

Procedure. Each subject was shown a sample 3 × 5 inch card containing two syllables and was instructed that he would receive a deck composed of similar cards and that he was always to choose one of the two syllables on each card. He was further told that the experimenter would say "right" or "wrong" after each choice, and that he was to try to be right as often as possible. He was then given the deck face down and was instructed to turn the cards one at a time, making his response for each. The placement of cards after each trial was arranged so that they could not again be seen.

After either 5 or 10 Outcome problems the experimenter stopped the subject and instructed him that there would now be a test of how much had been learned thus far. The subject was told that during the next few cards the experimenter would not say anything, that because this was a test he was to try to get 100% correct. The subject then proceeded to choose syllables on the next 10 cards (5 problems) with the experimenter saying nothing. After these 5 problems the experimenter announced that the learning would be resumed and presented outcomes during the next 10 problems. Test instructions then followed, etc. Ten Outcome problems continued to alternate with 5 Nonoutcome problems until 90 problems—60 with, 30 without outcomes—had been presented.

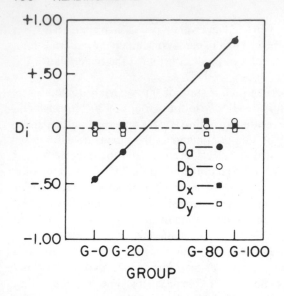

FIG. 1. The value of the D_i computed from the block of 60 Outcome problems for each group (the groups are ordered and spaced according to the percentage of problems on which the correct stimulus perservated for the two trials).

Results

Figure 1 shows the D_i, the difference between complementary Hs, computed from all the Outcome problems for each group. The figure shows that neither Predictions about positions nor Response-sets show greater excess in perseveration or alternation, i.e., the D_b, D_x, and D_y fluctuate around zero. The D_a, on the other hand, vary (linearly, oddly enough) from $-.47$ for G-0 (the subjects in this group Predict that the correct stimulus alternates for a minimum of 47% of the problems) to $+.80$ for G-100 (these subjects Predict that the correct stimulus repeats for a minimum of 80% of the problems).

The values of D_a and D_x may be inserted into Equation 2 to predict the number of Nonoutcome problems in which the same syllable will be selected for both trials. The prediction will be made for each group, so that T, the total number of Nonoutcome problems under consideration, will equal 600 (20 subjects × 30 Nonoutcome problems per subject). The predicted and obtained frequencies are presented in Figure 2. This figure has two noteworthy features. One is that the obtained values are exceedingly close to the predicted values. None of the discrepancies from the predictions are statistically significant. The other is that there is a bias in favor of repeating syllables. If a group had been run in which the experimenter caused the correct syllable to perseverate on 50% of the problems and to alternate on the other 50%, i.e., if the experimenter had said "right" and "wrong" totally at random, then one would predict (from interpolation in Figure 2, rather than from theoretical considerations) that the subject would repeat syllables for about 360 (= 60%) of the Nonoutcome problems. The fact that with this insoluble procedure D_a would appear to be about $+.15$ (from interpolation in

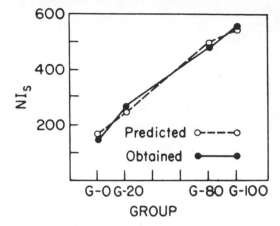

FIG. 2. Predicted and obtained NI_s for all the Nonoutcome problems for each of the four groups.

Figure 1) indicates that this repetition bias results primarily from the subject's tendency to Predict that the correct stimulus repeats rather than from a Response-set to repeat stimuli.

THE n-DIMENSIONAL PROBLEM

The preceding experiment demonstrates that for the two-trial simultaneous discrimination a close relationship exists between behavior during Outcome problems and during Nonoutcome problems. The model of mediating processes which has been elaborated provides a rationale for this relationship. In general, obtaining the H probabilities for one outcome condition permits a close prediction of the behavior patterns in the other condition.

The model was described, however, only for the situation in which two stimuli (for example, two different nonsense syllables) could occupy one of two positions: there were two dimensions with two values, or cues, for each dimension. The remainder of the paper will deal with transcending this limitation. It will be demonstrated how the model may be generalized to obtain H strengths at the outset of the n-dimensional learning situation.

The analysis for the n-dimensional problem will be reduced relative to the analysis described in the preceding sections for the two-dimensional problem. In that analysis two general categories of Hs were described: Predictions $(H_a, \ldots, H_{b'})$ and Response-sets $(H_x, \ldots, H_{y'})$. The category of Predictions also had two types of Hs: Predictions that the correct value of one of the dimensions repeated $(H_a$ and $H_b)$ and Predictions that the correct value followed a sequential pattern (specifically, for the two-dimensional problem, alternation: $H_{a'}$ and $H_{b'}$). The present model will be "reduced" in that it will attempt to evaluate only the first type of Prediction, i.e., only those Hs which are predictions that one of the values of one of the dimensions is repeatedly correct. Response-set Hs and Hs which are Predictions of more complex sequential events will be ignored. In effect the

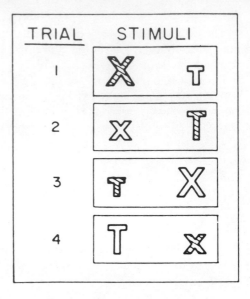

FIG. 3. Four trials of a four-dimensional problem.

assumption will be made that the most important type of mediating process which the adult human subject has at the outset of a problem of several dimensions consists in an attempt to locate the cue which is invariantly (within that problem) the basis for correct responding.

The assumption, incidentally, is not unique to the present treatment. In a common type of concept formation experiment the n-dimensional problem is employed and this assumption is more or less explicit in the analysis (for example, Brown & Archer, 1956; Bruner, Goodnow, & Austin, 1956; Grant & Curran, 1952; Hovland, 1952). For this reason the assumption will be referred to as the concept formation (CF) assumption. The model incorporating this assumption will be referred to as the CF model.

The a priori justification for the CF assumption comes from three considerations:

1. The preceding experiment showed that the Response-set H differences, D_x and D_y, were uniformly near zero. One could have assumed that the Response-set Hs were zero without seriously altering the predictions.

2. There is some evidence (Goodnow & Postman, 1955) that as the stimulus situation becomes multi-dimensional the subjects avoid complex sequence behaviors (resulting, for example, from single-alternation or double-alternation Predictions) in favor of locating that cue which is consistently to be chosen.

3. One may, by instructions and pre-experimental demonstrations, minimize Predictions that events follow complex patterns. Several investigators of concept formation have employed this technique (Archer, Bourne, & Brown, 1955; Bruner et al., 1956; Hovland & Weiss, 1953; Oseas & Underwood, 1952).

The CF model, then, will deal with the n-dimensional problem and will focus upon Predictions by the subject concerning that dimension which defines correct responding. While the model will be presented in general form for the n-dimensional problem it will be applied specifically to a four-dimensional problem. An example of such a problem is presented in Figure 3. The dimensions are form $(X$ versus $T)$, position (right versus left), color (white versus black), and size (large versus small). The figure shows one possible sequence of the various levels over the four trials. This sequence has the special property that each value of each dimension appears an equal number of times with every value of every other dimension. For example, T is black twice, large letters appear on the right twice, X is small twice, etc. Problems in which the dimensions show this kind of balance will be described as *internally orthogonal*.

THE CONCEPT FORMATION MODEL

As already stated, only Predictions that the correct cue repeats from trial to trial will be evaluated. For any given dimension there is only this one H. For the problem shown in Figure 3, for example, there are four Hs corresponding to the four dimensions. If the subject has a color H at the outset of the problem, he Predicts that one of the colors will be correct from trial to trial regardless of which form has that color, its size, or position. Similarly, if the subject has a size H, he Predicts that one of the two sizes will be correct from trial to trial. There are also, in this problem, a position H and a form H.

One task of the model will be to show how one may evaluate individually the n Hs which correspond to the n dimensions. In addition, a residual H will be determined demonstrating the pooled effect of other mediating processes. For purposes of simplicity it will be assumed that this Residual H is the pooled strength of Predictions about dimensions which are not part of the formal structure of the problem. Such dimensions might be movements by the experimenter, apparatus noises, a flickering light, etc.[3]

There are, then, $n + 1$ Hs to be described for the n-dimensional problem. For the four-dimensional problem described in Figure 3 there are five Hs:

H_a: The Prediction that form is the correct dimension and that the correct form will repeat.

H_b: The Prediction that position is the correct dimension, etc.

H_c: The Prediction that color is the correct diemsnion, etc.

H_d: The Prediction that size is the correct dimension, etc.

H_r: The Prediction that a non-recorded dimension is correct.

[3]This is an arbitrary interpretation of the Residual H. Certainly other processes could be occurring: Response-sets, more complex Predictions, periodic errors, as well as Predictions about unrecorded dimensions. The occurrence, if any, and contribution of each of these is completely unknown, nor have methods of disentangling them for the n dimensional problem been developed. The present assumption has the virtue of providing conceptual consistency and mathematical simplicity.

The probability of any of these Hs will be denoted by the corresponding subscript symbol. Thus, $P(H_a) = a$, $P(H_b) = b$, etc.

The Hs are related to behavior solely by the Prediction postulate described for the two-trial problem (the Response-set postulate is irrelevant for the CF model). The behavioral manifestations of the ith H follow directly from this postulate:

H_i: *The subject Predicts that one level of the ith dimension is correct and will repeat.*

Outcome-problem behavior: the subject makes his best guess as to which of the levels of that dimension is correct on Trial 1. If the response is correct (for example, if the experimenter says "right") the subject chooses the same level of the same dimension on Trial 2; if the response is incorrect (for example, if the experimenter says "wrong") the subject chooses the other level of the same dimension on Trial 2. This would, in general, be described as "Win-stay-Lose-shift with respect to the ith dimension."

Nonoutcome-problem behavior: the subject makes his best guess as to which of the levels of that dimension is correct on Trial 1. He chooses the same level of that dimension on all subsequent trials of the problem.

There is an important difference in the description of the behavior for Outcome and Nonoutcome problems. During Outcome problems behavior is stipulated only for the first two trials. This is because the effects of "rights" and "wrongs" from the second trial onward involve assumptions about resampling of Hs which are beyond the scope of the present model. The limitation of relevant Outcome problem data to the first two trials makes unfeasible, in a problem with even as few as four dimensions, the solution of the H probabilities in the usual manner, i.e., from Outcome problems. The reason is, of course, that behavior patterns resulting from different Hs inevitably overlap during the first two trials, making evaluations of the Hs ambiguous. Over Trials 1 and 2 of the problem illustrated in Figure 3 for example, behavior with respect to color would be identical with behavior with respect to size, as would the behavior with respect to form and position.

During Nonoutcome problems, on the other hand, behavior is specified for all trials of a problem. In the problem of Figure 3, a subject with a form H (i.e., H_a) would respond RRLL (or LLRR; described more generally as AABB). The Prediction postulate demands precisely this behavior. No other behavior could yield 100% correct if H_a were correct. Similarly, a subject with H_b would respond AAAA; a subject with H_c would respond ABAB; a subject with H_d would respond ABBA. This freedom to observe the manifestation of the initial H over several trials of a Nonoutcome problem permits the emergence of unique response patterns corresponding to each H. In the problem shown in Figure 3, one need only observe which of the four response patterns is occurring to determine which H the subject is holding. Thus, the H held by a single subject on a single (Nonoutcome) problem may be determined. Also, if one wishes to revert to probabilistic statements about the strengths of the various Hs, one need only present the problem to a large number of subjects. The proportion of subjects showing each of the response patterns provides probability estimates of the corresponding Hs.

In an internally orthogonal four-trial problem such as that shown in Figure 3 one may also determine when one of the class of H_r is occurring. Response patterns other than the four listed above may occur. For this problem, specifically, any combination of 3A's and 1B may also occur. Since they could not be produced by the four given Hs, these patterns will be interpreted as reflecting H_r.

By presenting a Nonoutcome problem of internally orthogonal structure, then, one may estimate the probabilities of all the various Hs described by the model. The Nonoutcome problem may be used to determine the H probabilities at a given point in a problem series. In the experiment to be described, for example, a large group of subjects receives a series of four trial problems. At various points in the series the group is subdivided, one half receiving an Outcome Problem, the other half receiving a Nonoutcome Problem. From the latter condition one may determine the probability of the Hs at the outset of the problem. The model assumes that these are also estimates of the initial H probabilities for the subjects facing the Outcome problem. The validity of this assumption will be demonstrated.

EXPERIMENT II

Method

Subjects. The subjects were 255 students from the experimental psychology courses at Indiana University. None of these subjects had participated in Experiment I.

Apparatus. Pairs of consonants of the alphabet were randomly selected to provide the stimulus forms for a given trial. The two letters were printed as transparent forms on an opaque background on a filmstrip negative. The pair of letters was printed four times with these variations: One of the letters was large and one was small; one was on the left and one on the right; the dimensions of letter, size, and position were mutually orthogonal, i.e., each level of each dimension appeared twice with each level of the other two dimensions. A color dimension was added by randomly selecting two hues from a set of seven transparent dies. (The hues were purple, blue, green, yellow, brown, red, and white.) The two colors were applied to the four reproductions of the pairs of letters, such that color was orthogonal to the other three dimensions. This produced the set of stimuli for the type of problem exemplified in Figure 3, i.e., four pairs of stimuli constructed from four mutually orthogonal dimensions. Twenty-four such problems were constructed. With a single exception, to be noted below, they were all internally orthogonal problems. There are six different types of 4-trial internally orthogonal problems, according to which dimension double alternates with respect to position (AABB), which single alternates (ABAB), and which follows an ABBA pattern. These six were randomly assigned to the 24 problems.

The filmstrips for the 24 problems were spliced together so that the problems could be presented conveniently in sequence. A pair of letters was projected by an overhead projector (Beseler Master Vu-Graph) onto a screen. Even in a well-lit room the letters appeared brightly with the appropriate hue. The larger of the two letters was approximately 6 × 3 inches when projected; the smaller letter was half that size. The letters were 2 inches apart.

Design. The subjects were divided into two groups of 127 and 128, respectively. Each group received a preliminary demonstration problem followed by the 24 problems of the experiment proper. The demonstration problem was constructed of the four dimensions indicated but was 14 trials in length. The 24 problems which followed this preliminary problem consisted of 18 Outcome problems with 6 Nonoutcome problems interspersed. One group (Group A) received the Nonoutcome condition on Problems 2, 6, 10, 14, 18, and 22; the other group (Group B) received the Nonoutcome condition on Problems 4, 8, 12, 16, 20, and 24. This design offered two advantages. First, H strengths, which are derived from the Nonoutcome procedure, could be obtained on every other problem. This permits a fairly detailed picture of changes in H probabilities over the problem series. Second, while one group of subjects is receiving a Nonoutcome problem (for example, Group B on Problem 20) the other group, which has had an almost identical history of problem solving experience in the experiment, is receiving an Outcome problem constructed of the same stimulus materials. The model permits prediction about behavior in the latter condition from the H information obtained from the former.

The latter feature provided the rationale for the one deviation from internally orthogonal problems during the experiment proper. The group receiving an Outcome problem when, at the same point, the other group was receiving a Nonoutcome problem did not necessarily receive an internally orthogonal problem. On these problems either zero, one, two, or all three of the remaining dimensions were confounded with the correct dimension. For example, if one dimension (for example, size) were confounded with the correct dimension (for example, color: green versus blue) then all blue letters would always be large (or always small). If all four dimensions were confounded, then the same letter would be large, blue, and on the left side on every trial of the problem. This variation in confounding expanded the range over which predictions could be made.

Procedure. The 255 subjects were run in 10 classes of approximately 25 students each. The first pair of stimuli from the preliminary problem was projected on the screen before the class while the initial instructions were read. The subjects were told that they were to decide which of the two stimuli was correct, that they were to indicate their choice by filling in the appropriate side (right or left corresponding to the location of the stimulus chosen) by the first answer space of an IBM answer sheet and that the experimenter would then indicate which stimulus was correct. They were further told that there would be a series of such stimuli and that this procedure was to be followed on each presentation. After all the subjects made their first response the experimenter pointed to the correct stimulus. Following this outcome presentation the next pair of stimuli appeared. The subjects responded and the experimenter again pointed to the correct stimulus. Fourteen trials took place in this manner. The forms for these preliminary trials were always the letters A and E, the colors were red and green, and the letters were of two sizes as described above. The experimenter always pointed to the larger letter on all trials for all subjects.

When the 14 trials were ended, the experimenter announced that the large letter was always correct and told the class that this was a demonstration problem. He then explicitly described the four dimensions (large or small, right or left, the two colors, and the two letters) and stated that as in the preliminary problem where the large stimulus was always correct one of these cues would always provide the correct basis for responding.

The experiment proper was then begun. Outcomes were always presented except when Nonoutcome problems were scheduled. During all Outcome problems the experimenter pointed to the correct stimulus after each trial. For Outcome Problems 1-12 one of the two colors always served as the basis for correct responding; on Problems 13-24 one of the two letters always served as the basis for correct responding. Thus, there were two concept formation learning sets: A color set followed by a form set. The second followed the first without any special announcement or break.

Before the first Nonoutcome problem (Problem 2 for Group A; Problem 4 for Group B) the experimenter announced that the next problem would be a test of how much had been learned thus far. The class was told that during the next problem the experimenter would not point to the correct stimulus after each trial, that because this was a test the students were to continue to try to get 100% correct. The next four trials followed without outcomes. These trials were followed by the next three Outcome problems. Test instructions were then given again (before Problem 6 for Group A; Problem 8 for Group B) followed by another Nonoutcome problem. Three Outcome problems continued to alternate with one Nonoutcome problem until all 24 problems had been presented.

Results

The H probabilities on every second problem are presented in Figure 4. These probabilities are directly equivalent to the proportion of subjects manifesting the response pattern corresponding to the H on each Nonoutcome problem. Thus the increase in c over Nonoutcome Problems 2-12 means that an increasing number of subjects are showing the response pattern corresponding to the color H on these problems. The figure shows how the probabilities of each H change, first during a color learning-set series (Problems 1-12) then during a form series (Problems 13-24).

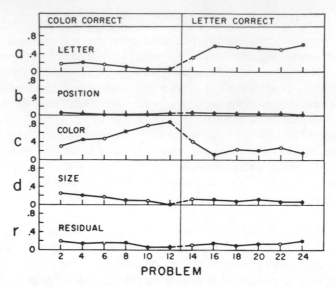

FIG. 4. The probability of occurrence of the various Hs (the open circles are for Group A; the filled circles are for Group B).

It is important to recall that each data point represented in this figure comes from a Nonoutcome problem, that the curves represent changes in response patterns recorded during problems when the experimenter is saying nothing. Furthermore, the points represent two different groups alternating on Nonoutcome problems. In spite of this unorthodox style of collecting data, the resulting curves are quite regular; the curves for c during Problems 2-12 and for a during Problems 14-24 appear very much like typical, i.e., Outcome problem, learning curves, and the curves for other Hs show regular, gradual extinction effects.

Certain details in this graph are noteworthy. The first is that H_b scarcely ever occurs. These subjects almost never Predict that position is the basis for solution. The reasons for this effect are unclear. It may occur either because the adult human subject generally avoids response to position in such a problem or because of the particular procedures employed in this experiment. What is important, however, is that the absence of consistent response to position means not only that $b = 0$ but that there is no Response-set to position, i.e., there is no manifestation of position preference. This represents further validation of the assumption that Response-sets are negligible with this type of subject.

The second detail is that when the learning-set changes there tends to be a small increase in the strength of already extinguished Hs; i.e., when the learning set shifts from color to letter, b, d, and R show a small increment in strength. Restle (1958) suggested that this might happen. The method provides a technique for quantitative analysis of the effect.

Third, more proficiency is achieved on the first learning set than on the second (c at maximum is .84; a reaches only .60). It is possible that color is more salient than letter, but again, the particular procedures must be considered. The letter problems came in the second half of a massed, and probably tedious, procedure. There was evidence that the subjects were tiring over the experimental session. One could have demonstrated this, although it was not done, by recording the number of yawns over the experiment. They clearly increased. It is possible, then, that the depression in the second learning-set function as well as some of the irregularities found in the second half of the data might disappear with a more distributed procedure.

Figure 4 portrays the information to be gathered by going beyond mere learning representations of data. Of course, this figure describes the H strengths from Nonoutcome problems. It is necessary now to consider its relevance to what traditionally has been of more universal interest, the Outcome problem.

During any even-numbered problem of Experiment II half the subjects received an Outcome problem while the other half received a similar problem without outcomes. Since the model deals with Hs at the *outset* of the problem one may assume, as has been done throughout, that the probabilities are the same for both types of problems. Therefore, if the probabilities are known for one type of problem they are, in theory, also known for the other. In theory, Figure 4, although derived from Nonoutcome problems, also describes the H probabilities at the outset of the corresponding Outcome problems. This assertion may be tested by using the H probabilities from each Nonoutcome problem to predict percentage correct on Trial 2 of each corresponding Outcome problem. From the data in Figure 4, in effect, the model can predict the traditional learning-set function: percentage correct on Trial 2 of successive problems.

The argument is straightforward:

1. On any Outcome problem one of the dimensions, and, therefore, one of the Hs is always designated as correct. The probability of the correct H (as inferred from the Nonoutcome problem) provides an estimate of the proportion of the subjects on the corresponding Outcome problem who, because they follow this H, would be correct on Trial 2. For example, on Problem 2 $P(H_c) = .32$. This means that 32 % of the subjects facing the Outcome condition on Problem 2 will make a correct response on Trial 2.

2. Zero to three dimensions may be confounded with the correct dimension during Trials 1 and 2 of the Outcome problem. Suppose, for the problem described in Figure 3, that color were the correct dimension. One dimension, size, is confounded with it over Trials 1 and 2. The probability of an H corresponding to such a confounded dimension provides an estimate of additional subjects who would be correct on Trial 2 of the corresponding Outcome problem. On Outcome Problem 2 also, size is confounded with color. $P(H_d) = .25$, so that in addition to the 32% mentioned above another 25 % would be correct on Trial 2.

3. All subjects holding an H about a dimension unconfounded with the correct dimension over Trials 1 and 2 (form and position in the example of Figure 3 and on the second Outcome problem) would, because of the "Win-stay-Lose-shift" character of the behavior required by the Prediction postulate, make an incorrect response on Trial 2.

4. For the proportion of subjects holding the Residual H it will be assumed that

half would be correct on Trial 2 and half would be incorrect. Since $P(H_r) = .18$ on the second problem, an additional 9% of the subjects would be correct on Trial 2 of the corresponding Outcome problem.

Thus, for Problem 2, percentage correct on Trial 2 is given as

$$\% \text{ Correct} = P(+_2) \times 100 = (.32 + .25 + .09) \times 100 = 66\%$$

In general,

$$P(+_2) = P(H_i) + \Sigma P(H_j) + \frac{P(H_r)}{2}$$

where $P(H_i)$ is the probability of the correct H, and $\Sigma P(H_j)$ is the sum of the probabilities of the Hs corresponding to dimensions confounded with the correct dimension over Trials 1 and 2.

Table 1 shows the dimensions which were confounded with the correct dimension during Trials 1 and 2 of the Outcome problems. It also shows in the right hand column, the resulting formulas for determining the theoretical $P(+_2)$ for each problem. From the information in Figure 4 one may obtain the numerical theoretical values. These have been obtained as percentages and are compared to the actual percentage correct in Figure 5.

Consider first the solid line. This connects the empirical percentage correct values, i.e., 100 (# right)/N. For all its irregularities it is a learning-set function, by definition (Percentage correct on Trial 2 over successive problems). The irregularities result, one should note, not from careless planning or sloppy procedure but rather, in large measure, from the deliberate confounding of dimensions. It was the task of the model to reproduce these irregularities.

The theoretical values are represented by the dashed line. The irregularities are well reproduced. Every change in direction of the curve is predicted. The H data, then, from the Nonoutcome problems permit generally good predictions of the performance at the outset of the Outcome problems. In this sense, the assertion that the H values portrayed in Figure 4 describe the values had an Outcome problem been presented receives some verification. A word of caution is needed, however. Three of the theoretical points (specifically at Problems 10, 22, and 24) are significantly different $(p < .05$ by χ^2 test) from the obtained points. The source of these differences, whether the model, or the procedure, is unknown.

DISCUSSION

A model has been presented which views the adult human subject as selecting, at the outset of a discrimination problem, one H from a set of Hs, where the H is defined as a mediating process. Within this general conception two variations of the model were considered. In the first the situation was restricted to the two-dimensional discrimination situation, but little restriction was imposed upon the type of H which the subject might hold. This permitted the detailed description of

TABLE 1
The Dimensions Confounded with the
Correct Dimensions over Trials 1
and 2 of the Indicated
Outcome Problems

Prob-lem	Correct dimen-sion	Confounded dimensions	Theoretical $P(+_2)$
2	color	size	$c + d + r/2$
4	color	position, size	$b + c + d + r/2$
6	color	form, position, size	$a + b + c + d + r/2$
8	color		$c + r/2$
10	color		$c + r/2$
12	color	position, size	$b + c + d + r/2$
14	form	position, size	$a + b + d + r/2$
16	form	position, color, size	$a + b + c + d + r/2$
18	form	position, color, size	$a + b + c + d + r/2$
20	form	position, size	$a + b + d + r/2$
22	form	color	$a + c + r/2$
24	form		$a + r/2$

Note.—Group B is receiving Outcome Problems 2, 6, 10, etc.; Group A is receiving 4, 8, 12, etc.

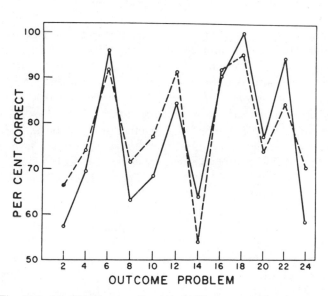

FIG. 5. The obtained (solid line) and predicted (dashed line) curves of the percentage correct on Trial 2 of successive Outcome problems.

two classes of Hs: Predictions and Response-sets. An experiment consisting of two-trial Outcome and Nonoutcome problems effectively demonstrated that for the two-dimensional situation the model accounts for the relationship between these two types of problems. The results also suggested that Response-sets Hs were not occurring.

The latter finding was employed in the second variation of the model. The omission of Response-set Hs from consideration helped simplify the model for application to the n dimensional problem. The application was restricted to the concept formation situation, i.e., to the setting in which it was assumed that the subject was attempting to locate that cue which provided the basis for correct responding. This variation permitted the specification of the H held by a single subject on any particular problem as well as statements about the probability of the Hs. A technique was demonstrated for validating the probability statements.

The general model has some special features and has uncovered some unique results which are worth stressing.

1. The H, rather than the specific choice response on a particular trial, is regarded as the dependent variable, i.e., as the unit of behavior affected by the reinforcements. This point of view has several advantages. First, as noted in the analysis of H behavior by monkeys (Levine, 1959b), the learning-set effect can be treated within the context of a conditioning theory. In the typical learning-set experiment the Prediction that one of the objects is correct and will repeat is the only H which receives 100% reinforcement beyond Trial 1. This feature produces the increase in "Win-stay-Lose-shift with respect to the object" relative to the other Hs.

Second, the paradox of alternation learning is eliminated. This paradox derives from the traditional view of reinforcement as increasing the probability of the last-made choice response. Consider a subject in Group G-0 in Experiment I. He responds by choosing one of two stimuli on Trial 1 of any problem. On half of the problems the experimenter will then say "right." This outcome is virtually universally regarded as a reinforcement of the response. But does it have this function? The subject typically chooses the other stimulus on the next trial. Therefore, the experimenter has reinforced one response yet has increased the probability that the subject will make the other response—a puzzling result by most definitions of the term "reinforcement." The resolution of this paradox by the present model is that the behavior affected by the reinforcements is not the choice response but the H selected, i.e., the Prediction of how events will proceed. In this particular example a series of outcomes reinforces the Prediction that the correct stimulus alternates.

Third, Experiment II makes it clear that learning may be occurring without being manifested in the record of correct choice response, i.e., in the traditional learning curve. The obtained percentage correct on Trial 2, represented by the solid line in Figure 5, shows no clear systematic increase over problems. One must analyze the changes in H strengths, as was done in Figure 4, in order to see the learning.

2. The definition of the H has been shifted from a behavior pattern to a mediating process of which the behavior pattern is a manifestation. The former definition was employed earlier in the model for monkeys. It was possible to define the H in this way because the experimenter utilized only a single procedure (presenting outcomes) resulting, with a given H, in a single behavior pattern. It would have been superfluous to assert that an H represented a Response-set or Prediction which resulted in the behavior pattern. The change was necessitated because the experimenter now employed two procedures: presenting and withholding outcomes. The behavior patterns defining an H previously (for Outcome problems) must, for some Hs, necessarily change when outcomes are withdrawn. For example, a subject with a strong "Win-stay-Lose-shift" habit must change his behavior during Nonoutcome problems, since "Win" and "Lose" are not available as stimuli for staying and shifting. By transferring the definition of the H from the response pattern itself to the determinants of the response pattern, i.e., to the mediating process, one was able to select intuitively reasonable postulates which permitted the specification of the change in the response pattern when outcomes were withdrawn.

3. A specific relationship exists between Outcome and Nonoutcome problems. This relationship is predictable from the model, in part because of the assumption that the same set of Hs determines behavior in both types of problems. This relationship was differently employed in the two experiments reported above. Experiment I simply demonstrated that the results predicted by the model in fact occurred. It demonstrated this for four differently treated groups receiving two-trials-per-problem learning sets.

Experiment II employed the relationship to determine Hs in a problem series from the Nonoutcome problems. The Nonoutcome problem became a "probe" to determine, for each individual subject, the H he was holding at the time.

4. A distinction is explicitly made between Predictions (manifested, during Outcome problems, in behavior contingent upon outcomes) and Response-sets (manifested in behavior which is always independent of outcomes). Hypothesis analyses up until now have overlooked the distinction. Krechevsky (1932a), for example, demonstrated Response-sets (position preference, stimulus preference) in rats but wrote as though the behavior were manifestations of Predictions. He characterized hypotheses as follows:

> an "hypothesis" is something that must be *verified* before it is persisted in. If the hypothesis does not lead to certain expected results it is soon dropped. "*If* this attempt is correct, *then* I should get such and such results, if I do not get such and such results then I must change my behavior." . . . The rat, in the maze or in the discrimination box, behaves in the very same way [pp. 529-530].

Note the dependence stipulated upon "results" (outcomes) as determiners of the response patterns. In fact, however, Krechevsky presented data only for behavior patterns which persist regardless of the outcomes, patterns which were Response-set manifestations.

This interpretation by Krechevsky caused Spence (1940) to retort hypotheses are far from what he [the writer, Spence] understands by the terms insightful and intelligent. Only *persistent* non-adaptative responses can attain the distinction of being hypotheses—for, in order to classify as a hypothesis, a response, although ineffective, must continue to be persisted in a certain minimum number of times. A maladaptive act which is speedily (intelligently?) abandoned cannot ever be a hypothesis [p. 287].

In effect, Krechevsky argued that all systematic behavior manifested an attempt by the subject to maximize his rewards; Spence's reply was that the behavior was of a different order. In terms of the analysis presented here Krechevsky was inferring Predictions from behavior patterns which are manifestations of Response-sets.

5. The prevalence of Response-sets in animals contrasts sharply with the present results. As just noted, Krechevsky found Response-sets in rats. Schusterman (1961) demonstrated similar Hs in chimpanzees, and Levine (1959b) and Harlow (1950) demonstrated them in monkeys. Response-set Hs are widespread among infrahuman animals. According to the experiments reported here, adult human subjects (specifically, college students) show no Response-set Hs. Thus, one could have assumed that these Hs were zero in Experiment I without hurting the quality of prediction; the explicit assumption in Experiment II did not seem to impair the effectiveness of the model; one Response-set commonly observed among animals, position preference, was clearly absent in Experiment II.

Although the model has these above mentioned features to recommend it, it does not yet stand as a comprehensive theory. There are several problems which remain to be solved. First the model deals with Hs only at the outset of problems. This restriction was made primarily because there is currently no basis for making assumptions about the effects of outcomes beyond Trial 2. A technique for investigating these effects will be needed before the model can be generalized. Second, in going from the two-dimensional (Experiment I) to the n-dimensional (Experiment II) problem the class of Hs was restricted to Predictions that the correct cue would repeat from trial to trial. While this restriction may be satisfactory for well motivated college students it is undoubtedly not adequate for application to all subjects. Children, for example, would probably require a model which measured both Predictions and Response-sets in the n-dimensional problem. Third, the definition of the Residual H is far from settled. The treatment of this H, that it was manifested by any response pattern not strictly conforming to a recorded dimension, was simple. The chief defect with this approach, however, is that it leaves out of account momentary sources of error, "slips" by a subject who has the correct (or any other) H. Because of this, the Residual H, as now measured, would increase artifactually with longer problems. It is anticipated that a more satisfactory treatment of Residual response patterns will be distilled as data accumulate. Finally, the various techniques of measuring mediating processes need to be refined and compared. Experiment II demonstrated that, for the n-dimensional problem, the Nonoutcome procedure may serve to determine the

Hs. M. Richter, at Indiana University, is currently developing the model to measure H strengths directly from Outcome problems of n dimensions. Another technique, one which is time-honored but not tested, is to utilize verbal reports. Several researchers (Bruner et al., 1956; Heidbreder, 1924; Verplanck, 1962) have had the subject state his hypothesis before each trial or certain trials. Insufficient attempt, however, has been made to investigate the relationship between the verbal response and the choice responses. The three techniques need to be developed, brought within the framework of the model, and compared.

READING NO. 13

THE BLANK TRIALS LAW: THE EQUIVALENCE
OF POSITIVE REINFORCEMENT AND
NONREINFORCEMENT[*]

By M. Levine
    H. Leitenberg,
    M. Richter

Levine (1963b) has recently described a model of hypothesis behavior by humans trying to solve simple discrimination problems. The model compares behavior during two types of problems: Outcome and Nonoutcome problems. An Outcome problem refers to the standard discrimination procedure in which stimuli are presented for a number of trials, the subject must make one of two choice responses after each stimulus presentation, and the experimenter presents an Outcome, e.g., says "right" or "wrong" after each response. A Nonoutcome problem follows exactly the same procedure except that outcomes are not presented, i.e., the experimenter says nothing after each response.[1] For the situation in which a problem lasts for exactly two trials the model yields the theorem that the probability of the subjects repeating their response from Trial 1 to Trial 2 during Nonoutcome problems is equal to the probability of the subjects repeating their response during Outcome problems when the outcome following the first trial is a "right."

Another way of stating this is: *During a Nonoutcome problem the subject behaves as though the experimenter were saying "right."*

Whereas the theorem was derived from a model describing behavior only over the first two trials of a discrimination problem, it is apparent that the theorem might have greater generality. That is, although the model is not developed to describe behavior throughout, e.g., a six-trial problem, one can still inquire as to the applicability to such a problem of the statement that "during a Nonoutcome

---

[1]It is becoming conventional (Koehler, 1961) to refer to trials without outcomes as "blank" trials. The phrase will be employed in that manner in this paper. A complete problem, however, consisting only of blank trials will be referred to as a Nonoutcome problem.

*Adapted from *Psychological Review*, 1964, **71**, 94-103. Copyright 1964 by the American Psychological Association. Reprinted by permission of the publisher.

problem the subject behaves as though the experimenter were saying 'right.' ''

This theorem was evaluated in four experiments. The first, which was intended as a direct test of the model, consisted in a series of discrimination problems each exactly two trials in length. The other three experiments provided a test simply of the generality of the theorem. They consisted in a series of modified double-alternation problems, a series of contingent-discrimination problems, and a single 40-trial guessing problem.

CONTINGENT DISCRIMINATION

In the contingent discrimination experiment two stimuli are presented, one of which has been defined as correct by the experimenter. The selection of a stimulus as correct depends (is contingent) upon the value of some other dimension. For example, the background upon which the stimuli are placed may be one of two colors (e.g., red or blue), with the following rule defining correctness: if the background is red then Stimulus A is correct; if the background is blue then Stimulus B is correct. This relationship holds throughout the problem.

A group of subjects received a series of such problems, each problem lasting for exactly four trials. On special test problems the group was subdivided, one subgroup receiving a Nonoutcome problem (E said nothing during all four trials), another subgroup receiving a (4+) problem (E said "right" for all four trials no matter which of the two responses the subject made). The theorem says that the distribution of obtained response sequences should be identical under these two conditions.

This comparison is the critical test of the theorem. It is possible, however, that the same distribution of response patterns would appear no matter what outcomes were presented. In order to check on this possibility, the distribution obtained during a Nonoutcome problem was also compared to the distribution produced when the E said "wrong" on a prescheduled basis.

Method

Subjects. The subjects were 120 students from the introductory psychology courses at Indiana University.

Apparatus. Seventy-two different three-letter nonsense syllables (selected from the 80%-93% association sections of Glaze's lists, 1928) formed the stimuli for 36 problems. A problem was constructed by selecting two syllables from this set and typing them on four cards, two of which were one color and two of which were a different color. The cards were selected from six colored sets of 3 x 5 cards (colored blue, green, yellow, orange, red, or white). The two colors employed for a given problem were randomly selected with the restriction that the same color not appear in two successive problems.

The two syllables were typed 1.5 inches apart in capital letters on the horizontal center line of the card. The position of the syllables was randomized with each syllable appearing twice on the left and twice on the right. The card colors either single-alternated or double-alternated over the four-trial problem.

Thirty-six four-trial problems, each utilizing two new nonsense syllables and two colors, were constructed. These sets of cards were put together to form a deck of 144 cards.

Procedure. Each subject was shown a sample 3 × 5 card containing two syllables and was instructed that he would receive a deck composed of similar cards, that he was to proceed through the deck one card at a time, and that he was always to choose one of the two syllables on each card. He was further told that the E would say "right" or "wrong" after each choice, and that he was to try to be right as often as possible. He then given the deck and was instructed to begin. After each trial the subject placed the card face down.

All subjects received five four-trial Outcome problems in which the correct nonsense syllable was always contingent upon the color of the card. During the sixth problem the subject received one of three different conditions according to the subgroup to which he had been assigned. One condition was a Nonoutcome problem. At the end of Problem 5 these subjects were instructed as follows:

"For these next few cards I am going to test you on what you have been learning. I want to see if you have learned enough to get the right word without my telling you whether you are right or wrong."

Problem 6 was then presented with the E saying nothing. The second condition was a (4+) problem. Without any announcement or change in procedure the E said "right" no matter which response these subjects made during the four trials of Problem 6. The third condition was a (1−, 3+) problem. The E said "wrong" to the first response followed by three "rights" to the following responses no matter which response these subjects made during the four trials of Problem 6.

The first six problems, then, consisted of five Outcome problems of a contingent discrimination type, followed by a test problem which could be either a Nonoutcome, a (4+), or a (1−, 3+) problem. The entire experiment consisted in six cycles of such a six-problem series. Each subject therefore received six test problems. During the first three and again during the last three test problems, he received each of the three test conditions. The conditions were organized for every three subjects to form a Latin square with Tests 1, 2, and 3, and again with Tests 4, 5, and 6.

Results

There are eight response sequences which a subject may manifest on any problem. For example, a subject may single-alternate his selection of syllables for the four trials (i.e., show abab), he may double-alternate (show aabb), perseverate (aaaa), etc. For each of the three types of problems the frequency distribution of the eight response patterns may be plotted and compared. The theorem says that the distribution from the Nonoutcome problems should be the same as that from

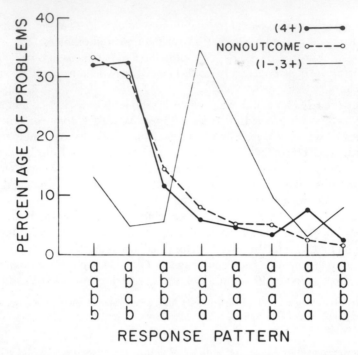

FIG. 1. Percentage of problems on which the eight response sequences occurred during each of the three conditions. (The response sequences are ordered according to the frequency during the Non-outcome problems).

the (4+) problems. It does not specify the relation of either of these to the distribution from the (1−, 3+) problems, but it suggests that the latter should be different.

The frequency distribution for each of the three types of test problems is plotted and compared in Figure 1. This figure shows three frequency polygons representing the relative frequency distributions of the response patterns for the three conditions. The data are combined for all 120 subjects on the two test problems of a given condition. Each curve, therefore, is based upon 240 problems. It will be seen that, as specified by the theorem, the match between the Nonoutcome condition and the (4+) condition is exceedingly close. It is equally clear that the (1−, 3+) condition yields an entirely different type of distribution. Thus, the similarity between the Nonoutcome and (4+) distributions is produced by the particular affinity of the two outcome operations involved (saying nothing versus saying "right") rather than by any stereotyped response sets by the subjects.

[Omitted here is a description of three other experiments (2-trial learning sets; double alternation; probability learning) comparing blank trials and "rights." They all yielded the same conclusion as the above study.   M.L.]

DISCUSSION

The finding has been consistently confirmed in four differently structured experiments that the behavior of subjects during trials when no outcomes are given is the same as the behavior of subjects when the experimenter says "right" following each response. Considering the crucial role attributed to "positive reinforcement" for altering response probabilities in contemporary theories of learning it is strange to find that the absence of reinforcement seems to yield exactly the same changes in response probabilities. "Right" has typically been treated as "fixating" a response, as making that response more likely to occur. Why has this effect not appeared in these experiments?

Levine's (1963b) model, from which the blank trials theorem was derived, suggests one solution to this problem. One relevant assumption in the model is that the unit of behavior directly affected by the outcome procedure is the subject's hypothesis (a mediating process defined as a prediction about what constitutes solution behavior) rather than his specific choice response. The hypothesis held produces either responses to selected cues (e.g., to nonsense syllables rather than positions in the above experiments) or the sequential organization of choice responses (e.g., alternation, win-stay-lose-shift, etc.) or both. The model also stipulates that each hypothesis is manifested in a specific response sequence, and that both "rights" and blank trials produce no changes in the subject's hypothesis and, therefore, no difference in the sequence of responses manifested. In contrast, "wrong" causes the subject to alter or reject his hypothesis, and thereby produces a very different response series.

This model accounts not only for the findings above, but for some puzzling findings from other experiments. Buss and Buss (1956), using the Wisconsin card Sorting Test, compared the effects of saying "right" versus "wrong" for correct and incorrect responses, respectively, with the effects of saying nothing versus "wrong" for these two types of responses. The theorem predicts no differences between the two groups and that is what Buss and Buss found (see also Buss, Braden, Orgel, & Buss, 1956). More striking, however, is the fact that in the nothing-vs.-"wrong" group almost all the subjects (14 out of 15) reached the criterion of 10 consecutive correct responses with the experimenter never saying a word! According to the theoretical ideas elaborated above, the subjects selected the correct hypothesis at the outset and the correct behavior pattern emerged undeterred. One other finding in this area comes from Buchwald (1959b). He has found that once a discrimination has been learned following the usual outcome procedure ("rights" versus "wrongs") the correct response does not extinguish (over 72 trials) when throughout extinction the experimenter says nothing. The blank trials law nicely predicts these results. A mediation process model nicely elucidates them.

7
PROBING FOR HYPOTHESES

From current perspectives, the most important detail of Reading No. 12 was the introduction of the blank-trial series as a probe for the H. This technique was demonstrated in four-dimensional problems with a set of four blank trials. The assumption was made that the eight simple Hs corresponding to the eight simple stimulus properties would predominate. The stimulus sequence was constructed so that each of these eight Hs yielded a unique response pattern during the series of blank trials. This construction permits inference of the H from the response pattern.

Little more was performed in Reading No. 12 than to demonstrate this technique and to suggest its validity. The next step was to apply this probe periodically during normal discrimination-learning tasks in order to investigate the dynamics of H testing. This step was taken, with the results appearing in Readings No. 14 (Levine, 1966) and 15 (Levine, Miller, & Steinmeyer, 1967).

These articles demonstrate the validity of the use of blank trials as a probe for S's H. The most fundamental validation derives from a feature insufficiently stressed within the articles. During four blank trials S may produce any one of 16 response patterns. Eight of these are patterns corresponding to the simple Hs; the remaining eight are patterns inconsistent with these Hs and with the theory as initially stated.* This feature provides a built-in null hypothesis: If during blank trials Ss were responding randomly, then the proportion of blank-trial sets showing simple H patterns should approximate 0.5. The obtained result was characteristically above 0.9. Other results also attested to the validity of the probe. The effects of feedback conformed to our everyday intuitions about H testing: Ss virtually always retained the H after a confirmation and rejected it after a disconfirmation; the solution H was not seen until S started the criterion run.

Readings No. 14 and 15, then, served to validate the blank-trial series as an H probe. In addition, these articles contain some of the revelations produced by

*In subsequent developments of the theory some of these "inconsistent" patterns are shown to reflect other systematic processes (See Readings No. 17 and 18).

probing. Thus, S's ability to deal with several Hs simultaneously could be demonstrated. The feedback "correct" was shown to do more than just confirm the H held. It also permitted S to eliminate incorrect Hs. These results suggested a mini-theory of S's manner of processing the stimulus-and-feedback information. Reading No. 15 contains not only the None-to-All effect but also the hint of coherence within dimensions. These articles, therefore, provided not only validation of the probe but examples of its usefulness. They also, as we shall see, motivated two sets of investigations. The first of these is described in Chapters 8 and 9; the other is presented in Chapters 10 and 11.

Reading No. 14
HYPOTHESIS BEHAVIOR BY HUMANS DURING DISCRIMINATION LEARNING[*]

By Marvin Levine

Data have accumulated rapidly (e.g., Bower & Trabasso, 1964; Kendler & Kendler, 1962; Levine, Leitenberg, & Richter, 1964) to indicate that choice responses made by the adult human during discrimination learning are organized by S's hypotheses (Hs). Levine (1963b) has further demonstrated that when the stimuli are multidimensional, i.e., differing in size, shape, etc. (see Fig. 1 for stimuli which vary in four dimensions), the particular H held by S may be inferred if outcomes are withheld for a few trials. The mechanics of such inference will be described below. The necessary assumptions are:

1. At the outset of a trial S selects an H from some set. This H is a "state," and may be thought of as a prediction by S. Thus, S may predict that the larger stimulus is correct (regardless of its shape, color, etc.) or that the stimulus on the left side is always correct, etc.

2. The set of Hs from which S samples is finite and is known exhaustively to E. In practice, it will be assumed specifically that each H is a prediction that one level of one of the dimensions is consistently correct. For the stimuli shown at the center of Fig. 1 there are, then, only the eight Hs indicated by the columns. The justification for this specific assumption will be presented below.

3. If no outcome is given following S's choice he keeps the same H for the next trial. During consecutive blank (i.e., no outcome) trials only one H will be maintained.

4. The S makes his choices in such a way that, if his H were in fact correct, he would always be right. For example, if an S predicts that one of the forms is correct he will choose that form, regardless of its size, color, or location, on every consecutive blank trial.

*Adapted from the *Journal of Experimental Psychology*, 1966, **71**, 331-338. Copyright 1966 by the American Psychological Association. Reprinted by permission of the publisher.

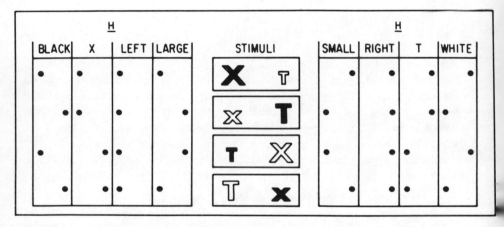

Fig. 1. Eight patterns of choices corresponding to each of the eight *Hs* when the four stimulus pairs are presented consecutively without outcomes.

This figure will be referred to several times throughout the book. For the reader's convenience, the figure also appears on the right-hand flap of the dust jacket.

Assumption 4 implies that over consecutive blank trials the pattern of responses will be perfectly correlated with the aspect of the stimulus corresponding to the *H*. The stimuli presented from trial to trial may be so constructed that the response pattern yielded by each *H* is unique. The four stimulus pairs at the center of Fig. 1 are so constructed. Suppose these stimuli are presented as four consecutive blank trials. The response patterns corresponding to the eight possible *H*s are shown in the columns of Fig. 1. If, e.g., *S* predicts that black is the basis for solution his responses will show the simple position-alternation pattern indicated in the column marked "black" (since the black stimulus also follows simple position alternation).

The response patterns described in Fig. 1 show either two or four responses to one side. According to the assumptions, no $3-1$ combinations should occur. To treat the possible appearance of the eight $3-1$ patterns the following will be assumed:

5. On any trial *S* has a certain constant probability of choosing incorrectly. For example, an *S* who predicts that the left side is the basis for solution may, "by accident," choose the right side on some trial. One such incorrect choice in a set of four blank trials will produce a $3-1$ pattern. In practice, this probability is very small (of the order of .02) and this assumption may, with little distortion to the results, be ignored. It is necessary, however, for the complete treatment of all the data.

Unlike other hypothesis models (Bower & Trabasso, 1964; Restle, 1962) the present assumptions include nothing about the effects of outcomes ("right" and "wrong"). These effects were studied here empirically.

Method

Subjects.   Eighty volunteers from the introductory psychology courses served as *S*s. One other *S* was discarded because of failure to solve any of the preliminary problems.

Materials and procedure.   The experiment consisted of a series of four-dimensional discrimination problems with stimuli of the sort illustrated in Fig. 1. The stimuli were drawn in color 1½ in. apart on 3 × 5 in. cards. The large letter was 1 in. in height; the small letter was ½ in. A problem was composed of a set of stimulus cards all containing the same two letters and two colors. Different problems used different pairs of letters and of colors.

In order to meet Assumption 2, that *S* chooses only the eight simple *H*s described in Fig. 1, a preliminary instruction-and-problem phase preceded the experimental series of problems.

The *S* was seated across from *E*, was shown a sample stimulus card, and received the following instructions:

> In this experiment you will be presented with several easy problems. Each problem consists of a series of cards like this one. Each card will always contain two letters, and the

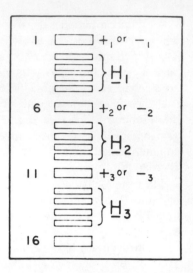

FIG. 2. A schematic of the 16-trial problem showing the trials on which E said right or wrong ($+_i$ or $-_i$) and the blank trials from which the hypotheses (H_i) were inferred.

letters will be of two colors. You will also notice that the letters are of two different sizes, and, of course, that one letter is on the left and one is on the right. Every card will be like this one except that the letters and the colors will be different. One of these two stimuli is "correct" in the sense that I've marked it here on my sheet. For each card I want you to tell me which of these two you think is correct and I'll tell you whether you're right or wrong. Then you go on to the next card, again you make a choice, and again I'll tell you whether you are right or wrong. In this way you can learn the basis for my saying "right" or "wrong." You can figure out whether it's because of the color, the letter, the size, or the position. The object for you is to figure this out as fast as possible so that you can choose correctly as often as possible.

The first problem consisted of 10 trials in which the color (green) was the basis for solution. The S received the deck face up. He responded to the top card, the appropriate outcome was given, and he then turned the card face down out of the way. This procedure was followed for all 10 trials. The E then asked S what the solution was. The S who said "green" received the instructions for the next problem. An S who verbalized any H other than the eight simple ones was told, "The problem is not as complicated as that. One of the letters, colors, sizes, or positions is consistently correct throughout." The nonsolving S then redid that problem. If he did not solve it the second time he was told simply that the green letter was always the correct one.

The S was then instructed for the next three preliminary problems with this statement:

In the last problem I said right or wrong after each card. For the next problem I will not always tell you whether you are right or wrong. After some cards, I'll say nothing. Don't let that disturb you. Try to be right all the time.

The E also reiterated that one of the simple solutions would be consistently correct. The three problems were then presented. These had sets of blank trials interspersed among the outcome trials. For all *S*s large size, the letter O, and the left position were respectively correct.

The experimental problems.   Each *S* then received 16 16-trial problems in which an outcome was always presented at the first, sixth, and eleventh trial. The stimuli for each problem were arranged with special restrictions. In a four-dimensional simultaneous-discrimination problem there are exactly eight different stimulus pairs which may be presented. These may be grouped into two different sets of four pairs, the dimensions being perfectly counterbalanced within each set. Figure 1 shows such a set in which each level of every dimension appears exactly twice with each level of every other dimension. Such a counterbalanced set of stimulus pairs is described as *internally orthogonal*. The remaining set of four stimulus pairs may be produced by simply interchanging the positions of each stimulus. For example, for the top pair, the small white T would be placed on the left and the large black X on the right. This new set of four pairs will also be internally orthogonal. Referring to one set as Set A and the interchanged set as Set B, Set A was used for all blank trials. That is, Trials 2-5 were composed of the four Set A stimuli, as were Trials 7-10, and Trials 12-15. The trial-to-trial order was different for each of the three sets. Set B was used for the remaining (outcome) trials. This arrangement had two virtues: The *S* never encountered a specific stimulus pair to which an outcome had previously been given, and the outcome cards, as well as the blank-trial sets, had the property of internal orthogonality.

The *E* said "right" or "wrong" on Trials 1, 6, and 11 according to a prearranged schedule and regardless of *S*'s response. Each of the eight possible right-wrong sequences which could occur on three trials was assigned to each of the first eight problems and again to each of the last eight problems. The sequences were assigned to different problems for each eight *S*s, forming 8 × 8 Latin squares. Trial 16, the last trial of each problem, was treated separately: The *S* was told right on half the problems; nothing was said on the other half. Figure 2 shows a summary of the procedure.

RESULTS AND DISCUSSION

The blank-trials data.   The data from the sets of four blank trials fall into two classes: the eight patterns conforming to the specified *H*s, (cf. Fig. 1) and the eight patterns not conforming (the 3−1 patterns). The *H* patterns appear on 92.4% (3,550 out of 3,840) of the four trial sets. Thus, *S*'s behavior is strongly systematic, in the form predicated by the first four assumptions. The fifth assumption stipulates that *S* has a small probability of making an error on any one trial. This value, calculated from the result that 7.6% of the patterns are 3−1 patterns, is .02. Further verification of the assumptions comes from the response on each outcome trial. Each set of blank trials permits inference of the *H* which, in turn, permits *E* to predict the next response. For example, if the four-trial pattern indicates that *S* is hypothesizing that the large stimulus is correct, it is necessary only to see on which

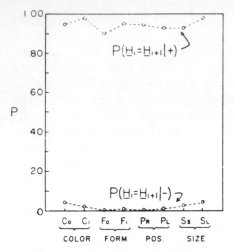

FIG. 3. The probability that an H is repeated after E says right (top curve) and wrong (bottom curve), when H_i is $C_0, C_1, \ldots, S_L$.

side the large stimulus is appearing in the next trial to predict the next response. This prediction was made for all the interpretable patterns (i.e., the non-$3-1$ patterns) and was correct 97.5% (3,461 out of 3,550) of the trials. Given that 2% of the responses will be erroneous on any one trial, this set of predictions is essentially perfect.

The effects of outcomes.   The consistency of these data attests to the plausibility of a general H model. Further confirmation can come from consideration of commonly presumed properties of H testing. Connotations of the concept of H testing are that an H when confirmed is retained for further testing, and when disconfirmed is rejected for another. Indeed, these connotations are incorporated as assumptions in Restle's (1962) theory. He assumes that when S is told right he keeps the H sampled; when he is told wrong he returns the H to the set and takes a new random sample. These presumed effects of right and wrong may be directly determined by comparing the Hs before and after each outcome. These effects are shown in Fig. 3. The top curve describes the probability that two successive Hs (the first and second or the second and third) are the same when E said right after the response on the intervening outcome trial.[1] The overall proportion, based on 1112 cases, is .95. The bottom curve in Fig. 3 shows the analogous set of probabilities when a wrong was said. The overall proportion, based on 1,027 cases, is .02. It is evident that the single outcome pushes S to one of two extremes. The H is conditioned and extinguished, so to speak, with almost perfect efficiency.

This result shows that Restle's assumption, that the effect of right is to cause S to

---

[1]The curve was computed only from the interpretable response patterns. The precise probability estimated is $P(H_i = H_i + 1)$ *given* a right on the intervening outcome trial, the response pattern on Set i or $i + 1$ is not $3-1$, and the response on the intervening outcome trial is consistent with (i.e., predictable from) H_i. Except that a wrong is given on the intervening outcome trial, the bottom curve in Fig. 2 is based on the same conditions.

keep his H, is reasonable for the present situation. His assumption about the effect of wrong, however, is not. He assumes that S resamples with replacement, which implies that the mean of the bottom curve in Fig. 3 should be .125. The mean, of course, is much lower than this, indicating the S seeks a new H without first replacing the old. Further substantiating a nonreplacement assumption is the result that the rejection of an incorrect H lasts beyond one outcome trial. If wrong is said after both the first and second H, H_3 not only will be different from H_2 but will also tend to be different from H_1: $P(H_3 = H_1 \mid -_2-_3) = .04$.

The foregoing has established that the H is a viable concept. Hypotheses are detectable from choices and their responsiveness to outcomes is measurable. It is possible now to go beyond this description to the delineation of more complex processes. In order to appreciate the significance of the phrase "more complex processes" it is valuable to reconsider Restle's theory. In it whenever S resamples, i.e., following a wrong, he does so after replacing his hypothesis in the H set. After a wrong, S never analyzes the previous information received, and does not, therefore, reject Hs from consideration. In effect, the size of the set from which S resamples is constant and is the same as it was at the outset of the experiment.

The simplicity of this view provides a useful background against which to evaluate the ability of S to analyze information. As an illustration of such information analysis consider the selection of H_1 after E says wrong on Trial 1. By the nature of the stimuli four Hs are characterized as wrong and four by implication are right. The probability that H_1 is one of the four Hs designated as correct is found to be .873. If this probability were 1.0, the number of Hs from which S resampled, $N(H_1)$, would be a maximum of four; if it were .80, $N(H_1)$ would be a maximum of five (four correct Hs out of five). These results follow from the assumption that the probability of choosing one of the four Hs defined as correct after Trial 1 is equal to four divided by $N(H_1)$. Symbolically, $P(H_1+) = 4/N(H_1)$. Since $P(H_1+) = .873$, $N(H_1) = 4.6$. This value should, of course, be interpreted as the mean size of the functional H set when S resampled, i.e., after E said wrong, on Trial 1. It is natural to inquire next whether S utilizes information received over several previous trials when subsequently resampling. One expects, of course, that with succeeding outcome trials S can learn that more and more Hs are incorrect and, correspondingly, can reduce the size of the functional H set. When he resamples after a wrong, the later the wrong appears the smaller should $N(H_i)$ be. The equation just given generalizes quite naturally to $P(H_i+) = N(H_i+)/N(H_i)$, where $N(H_i+)$ is defined as the number of logically correct Hs after the ith outcome. With internally orthogonal stimuli $N(H_i+)$ is four after one outcome, two after two outcomes, and one after three outcomes. $P(H_i+)$ is taken from the obtained proportion of H_i which are logically correct.

The possible systematic reduction in $N(H_i)$ is not unlike the process described by Bruner, Goodnow, and Austin (1956) as focusing. In their experiments Ss worked on similar problems but were instructed to state (by writing symbols) their Hs at each trial. The focusing Ss wrote in such a way as to retain at each successive

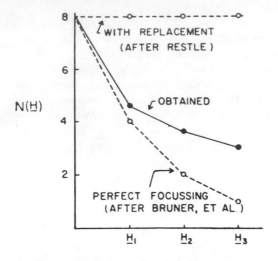

FIG. 4. The size of the set, $N(H_i)$, from which S is sampling H_i immediately following a wrong, i.e., after $-_i$; see text for the determination of $N(H_i)$.

trial only those Hs indicated as correct on all the preceding trials. As Hs were shown to be incorrect they were permanently rejected. In the present experiment, because the stimuli are internally orthogonal, each outcome would permit a perfect focuser to reduce $N(H_i)$ by half. The task, then, of determining $N(H_i)$ after each wrong is essentially the task of determining the extent to which this focusing process occurs during the first three outcome trials of the present experiment.

The value of $N(H_i)$ following a wrong at the ith trial is presented in Fig. 4. This figure contrasts the obtained curve with that to be obtained if no information from outcome trials were utilized in resampling (the top curve) and that to be obtained if all Ss were perfect information retainers and analyzers (the bottom curve). A steady reduction in $N(H_i)$ is seen, although Ss are by no means perfect focusers. Each point is based on almost 600 observations, and the decrease is highly reliable. Thus, S is not only rejecting the H manifested after a wrong (cf. Fig. 3) but is rejecting other Hs not manifested.

The last finding evaluates the degree to which S retains and analyzes earlier information when he resamples, i.e., when E has just said wrong. The effects of a right will now be considered in greater detail. Figure 3 compellingly suggested that when E said right S simply retained the same H he had manifested. There is evidence, however, that S is doing more than this, that he is attempting to store the information of the trial and to collate it with that of previous outcome trials. He is, in a word, focusing. Figure 5 shows the probability of selecting H_3 correctly, after a wrong on the third outcome trial, as a function of the number of rights announced during the first two outcome trials. It is clear there that the more often E previously said right the more likely S is to select the only H consistent with all the preceding information. Since the probability of choosing the correct H is one (the number of logically correct Hs after three outcome trials) out of $N(H_3)$, $N(H_3)$ is the reciprocal of the obtained probabilities. For convenience this is scaled at the right

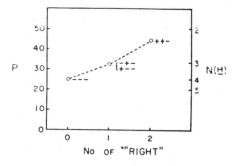

FIG. 5. The probability that H_3 is the correct H following wrong on Trial 3 and with 0, 1, or 2 rights on the first two outcome trials.

of Fig. 5. $N(H_3)$ decreases from four after zero right to a mean of 2.25 after two right. The S, it is clear, not only uses the outcomes to reject several incorrect Hs, but he rejects more when he has been told right than when he has been told wrong. This effect has also been obtained by Richter (1965) in an experiment without blank trials. He found that the more the S received information by being told right rather than wrong, the more likely he was to be correct on a test trial. These results contradict an important implication in recent mathematical models. Bower and Trabasso (1964) and Estes (1964) have noted that their models imply that learning occurs only on errors. This statement has reference to the process portrayed in Fig. 3, in which S resamples Hs, and can go from the incorrect to the correct H, only when wrong. Figure 5 shows, however, that S not only is learning, in the sense of eliminating incorrect Hs from the total set, when right, but that he learns more effectively when right than when wrong.

Outline of a theory.   It was assumed at the outset only that S samples Hs and retains the H during blank trials. Clearly, other processes must be postulated to account for the effects of outcomes, particularly for the results that the size of the set was smaller after each successive outcome (cf. Fig. 4) and that the reduction was performed more efficiently following a right than following a wrong (cf. Fig. 5). These results, data from other experiments, and postmortems with Ss suggest the nature of these processes.

1. The S codes the stimuli paired with an outcome. The coding process is probably of the sort proposed by Haber (1964), and by Glanzer and Clark (1964). Thus, S on being presented with a pair of stimuli (e.g., a large black X on the left and a small white T on the right), may silently rehearse "large black X on the left."

2. The S codes aspects of only the stimulus chosen. More specifically, he codes the intersect of the functional H set and the stimulus chosen. Consider these examples: (*a*) Example 1: On the first trial of a problem the pair of stimuli are a large black X on the left and small white T on the right. If the functional set initially consists in all eight Hs, S choosing the left stimulus will memorize, i.e., code, "large black X on the left"; S choosing the right stimulus will code "small white T on the right." (*b*) Example 2: Suppose the stimuli just described are

presented on the third outcome trial and S, from the previous two outcome trials, has eliminated everything but small, black, and X. He would code the intersect of this set with the stimulus chosen: Upon choosing the left stimulus he would code "black X"; upon choosing the right stimulus he would code "small."

3. Outcomes produce their effects upon the coded material. (a) If E says "right" S now stores the material just coded as the new functional H set, i.e., as the total set of correct Hs. This automatically eliminates without further effort the incorrect Hs. In Example 1, above, S who chose the left stimulus and was then told right might simply continue to rehearse "large black X on the left." (b) If E says wrong S must recode. He does this by eliminating the just-coded material from the functional H set, (or to put it another way, he finds the complement of the just-coded material in the H set held). Consider again Example 1. After a wrong on Trial 1, S must perform what the reader performs when told "large-black-X-on-the-left is wrong. What is right?" He must find the other levels.

A wrong, with the consequent need for recoding, produces three disadvantages relative to the effects of right. The recoding requires time, the translation may be incomplete, and the material first coded may not be completely erased. Following a wrong, therefore, the new functional H set will be more likely to have a larger proportion of incorrect Hs than following a right. This, of course, is precisely what was demonstrated in Fig. 5. One would expect also that too short an intertrial interval, i.e., between the wrong and the next stimulus, would cut down the recoding time and would, therefore, impair learning. This result, although in the context of a four-response, successive-discrimination experiment, has been obtained several times by Bourne and Bunderson (1963) and Bourne, Guy, Dodd, and Justesen (1965).

In conclusion, it is proposed that a theory of information processing is needed to account for the present results. The presumed processes are: (a) the S codes the stimuli followed by an outcome; (b) he codes only the intersect of the stimulus chosen and the H set held; (c) if told right S takes the material just coded as the new H set from which to sample; if told wrong he tries to recode, i.e., tries to select for rehearsal and storage the complement of the just-coded material.

Reading No. 15
THE NONE-TO-ALL THEOREM OF HUMAN DISCRIMINATION LEARNING*

By Marvin Levine
   Paul Miller
   Charles H. Steinmeyer

According to H theory S samples from a set of Hs and responds on the basis of the selected H. It is generally assumed that outcomes affect the H sampled. If, after the response, E says "right" or says nothing, S keeps his H for the next trial; if E says "wrong" S abandons his H and resamples. This conception implies that when the correct H is sampled S should make no further errors. Any error, therefore, indicates that at any previous trial only irrelevant Hs have been sampled. Thus, prior to the last error the correct H is never sampled; following it the correct H is held exclusively, producing, of course, the criterion run of correct responses. This description of H-sampling behavior before and after the last error will be referred to as the none-to-all theorem. The purpose of the present research was to investigate this theorem directly, to determine the H held after each trial and to see whether the probability of appearance of the correct H jumps from zero to one.

The H was determined by the blank-trial method developed by Levine (1966). If sets of four blank trials alternate with outcome trials, during a long discrimination problem one may derive both a learning curve and a hypothesis curve. The percentage correct on each outcome trial yields the learning curve; the percentage occurrence of the correct H at each blank-trial set describes the hypothesis curve. The latter provides a direct test of the none-to-all theorem.

EXPERIMENT I

Method

Subjects.   Eighty students from the introductory psychology course at Indiana University served as Ss.

*Adapted from the *Journal of Experimental Psychology*, 1967, **73**, 568-573. Copyright 1967 by the American Psychological Association. Reprinted by permission of the publisher.

Materials and procedure.   Four decks of 91 3 × 5 cards were constructed. Each card contained stimulus pairs like those employed by Levine (1966). The cards for any one deck all contained the same two letters and two colors; each deck contained a different pair of letters and of colors.

The decks were used for four 91-trial problems. Trials 1, 6, 11, . . . , 91 were outcome trials; Trials 2-5, 7-10, 12-15, . . . , 87-90 were blank trials. The stimuli for each set of 4 blank trials were internally orthogonal, i.e., each level of each dimension appeared exactly twice with each level of each other dimension (cf. the stimuli of Fig. 1 in Levine, 1966). In a four-dimensional simultaneous-discrimination problem eight different stimulus pairs may be constructed. These may be divided into two different internally orthogonal groups. One group was used for each set of blank trials. The trial-to-trial order varied within each set. The other group was used for successive sets of four outcome trials. The trial-to-trial order also varied for each outcome set with the restriction that the first card of a set could not be the same as the last card of the preceding set.

At the outset of the experimental session Ss had been instructed that the eight levels of the dimensions would provide the basis for solution of the problems. They then received a series of preliminary practice problems and short problems during which outcome trials alternated with sets of 4 blank trials. The four problems under present consideration then followed. These problems had as solution one level from each of the four dimensions. The sequence of these was counterbalanced with every four Ss to form 4 × 4 Latin squares. Each problem was continued until S reached a criterion (14 correct responses out of 15) or until the 91 trials were presented.[1] Of the 320 problems presented, 14 had to be disqualified because of E error. These were not replaced.

Results

On any set of 4 blank trials an S may show one of 16 possible response patterns. Eight of these are manifestations of the eight Hs stipulated by the instructions; the others reflect other processes. If Ss were responding in a thoroughly irrelevant way, then, of course, the eight H patterns should tend to occur 50% of the time. They occur on 95.1% (1862/1958) of the blank-trial sets showing that the behavior was strongly organized by the H-sampling process.

A precriterion learning curve and H curve were obtained. The learning curve is based only on the outcome trial data. The outcome trial on which the last error occurs (OTLE) is taken as Trial 0, the outcome trial preceding this is −1, the next

[1]The "imperfect" criterion requires some explanation. Preliminary work had shown that Ss occasionally choose incorrectly (relative to their H) "by accident." One sees this directly in an S who, during a series of blank trials, will blurt out something like "Oops! That last response was a mistake. Is it too late to change it?" Levine (1966) has shown that the probability of an "Oops!" error is low (on the order of .02). During the present experiment in only six problems was an error made within a string of 15 correct responses. It would appear that these errors, though infrequent, are of a different order from the errors resulting from incorrect Hs and could, by occurring after 10 or 12 consecutive correct responses, seriously obscure the description of the H-testing process.

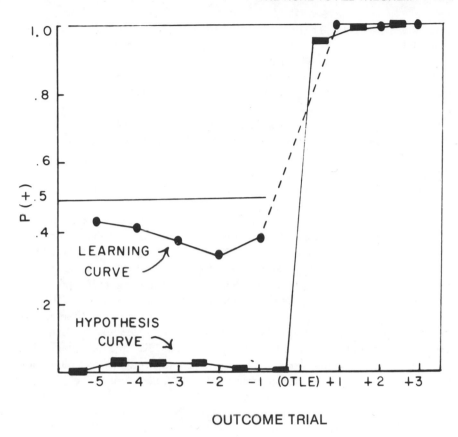

FIG. 1. Learning and hypothesis curves showing, respectively, the proportion of correct responses on the outcome trials and the proportion of correct *H* patterns.

preceding outcome trial is −2, etc. The proportion of correct responses on each of these trials is obtained. These values are plotted as the circles in Fig. 1. The data come only from those problems in which the last error occurred on the fourth outcome trial or later. The *N* ranges from 131 on Trial −1 to 74 on Trial −5. The pre-OTLE part of the curve shows two clear features: Not unexpected is the stationarity (cf. Bower & Trabasso, 1964); rather startling is the result that the probability of a correct response in this two-response task is significantly and consistently below .5 ($p = .38$).

The *H* curve, showing the proportion of times that the correct *H* occurred, is based only on the blank-trial data. The blank-trial set just preceding the final error is represented in Fig. 1 by the rectangle just preceding the OTLE, the next set back precedes −1, etc. The probability that the correct *H* appears, based on all the precriterion *H*-patterns (841), is .011. It appears directly, then, that the theorem, that the *S* does not hold the correct *H* prior to the OTLE, is valid for the present experimental situation. The other side of the theorem, that following the OTLE S holds only the correct H, also appears to be valid here. This conclusion, however, is a truism since the responses during these four-trial sets were part of the definition of the criterion run. The next study eliminates this artifact. Note, however, the small deviation from $p = 1.0$ at the first set after the OTLE.

One other characteristic of H sampling may be seen in these data. Glanzer, Huttenlocher, and Clark (1963) and Kendler and Kendler (1962) have proposed that Ss respond primarily to dimensions. While Hs within the present model correspond to values within dimensions it is, nevertheless, possible that whole dimensions are present or absent within the set from which S samples. For example, Ss may forget (i.e., omit from the functional H set) not individual levels but the dimension itself.

Figure 1 shows that Ss almost never sample the correct H (e.g., "small") during the precriterion trials. What is the probability, q, that they sample the complementary H, that dealing with the other level of the dimension (e.g., "large")? In the 717 H patterns appearing before the OTLE -1, $q < .02$. Thus, S shows neither the correct H nor its complement. The remaining six Hs appear 97% of the time. This result holds until (and not including) the blank-trial set just prior to the OTLE. At this set, $q = .17$. This implies that S, when he first samples the neglected dimension, may first test the incorrect level—which perforce leads to an error on an outcome trial—and then shift to the other level and the criterion run. On most of the problems, however, S, when he turns to the correct dimension, also recalls enough of the past information to select the correct level.

EXPERIMENT II

Because of the counterintuitive, subchance character of the precriterion learning curve it was decided to replicate the study. Another condition, however, was added. To check on the possibility that the unusual procedure of blank trials contributed to the suppression effect, two conditions were presented: problems with and problems without the blank-trial sets.

Method

Subjects.   Thirty-two students from the introductory psychology course at Indiana University served as Ss. None of these had served in Exp. I.

Materials and procedure.   Eighteen decks, each containing a different pair of letters and of colors, were constructed. Nine of these had 24 cards (the short decks), the other nine had 116 cards (the long decks). The short decks consisted of four internally orthogonal stimulus cards repeated six times. With each repetition the sequence of the four cards was varied, with the restriction that the first card of a set could not be the same as the last card of the preceding set. The construction of the long decks was similar to that of the decks in Exp. I. Cards 2-5, 7-10, etc., consisted of the same four internally orthogonal card types throughout. The remaining four card types were used for Cards 1, 6, 11, etc. (the 24 outcome trials). Those 24 cards had exactly the same counterbalanced structure as the cards of the short decks.

At the outset of the experimental session each S was shown a sample card, was instructed about the four dimensions, and was told that one of the aspects of the four dimensions would be the basis for choosing correctly. A short problem was then presented, with an outcome given after every response. If S did not solve this problem the eight possible solutions were reviewed. He then received instructions for the next problem. He was informed that there would be trials during which E would say nothing, and was told to try to be correct all the time. The second preliminary problem, a long problem, was then presented. Outcomes were given after every fifth response. This was followed by the experiment proper, eight short problems alternating with eight long problems. Each of the eight simple solutions was assigned to each of the eight problems of both types.

The S received each problem until he reached a criterion of correct responses on six consecutive outcome trials, or until he went through all the cards in the deck. This same criterion was applied to both the short and long problems.

Results

Again the responses during the blank trials were highly organized as stipulated by the H model. The eight H patterns occurred on 95.4% (2303/2414) of the blank-trial sets.

In all other respects also, the results duplicated those of Exp. I. Figure 2, based on all problems in which the OTLE occurred on or after the fourth outcome trial, shows the pre- and post- OTLE learning curves for both types of problems and the H curve from the long problems. Both learning curves manifest the stationarity and the suppression of performance (for the short and long problems, $p(+) = .39$ and .36, respectively). These effects, therefore, are obviously not related to the presence of blank trials and must be explained in terms of the characteristics of the outcome trials.

The H curve shows the none-to-all effect: The probability of the correct H before the OTLE is .02; following that critical trial there is a leap to virtually perfect H selection. The description of H performance after the OTLE is here independent of the presence of criterion responding, since the criterion was defined solely in terms of outcome responses. That criterion responding follows from S holding the correct H is clearly implied. There appears again the curious deviation from perfect H selection at the four-trial set between the OTLE and the start of the criterion run.

Not only does the correct H rarely occur before the OTLE but the probability, q, of the complementary H is equally low: up to the set at OTLE -1, $q = .018$. At the set just preceding the OTLE, $q = .16$. The conclusion, therefore, is confirmed

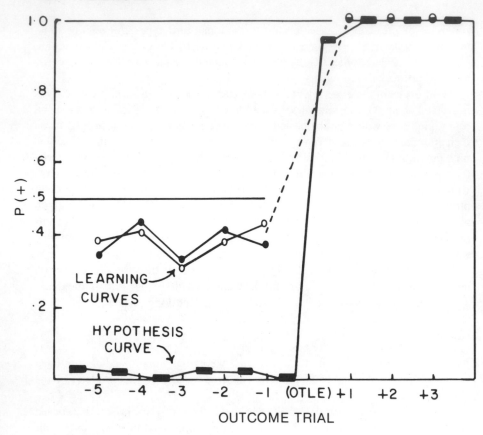

FIG. 2. Learning and hypothesis curves. (The open circles represent data from the short problems; the solid circles and rectangles represent the long problems.)

that the correct *dimension* is omitted. When S does consider it, he is more likely to select the correct level.

DISCUSSION

These experiments demonstrate, as did the preceding in this series (Levine, 1966), that when the H set is restricted and blank-trial probes are used, S's H-testing characteristics emerge simply and reliably. Specifically, the present experiments show the none-to-all sampling of the correct H which underlies the stationary backwards learning curve. In addition, the paradoxical effect was found that in a two-choice task, less than 40% of the precriterion responses were correct. The remainder of the discussion will be devoted to explaining this suppression of performance. It will be demonstrated that it, too, follows from the theory of H sampling, that the suppression appears when the processes described by the theory occur with the stimuli of the present experiments. The key theoretical assumptions are: (*a*) When *S* holds an *H* and, following his response, is told "right" he holds that *H* for the next trial. (*b*) When he is told "wrong" he resamples from the set for the next trial. (*c*) During precriterion responding *S* samples neither the correct *H* nor the complementary *H*. In the problems presented here, therefore, he is sampling during the precriterion phase from at most only six *H*s. The important feature of the stimuli is that they were internally orthogonal over sets of four outcome trials. Such stimuli have two special characteristics[2]: (*a*) No attribute is paired with the correct attribute for more than two consecutive trials. (*b*) For any two trials only one attribute is so paired.

The learning curve prior to the OTLE (taken throughout as Trial 4 or beyond) may now be derived. On Trial 1 three of the six *H*s in the functional *H* set must lead to the correct choice, three to the incorrect choice. Therefore, $p(+_1) = .5$. Performance on Trial 2 depends upon the outcome on Trial 1. Suppose a correct response occurred on Trial 1. This means that *S* held one of the three *H*s paired with the correct *H*. On Trial 2 only one of these will remain paired. The other two must lead to a wrong response (for the Stimuli in Fig. 1 of Levine, 1966, if "black" is correct and *S* makes the correct response on Trial 1, he is holding either "large," "X," or "left." Only "large" will again be correct on Trial 2). Since *S* keeps his *H* after a "right," $p(+_2 \mid +_1) = .33$.

Given an error on Trial 1, predictions of Trial 2 performance are not so simple. It is assumed that *S* resamples from the *H* set, but no assumption has been made about how many *H*s he first eliminates. One extreme possibility is that he eliminates nothing, i.e., that he returns the *H* to the set before resampling. This, Restle's (1962) "wrongs" assumption, while not generally valid (Levine, 1963a, 1966; Trabasso & Bower, 1966), provides a useful limiting condition. It will be referred to as the Reject-O assumption. At the other extreme, *S* may reject all the three *H*s called "wrong." Suppose, for example, that "black" is correct and that *S*, faced with the first stimulus in the aforementioned figure, starts with the *H* "choose the smaller." After making the right-hand response and being told "wrong" he would avoid trying not only the smaller form but also "right-side" and "T." This will be described as the Reject-3 assumption.

After being told "wrong" on Trial 1 the *S*, according to the Reject-O assumption, resamples from all six *H*s. Therefore, $p (+_2 \mid -_1) = .5$. According to the Reject-3 assumption he resamples only from those *H*s which were correct on Trial 1. Only one of these will again be correct on Trial 2, i.e., $p(+_2 \mid -_1) = .33$. The overall (unconditional) probability of a correct response on Trial 2 is given by

$$p(+_2) = [p(+_2 \mid -_1) + p(+_2 \mid +_1)]/2.$$

For the Reject-O and Reject-3 assumptions, respectively, these values are .415 and .33.

---

[2]An example of the stimulus sequence will be found in Fig. 1 of Levine (1966).

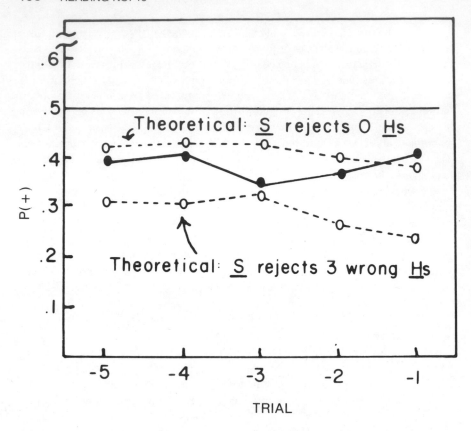

FIG. 3. The obtained (solid circles) and the theoretical (open circles) backwards learning curves.

In analogous fashion one may obtain the theoretical probabilities at each successive trial. This has been done both with the Reject-O assumption and with the Reject-3 assumption. The resulting theoretical precriterion learning curves are shown in Fig. 3. Both variants of the theory predict suppressed performance, the Reject-3 assumption predicting fewer correct responses than the Reject-O assumption. Regardless, then, of how much S remembers from the preceding incorrect trial, the theory predicts below-chance performance. The obtained curve falls between the two extremes suggesting that S remembers some but not all of the information on an error trial.

In conclusion, then, the suppressed character of the precriterion learning curve follows from the assumptions above, when this H-testing process occurs with the orthogonal stimuli of the present experiment. An additional irony was also suggested: As seen in Fig. 3, the theory predicts that during presolution responding the better S processes information the worse his performance will be.

8

FURTHER APPLICATIONS
OF BLANK TRIALS

The blank-trial probe provided an aperture through which underlying processes could be viewed. Judicious application of this probe revealed not only the specific H held, but some of the dynamics by which Hs were sampled and information was processed. When a window facing out into a new terrain is discovered, an obvious research strategy is dictated: look through the window. Similarly, with a new probe, one explores in a variety of ways to see the new phenomena. A few straightforward explorations were carried out. Heretofore, blank trials were employed with four-dimensional (4-D), two-response tasks. Two studies were subsequently performed in which the probe was applied to eight-dimensional (8-D) and three-response problems, respectively. These may be briefly described.

The 8-D problem (Levine, 1969b).   The previous data (Levine, 1966) had demonstrated that the zero-memory assumption was incorrect. A criticism was subsequently directed at that study, to the effect that memory effects were obtained because the task was relatively simple. The problems were constructed from four dimensions whereas confirmations of the zero-memory assumption had come from tasks with five or six dimensions (cf. Reading No. 11). I decided, therefore, to apply the blank-trial analysis to 8-D problems. So complex a problem would, of course, speak to the criticism. It had, however, another virtue. With this difficult a problem Ss would make substantial numbers of errors. Since S virtually always tries a new H after an error, one could study resampling of Hs for several trials into a problem.

The experiment, in many ways, paralleled the 4-D research. The Ss first received preliminary practice problems, and then a series of experimental problems, each of which had feedback trials followed by sets of blank trials. The chief differences were that these, of course, were all 8-D problems, and that each problem consisted of six feedback trials. Incidentally, an inordinate number of blank trials is not needed to probe for the simple Hs in 8-D problems. A set of five blank trials (one more than employed with 4-D problems) permits determination of each of the 16 simple Hs as well as of inconsistent patterns.

The previous results were basically replicated. The H was virtually always repeated ($p = .94$) when a "right" was given, and virtually never repeated ($p = .01$), given a "wrong." The size of S's set, estimated according to the routine described in Reading No. 14, declined from 16 Hs to about 6 Hs after the second feedback trial (F_2). Thus, these gross measures indicated that here, too, S remembered previous information when he resampled.

These longer problems permitted a more subtle analysis of S's memory. For example, one could investigate his memory for disconfirmed Hs across the six trials of the problem. It was demonstrated that when the initial H, H_1, was disconfirmed (i.e., when S was told "wrong" at F_2), that H was avoided throughout the problem: The probability that H_1 was resampled was .005 after F_2 and drifted to .029 after F_6. By similar measures S's memory for all disconfirmed Hs could be determined and was found to be good.

The S's memory for the stimuli of individual feedback trials was also determined from the H-probe data. A typical serial-position curve was obtained: Ss tended to remember some of the stimulus information both from the first and from the most recent trials. No memory was evident for intermediate stimuli. The data strongly supported the view (Glanzer & Cunitz, 1966) that the primacy and recency effects were long- and short-term memory effects, respectively.

The results, therefore, not only demonstrated memory effects in this more complex problem, but suggested that Ss remembered Hs primarily, that most of the stimuli (all but some of the first and last) were forgotten.

The 3-value problem (Gumer & Levine, 1971).   This experiment differed from the preceding experiments in seemingly minor details. These variations, however, permitted some novel effects to emerge. The Ss received a series of 4-D problems, each of which was 18 feedback trials long. Instead of the usual two-valued alternative, three-valued stimuli were presented. The S might see, for example, a small, red "X" on the left, a large, blue "T" in the center, and a medium-sized, yellow "M" on the right. He chose one of the three alternatives and, as usual, was told "right" or "wrong." The standard routine of pretraining, blank-trial probes, etc. was instituted with one other detail added: Whereas previously the first H probe (H_1) was inserted just after the first feedback trial (F_1), here an additional blank-trial H probe (H_0) was presented at the very outset of the problem i.e., before F_1. The experiment was performed in this way in order to obtain further evidence concerning the *dimension coherence* described in Reading No. 15. In that study, it will be recalled, not only was the solution $H(H+$, e.g., large) rarely seen during precriterion responding, but the other H on the same dimension ($H-$, e.g., small) was equally infrequent.

The present results confirmed this affinity of Hs within a dimension. As before, the Hs for the values (here three of them) of the relevant dimension rarely appeared during precriterion responding. Thus, before S solved the problem, the entire dimension tended to be absent from his sample. An additional demonstration of dimension coherence came from the use of H_0. On problems in which S was told "wrong" at F_1 (which thereby disconfirmed H_0), the next H, H_1, came from the same dimension more than half the time. This of course, is well in excess of chance (.25). Similarly, when S was told "wrong" on the first two feedback trials, H_0, H_1, and H_2 tended to come from the same dimension. Dimension coherence was, therefore, seen both in the absence of the relevant dimension during precriterion responding and in the dimension-related sequence of observed Hs.

The remaining applications of blank-trial probes are less exploratory and more concerned with the properties of probes. Reading No. 16 is noteworthy as the only article published by me which was prompted by an undergraduate. Fundamental to the use of the blank-trial probe is the assumption (see Reading No. 14), that S retains his H in the absence of feedback. This assumption is necessary, of course, for the inference of a single H from a few blank trials. Fred Frankel, then a senior at Stony Brook, bounded up one day with, he said, a test of the theory. He noted that the blank-trials assumption sets no limits on the length of the run of blank trials and that, therefore, even with as many as 30 consecutive blank trials we should see a single H. Fred's beaming face when he concluded this argument contrasted sharply with my anxious heart. Had this kid spotted a vulnerable point in the theory? Suppose Ss changed Hs during a blank-trial series. In the course of 30 such trials these shifts (or some other irregularities) would surely emerge irrefutably. At best, this elegant theory would have to be encumbered with *ad hoc* assumptions. At worst—well, that was too painful to contemplate. Of course, there was no choice. One can't command the disappearance of challenging ideas. But what if Ss should . . . I masked these grim thoughts with a smile and managed, in my best professorial style, something like, "Say, Fred, that's a first-rate suggestion. Let's plan a study."

As will be seen in Reading No. 16, there were no dire consequences. Despite my momentary lapse of faith, 30 blank trials yielded results nicely consistent with the theory. Furthermore, as frequently happens with novel experiments, new details were introduced and new insights were afforded. In particular, a post-experimental verbal probe was added which became useful in evaluating the choice-response protocols. This result, in turn, started us thinking more seriously about the verbal probe and led to the following application of blank trials.

Validation of the verbal report (Karpf & Levine, 1971).   The H may be regarded as a state of the S, a state which is probed for by a set of blank trials. An interesting question is whether this state is describable by S, i.e., whether he can accurately tell us his H. Adapting Skinner's (1957) *tact* concept, these verbal reports were referred to as *introtacts*. Short problems (each consisted of exactly four feedback trials) were presented under three conditions: (1) A blank-trial probe was presented before each feedback trial, as well after the fourth feedback trial; (2) introtacts replaced blank trials, i.e., S was requested to state his H before each feedback trial and after the fourth feedback trial; (3) no probes were employed before each feedback trial; S was asked to state the solution after the fourth trial. Thus, in the first two conditions H_0 - H_4 were obtained; in the last condition only H_4 was obtained.

The same set of questions (e.g., the probability that S repeats his H, given "right" and given "wrong," the frequency distribution of the 8 Hs at H_0, etc.) was asked separately in the blank-trial and in the introtact conditions. Both conditions yielded the identical configurations of results. The same picture of H testing emerged whether one used blank-trial probes or verbal probes. Furthermore, the probing process, in general, appeared to leave undisturbed the problem-solving performance: The proportion of problems solved in the blank-trial, introtact, and no-probe conditions was .76, .76, and .80, respectively. The differences were not significant.

The H has been characterized as an underlying state of the S. The covert state, furthermore, is presumed to change in lawful ways. This general conception is confirmed by the results above: Each of two clearly different operations—presenting blank trials or having S provide an introtact—leads to the identical description of the underly processes. A corollary conclusion is that for this situation the verbal report is a valid manifestation of the state characterized as "holding an H."

The remaining article in this group (Reading No. 17) is an offshoot from the main branch. It describes not a novel exploration with blank trials, but a modest change in theoretical conception required, in part, by the blank-trial results. While these results started me thinking about an enlarged H-sampling conception, other data were accruing which suggested this same conception. Reading No. 17 reviews these data and concludes that Ss must be sampling more than one H at a time. This view, of course, needs to be squared with the fact that a single H is seen during a series of blank trials. A revised sampling assumption is presented which integrates this apparent discrepancy.

Reading No. 16
HUMAN DISCRIMINATION LEARNING:
A TEST OF THE BLANK-TRIALS ASSUMPTION*

By Fred Frankel
   Marvin Levine
   David Karpf

To account for data from multi-dimensional discrimination problems, Levine (1966, 1969b) has presented a model based upon three assumptions: (1) *The Basic Assumption:* The *S* samples an *H* from some universe of *H*s; the sampled *H* determines the choice response. This assumptionn is made by all *H* theorists. (2) *The Blank-Trial Assumption:* *S* responds according to a single *H* during a series of blank trials. If, for example, *S*'s *H* at some point in the problem is "Choose the larger stimulus" and if, starting at that point, *E* says neither "right" nor "wrong" for a series of trials, the *S* selects the large stimulus consistently for those trials. (3) *The Composition Assumption:* The universe of *H*s is finite and its composition is known to the *E*. In practice, this last assumption is fulfilled by limiting the number of possible solutions and by enumerating these solutions to *S*.

Levine (1966) and Levine, Miller, and Steinmeyer (1967), using blank-trial sets four trials in length, found that the response patterns reflected the *H*s specified by the composition assumption about 90% of the time. This result, replicated and extended by Ingalls and Dickerson (1969), Erickson (1968), and Levine (1969b), attests to the validity of the model in general and of the blank-trials assumption in particular. A more stringent test, however, occurs with a longer series of blank trials, where random responding may be even more clearly differentiated from systematic behavior because of the extreme unlikelihood that the two will yield similar response patterns. The model makes no qualifications as to length of series. It predicts, for example, that even with 30 consecutive blank trials, the responses should reflect a single *H*.

This test was carried out in two experiments. In both of these experiments, *S*

*Adapted from the *Journal of Experimental Psychology*, 1970, **85**, 342-348. Copyright 1970 by the American Psychological Association. Reprinted by permission of the publisher.

received a few four-dimensional, discrimination problems with 30 consecutive blank trials interposed once within each problem.

EXPERIMENT I

In this experiment, the 30-blank-trial probe (referred to, hereafter, simply as the 30-probe) was presented after two feedback trials. The composition of the set of Hs was such that two outcomes logically eliminated all but two possible Hs. The model, of course, predicts that only one H will appear.

Method

Subjects.   Thirty-two undergraduates participated in order to fulfill a requirement in the introductory psychology course.

Problems.   Four experimental problems were each constructed from 36 slides. Each slide contained a pair of letters varying along four dimensions: from ("E" vs. "O"), size (one letter was twice as large as the other), color (one letter was black, the other was white), and position (one letter was on the left, one was on the right). Three of the slides were designated for the feedback trials; the remainder served for blank trials. The sequence within a problem was always 2 feedback trials, 29 blank trials, 1 feedback trial, and then 4 more blank trials.

The feedback was preprogrammed: The S was told "right" or "wrong" according to a prearranged schedule regardless of his response. Four feedback patterns were used. Letting $+_i(-_i)$ stand for right (wrong) on the ith trial, these patterns were: $+_1 +_2 +_{32}$, $+_1 +_2 -_{32}$, $-_1 -_2 +_{32}$, and $-_1 -_2 -_{32}$. These four patterns were assigned to the four experimental problems in advance. The sequence in which the four problems appeared varied for each S, forming a Latin square with every four Ss.

In addition to the four experimental problems, a set of six preliminary training problems were constructed from the same four dimensions. Five of these problems were 12 trials long; the sixth had 21 trials. All six problems had legitimate solutions. The first four problems, containing only feedback trials, had one solution from each of the four dimensions. The fifth and sixth problems, for which the solutions were always "E" and "small," respectively, contained blank trials. In Problem 5, only Trials 1, 2, and 6 were feedback trials; in Problem 6, Trials 1, 2, 6, 17, and 21 were feedback trials.

Procedure.   The stimuli were rear-projected onto two, 4×6 in. translucent Plexiglas windows mounted in a large plywood panel. The S was seated before the stimulus windows and a typical slide was turned on. The E pointed out the four dimensions, enumerated the eight possible solutions, and demonstrated the response, a press of the window containing the selected stimulus. The first four preliminary problems, containing only feedback trials, were then presented. Following these, S was told that subsequent problems would have occasional runs

TABLE 1
Frequency with Which The Various Numbers
of Responses Occurred Consistent with
One of the Eight Hs

Number of responses	Number of problems
30	109
29	9
28	2
27	4
26	1
25	1

of trials during which he would receive no information as to the correctness of each response. These were characterized as test trials during which S was supposed to try to be correct. The two remaining preliminary problems were then given. The E always announced the solution after each of the six preliminary problems. Following these, the four experimental problems were presented without comment by E.

During a feedback trial, the appropriate feedback word ("right" or "wrong") was illuminated for one second immediately after the window was pressed. The next slide appeared one second after the feedback word went off. On blank trials, the next slide appeared one second after the response occurred.

Results

Each of the four experimental problems contained 30 consecutive responses uninterrupted by feedback (the 29 blank trials and the responses to the next feedback trial). Of the resulting 128 30-probes (32 Ss with four problems per S), 2 contained unusual, although systematic, response patterns and will be discussed separately. Of the remaining 126 protocols, the chief result is that 109 showed one of the eight H patterns consistently, without a single deviation. An additional 9 showed a single error (29/30 consistent H-pattern responses). The complete distribution is shown in Table 1, which reveals a total of 34 discrepant responses. These results validate the blank-trials assumption to an astonishing degree. The probability of a response discrepant with the assumption is estimated by $34/(126 \times 30) < .01$.

Scanning the protocols containing these errors revealed nothing systematic. The errors seemed to reflect a small degree of noise in the response system. Grouped together, however, they did manifest two small nonrandom characteristics. Figure 1 shows a plot of the number of errors as a function of trials in the 30-probe. There is a tendency for the errors to occur in the early trials. The null hypothesis, that the errors are random events which are equally distributed within the first, second, and third sets of 10 trials, was tested by x_2 and rejected, x_2 (2) = 18.4, $p < .01$. These errors also tended to occur in 30-probes that followed negative feedback trials: from a total of 17 30-probes containing at least one error, 13 came

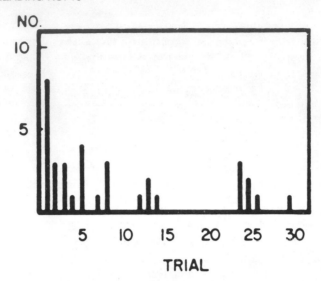

FIG. 1. Locus of discrepant responses
during the 30-probe.

after negative feedback on the first 2 outcome trials ($-_1-_2$). The null hypothesis, that the errors are random events which are equally distributed between $+_1+_2$ and $-_1-_2$ outcomes, was tested by x_2 and rejected, $x_2(1) = 4.76$, $p < .05$. Levine (1969b) has noted a similar result, that more inconsistent blank-trial patterns occur after a "wrong" than after a "right."

Of the two special protocols referred to previously, one showed simple alternation between the letters "O" and "E," without exception, for the 30 trials. On this problem, S had been told "right" after the thirtieth response. The alternation pattern then continued for the remaining 4 blank trials. This behavior, therefore, violates the composition assumption, but is additional support for the blank-trials assumption. The remaining protocol is not so easily disposed of. This S, on his third problem, went to the right side consistently for the first 11 blank trials, then went to the small letter for the remaining 18 responses. Thus, it appears that this S changed Hs midway. We will return to this problem in the second study.

Turning away from this pair of problematical results to the more agreeable 126 protocols, a question may be raised concerning the information held by S during the 30-probe, when he manifested a single H. After two feedback trials, only two Hs are possibly correct, i.e., are logically consistent with the information on those two trials. On 102 of the protocols, the H manifested was one of these two correct Hs. The question may be raised for these problems, whether S was also holding (though not manifesting) the other correct H. The probability that this occurred may be estimated from the effects of the third feedback trial. The stimuli were such that the third feedback always disconfirmed exactly one of the two logically possible Hs. On those third-feedback trials when S was told "wrong," the H manifested during the 30-probe is disconfirmed; the other is confirmed and is the only remaining correct H. It may be inferred that this other H had been latent (i.e., held by some Ss but not manifested) during the 30-probe if it appears with greater-than-chance frequency during the subsequent four-blank-trial probe. The estimated probability that S shows the correct H following "wrong" on the third feedback trial (given that he showed one of the correct Hs during the 30-probe) is .42 (18/43). This proportion is significantly ($z = 2.36; p < .01$) higher than .25, the probability that S will choose the correct H if he remembers only the information from the third outcome trial. Thus, in at least a few instances during the 30-probe, Ss may be regarded as holding two Hs though manifesting only one.[1]

EXPERIMENT II

The preceding experiment demonstrated the validity of the blank-trials assumption, but in a fairly restricted context. First, all of the 30-probes occurred after two feedback trials. Second, in the interest of fulfilling the composition assumption, S was pretrained with instructions and with six preliminary problems. In the present experiment, responding during the 30-probe was studied under more general conditions. First, the 30-probe was presented after the first, second, or third feedback trial. Second, the composition assumption was dispensed with: one group of Ss were given no instructions about the range of solutions.

The omission of the composition assumption poses, of course, a technical problem. The logic of inferring the H from the response pattern rests upon this assumption. To solve this problem a different routine was undertaken. The S was asked at the end of the experiment how he had responded during each of the 30-probes. It was assumed that S's statement revealed the H he had selected from the now possibly infinite universe of Hs. The 30-probe was then studied to determine whether, as the blank-trials assumption stipulates, S had responded consistently during the blank trials with this verbally reported H.

In order to dispense with extensive instructions, therefore, a substitution was made: the composition assumption was traded for an expectation about verbal reports, that S could accurately describe the basis for his responding during the 30-probe. The results, in part, evaluate this expectation.

It is appropriate at this point to describe an enlargement of the model which has taken place recently. Several authors (e.g., Erickson, Zajkowski, & Ehmann, 1966; Levine, 1969b; Restle, 1962; Trabasso & Bower, 1968) have assumed that

---

[1] The test of significance depends upon the null hypothesis one employs. The hypothesis in the text is predicated upon Gregg and Simon's (1967) "Local consistency" assumption. Another plausible null hypothesis is that S remembers only the information from the third feedback trial, but rejects the *dimension* containing the just disconfirmed H (cf. "Local consistency with local nonreplacement" by Gregg & Simon). In this case, the chance probability of selecting the correct H is .33. The obtained value is still larger than this although not significantly so ($z = 1.02, p > .05$).

S holds and evaluates not one but several *H*s simultaneously. Levine (1970) reviewed a variety of data which favored this conception and proposed a supplementary response rule: the *S* takes one *H*, a *working H*, from the sample as the basis for his response. This is the *H* described in the basic assumption and to which the blank-trials assumption applies. This subset-sampling conception and the working-*H* response rule would account for the final results of Exp. I, that some *S*s may have been holding two *H*s although they showed only one during the 30-probe.

Levine (1970) also presented evidence that *S*s occasionally employ another response rule, coined the "majority rule" by Richard, Lépine, and Rouanet (1969). For an example of this rule, assume *S* holds three *H*s in his sample; he would on any one trial make that response favored by any two of these *H*s. Levine showed that this response rule tended to be employed about 3% of the time on blank-trial probes immediately after the first feedback trial. This is the most likely locus of occurrence of this rule, since during a four-dimensional problem *S*s tend to have three or four *H*s in their subset after one feedback trial. Because 30-probes are presented after the first feedback trial in this next experiment, one should be alerted to majority-rule as well as to single-*H* behavior in considering the results.

Method

Subjects.   Forty-eight undergraduates from the introductory psychology course served as *S*s in order to fulfill a course requirement.

Problems.   Four types of problems were constructed, each problem from 33 slides. While all four problem types consisted of four-dimensional stimuli, each type was based upon different dimensions. Thus, there were: (*a*) a *geometrical-form* problem, whose dimensions were shape (square vs. triangle), thickness of contour (thin line vs. ⅜-in. band), texture of contour (solid vs. dashed), and direction of an inscribed arrow (pointing up vs. pointing down); (*b*) a *flower* problem, with tulip vs. daisy, a long stem vs. a short stem, etc.; (*c*) a *car* problem; and (*d*) a *letter* problem (similar to the stimuli of Exp. I).

Within each problem, the 33 slides consisted of 4 feedback-trial slides and 29 blank-trial slides. The latter (the 30-probe) followed 1, 2, or 3 feedback slides, according to the following plan: In the geometrical-form problem, which was employed only as a preliminary problem, the 30-probe appeared after the second feedback trial. Within the flower, car, and letter problem types, the locus of the 30-probe varied factorially, generating nine unique problems.

Each *S*, then, received the geometrical-form problem followed by three other problem types. In each of the latter, the 30-probe occurred after a different feedback trial. The three problem types, the three probe placements, and three orders of occurrence of each of these variables were counter-balanced with every three *S*s, in a Greco-Latin square.

Procedure.   The *S*s were divided into two groups, an Informed (I) and Noninformed (NI) group Every *S* was shown a stimulus from the geometrical-

TABLE 2

Frequency with Which the Various Numbers
of Responses Occurred Consistent
with One of the Eight Simple *H*s

Number of responses	Group	
	Informed	Noninformed
30	48	31
29	7	8
28	2	5
27	3	3
26	1	4
25	1	2
Special problems	10	19

form set, was told about the mechanics of response and feedback, and was instructed to choose correctly as often as possible. All *S*s were also informed that for several responses they would not be told whether they were right or wrong. The *S* was further instructed that these (blank trials) were a test of learning and that he was to try "to get 100 per cent correct" on these trials. The NI *S*s were given no further instructions; the I *S*s were told about the eight features of the stimuli, that one and only one of the eight features would be the solution throughout any one problem. The *S*s in both groups then received the preliminary problem, consisting of 2 feedback trials, 29 blank trials, and 2 more feedback trials. At the end of this problem, the solution was announced to the I group but not to the NI group. Each *S* then received the three problems of the experiment proper. The solutions were not announced to any of the *S*s following each of these problems.

At the end of the experimental session, *S* was reminded of each problem ("Do you remember the problem with 'flowers'?"), and was asked on what basis he had responded during the run of blank trials. Following *S*'s statement, *E* further asked whether he used this rule consistently, i.e., for every response during that run.

Results

The results were analyzed according to the following plan: As in Exp. I, the 30-probe was inspected for *H* behavior. If 25 or more of the responses were to one of the eight stimulus values, then the problem was categorized as an instance of *H* behavior. For such problems, called *normal,* the verbal protocols were not consulted (except in connection with subsequent analyses, discussed subsequently). If, on the other hand, fewer than 25 of the responses were to each one of the stimulus values, the problem was categorized as *special*. The verbal protocol was then read in the hope that it might indicate the determinant of *S*'s responses.

The normal problems.—Table 2 shows the frequency distributions of responses consistent with one of the eight stimulus values for the Informed and

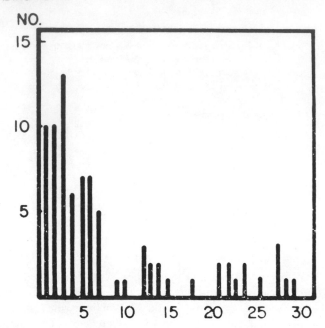

FIG. 2. Locus of discrepant responses during
the 30-probe of the normal problems.

Noninformed groups, separately. The table reveals that even where the instructions about solutions are minimal or absent, Ss are largely constrained to employ the eight simple Hs. Thus, even the Noninformed group shows the simple Hs on 74% (53/72) of the 30-probes.

The reduction in the instructions produces two effects: The number of special problems increases (comparing the number of normal and special problems in each of the two groups of Exp. II yields $\chi^2 = 2.77, p < .05$); also, the error distribution of normal problems shows more dispersion (e.g., significantly fewer problems in the Noninformed group showed 30 consistent responses, $z = 1.97, p < .05$). Even in the Noninformed group, however, there is both a high proportion of normal problems and a strong skewness to the distribution.

If the normal problems for both groups are combined, there are 36 protocols with 1-5 discrepant responses, producing a total of 82 discrepant responses. Plotting these by their position in the 30-probe yields the results in Fig. 2. The comparable results from Exp. I, that the response errors are more frequent early in the blank-trial series, are clearly replicated (cf. Fig. 1).

Neither of the two variables, problem type, and number of feedback trials preceding the 30-probe, showed any important effects. The number of normal problems appearing in the nine cells of the 3 × 3 matrix (3 Problem Types × 3 Numbers of Feedback Trials) is generally uniform: the smallest cell frequency is

TABLE 3

Frequency of the Various Systematic Response
Patterns during the 30-Probe

Group	Normal problems	Special problems			
		Majority rule	Shift H	New H·	Re-sidual
Informed	62	6	0	0	4
Noninformed	53	9	4	1	5

11; the largest is 15. The marginal totals show no large, systematic, or significant variation.

The special problems.   The special problems, of course, are not necessarily negations of the blank-trials assumption. They may contain systematic modes of behavior other than the eight simple Hs. The verbal descriptions about these problems revealed three such modes.

1. Majority-rule behavior. The S holds 2, 3, or 4 Hs simultaneously and chooses the side dictated by the majority of these. (E.g., "It could be daisy, three leaves, or ragged-shaped leaves. If it had all three I chose it; if it had two out of the three I chose it.")

2. Shift Hs. The S predicts E will change the solution during the problem. (E.g., "It started with two leaves then changed to three leaves.")[2]

3. New Hs. The S describes an H not in the set. (E.g., "I switched [S here means alternated] from one side to the other.")

After reading the verbal protocols of the special problems, the E studied the corresponding 30-probes for the indicated pattern. Table 3 shows the frequency with which the special problems fell into the various categories. The last category, *residual*, shows the number of protocols which could not be classified, neither on the basis of the response patterns themselves nor after consulting Ss' verbal statements (which were occasionally uninterpretable). All of the special problems falling in the other three categories showed at least 27 out of the 30 responses consistent with the indicated pattern.

The verbal reports.   The Ss' statements were useful during the special problems in searching for organization of the 30 responses. Their validity may also be evaluated from the normal problems. On 79 of these problems, all the responses in the 30-probe were consistent with one of the eight simple Hs (cf. Table 2). The S subsequently stated this particular H for 77 (97%) of these problems. On the

---

[2] A statement describing a shift H is typically ambiguous. For example, from the statement, "Started off with serrated leaves—then changed to three leaves," it is not clear whether S's H was that the solution changed midway or whether S held two simple Hs and switched them midway. Because this behavior appeared only with the NI group, the more harmonious interpretation is tentatively made that S held a single H involving a shift in solution.

remaining 2 problems, S stated a different simple H for 1; for the other, the verbal report contained reference to three different Hs and was unclear.

There were 28 problems with 27-29 consistent responses. On 27 (96%) of these problems, S stated the corresponding simple H. On the remaining problem, with 29 responses consistent with a simple H, S stated an inappropriate majority rule. In general, Ss did not tend to report the sporadic errors in responding for these 28 problems. When asked whether they were consistent in their responses over these 30 trials, only seven times (25%) did Ss remark that they had made an occasional error.

DISCUSSION

The present experiments further substantiate the validity of Levine's (1966, 1969b) general H model. The more recent version of the model stipulates that during blank trials, either one simple H or majority-rule responding will appear. In all but 14 (the residual and shift patterns) of the 272 problems of Exp. I and II combined, Ss demonstrated quite consistent adherence to one of the two response rules. Of these 258 problems, 15 manifested the majority rule and 243 the single, working-H response rule.

The degree to which a single H appears over the blank trials depends upon the degree of preliminary training. In Exp. I, where both explicit instructions and a large number of preliminary problems were presented, 98% (126/128) of the protocols showed at least 25 responses to one of the stimulus values. When Ss were informed of the H set but only presented with one preliminary problem (Exp. II, Group I), 86% (62/72) of the protocols displayed an H within the specified set. Finally, when no information was given as to the H set (Exp. II, Group NI), 74% (53/72) were normal problems.

The last datum reflects the perceptual effects of the attribute values corresponding to the eight simple Hs. These attribute values have visible self-contained qualities and undergo independent rearrangement with each other from trial to trial. These characteristics evidently cause the attribute values to serve as the basis for Hs a substantial proportion of the time. It also is evident, however, that if one wishes to fulfill more perfectly the composition assumption, to know, that is, that all Ss are working only with the specified set of Hs, then one must enhance the perceptual effects with pretraining.

The increase in amount of pretraining was also accompanied, during the normal problems, by a decrease in the number of responses discrepant from a single H. In Exp. I, .9% (34/30 × 126) of the responses were thus discrepant; in Exp. II for Group I, 1.6% (29/30 × 62) and for Group NI, 3.3% (53/30 × 53) were not consistent with one of the eight simple Hs.

Surprisingly, these errors showed a tendency to occur at the beginning of the 30-trial probe. This suggests that the accuracy of the usual 4-trial probe may be enhanced not only by pretraining, but also by placing "dummy trials" at the beginning of the 4-trial series. These dummy trials would be discarded before analysis. The virture of this procedure is a topic for further research.

Reading No. 17
HUMAN DISCRIMINATION LEARNING: THE SUBSET SAMPLING ASSUMPTION*

By Marvin Levine

Restle (1962) presented three models of which the first assumed: (a) The subject begins a learning task with a universe of hypotheses from which he draws one. This hypothesis dictates his response. (b) When the subject is told "right" after a response, he keeps his hypothesis for the next trial. (c) When he is told "wrong" he returns his hypothesis to the set and randomly draws a new one.

The third assumption, called the zero-memory assumption, because it permits the subject to resample the hypothesis he has just rejected, has been refuted by a variety of results (Erickson, 1968; Levine, 1963a, 1966; Trabasso & Bower, 1966) and has since been disavowed by everyone. Alternative treatments may be found by Gregg and Simon (1967), Levine (1966, 1969b), Restle and Emmerich (1966), and Trabasso and Bower (1966, 1968). The zero-memory assumption, therefore, is not treated here. However, a feature contained in the first and third assumptions, that the subject samples only one hypothesis at a time, also requires reconsideration. The present argument is based upon a review of this single-hypothesis feature.

Restle's two other models differed from the first in one important detail: They assumed that the subject sampled either a few or all of the hypotheses. He further demonstrated that all three models yielded the same theorems, that the predictions generated were independent of the number of hypotheses sampled (an effect, incidentally, dependent upon the zero-memory assumption). This theoretical demonstration, and the fact that no data were available on which to base a decision, led subsequent investigators initially to employ the simplest assumption, that the subject sampled one hypothesis (cf. Bower & Trabasso, 1964; Erickson, Zajkowski, & Ehmann, 1966; Levine, 1963b, 1966). A variety of results have recently appeared, however, which suggest that the subject is sampling more than

*Adapted from *Psychological Bulletin,* 1970, **74,** 397-404. Copyright 1970 by the American Psychological Association. Reprinted by permission of the publisher.

one hypothesis and which have led theorists to postulate multihypothesis sampling. The aim, then, of this article is to evaluate the single-hypothesis assumption, to present an alternative, and to marshall the evidence favoring this alternative.

REVISION OF THE BASIC ASSUMPTION

A desideratum of hypothesis theory is the specification of the subject's hypothesis. Levine (1966) developed a model which permitted this specification. The model began with the basic assumption, similar to Restle's first assumption, that the subject started with a set of hypotheses and selected one (note the single-hypothesis assumption) which determined his response. Rather than assumptions about the effects of feedback, Levine employed a blank-trials assumption: When the subject is told nothing after his response he keeps his hypothesis for the next trial. A third assumption, the composition assumption, was added: The universe of hypotheses from which the subject samples is finite and is known to the experimenter (this last assumption is typically fulfilled by training and instructing the subject). These three assumptions permit one to infer the subject's hypothesis from a short series of blank trials.

In the experiment of interest here, Levine (1966) presented these blank-trial probes after each of the first three feedback trials. The main findings were: 92.4% of the probes showed the hypothesis patterns; the subject virtually always ($p = .95$) repeated a hypothesis following a "right" feedback; the subject virtually never ($p = .02$) repeated his hypothesis following a "wrong" feedback. These results are consistent with Levine's assumptions and with the usual connotations of hypothesis testing. The next result, however, introduces the complication.

Levine obtained the proportion of hypotheses which were correct whenever the subject resampled for a new hypothesis, i.e., whenever he had just been told "wrong". The reciprocal of this proportion of correct hypotheses gives the average size of the hypothesis set from which the subject is sampling.[1] Obtaining this estimate after each "wrong" feedback trial, Levine found that the set size decreased from eight hypotheses at the start of the problem to approximately three hypotheses after the third feedback trial (F_3). These estimates, of course, are average values. Some subjects process the information perfectly; that is, they always show the correct hypothesis after F_3. For these subjects the set contains only one hypothesis, the correct hypothesis, after the third feedback trial. Obviously, these perfect processors are testing more than one hypothesis per trial. Starting with the full set of eight hypotheses, these subjects must eliminate four

---

[1]Consider a subject who was told "wrong" at the ith feedback trial (F_i) and must resample for a new hypothesis. If there are N_1 hypotheses in the set from which the subject samples (1 correct hypothesis and $N_1 - 1$ incorrect hypotheses) then the probability of the subject selecting the correct hypothesis, $H+$, is given by

$$P(H_1 = H+ \mid F_1 = -) = 1/N_i.$$

Since $P(H_i = H+ \mid F_i = -)$ may be estimated from the data, the size of the set may in turn be estimated from its reciprocal.

hypotheses after F_1, two more hypotheses after F_2, and the remaining incorrect hypothesis after F_3. Levine adapted the term "focusing" from Bruner, Goodnow, and Austin (1956) to characterize this process. The majority of subjects are not quite so perfect. On the other hand, they do considerably better than testing just one hypothesis per trial. The general scheme that emerges, then, is as follows: The subject takes a subset of several hypotheses simultaneously, eliminating from this subset those which are inconsistent with the information. A perfect focuser takes the universe as his initial subset and eliminates the seven incorrect hypotheses by the third feedback trial.

This picture, which emerges from the analysis of the hypotheses obtained with blank-trial probes, is not consistent with the single-hypothesis assumption made to justify blank trials as probes. To put it another way, over a series of blank trials, subjects show one hypothesis; over a series of feedback trials, however, they manifest the analysis of several hypotheses simultaneously. This discrepancy leads to a revision of the basic assumption as follows: At the outset of a problem, the subject samples a subset of hypotheses from the universe. He then takes one of these as his *working hypothesis*. The working hypothesis is the basis for his response (and is the hypothesis to which the blank-trials assumption applies).

The subset contains those hypotheses that will be processed (and, when appropriate, eliminated) after each feedback. The processing occurs after both those responses called "right" and those called "wrong." The data reveal, however, this difference in the processing: following a "right" the same working hypothesis is retained, although other hypotheses in the subset may be discarded; following a "wrong" the working hypothesis is one of the hypotheses discarded. In the latter case, therefore, the subject must choose a new working hypothesis. He does this by selecting one of those remaining in his subset. If, however, the subset has gone to zero (if, for example, the "wrong" disconfirms not only the working hypothesis but all the hypotheses which were in the subset), then the subject must take a new subset and a new working hypothesis from this subset.

The revised basic assumption is clearly in two parts. The first describes the subjects' mode of sampling and is referred to as the subset-sampling assumption. The second, dealing with the working hypothesis, describes how the overt response is made and is referred to as the working-hypothesis response rule. The two aspects may be illustrated by having the subject speak aloud during these problems. They frequently say something like, "It could be 'large,' 'black,' or 'X.' I'll try 'large.' "

FURTHER EVIDENCE
FOR THE REVISED BASIC ASSUMPTION

The Choice-Latency Discrepancy

According to the single-hypothesis assumption, the subject is in two states: he samples incorrect hypotheses and makes correct responses only by chance, or he

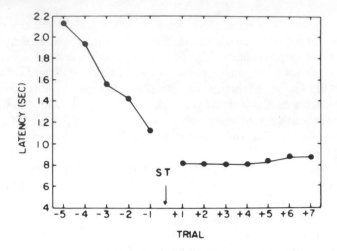

F<small>IG</small>. 1. Mean latencies at successive trials before and after the solution trial (ST).

samples the correct hypothesis and thereafter makes only correct responses. The trial of the last error marks the transition between the two states. Bower and Trabasso (1964), using traditional problems (no blank trials), showed that the trial of the last error was indeed a pivot around which the predicted discontinuity appeared. They showed that the proportion of correct responses at each trial before the trial of the last error was constant at about 0.5. After the trial of the last error, the proportion, of course, was 1.0 by definition.

Latencies should also reflect this discontinuity. As Erickson et al. (1966) pointed out, latencies after the trial of the last error should be constant and should be lower than the average latency before the trial of the last error. The constancy, however, does not obtain. Erickson et al. and Falmagne (1970) showed that the latency during the criterion run is gradually decreasing over trials. Thus, a puzzle was posed. Choice responses seemed to reflect the two-state conception (based on the single-hypothesis assumption); latencies showed decreases suggesting changes occurring when the subject was in the second state (i.e., when the subject held, presumably, only the correct hypothesis).

The discrepancy is resolved by shifting to the subset-sampling assumption. With this assumption, the trial of the last error is interpreted as that trial at which the subject first takes the correct hypothesis as his new working hypothesis. There will, typically, be other hypotheses in the subset that he is monitoring. During the next few trials he is reducing his subset until none but the working hypothesis remains. Trabasso and Bower (1968), who also have shifted to a version of the subset-sampling assumption, made the suggestion that latency is correlated with the number of hypotheses in the subset to be evaluated. This implies the result of Falmagne and of Erickson et al. that latency decreases during the criterion run. The decrease should occur until only the working hypothesis remains.

Levine (1969a) pointed out that this argument has a corollary. If the trial of the last error is that trial at which the subject first takes the correct hypothesis as his working hypothesis, then there is a later trial at which the last of the incorrect hypotheses in the subset is eliminated. At that trial, the solution trial, the subject first holds only the correct hypothesis. The solution trial, then, is a pivotal trial. Before it the subject has a decreasing subset containing more than the working hypothesis; after it the subject holds only the working hypothesis. The latencies should reflect this two-state character by a two-part curve: from the trial of the last error to the solution trial the latencies should decrease; beyond the solution trial the latencies should be constant. Because the solution trial occurs at different trials for different subjects, averaging at each trial after the trial of the last error obscures the discontinuity and yields a decay-like curve. Averaging, however, before and after the solution trial separately should yield the two parts clearly.

The two-part implication could be tested only if the solution trial could be located. Levine tried a simple expedient. A bell was placed near the subject engaged in a four-dimensional discrimination-learning problem. He was told that he should ring the bell when he knew the solution and should continue responding. If the subset-sampling assumption is correct and if the trial on which the subject sounds the bell is indeed the solution trial, then averaging the latencies around this trial should yield the two-part curve.

Figure 1 shows the latencies during the criterion run at each trial before and after the solution trial. The two-part curve emerges clearly. Levine further showed that the two parts appear no matter how many trials after the trial of the last error the solution trial occurred.

The latency results are, thus, consistent with the revised basic assumption: the reduction in latency reflects the reduction of the hypothesis set until only the working hypothesis remains. It is after this point that the latencies are constant.

The Redundant, Relevant Cues Experiment

Another result critical of the single-hypothesis sampling assumption comes from concept-identification problems with redundant, relevant cues. As the name implies, there is not one but two solutions to these problems. For example, triangles are always black (circles are always white), and both are made relevant so that either the hypothesis ''sort by form'' or the hypothesis ''sort by color'' would produce criterion performance. The single-hypothesis assumption implies, of course, that the subject could solve with either one or the other hypothesis but not with both. Trabasso and Bower (1968) carried out two pilot studies to test this implication. The problems in these studies were constructed from several attributes, two of which were relevant and redundant. After a subject showed 10 successive correct responses, he was presented with two tests (two series of blank trials) to see what he had learned. In each test, one of the relevant attributes was eliminated, permitting the experimenter to observe whether the subject sorted properly with the remaining relevant attribute.

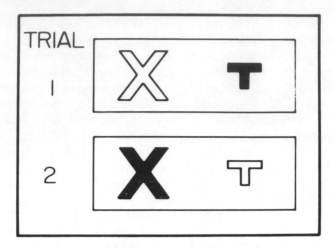

FIG. 2. Two pairs of four-dimensional stimuli in which three of the dimensions are confounded.

Trabasso and Bower's description of the results and their concluding statements are very apt for the present thesis:

> . . . a typical subject might classify the sixteen test cards for color (with shape neutralized) correctly, whereas on the sixteen test cards for shape (with color neutralized) he would classify at the chance level, eight correct and eight incorrect. Such individual data cause no equivocation in classifying this subject as having learned differential responses to color but not to shape.
>
> An important feature of the pilot results was that a significant proportion of the subjects learned *both* relevant attributes, a clear contradiction of our prior assumption of single-attribute sampling [pp. 68-69].

They subsequently confirmed this last result and revised their version of hypothesis theory to include sampling of subsets of hypotheses. They pointed out that just after the trial of the last error the subject's subset may contain only one or both of the correct hypotheses. If it contains only one, then the subject will respond correctly to one of the tests but not to the other; if it contains both, then he will respond correctly on both tests.

These results, completely consistent with the present revised basic assumption, nevertheless hold an interesting implication for that assumption. The subject, employing one particular working hypothesis, can also employ another hypothesis in the subset if the situation so requires it. Evidence that hypotheses other than the working hypothesis are available for use in responding is supplemented in the next section of this review.

Majority-Rule Phenomena

The evidence so far was presented in support of the subset-sampling assumption and was consistent with—if not in support of—the working-hypothesis rule. There are other sets of data that support the subset-sampling assumption but that imply a different response rule. Assume that the two stimuli in Figure 2 are presented on the first two feedback trials of a problem. Notice that the second-trial stimuli are almost the same as the first-trial stimuli: only the color has shifted. Because three of the dimensions remain confounded, and one has changed, these stimuli will be said to show a 3-1 shift. Assume further that the subject has responded to the left side on trial one, was told "correct," and now holds the subset "large, white, X, or left." According to the working-hypothesis rule, one of these will be the basis for his response on the next trial. This implies that he should respond to the right side 25% of the time (when "white" had been selected as the working hypothesis) and to the left side 75% of the time (when "large," "left," or "X" had been selected as the working hypothesis). The subset-sampling assumption, however, permits another mode of response. The results in the preceding section suggested that all the hypotheses in the subset may be available to the subject for use in responding. If so, the subject might, on any one trial, make that response which he believes has the best chance of success. He may, that is, make that response which is dictated by the majority of the hypotheses in his subset. Richard, Lépine, and Rouanet (1969) recently incorporated such a response rule in a general hypothesis model and have dubbed this the *majority rule*.

Two sets of data indicate the operation of a majority rule. Richter (1965) presented to 40 subjects 16 four-dimensional problems in which the first two trials formed a 3-1 shift (cf. Figure 2). The subset-sampling assumption *cum* working-hypothesis rule predicts that subjects who were correct on Trial 1 will choose the three-side (the side with three correct hypotheses) 75% of the time. The majority rule would produce choice of the three-side 100% of the time. Richter found that the three-side was chosen on 85% of the trials. This suggests that the majority rule is at least occasionally employed in this specific sequence.

A second datum comes from Levine's experiment with blank trials. It was demonstrated that, in a set of four blank trials, eight different response patterns corresponded to the eight simple hypotheses (cf. Fig. 1 of Levine, 1966). It was also noted that a subject may show any 1 of 16 response patterns, of which only 8, the hypothesis patterns, are perfectly correlated with the eight stimulus attributes. The other 8 may be characterized as inconsistent patterns. The four blank-trial stimuli after the first feedback trial were so ordered that a subject who followed the majority rule always produced a specific one of the 8 inconsistent patterns. Since this is not one of the hypothesis patterns, its frequency could be independently determined.

It was reported earlier that the hypothesis patterns appeared on 92.4% of the blank-trial sets. In this experiment, therefore, the working-hypothesis rule is clearly predominating. It is possible, however, that the majority rule accounts for some part of the remaining 7.6% of the patterns. These inconsistent patterns can occur in eight different ways, each one some permutation of three responses to one side and one response to the other. The majority rule yields exactly one of these. If this rule is not operating at all, then the eight inconsistent patterns should occur equally often, that is, on the null hypothesis, the majority-rule pattern should account for only 12.5% of these inconsistent patterns. This particular pattern, however, constituted 38.3% (44/115) of the inconsistent patterns ($z = 8.6, p <$ .01) that followed the first feedback trial. Thus, the majority rule is operating here too, although it is much weaker than in Richter's study.

CONCLUSION

The various experiments reviewed all confirm a subset-sampling assumption, that the subject monitors and evaluates several hypotheses simultaneously during discrimination learning. The accompanying working-hypothesis rule is not as clearly established. The data from the blank-trials, the latency, and the reduntant, relevant cues experiments support a working-hypothesis rule; some of the data, however, imply a majority rule. It is probably incorrect to expect that one of these rules is wrong, one is right, and that future research will determine the winner. Rather, the evidence suggests that subjects use either rule and that it is the task for future research to determine when each occurs.

9

THE START OF THE CHILD PROGRAM

This section belongs with the preceding chapter, since it describes further exploration with the blank-trial probe. The use of children as Ss, however, produced a theoretical departure divergent enough to warrant separate treatment.

A comparison of the H model presented for the monkey (Levine 1959b, Reading No. 8) and for the college student (Levine 1966, Reading No. 14) reveals an important difference. In both, the H is defined as a source of systematic responding. However, for the monkey the Hs are primarily *Response-Sets*, response tendencies (e.g., Position Preference) that persist mechanically, regardless of the feedback; for the adult human the Hs are all *Predictions*, tendencies that change with disconfirmations.* Available evidence suggested that children would require an enlarged model encompassing both types of Hs. I delayed, therefore, the study of discrimination learning by children, although this seemed like a natural direction in which to carry the investigation. A second reason for the delay was more personal. I had had no experience with children as Ss, a formidable literature was already developing, and the adult human research, which had strong momentum, demanded my attention. These personal obstacles were happily reduced at about the time that I felt ready to confront the enlarged theoretical issues. In 1968 I was joined in the project by Barry Gholson, a post-doctoral Fellow trained in child research. He immersed himself in H theory and in the techniques associated with the multidimensional discrimination task, especially the use of the blank-trial probe. Together we planned an initial experiment with children.

Rather than mimicking one of the experiments designed for the adult human, we adapted the procedures for young children. The initial experiment entailed fairly long problems, thereby increasing the likelihood that S would achieve solution. We decided to use automated procedures (cf. Levine, 1969a), but instead of having the words "right" and "wrong" light up, a light appeared over the correct

*See Levine, 1963a (Reading No. 12), for a discussion of these types of Hs.

response alternative. The most important change concerned the blank-trial stimulus sequence. It will be recalled that for 4-D problems a simple *H* appeared from the four blank trials as either four responses to one side (a 4-0 pattern) or two responses to each side (a 2-2 pattern). The stimulus sequence was such that any 3-1 response pattern was inconsistent with any stimulus pattern and, therefore, did not reflect a simple *H*. Gholson pointed out that this arrangement posed a special problem with children. The literature suggested that young children tended to show two types of Response Sets. They would perseverate on position (producing, during blank trials, a 4-0 pattern) or alternate on position (producing a 2-2 patter If these patterns were to be (erroneously) interpreted as Prediction *H*s, i.e., as 4-υ and 2-2 patterns from adults had always been interpreted, then some peculiar conclusions would be drawn about *S*'s information-processing characteristics. Furthermore, these Response-set *H*s would be hopelessly confounded with Prediction *H*s. Thus, a single-alternation pattern could result either from mechanical position alternation or from *S*s consistently choosing the stimulus component that, for the given set of blank trials, happened to alternate positions.

Gholson not only foresaw these problems, but had a simple solution at hand. Change the stimulus sequence, he proposed, so that the eight 3-1 response patterns each conformed to a simple *H*. (See Fig. 1 of Reading No. 18 for an example.) With such a sequence the eight 4-0 and 2-2 patterns are inconsistent with the eight simple *H*s and would normally be of little interest. With the children, however, four of these patterns, the two 4-0 patterns and those two 2-2 patterns that single-alternated, would reflect the Response-sets. Thus, the confounding could be eliminated. The Response-set *H*s could be catalogued alongside the Prediction *H*s, and these latter could be more readily interpreted. Needless to say, this change was incorporated. As Reading No. 18 shows, this seemingly trivial alteration in stimulus sequence yielded clear results and facilitated the expansion of the theory.

This expansion came about precipitously. For several years now it was clear that adult *S*s changed *H*s after a disconfirmation. Through these years the thought would occur to me occasionally that the *S*s were probably not changing *H*s willy-nilly, but might be following some overriding plan. If this were the case, it would follow that, during a series of disconfirmations, the sequence of *H*s should have some systematic character. While this idea seemed plausible, nothing inspired me to develop it. I merely tucked it away. When, however, the children's protocols started coming in, the systematic character of their *H* sequences fairly leapt out at us. One would repeatedly see types of simple *H* sequences. This provided the needed push. The System (*Sy*) analysis was completed within a few weeks. The results are presented in Reading No. 18. Details of the analysis may be found in the Appendix.

Following publication of this article I realized that it contained an interesting implication. When invited to speak about this material, I dramatized this implication by beginning the talk with a little puzzle. This goes as follows:

"Imagine that we present the standard four-dimensional simultaneous-discrimination problem to a large number of second-grade children from a good suburban school. Each child will receive a problem 10 feedback trials in length. There are no blank trials. He will have been instructed about the eight possible solutions and will have received preliminary training problems. You, I might add, know nothing about the details of the problem that the children will receive. That is, you do not know the particular stimuli that the children see or the solution to the problem. I am interested only in those problems in which the children are told "wrong" on trial 2. This will be the case for approximately 50% of the problems. These children will be selected out; our concern will be only with them.

"Suppose, further, that we have all conceivable information about each child. We have taken all sorts of physiological measures and can describe each of these. We have given all sorts of paper-and-pencil tests and can give you any score. If there are any questions you wish to ask of the child, these questions have already been asked and we can give you the answers. The only restriction is that you must obtain the information before the start of trial 3.

"Here now is the puzzle: What physiological or test information do you want, or what questions do you wish to ask of the child, that will enable you to predict whether or not he will solve the problem (i.e., will choose correctly on the last five trials)?

"Remember that you know nothing about S's problem. You are considering only cases where S is told 'wrong' on trial 2, and you must obtain the information before the start of trial 3. What information will aid in your prediction?"

One answer to this question is implied by the Sy analysis described in Readin No. 18. A test of this implication, derived from a pilot study just completed in my laboratory, is presented in the Addendum following the Reading.

Reading No. 18
HYPOTHESES, STRATEGIES, AND STEREOTYPES IN DISCRIMINATION LEARNING[*]

By Barry Gholson
Marvin Levine
Sheridan Phillips

While the assumptions of H theory have proven quite useful in the description of the behavior of the adult human, it has typically been assumed that the discrimination-learning behavior of children is best described by S-R continuity models of either the more conventional single link or mediational type (e.g., Dickerson, 1967; Eimas, 1967; Kendler & Kendler, 1962, 1968, 1969; Osler & Kofsky, 1965; Spiker, 1970; Zeaman & House, 1963). A few recent investigators have, however, begun to question the utility of the S-R models in describing the behavior of children. Weir and Stevenson (1959), for example, suggested that by about fourth grade children might begin to develop and test complex Hs in attempting to solve simple discrimination-learning problems. Others (Friedman, 1965; Harter, 1967; Ingalls & Dickerson, 1969) have also suggested that H testing begins at about the fourth grade level, and Eimas (1969) has proposed that even second graders might sometimes test Hs in solving these problems.

Eimas (1969) and Ingalls and Dickerson (1969) replicated Levine's (1966) experiment in research with children. Eimas' Ss were from grades 2, 4, 6 and 8; Ingalls' and Dickerson's were from grades 5, 8 and 10. Eimas reported that the mean percentages of blank-trial probes conforming to simple Hs were 71, 73, 77 and 79 for children of grades 2, 4, 6 and 8, respectively. Although each of these scores differed significantly from the chance level of 50%, these Ss were not showing H patterns with nearly the consistency of adults. Eimas also reported that, among second grade Ss, two successive Hs were the same only 60% of the time when feedback on the intervening trial was positive but this percentage increased with age (cf. Levine's 95% among adults). Further, he found that the probability of repeating an H following negative feedback was 15-18% among the school age

*Adapted from the *Journal of Experimental Child Psychology*, 1972, **13**, 423-446. Copyright 1972 by Academic Press, Inc. Reprinted by permission of the publisher.

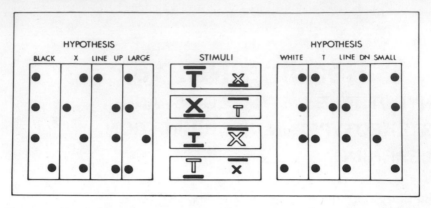

FIG. 1. A stimulus sequence which permits inference of the eight simple Hs from 3-1 patterns of responses (note that position is not one of the four specified dimensions).

children (cf. Levine's 2% among adults). Generally speaking, Ingalls and Dickerson (1969) obtained better performance from their fifth and eighth grade Ss as did Neussle (1971) among fifth and ninth grade children. Thus, recent research using blank-trial probes suggests some promise for adapting the technique to children. But, at least under the exact procedures employed by Levine (1966), H theory finds less support among children than among adults.

EXPERIMENT I

A careful analysis of the construction of the blank-trial probes used in the recent child research suggests a potential problem. In each study the response patterns corresponding to two of the simple Hs were position-alternation patterns. Also, position ("left" and "right" side) was a dimension used in each problem. Further, it is well-known that children are frequently observed to display spontaneously such response sets as position alternation and perseveration (See Fellows, 1968, for some of this literature), particularly in two-choice problems. Therefore, if these response sets are occurring in this research, they would be misinterpreted as simple Hs.

The design of Exp. I eliminated this confounding by using five-dimensional stimuli (cf. Fig. 1), by omitting the two positions from the set of solutions and by appropriate pretraining. In addition, simple Hs always corresponded to three responses to one side and one response to the other side (3-1 patterns). The four stimulus pairs in Fig. 1 contain this feature. With this type of blank-trial probe position-response sets are easily distinguished from simple Hs.

The present study differed from the related child research in still another way. The studies described above used relatively short problems containing only three or four feedback trials, with E saying "right" and "wrong" according to a prearranged schedule regardless of the child's response. Experiment I used a series of longer problems with real solutions, determined prior to S's appearance at the laboratory.

Method

Subjects.   The Ss were 50 second graders (mean CA = 7:6), 50 fourth graders (mean CA = 9:7), 50 sixth graders (mean CA = 11:6), and 50 college students (age 17-24 years). The elementary school children were drawn from the Scraggy Hill Elementary School in the semirural community of Port Jefferson on the north shore of Long Island. This population is predominantly middle class.

The Ss who participated in the experiment were required to solve at least two of four-pretraining problems. Seven Ss, six second graders and one fourth grader, were replaced for failure to meet this criterion.

Stimulus materials and equipment.   Each S was presented individually with a series of four-dimensional discrimination-learning problems using stimuli of the sort illustrated in Fig. 1. The same four dimensions were employed in each problem but each used a different pair of forms.

Stimuli were projected from behind a large interface which hid the apparatus from S's view. The stimuli appeared on two 4 × 5½-in. screens mounted 1¼ in. apart on the interface. The figures, when projected, were about 5 in. apart. The small figure was 1 in. high and the large figure 2 in. high.

Mounted ½-in. above each screen was a 4 × 2½-in. opaque cover which completely enclosed a red bulb. On feedback trials, as soon as S responded (touched one of the two screens), both covers lifted and the red light mounted over the correct stimulus was illuminated. The feedback lamp remained lit for 3 sec *with* the stimuli still in S's view. The feedback lamp was extinguished, the covers closed, and the stimuli disappeared from S's view simultaneously at the end of the 3-sec interval. On the blank trials the covers remained closed, and the stimuli were extinguished immediately upon S's response. The intertrial-interval was always 1 sec.

Pretraining.   In order to introduce the four bivalued dimensions and blank trials, a preliminary instruction and pretraining period preceded the main experiment. Upon receipt of the first pair of stimuli the eight Hs were described to S along with the response required on each trial, the mechanics of the covers, and the meaning of the feedback lamps. The first pretraining problem consisted of 16 feedback trials; the solution was "white." After completing the problem, S was asked to verbalize the solution. If he gave the correct solution he was told "very good" and went on to the next problem. If he did not give the correct H, the problem was re-presented and E gave a hint: The S was told to try the two colors, to see if the answer was either black or white. If the problem was not solved this time, the correct answer was stated and the next problem was presented. This procedure was continued throughout pretraining.

The second pretraining problem also consisted of 16 feedback trials. The answer was "large." The third pretraining problem introduced blank trials. It consisted of 16 feedback trials and eight blank trials. The S was told that on some trials the covers over the lights would not open, that E would still know if the response was correct, and that he (S) was to attempt always to be correct. The correct H was one of the forms. The last preliminary problem consisted of 16 feedback trials with 24 blank trials interspersed in sets of four. The solution was "line up."

   Experimental problems.   Each S then received a series of six 76-trial problems in which feedback was always presented every fifth trial from trial one through 76. Thus, there were 16 feedback trials and 15 sets of four blank trials.

   The stimuli for each problem were arranged with special restrictions (see Levine, 1966): Using the four relevant bivalued dimensions there are exactly eight different stimulus pairs possible. The pairs were arranged into two sets (Set A and Set B). In each set each level of each dimension is exactly counterbalanced with each level of every other dimension. Set A was used to construct blank-trial probes. The four stimulus pairs in each probe were arranged so that each of the eight simple Hs would yield a 3-1 response pattern, i.e., three responses to one side and one response to the other side (see Fig. 1). This arrangement eliminated any correspondence between the eight specified H patterns and response-set patterns (i.e., 2-2 and 4-0 patterns did not correspond to simple Hs). Set B stimuli were used for feedback trials. The problems were so constructed that each series of three feedback trials logically defined the solution H. Within the restrictions specified above, the stimuli of both sets were ordered randomly.

   The solution H for each problem was selected randomly from the eight possible Hs and S received feedback in accord with the predetermined solution. In each problem, S continued responding until he met a criterion of five successive correct feedback trials. He was then told the solution and presented with the next problem. If he did not reach criterion by the 76th trial, he was told the solution and began the next problem.

Results and Discussion

   Blank-trial data.   Data from the blank-trial probes fall into two classes: the eight (3-1) patterns dictated by the specified Hs (see Fig. 1), and the eight (2-2 and 4-0) patterns not consistent with those Hs. The mean percentage of consistent H patterns on blank-trial probes for grades two, four, and six, and for adults were 88.4, 89.3, 92.4 and 92.8, respectively. Each of these scores differed significantly from 50%, the score expected if Ss were generating responses randomly ($p < .001$ in all cases). Comparable percentages for just those blank-trial probes occurring prior to the (feedback) trial of the last error (abb. TLE) were examined. These percentages were 83.8, 84.0, 89.2 and 84.9 in order of increasing age. A single-classification analysis of variance revealed no significant effects due to age.

   Thus, the behavior of elementary school children, as well as adults, was strongly systematic. Some inconsistent patterns were observed, however, in each age group. A possible means of explaining the presence of these inconsistent patterns concerns the role of such response sets as position preference and position alternation. As noted above, children's choice responses in two-alternative learning situations are sometimes determined by these response sets. This suggested further scrutiny of the blank-trial probes in which inconsistent response patterns (2-2 and 4-0 patterns) were observed. These probes were separated into four discrete categories of left (L) and right (R) responses: (a) position perseveration (LLLL and RRRR); (b) position alternation (LRLR and RLRL); (c) doubles (LLRR and RRLL); and (d) residual (LRRL and RLLR). If these patterns were not being produced by any systematic process, then 25% of these patterns should fall into each of the four categories. If, on the other hand, these patterns were dictated by position alternation and perseveration response sets, virtually all inconsistent patterns should fall into these two categories.

The analysis revealed a small but significant category effect at each age level $(x^2(3) < 11.48, p < .01$, in all cases), reflecting a tendency for more inconsistent patterns to fall into the position-alternation category (about 36%) than in any of the other three. This suggests that some systematic responding was occurring during inconsistent blank-trial probes. On the other hand, there was about equal number of observations in the position perseveration (22%), doubles (19%), and residual (23%) categories. Thus, although there was some tendency for choice responses in inconsistent probes to alternate, response sets did not generally account for the inconsistent response patterns observed in the present study.

The effects of feedback. Commonly held assumptions of H theory are that S retains an H when given positive feedback following his choice response, but abandons his H and resamples following negative feedback. These assumptions can be examined in the present study by looking at all cases in which two consecutive blank-trial probes revealed consistent H patterns. The probability for each age group that two successive Hs were identical when the intervening feedback information was positive, $P(H_i = H_{i-1} \mid F_i = +)$, can be seen in the left column of Table 1. The number of observations upon which these probabilities were based ranged from 1105 to 1185. These data lend strong support to the usefulness in describing the behavior of children of the assumption that an H is retained when the choice response is followed by positive feedback information. The tendency to switch Hs following positive feedback, while small in each age group, decreased significantly with increasing age $(x^2(3) = 61.1, p < .01)$. Ingalls and Dickerson (1969) reported similar findings.

The probability that two successive Hs were the same given that the intervening feedback information was negative, $P(H_1 = H_{i-1} \mid F_1 = -)$, may be seen in the last column of Table 1. The number of observations upon which these probabilities were based ranged from 397 for adults to 854 for second graders. The overall age effect was significant, $(x^2(3) = 29.51, p < .01)$. There was no significant difference, however, between children in grades two, four and six. Thus, it

TABLE 1

The Proportion of Times That H_{i-1} Was Repeated When S's Feedback-Trial Response Was Correct ($F_i = +$) or Wrong ($F_i = -$)

Group	$P(H_i = H_{i-1}|F_i = +)$	$P(H_i = H_{i-1}|F_i = -)$
Grade two	.93	.08
Grade four	.94	.10
Grade six	.97	.07
Adults	.99	.01

appears that Ss at all age levels tend to abandon an H when feedback information is negative, but that children of elementary school age might tend to sample with replacement (Restle, 1962), i.e., might return a disconfirmed H to the total set of possible Hs before randomly resampling a new one. If this *zero memory* assumption is true, then, using stimuli with four bivalued dimensions, the expected probability of immediately repeating a disconfirmed H would be 12.5%. Support for this assumption that young children do sample with replacement comes from Eimas (1969), who reported that the probability of an S immediately repeating a disconfirmed H ranged from 15 to 18% and from Ingalls and Dickerson (1969), who reported a corresponding value of about 9%.

The appropriateness of the zero-memory assumption in the present study can be determined by a different approach. If on a given feedback trial an S were to choose the large, black, T, with a line on the top, and the feedback were negative, then all four of these Hs would be disconfirmed, not just the H that dictated the response. This would, in effect, reduce the set of possible correct Hs to four. An S who is *locally consistent* always resamples from among those Hs which were consistent with the stimulus that was positive on the last feedback trial. If the zero-memory assumption holds, on the other hand, then the H observed following negative feedback should be locally consistent only 50% of the time. The percentages of Hs that were locally consistent following negative feedback were 89.3, 87.9, 91.4 and 96.4 for grades two, four, six and adults, respectively. Each of these values differed significantly from the 50% value ($p < .001$, in each instance) predicted by the zero-memory assumption.

Thus, examination of two different average measures of memory for feedback-trial information among the elementary school children leads to two contradictory conclusions. On the one hand, these children appear to have forgotten the very H which was just tried and disconfirmed, resampling it with about the frequency expected if they were randomly resampling from the full set of eight Hs (zero memory). On the other hand, these same children appear to eliminate all four disconfirmed Hs 90% of the time following negative feedback (local consistency). Thus, the tendency to repeat an H given negative feedback must be explained in some way other than "zero" memory. One possibility is that a few Ss in each grade might have adopted a primitive style of responding. For example, any S who displayed a stimulus preference, i.e., an S whose choice responses were always dictated by a single H, independent of feedback, would always repeat an H following negative feedback. Examination of protocols of individual Ss suggested that this might be the case. Among the 150 school age children, 20 Ss accounted for 60% of the cases in which a disconfirmed H was immediately repeated following disconfirmation. At the other extreme, 72 Ss *never* repeated an H following negative feedback, and 32 more did so only once. Thus, at each age level a few Ss whose responses were determined by a stimulus preference, accounted—when averaged in with the remaining Ss—for the apparent applicability of the zero-memory assumption as a resampling rule. The remaining Ss, however, tended to resample Hs according to a local consistency rule. Some implications of this finding are treated more extensively below (see section on Hypothesis-Sampling Systems).

The results of Exp. 1 strongly support the conclusion that the assumptions of H theory provide a useful description of the behavior of young children, as well as of adults, in the discrimination learning problem. Several considerations, however, led to a further examination of the data. First, although Ss at all age levels behaved according to the assumptions of H theory, the proportion of problems solved varied with age. The percentages solved were 64.5, 70.3, 80.5 and 96.2 in order of increasing age. Second, as noted above, an odd contradiction appeared in the data. The elementary school children repeated a just-disconfirmed H so frequently that they appeared to resample with zero memory. But they were also locally consistent, i.e., resampled 90% of the time from among only the four Hs that were consistent with the positive stimulus on the preceding feedback trial. Finally, the individual S protocols suggested that the sequences of Hs from one blank-trial probe to the next were not haphazard, but appeared to be determined by specifiable problem-solving styles. These considerations led to the expansion of H theory which is treated in the next section.

Hypothesis-Sampling Systems: Strategies and Stereotypes

Blank-trial probes are used not merely to determine whether Ss use Hs in solving problems, or to collect facts about Hs, but to elucidate a theoretical conception about how Hs are used in solving discrimination-learning problems. This theory was developed to account for the behavior of adult humans (more specifically, college students) and has restrictive features appropriate to these Ss. For the most fruitful application of H theory to young children, these restrictions should be made explicit. First, the theory views S as processing information in an effort to arrive at the solution to the problem at hand. Thus, the H may be viewed as a prediction made by S about the behavior that will lead to solution. For example, S may predict that the large stimulus is the basis for choosing correctly. He would then test this H, or prediction, by choosing the large stimulus. If, after the choice response the feedback indicated that the response was correct, the prediction would be confirmed and the H retained for the next choice. If, on the other hand, the feedback was negative, the H would be disconfirmed and rejected, and a new H selected for the next choice response.

Early in the development of H theory, however, theorists (Fellows, 1968; Levine, 1963b; Reese, 1963) characterized another type of routine that S might follow. Consider, for example, an S who has a stimulus preference. He might choose the large stimulus for many trials not because he is testing the H "the solution is 'large'," but simply because he "likes" the large stimulus. Levine labeled these latter determinants of the behavior as *Response-set H*s (as opposed to the information-processing determinants, called *Prediction H*s). The key distinguishing feature between Response-set and Prediction Hs is behavioral. As noted above, Prediction Hs are sensitive to disconfirmations. Response-set Hs, on the other hand, are notoriously insensitive. Perusal of the literature on learning in children indicates that these Ss frequently show position-alternation, position-perseveration, or stimulus-preference Hs for long strings of responses despite repeated negative feedback.

As Levine (1963b, 1966, 1969b) demonstrated, however, such Response-set Hs are absent from the behavior of the adult human. Consequently, because modern H theory was developed to account specifically for adult behavior, no conception of Response-set Hs was included in current theories. In all major statements of H theory, then, the S is viewed as engaging in one general type of activity: He is processing information, i.e., testing out prediction Hs in an attempt to arrive at the solution. In order to describe the behavior of young children, however, the information processing conception must be supplemented to include Response-set Hs as well.

A second conception within contemporary H theory is that S may test more than one H at a time. As a consequence, theorists have attempted to estimate the number of Hs that S is sampling (cf. Levine, 1967; Trabasso & Bower, 1968). These measures, however, yield average values of the set size. Some Ss might eliminate one H per disconfirmation; others might eliminate all disconfirmed Hs at each trial. Instead, therefore, of seeking an average value, one might speculate that there are (at least) two systems, or strategies, in H processing. Bruner, Goodnow and Austin (1956) referred to their own version of these two strategies by characterizing Ss as "partists" and "wholists." Generally speaking, however, this distinction has not been universally maintained. In contemporary H theory S is viewed as working with some variable number, n, of Hs. The value of n is merely a parameter in an otherwise standard theory. Within this framework it is sensible to ask about average values of n.

When one works with children, however, the qualitatively different processes that are observed preclude simple averaging. As was seen earlier, when the zero-memory assumption was examined, ignoring stimulus preferences led to the erroneous conclusion that the children sampled a single H and forgot it as soon as it was disconfirmed. This was an indication that a model which ignored Ss' system of responding was at worst wrong and at best superficial. A survey of *S*s' protocols also suggested that the *H*s were occurring in other systematic sequences. These indications made questionable the assumption that *S*s choose randomly a set of *H*s of size *n*. The alternative is that *S*s' *H* selection follows some plan. With this view, *E*'s task is not to seek some average value of overall performance but to categorize performance on each problem in terms of the plan or *System* (abb. *Sy*) employed, where a *Sy* is defined as the determinant of the sequence in which *H*s are manifested.

If one wishes to categorize a performance according to certain features he first needs some technique that permits him to detect those features. If *S*s have different *Sy*s, how may these be detected? The technique is analogous to the method for detecting *H*s. An *H* is inferred from a sequence of responses. Similarly, a *Sy* may be inferred from a sequence of *H*s. Two extreme examples will illustrate the general logic. Consider first an *S* who starts a problem with a stimulus preference, e.g., for the "large stimulus." Consider, also, only those problems in which *S* received positive feedback on the first feedback trial and negative feedback on the next two (i.e., $F_1 = +$, $F_2 = -$, $F_3 = -$). One inspects the *H*s after each feedback trial. This hypothetical *S* (with a preference for large stimuli) will manifest "large" on H_1, H_2, and H_3. Conversely, from such a perseverative *H* sequence one infers a stimulus-preference *Sy*. At the other extreme, consider a maximally efficient *S* (referred to as a "focuser"), one who starts with all eight *H*s, eliminates four at F_1, two more at F_2, and the final incorrect *H* at F_3 leaving only the correct *H*, *H* +. For this *S*, H_1 will be consistent with the feedback information at F_1, H_2 will be different from H_1 and will be consistent with the information at both F_1 and F_2, and H_3 will be *H* +. When this pattern appears in the data, one infers a focusing *Sy*.

These, then, are two very different *Sy*s and their behavioral manifestations. What other *Sy*s may one look for? Unfortunately, there are no *a priori* rules specifying the various possible *Sy*s. They are undoubtedly different for different types of *S*s and for *S*s of different ages. A survey of *H* sequences in the various protocols of Exp. 1 suggested four *Sy*s. Table 2 contains the names, a brief description, and the manifestations of these four.

The first row shows Stimulus Preference, which has already been described.

The second row shows Hypothesis Checking. It is assumed here that the eight *H*s are ordered by *S* into the pairs of *H*s from each of the four dimensions, as though *S* imagines a list of the pairs of *H*s. He goes through this list, testing each *H* in turn, one dimension at a time. Thus, he tries an *H*, then, if it is disconfirmed, he tries its complement (op*H*, the opposite *H* on the same dimension). If that is disconfirmed he tries an *H* from another dimension, then its complement, etc. It is further assumed that the *H*s are sampled in a locally consistent manner, i.e., consistent with the information in the last disconfirming trial.

The third row shows Dimension Checking, a somewhat more sophisticated *Sy*. Here again *S*s proceed one dimension at a time, but they show what Erickson (1968) has termed "local nonreplacement and local consistency." Here, in

TABLE 2

The *Sys*, Their Definitions, and Manifestations (Note: H_i = an H from the ith Dimension; opH_i = the other H from the ith Dimension; H_j = an H from the jth Dimension; etc.)

SY	Definition	Example of manifestation							
		F_1	H_1	F_2	H_2	F_3	H_3	F_4	H_4
Stimulus preference	*S* stays with one *H* even though it is disconfirmed	+	H_i (Large)	—	H_i (Large)	—	H_i (Large)	—	H_i (Large)
Hypothesis checking	*S* checks all *eight hypotheses* systematically, one dimension at a time	+	H_i (Large)	—	opH_i (Small)	—	H_j (White)	—	opH_j (Black)
Dimension checking	*S* checks all *four dimensions* systematically, one dimension at a time	+	H_i (Large)	—	H_j (White)	—	H_k (Bar down)	—	H^+ (T)
Focusing	*S* eliminates immediately all logically disconfirmed *H*s	+	H_i (Large)	—	H_j (White)	—	$(H_k = H^+)$ (T)		

addition to local consistency, it is further assumed that when an H held is disconfirmed at or after the second feedback trial, S recognizes that it is logically impossible for the other H on the dimension to be correct. To put it another way, if some H, H_j, is held by S he can recognize that because H_j was consistent with the feedback at the time of its selection, its complement must of necessity have been inconsistent with the feedback at that time, and hence cannot be the solution. According to this Sy, then, S goes through the dimensions one at a time, manifesting only one H per dimension.

The bottom row of the table shows the Focusing Sy, which was described earlier. Using this Sy an S chooses Hs which are not only locally consistent but consistent with all the preceding feedback trials. The H after the third feedback trial is, of necessity, the solution.

It is worth noting that the four Sys of Table 2 divide into two classes. Just as Hs were divided (Levine, 1963b) into Predictions and Response-sets, so Sys may be analogously divided into Strategies and Stereotypes. A Strategy is a Sy based upon Prediction Hs, a Sy which, in principle, will ultimately lead S to the solution. The last three Sys in Table 2 all have this character. A Stereotype, on the other hand, is based upon Response-set Hs and lacks this solution-achieving feature. Here S persists in the same H despite repeated disconfirmations and will never (so long as he maintains this mode of behavior) arrive at the solution to the problem. Clearly, Stimulus Preference fits this description. Other Stereotypes will be considered in connection with Exp. 2.

The data from Exp. 1 were categorized into these four Sys. Before proceeding to these data, some qualifications should be noted. First, Table 2 shows sequences of four Hs, but this is for illustrative purposes. In general, the sequence of Hs should be long enough that the various Sys may be disentangled and short enough that the possibility that S changes Sys within the sequence is minimized. A sequence of three Hs meets these two criteria. Second, when the sequences consisting of the first three Hs are considered, there are sequences of Hs besides those shown in Table 2 which might occur (e.g., for the F sequence $+_1$, $-_2$, $-_3$, there are eight others: H_i, H_j, opH_j; or H_i, H_i, H_j; etc.). The existence of these sequences provides a kind of null hypothesis: If Hs are being randomly generated, the non-Sy sequences should occur at least as often as the Sy sequences described above. If, on the other hand, the present analysis is absolutely correct then only the four sequences shown in Table 2 should occur. The remaining eight should never occur. Finally, Table 2 uses the feedback sequence $+_1$, $-_2$, $-_3$. The analysis was performed for the four feedback sequences containing an error at the third trial.

Figure 2 contains the relative frequencies of the Sy sequences for the four groups. Each frequency distribution is based on about 90 problems. The three broken curves are from the elementary school children and are all similar. Among these three groups the only Sy which varies monotonically with age is Focusing but the differences here are no greater than the differences at the other Sys, which are not systematically ordered. These data suggest that 2nd-6th grade Ss approach

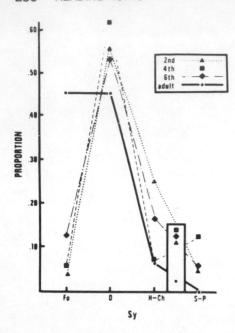

FIG. 2. The frequency distribut over the four *Sys*, ordered from to least sophisticated.

these problems in the same way. The only reservation to make to this surprising conclusion is that *S*s were screened during preliminary problems. Consistent with the procedure employed in previous studies, those *S*s who did not solve two of the preliminary problems were dropped from the study. Most (6 out of 7) of these were second-graders. This screening procedure would obviously tend to equalize the groups. The next study eliminates the effects (quite minor, as will be seen) of this screening procedure.

That the peaked curve of the groups of children is not an inevitability of the method is seen by the solid black line, representing the adults. These *S*s show only Strategies (Stimulus Preference never occurred), with Focusing the modal *Sy* and the two most efficient *Sys* appearing on more than 90% of the problems. The adults differ clearly and sensibly from the elementary school children, who do not appear to differ much among themselves.

Another datum concerns the residual *H* sequences, those which did not reflect any of these four *Sys*. With one exception these virtually never occurred (each occurred about one time per hundred problems). However, one sequence, H_i, H_j, opH_i (given $-_2$, $-_3$), occurred with appreciable frequency in each of the three groups of children. Its relative frequency is shown in the insert in Fig. 2 between Hypothesis Checking and Stimulus Preference. Its potential significance was investigated further in Exp. 2. Despite this one puzzling wrinkle, the results of the *Sy* analysis were sufficiently well ordered to compel confidence that the routine underlying *H* testing may be detected from the *H* sequence. Experiment 2 was designed, in part, as a further investigation of the *Sy* analysis.

EXPERIMENT 2

Experiment 1 demonstrated the general usefulness of H theory in describing the behavior of elementary school children (as young as 7 years) in discrimination-learning problems. One purpose of Exp. 2 was to explore the usefulness of this theoretical conception of behavior with even younger (5-year-old) children. Another purpose was to examine further the Sy analysis described above.

As noted above, earlier research led to the expectation that many of the response patterns observed in the blank-trial probes of Exp. 1 might be dictated by position-alternation and perseveration Response-set Hs. The experimental results, however, were not consistent with that expectation. It is possible that by second grade the dominance of such Response-set Hs is reduced. On the other hand, younger (e.g., 5-year-old) children might show such response patterns with some frequency. This consideration suggested that a radical change in the Sy distribution might occur between kindergarten children and second graders. Accordingly, Exp. 2 was planned for purposes of comparing these two groups.

Another possible reason for the low frequency of Response-set Hs among the second graders of Exp. 1 was that six Ss had been eliminated for failure to meet a pretraining criterion. It was thought that these Ss' responses might have been determined by such Response-set Hs and that this had led to their rejection. Therefore, no Ss were eliminated from Exp. 2 because of pretraining criteria.

The Ss in this second experiment received problems basically similar to those in Exp. 1. Thus, each S received preliminary training problems with instructions about the eight possible solutions, followed by the series of experimental problems containing blank-trial probes. There were, however, certain important differences incorporated in the present procedures, differences which, it was hoped, would facilitate the Sy analysis. A Sy emerges from the sequence of Hs which appear after Ss receive negative feedback. A series of such negative feedback trials are ideal in this respect. In order, therefore, to collect data most efficiently for the Sy analysis the problems were short and feedback was "preprogrammed": No matter which response S made it was characterized as wrong during the first few feedback trials of most of the problems.

Method

Except as described below, the method of Exp. 2, including instructions and pretraining, was identical to Exp. 1.

Subjects. The Ss were 48 second grade (mean CA = 7:4) and 48 kindergarten children (mean CA = 5:4) who were students at Scraggy Hill Elementary School in Port Jefferson, NY. No S had participated in any of the previous research.

Experimental problems. The first nine experimental problems were each 25 trials long. Trials 5, 10, 15, 20 and 25 were feedback trials. Blank-trial probes like the one in Fig. 1 were presented before each feedback trial.

Feedback was preprogrammed. Six sequences of positive feedback ($+$, the light over the selected stimulus flashed on) and negative feedback ($-$, the light over the other, nonselected, stimulus flashed on) were developed. The sequences $----+$, $---++$, and $+++++$ were each assigned to two problems; the sequences $++-++$, $+--++$, and $-+-++$ were each assigned to one problem. The order in which these nine problems were presented was randomized separately for each S at each age level.[1]

Results and Discussion

Blank-trial data.   There were 2,160 blank-trial probes at each age level. Second grade children generated consistent H patterns on 80.1% of these. This score, which differed significantly from the chance level of 50% ($z = 27.88$, $p <$ .001), compared favorably with the corresponding second-grade datum of Exp. 1. The percentage of consistent Hs among kindergarten children was 42.0, which was significantly below chance expectation ($z = 11.15$, $p < .001$).

In order to determine the extent to which the choice responses of the kindergarten Ss were determined by position-alternation and position-perseveration Response-set Hs, the 1,254 inconsistent blank-trial probes were analyzed into the four possible categories. These categories and the percentage of observations in each were: (a) position perseveration (LLLL or RRRR), 25.6%; (b) position alternation (LRLR or RLRL), 58.5%; (c) doubles (LLRR or RRLL), 4.7%; and (d) residual (LRRL or RLLR), 11.1%. Thus, taken together, position perseveration and alternation accounted for 84.2% (1,056 of 1,254) of the inconsistent blank-trial probes, while the two remaining categories, taken together, accounted for only 15.8%. Results of a similar classification of the inconsistent patterns among second graders were essentially identical to Exp. 1. It appears, then, that the kindergarten Ss' inconsistent response patterns were not generated randomly, but instead, were determined by Response-set Hs.

The effects of feedback.   The second graders responded in the same way to positive and negative feedback as in Exp. 1. These Ss maintained an H 89.3% of the time when feedback was positive and 10.7% of the time when feedback was negative. Among the kindergarten Ss, the simple Hs observed in two consecutive blank-trial probes were the same 78.8% of the time when intervening feedback was positive. The H was also maintained 45.6% of the time when intervening feedback was negative, clearly beyond the 12.5 stipulated by "zero" memory.

The present problems contained a blank-trial probe (H_0) prior to the first feedback trial. With this procedure one can determine the degree to which second grade children categorize Hs in terms of dimensions. If dimensionality does direct choice responses among these Ss, then in the sequence H_0, $F_1 = -$, H_1, the new H should tend to be the complement of the initial H. If, on the other hand, children of

[1] A final problem presented each S was not included in the data analysis. In this problem, S was given only positive feedback and was assured throughout by E that his performance was very good.

this age do not work with dimensions but choose randomly from the four locally consistent Hs, then the expected value would be 25%.

The observed value was 53.3% which differed significantly from chance ($p <$ .001). This result compares favorably with similar findings reported for adult Ss (Andrews, Levinthal & Fishbein, 1969; Gumer & Levine, 1971). It appears, then, that second grade children do, as suggested by mediational (e.g., Kendler & Kendler, 1962) and attentional (e.g., Zeaman & House, 1963) theory, categorize Hs in terms of dimensions.

Sy analysis.   Because position alternation and perseveration did not occur with any appreciable frequency among the elementary school children and adults of Exp. 1, the only Stereotype described in Table 2 was Stimulus-Preference. However, the analysis of inconsistent response patterns by kindergarten children, and inspection of individual S protocols indicated that the Sy analysis described in Table 2 should be expanded to include Position-Alternation and Position-Perseveration Sys. The same criteria were used in assigning H sequences into these Sy categories as with the other Sy categories: The Sy had to appear throughout H_1, H_2, and H_3; $F_3 = -$; etc.

Figure 3 contains the relative frequencies of each of the six Sy sequences for each age group. The abscissa of Figure 3 may be thought of as a continuum of Sy sophistication, ranging from the most effective Strategy (Focusing, Fo), to the least appropriate Stereotypes [Position-Alternation (P-A) and Position-Perseveration (P-P)]. The chief result, of course, is that the two distributions scarcely overlap. The second grade Ss show basically the same distribution as the corresponding group in Exp. 1 despite the differences in procedure, *viz.*, no Ss were screened out this time, feedback was preprogrammed and the problems were shorter. The kindergarten children, on the other hand, approach these problems in a dramatically different fashion. They show steady stereotypic responding not only within problems but on practically all (94%) of the problems. Whether this inappropriate style of responding is inevitable by such young children is a question for future research. The possibility of training such Ss to use Strategies, i.e., the possibility of shifting the distribution to the left, will be explored.

In general, only Sy sequences tended to occur. The chief exception again was H_i, H_j, opH_i, shown in the insert. The second-grade children showed this pattern about as often as before. The fact that this sequence is produced only by the older school children but not by either kindergarten children or adults (cf. Fig. 2) suggests that it reflects some bona fide but primitive or imperfectly performed Strategy.

CONCLUSIONS

The chief argument of this essay is for an expansion of H theory. As it developed during the last decade, the theory contained two tacit restrictions: that S sampled Hs randomly (or indifferently among those not rejected) and that these Hs

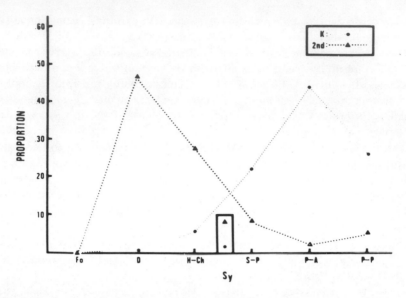

Fig. 3. The frequency distributions over the *Sy*s for the kindergarten (K) and second grade (2nd) *S*s.

were always Predictions. The proposed revision has *S* sampling *H*s not randomly, but according to some plan or general determinant here called a *Sy*. The revision also assumes that the *H*s may be manifestations of Response-sets as well as of Predictions.

This new conception permitted the development of a technique for inferring the *Sy* occurring on a particular problem. This, in turn, permitted a fine-grain analysis which revealed reasonable and illuminating developmental changes. Thus, kindergarten children showed primarily Stereotypes related to position, a dimension which had been explicitly eliminated from the problems. Elementary school children showed some Stereotypes but these were primarily to the dimensions specified as possibly relevant. These *S*s also manifested an inefficient Strategy (Hypothesis Checking) and rarely showed the most efficient Strategy. The college students, on the other hand, revealed virtually nothing but the two most efficient *Sy*s. Replicating earlier findings, they never showed any Stereotypes.

The results are clearly sensible and attest to the promise of the enlarged *H* theory. There are, however, some attendant problems which may be noted in closing. First, whereas the task and *Sy* analysis distinguished decisively between kindergarten pupils, older children and college students, few systematic differences appeared among the second, fourth and sixth grade *S*s. It may be that differences will appear with more sensitively designed experiments, but one must await those experiments. Second, the *Sy* conception has *S* proceeding through the set of *H*s perfectly according to some rule. No qualifications were placed upon his performance other than to limit the observation to a short (three-*H*-probe) sample of his behavior. Specifically, no forgetting or break in the routine was allowed for, at least through the first three probes. This, on the face of things, seems unrealistic particularly in the light of Ingall's and Dickerson's finding, that children do not generally remember (manifest) all the stimulus dimensions. An obvious next step in the development of the theory is to detect not only S's mode of systematically selecting Hs but the subset of Hs to which he confines himself. The third problem may be a consequence of the failure to integrate with the Sy analysis the possibility that S forgets dimensions. One sequence not stipulated by any of the Sys (H_i, H_j, opH_i) recurred in the two experiments. It may reflect an S who is working with (i.e., remembers) only two dimensions or who, after F_3, has forgotten that he tried the ith dimension. In either case it adds to the conviction that a theoretical synthesis of memory and Sy processes will be fruitful. Finally, it may be noted that the method of analysis is cumbersome. Because a Sy is inferred from a sequence of three consecutive Hs, S must make 15 consecutive choice responses consistent with his Sy in order for the appropriate inference to be made. Many problems are unusable because the feedback sequence is inappropriate or because S was distracted and accidentally responded incorrectly. As a consequence, typically less than half the problems are classifiable.

Because of these considerations the analysis presented above is intended as an introductory statement rather than as a definitive conception. It is hoped that its promise will stimulate further development of the theory and streamlining of the technique.

ADDENDUM TO CHAPTER 9

We are now prepared to consider the puzzle presented earlier in this chapter.

One difficulty with the Sy analysis described in Reading No. 18 is that it is cumbersome. First, before a problem can be categorized several conditions must hold: S must be told "wrong" at F_3 and, for strategies, the Hs must be interpretable and locally consistent. These requirements reduce the number of classifiable problems to about one-third of all problems presented. Second, the large number of blank trials take time and limit the number of problems that may be presented. A more efficient probe seemed desirable. Sheridan Phillips, a graduate assistant in our child research since its inception, explored having children state Hs in place of the blank-trial probe.* This technique, if successful, would permit presentation of many more problems per S. She first tried out this technique with two groups of Ss, second- and sixth-grade children. Preliminary data appeared promising. More germane to the present analysis, these data provided one answer to the puzzle presented above.

The rows of Table 2 in Reading No. 18 are ordered according to increasing

*Phillips' Ph.D. thesis, which is devoted to a systematic study of this topic, will be duly reported elsewhere.

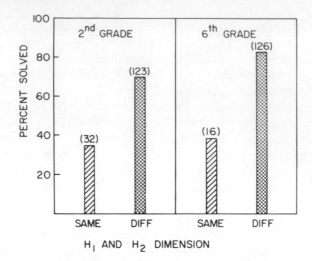

F<small>IG</small>. 3. The percentage of problems solved by second- and sixth-grade children when H_1 and H_2 came from the same dimension or from different dimensions. The number above each bar shows the number of problems in that category.

sophistication. The Sys in the top two rows are relatively primitive; those in the bottom two rows are quite efficient. Note that in the top two rows the Hs before and after $F_2 = -$ (i.e., H_1 and H_2) are both from the same dimension. With the more efficient Sys, however, H_1 and H_2 come from different dimensions. One answer to the puzzle, then, is to ask S two questions: Just before F_2 ask S, "What do you think the solution is?" Ask the same question again just after F_2. (Remember, we are considering only problems with $F_2 = -$.) According to the theory, if both answers refer to the same dimension, S is following an inefficient Sy and should be unlikely to solve the problem; if both come from different dimensions S should be likely to solve the problem.

All protocols with $F_2 = -$ were selected out. For each grade, the percentage of problems solved when H_1 and H_2 came from the same dimension was compared to the percentage solved when H_1 and H_2 came from different dimensions. This comparison is shown separately for each grade in Fig. 3. It is seen there that when H_1 and H_2 are from the same dimension the Ss solve half as many problems as when H_1 and H_2 are from different dimensions. The result is the same for both grades. It is possible, then, to tell from information quite early in the problem how S will perform on that problem. The expanded theory of Reading No. 18 pointed to the critical information.

The apparent similarity between the second- and sixth-grade results is intriguing. The percentage solved in each H_1 - H_2 condition is about the same in both age groups. It would appear that a primitive Sy leads S to poor performance regardless of his age. The S is either "with it" or is not. This is not to say that the sixth graders as a group are equal to second graders. Above each bar in Fig. 3 is the total number of problems in the particular category. It is seen there that, compared to the second-grade problems, a much larger proportion of the sixth-grade problems had H_1 and H_2 from different dimensions. Thus, the sixth graders are more likely to show a sophisticated $H_1 - H_2$ sequence. The data suggest, however, that those (few) sixth graders who start the problem badly are no more likely to solve than their second-grade counterparts.

10
WHEN S FAILS TO LEARN

The initial experiments employing the blank-trial probe (Readings No. 14 and 15—see Chapter 7) led to two lines of research. On the one side was the variety of probe applications, described in the preceding two chapters. On the other side, research was stimulated by the curious finding described in Reading No. 15: In the two-response task, Ss who had not yet solved the problem were choosing the correct alternative much less than half the time. The next two chapters will describe the research that evolved from this result.

Whereas this finding was reported with appropriate scientific austerity, its discovery was less formal. While I was running one of the Ss, a shy freshman who was not solving one of the problems, a note of embarrassment crept into an otherwise impersonal situation. I was telling her that she was wrong much too often. She appeared to be so bad at the task that she couldn't even guess correctly—I worried, at any rate, that she might be feeling something like this. Fortunately, she solved the succeeding problems. That brief emotional interaction alerted me, however, to something peculiar that was happening. A scan of all our available data confirmed the odd fact that during unsolved problems Ss chose correctly between the two alternatives less than 40% of the time. This fact prompted a return to the theory in search of an explanation.

This *precriterion suppression* could be derived (1) by assuming that S tests Hs according to well-documented routines (primarily that S keeps confirmed Hs, rejects disconfirmed Hs, and holds neither the solution H nor its compliment before the TLE—these processes were demonstrated in Readings No. 14 and 15) and (2) by using my thoroughly counterbalanced stimulus sequences (it will be recalled that S received "internally orthogonal," rather than random, stimulus sequences). Rudimentary examples of the derivations may be found in the Discussion of Reading No. 15.

In deriving the effect, my concern, of course, was with pre-TLE performance. The problem was to derive the probability of a correct response on trial n given that S made an error on some later trial. Two considerations, however, caused me to shift from such data, i.e., from normal problems that S solves late (or doesn't solve), to insoluble problems. First, I found it congenial to think of the nonsolving S as having forgotten—or in some way having blocked out—the relevant dimension. It was as though "large" were the solution but the difference between large and small size was virtually indiscriminable. I started to toy with that conceit, imagining a 4-D problem in which the large stimulus was 1.0 inch and the small stimulus was .99 inch, with "large" the solution. Such a problem would be clearly insoluble. Most importantly, the theorems that applied to precriterion behavior should obviously also apply to behavior in this problem. Technically, the S (unless he thought to take a ruler and measure the stimuli) would always be in the "precriterion" state.

The second consideration that encouraged the use of insoluble problems was suggested by a mathematician acquaintance. I was discussing with him the derivation of the precriterion performance curve, i.e., of the probability of a correct response given that S made an error at some later trial. This arrangement of having an event (the probability of a correct precriterion response) conditional upon an event later in time (the subsequent error) troubled him. He suggested that the derivation would be simpler if everything could move forward in time. As mentioned above, I had already contemplated the theoretical identity between S in the precriterion state and S in an insoluble problem of the sort described above. I further recognized that with insoluble problems one avoided this conceptually awkward stipulation "given a subsequent error." I decided, therefore, to test the theory by using insoluble problems.

Another virtue of insoluble problems was that precriterion responding now came under E's control. He didn't have to wait for S to fail to solve a problem. As a consequence all Ss contributed "precriterion" data, not just the poor Ss. This apparently minor consideration made possible the test of an interesting theorem. According to the theory, the better an information processor S is—the faster he solves normal, soluble problems—the worse he should do on these insoluble problems. This theorem is expressed in Fig. 1 of Reading No. 19, which shows that the better S's assumed memory (i.e., the greater the number of incorrect Hs S can reject at each trial) the lower the predicted percent correct.

It would be hard to test this theorem if one had to rely on S failing to solve normal problems: The best Ss would rarely fail to solve a problem. All Ss, however, could provide insoluble-problem data. The obvious experiment required that an occasional insoluble problem be inserted in a long sequence of soluble problems. Good and poor Ss could be separated, based upon the soluble-problem data. The theorem, that the better Ss would do worse on the insoluble problems, could be tested by observing the performance of these two subgroups on the insoluble problems. Reading No. 19 describes the use of insoluble problems and the test of this theorem.

After this article was published, I began to feel that I had been a bit too casual in assuming that precriterion responding and insoluble-problem responding were equivalent. Demonstrating the similarity between both kinds of responding would be a small step, but one worth taking. A then student of mine, William Glassman, and I planned a study to compare these two types of behavior. This investigation seemed, at first, relatively perfunctory. Lurking around this experiment, however, were certain conceptual enigmas that had been haunting me since the discovery of the precriterion suppression Consider an S who continues to make errors for several (e.g., 20) trials of a normal, i.e., soluble, problem. I characterized this S as sampling, during the precriterion trials, from a domain of Hs having two properties: It does not contain the Hs from the relevant dimension, and it is small (6 Hs in 4-D problems; 14 Hs in 8-D problems).* Thus S is sampling from a small domain of Hs, all of which are incorrect. It frequently happened that such an S ultimately solved the problem. What prompted him to break out of that incorrect set? Suppose S tested all the Hs in the incorrect domain and came to recognize that they were, in fact, all incorrect. The incorrect domain would, so to speak, become empty. What would S do next? Suppose the incorrect domain were very large. Is it possible that sampling of the correct H would be inordinately retarded? An earlier experiment (Ress & Levine, 1966), concerning Einstellung in discrimination learning, suggested that that would indeed be the case.

The theoretical framework for answering these questions began to take shape at the time that Glassman and I were working out the comparison between presolution and insoluble-problem behavior. This experimental comparison soon became embedded in a significant enlargement of H theory. The experiment and the expanded conception are described in Reading No. 20.

*I was still thinking of the S during precriterion responding as having "forgotten" the relevant dimension. This is not intended as hard theory. At the time, however, I found it fruitful.

Reading No. 19
THE PRESOLUTION PARADOX IN
DISCRIMINATION LEARNING *

By Marvin Levine
    Robert M. Yoder
    Joel Kleinberg
    Jay Rosenberg

Levine (1966), in an analysis of H behavior during discrimination learning, employed stimuli varying in form, color, size, and location. The sequence of stimuli were internally orthogonal, i.e., during four consecutive feedback trials each letter was black twice, large stimuli were on the right-hand side twice, etc. Levine, Miller, and Steinmeyer (1967), using these stimuli, discovered an unexpected property in the choice behavior of adult humans: prior to the trial of the last error (TLE) the probability of a correct choice was .38, significantly less than .5.

It is possible to show that the commonly held assumptions of H theory predict this performance suppression. These assumptions are[1]:

1. The S, in trying to solve a problem, selects an H from some set and responds on the basis of that H. For example, S may predict that "large" is the correct basis for choosing. He would, then, choose the side containing the larger form.

2. Given demonstration problems and appropriate instructions, S samples only from the Hs corresponding to the stimulus levels. Thus, S predicts that large, or x, etc., is correct. He does not employ Hs about conjunctions of cues or about complex sequences.

3. During presolution responding S samples neither the correct H nor the other H on the same dimension. Thus, if "right side" is the solution, before the TLE S tries neither the H right side nor left side. Before the last error S may be regarded as sampling from, at most, the remaining six Hs.

4. If S's response is followed by a positive outcome (e.g., E says "correct") he keeps his H for the next trial.

---

[1]Although these are listed here as assumptions they all have direct empirical support. See Levine (1966) and Levine et al. (1967) for the experimental results.

*Adapted from *Journal of Experimental Psychology,* 1968, **77,** 602-608. Copyright 1968 by the American Psychological Association. Reprinted by permission of the publisher.

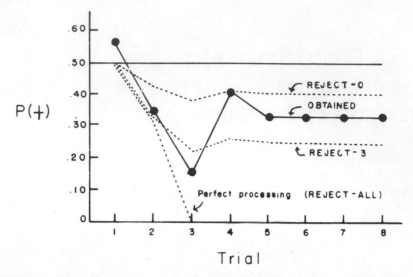

FIG. 1. Theoretical (dashed lines) and obtained (solid line) curves of performance during insoluble problems.

5. If S's response is followed by a negative outcome (e.g., E says "wrong") he abandons his last H and resamples. He might do this in several ways, all of them falling along a continuum of amount remembered. These alternatives will be considered for S prior to the TLE, when he is sampling among six Hs (cf. assumption 3, above). (a) the Reject-0 assumption: at one extreme S may remember nothing, not even the H he just rejected. He would, in effect, return this H to the set and, before the TLE, resample from the full set of six Hs. This is the assumption made by Restle (1962) and by Bower and Trabasso (1964); (b) the Reject-1 assumption: he may remember that this one H is wrong and resample without replacement, i.e., from among five Hs; (c) the Reject-3 assumption: he might notice that the negative outcome following his response logically disqualified as many as three Hs. Following any error he resamples from a reduced, but fixed, number of Hs. This is similar to the assumption by Trabasso and Bower (1966); and (d) the Reject-all assumption: in addition to the Hs disqualified by a "wrong," he might remember additional Hs disqualified on earlier trials and could, therefore, reduce the set still further. At the extreme his memory would be perfect and he would sample only from the set of logically correct Hs. This would correspond to the performance of focusers as described by Bruner, Goodnow, and Austin (1956, pp. 129-134).

Applying this theory to problems with internally orthogonal stimuli yields the prediction that S will be correct on less than 50% of the presolution trials (see Levine et al., 1967). This prediction holds for all variants of Assumption 5. A second prediction is that the better S's memory, as characterized by the scale of Assumption 5, the worse he will do. These predictions are represented by the family of theoretical curves in Fig. 1. The present experiments were designed to test these two predictions.

An inadequacy with presolution data is that they heavily represent slow learning. For example, protocols with no or only one error cannot be used. A better technique, which does not exclude data and for which the five assumptions, above, are applicable, is to rely on insoluble problems. During such problems the solution depends upon a hidden dimension, i.e., upon one which is not represented is S's H set. All Ss are in the presolution stage throughout the whole problem.

EXPERIMENT I

During this experiment the hidden dimension was established by instructions. The S was told only about the form, color, and size dimensions. Nothing was said about the positions as possible solutions. Also, to enhance the instructions, several problems were first presented in which one of the six stipulated Hs was the solution. It was felt that after these instructions and preliminary problems S would have an H set consisting of the six instructed Hs (cf. Assumption 3).

A methodological problem exists with this technique. During an insoluble problem an S could conceivably learn and remember that all six Hs were disconfirmed. In other words, he could, after a few trials, have an empty set. Two problems with this situation are that H theory has no assumptions to cover it and, less formally, that S would recognize that the rules given in the instructions were not holding. To avoid such perfect information processing by S the trials, rather than being S-paced, were presented at a 2-sec rate. This turned out to be a satisfactory solution to the problem.

Method

Subjects.   Forty-four undergraduates served as Ss. Twenty of these were volunteers from the beginning psychology course; 24 were paid Ss attending the summer session.

Materials.   A Kodak Carousel slide projector presented the stimuli. An Atcotrol timer controlled the projector so that slides could be presented at a 2-sec rate. Slides were constructed of four-dimensional stimuli similar to those employed by Levine (1966). The slides were arranged into sets of eight, each such set comprising the materials for a problem. The eight slides were grouped into two sets of four internally orthogonal stimuli so that they had these characteristics throughout: no dimension could be correlated with any other dimension for more than two trials and only one pair of dimensions was so correlated for two trials. Opaque slides were placed after each set of eight to mark the end of one problem and the start of the next.

Procedure.   A sample slide was shown and three dimensions, the two letters, the two sizes, and the two colors, were pointed out (the two positions were never mentioned). The S was told that he would receive some short problems in which a series of such slides would be shown, that he always had to choose one of the two alternatives by saying one of the two letters, and that he would always be informed

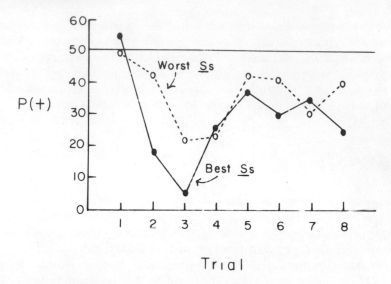

FIG. 2. Performance by the 10 best and the 10 worst *S*s (defined by the number of soluble problems solved) on the insoluble problems.

whether he had made the correct response. The correct response, he was told, would always depend upon one of the six attributes. He was further instructed that the slides would appear at a fast rate and that he was to respond rapidly. Three sample problems were then presented, the three described dimensions each contributing one of the solutions. After these three problems *S*'s questions were answered and the six solutions reiterated.

The experimental problems followed. The first five had legitimate solutions, the sixth had a position solution. Following this, five more series of six problems each were presented, five with a legitimate solution, one with a position solution. There were, then, 30 legitimate eight-trial problems and 6 insoluble eight-trial problems (Four *S*s solved one of these 6 insoluble problems. These were discarded. The next experiment eliminates the need for even this small degree of selection.) The 2-sec rate posed no problems. The *S*s virtually always responded (the probability of no responses was less than .01) and *E* always said "right" or "wrong" within the 2-sec interval.

Results

Figure 1 shows three theoretical curves and the obtained curve. The theoretical curves embody the two predictions: (*a*) all versions predict below chance responding starting at Trial 2, and (*b*) the better the processing the worse the predicted performance. Note, also, that the curve for the Reject-all assumption stops at Trial 3. At this trial the perfect processor, having eliminated all six Hs, will face an empty set. H theory has no assumptions for this contingency.

The first prediction is confirmed by the data in Fig. 1. The obtained curve, averaged for all 40 Ss on the six insoluble problems, clearly shows below chance responding and tends to fluctuate between the Reject-0 and Reject-3 condition.

The second prediction may be tested by comparing the function for the best and poorest information processors. The best and worst may be independently specified on the basis of performance during the soluble problems. Those 10 Ss showing the most solutions and those 10 showing the fewest solutions during the soluble problems were separated out. Performance on the insoluble problems was then plotted separately for the two groups. As demonstrated in Fig. 2 the better Ss show greater performance suppression on Trials 2 and 3 than the poorer Ss. This difference, significant at the .01 level for each of the two trials, verifies the second prediction. Note also that the better Ss are virtually perfect information processors (cf. the Reject-all curve in Fig. 1). This means that after the first two trials they rejected all but one H, the one correlated with the correct position on Trials 1 and 2. This H, of necessity, leads to an error on the third trial and is also disconfirmed. These Ss, then, by Trial 3 have eliminated all six Hs as possible solutions. If one assumes that S "recycles" and starts checking the six Hs again, it is apparent that he does so with reduced efficiency. From Trial 4 on, his performance is like that of the poorer Ss.

EXPERIMENT II

The preceding experiment verified the two predictions of H theory but had certain imperfections. First, because six-H problems are so simple for college students, a compensatory difficulty was added by presenting the stimuli at a peculiarly high (2 sec.) rate. Second, the assumption that one could eliminate a dimension by instructions alone was not entirely perfect; four Ss, it will be recalled, solved an "insoluble" problem. Finally, the experiment was run with stimuli for which the prediction of performance-suppression was already found to hold (Levine et al., 1967). Some demonstration of the generality of the effect is clearly desirable. These three considerations suggested the use of problems with more dimensions. These not only permit presentation of the stimuli at a more usual pace but change the stimuli and stimulus sequences with which the phenomenon was discovered. Finally, by defining the correct response for each trial on the basis of a dimension which is subsequently removed, a genuine insoluble problem is created.

Method

[Omitted here is an experiment consisting of 8-D soluble problems and 7-D insoluble problems. The results shown in Figs. 1 and 2 were replicated.   M. L.]

DISCUSSION

The present data confirm the two predictions of the H theory previously outlined. With internally orthogonal stimulus sequences presolution (or insoluble problem) performance is impaired. The better the S the more it is impaired. Since this impairment does not occur when randomized stimulus sequences are employed (Bower & Trabasso, 1964; Erickson, Zajkowski, & Ehmann, 1966) the effect would appear to depend upon the restrictions of the stimulus sequences, i.e., the orthogonality. With the stimuli of the present experiments no dimension could be correlated with any other dimension for more than two (Exp. I) or three (Exp. II) trials. In particular, no dimension is correlated for very long with the correct (hidden) dimension and any H very quickly leads to an error. With randomized stimuli irrelevant dimensions are correlated with the correct dimension for runs of varying length. Thus, one can hold the incorrect H and still make the correct response for several consecutive trials. The number of correct responses produced when dimensions are correlated for several trials would offset the decrement in performance when dimensions alternate frequently with the correct one. This suggests that the level of presolution responding found in these and the other experiments follows a general rule: the more correlated the dimensions with the correct (or hidden) dimension the higher will be the level of presolution (or insoluble problem) responding.

Reading No. 20
HYPOTHESIS THEORY AND NONLEARNING DESPITE IDEAL S-R-REINFORCEMENT CONTINGENCIES*

By Marvin Levine

A college student appears at the laboratory and is given a simple learning task. He is instructed to respond to each of a series of stimuli with any one of a limited set of responses. After some (preselected) response the experimenter (*E*) says "right," after the others he says "wrong." The well-known experimental result is that the selected response increases in relative frequency.[1] For more than half a century this finding has been so ubiquitous that it has been twice codified, as the Law of Effect and as the Reinforcement Principle.

The phenomenon, however, is not absolutely reliable. There are at least two classes of results indicating that learning does not always take place. The first comes from studies concerned with the role of awareness in learning. Several authors (e.g., Dulaney, 1961; Spielberger & DeNike, 1966) have identified subsets of subjects (*S*s) showing no change in response probability throughout the task. The second comes from investigations of transfer of learning from a first to a second discrimination problem (e.g., the reversal-shift procedure). The authors typically report the elimination of several *S*s who, after an inordinately long number of trials, still had not learned the first problem. It appears, then, that nonlearning certainly occurs. The experiments below will demonstrate that it occurs even with well-motivated *S*s for whom all the relevant information is available and unambiguous. The purpose of this article, however, is not merely to

---

[1]More typically, *E* says "right" only to certain responses in the presence of certain stimuli. For example, *E* may say "right" to *S*'s response "alpha" only if triangles are part of the stimulus complex. Otherwise he says "right" only to the response "beta." While it is always more accurate to speak of *E*'s feedback as contingent on certain responses *in the presence of certain stimuli*, the italicized phrase will generally be omitted. It should, however, be understood as given throughout.

*Adapted from *Psychological Review*, 1971, **78**, 130-140. Copyright 1971 by the American Psychological Association. Reprinted by permission of the publisher.

FIG. 1. A simultaneous-discrimination stimulus constructed from eight dimensions (letter, A-T; letter size, large-small; letter color, black-white; underline, solid-dashed; border shape, circle-square; border number, one-two; border texture, solid-dashed; spots, one-two).

substantiate this finding, but to present a theory which accounts for this and related results.

Hypothesis theory has been vigorously developed in recent years. Some detailed specifications of the theory will be given below, along with a review of the data on which the specifications are based. However, it will be useful first to have a clear description of the initial task to which the theory will be applied.

Several 12-trial multidimensional simultaneous-discrimination problems were constructed. Each trial was initiated by the display of two stimulus patterns (cf. Figure 1). One pattern consisted of a set of values from each of eight two-valued dimensions; the other pattern consisted of the complementary values of the dimensions. From trial to trial the dimension values shifted from one pattern to the other so that on some trial the T might be large, surrounded by one solid circle, etc. The shifting of values from trial to trial followed these rules: (*a*) on each pair of adjacent trials, values from four dimensions remained paired together (i.e., were on the same side for both trials) while the values from the other four dimensions were changed (shifted sides from one trial to the next); (*b*) no two dimension values stayed paired with each other for more than three consecutive trials (e.g., A's could not be large more than three times in a row, circles could not be paired with the solid underline more than three times in a row, etc.); (*c*) for any dimension value there was one and only one other value paired for the three trials.

The experimental problems were basically of two types: 12-trial 8-dimensional (8-D) problems with legitimate solutions and 12-trial 7-D insoluble problems. The latter were formed by selecting the solution from 8-D stimuli and by then eliminating the relevant dimension. Suppose, for example, that (before the experiment began) "single spot" was selected to be the solution. The *E* noted on which side the single spot occurred on each of the 12 trials—choice of this side would be correct. He then made 12 new stimuli, identical to the old except that the spots were omitted from both of the stimulus patterns. The *S* received eight such insoluble problems distributed throughout 24 legitimate problems.

The *S*s were first shown examples of the stimuli and were carefully instructed about the eight dimensions. They were told that they were to select one of the two patterns and that after each choice E would indicate the correctness of that response. They were further told that the solution (i.e., the basis for responding correctly) on any one problem was one of the 16 attribute values (8 dimensions $\times$ 2 values per dimensions) and that they were to try to be correct as often as possible. The S was then given several practice problems (both 7-D and 8-D—all soluble) followed by the 32 (24 soluble, 8 insoluble) experimental problems.[2]

In the results, three types of problems can be characterized: legitimate 8-D problems which are solved (defined as having correct responses on Trials 10, 11, and 12)—these will hereafter be ignored; legitimate 8-D problems which are unsolved (defined as having an error on one of Trials 10, 11, or 12); and insoluble 7-D problems, which, of course, S cannot solve. It is the comparison of performance on these last two types of problems which is of interest. Before presenting this comparison, however, the theory will first be reviewed.

THE THEORY OF INSOLUBLE AND UNSOLVED PROBLEMS

The necessary assumptions are:

1. The basic assumption: The S selects an H from some universe and responds on the basis of that H. For example, S may predict that circles are the basis for choosing. He would then choose the side containing the circle. This is a primitive axiom, although support for the second part, that the H directs the response, is found by inserting blocks of blank (i.e., no feedback) trials into normal problems. Frankel, Levine, and Karpf (1970) have shown that Ss virtually always respond to a single attribute value for as many as 30 consecutive blank trials.

2. The composition assumption: The universe from which S samples contains only those Hs corresponding to the stimulus levels. The S predicts that "large" or "T," etc., is correct. He does not employ Hs about conjunctions of cues or about complex sequences. This assumption, clearly, is a function of E's instructions and of the preliminary practice problems. By altering these, the assumption can be changed without affecting the rest of the theory. The last set of experiments described below employs a different composition assumption (and, concomitantly, entails different pretraining). The important feature of the present assumption is that for insoluble 7-D problems, S's universe consists of 14 Hs.

3. Presolution responding: Prior to solving the problem (as manifested by a string of successive correct responses) S samples neither the correct H nor the other H on the same dimension. Thus, if "large letter" is the solution, before the criterion run—or during unsolved problems—S tries neither the H "large letter" nor "small letter." This assumption is based on fairly direct experimental support. Levine, Miller, and Steinmeyer (1967), probing for S's H after each trial, showed that prior to solving, Hs from the relevant dimension virtually never appeared. The

[2]For a more complete review of this experiment, see Glassman and Levine (1972).

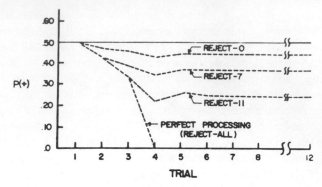

FIG. 2. The family of theoretical curves, each of which corresponds to the particular memory assumption added to the theory.

important feature of this assumption is that during unsolved 8-D problems, S's universe consists of 14 Hs.

It is hoped that the reader has noticed the congruity between the last two assumptions: During both insoluble 7-D and unsolved 8-D problems, the S is sampling from a universe of 14 wrong (irrelevant) Hs. In both cases, the correct H ($H+$) and the complement of $H+$ are outside the set from which S is sampling. This similarity in theoretical state in turn implies that the behavior under the two conditions should be similar. This, then, is the first prediction of the model, that the trial-by-trial behavior should be the same during both an insoluble 7-D problem and an unsolved 8-D problem.

The next two assumptions will permit further refinement of this prediction and some specification of the details of that trial-by-trial behavior.

4. Affirmative feedback: If S's response is followed by a positive outcome (e.g., E says "correct"), he keeps his H for the next trial. Probing for the H after each trial, Levine (1969b) showed that, with the present procedure, this assumption almost always held ($p \approx .95$).

5. Negative feedback: If S's response is followed by a negative outcome (e.g., E says "wrong"), he abandons his last H and resamples. Levine (1969b) showed that this assumption also virtually always held ($p \approx .99$). Several proposals have been made concerning S's mode of resampling following a "wrong." A few of these will be described here. All of these alternatives can be ordered along a memory continuum describing how much S remembers from past trials. Each proposal will be illustrated by an S sampling from a universe of 14 wrong Hs.

(a) Reject 0: At one extreme, S might remember nothing, not even the H just disconfirmed. He would, in effect, return this H to the set and would resample from the full universe of 14 Hs. This assumption, first made by Restle (1962), has been shown to be generally false (Levine, 1966; Restle & Emmerich, 1966). It is included here, however, as one end of the memory continuum.

(*b*) Reject 7: The *S* might remember all the *H*s corresponding to the stimulus pattern he just chose and might recognize that they are all disqualified by the negative feedback. He resamples, in effect, from the seven *H*s consistent with the information on the trial just past. Also, he does not utilize information from earlier trials. Gregg and Simon (1967) dubbed this the "local consistency" rule. Trabasso and Bower (1968) have employed this assumption.

(*c*) Reject 11: The *S* might sample from *H*s consistent not only with the just-past trial but with the preceding trial as well. With the stimulus sequences of the present experiment, this always means that *S* ignores 11 *H*s when resampling after a "wrong." This two-trial consistency check is part of an assumption proposed by Trabasso and Bower (1966).

(*d*) Reject all: The *S* might remember more than just two previous trials and could, therefore, eliminate more incorrect *H*s. At the extreme, his memory would be perfect and he would always sample among logically correct *H*s. This corresponds to the performance of focusers as described by Bruner, Goodnow, and Austin (1956, pp. 129-134). This poses an interesting psychological problem in the present context. The stimulus sequences are such that by the fourth trial of a problem all 14 *H*s are disconfirmed. The focuser facing an insoluble problem has an empty universe after Trial 4. Some suggestions concerning the behavior of *S* in this circumstance will be made later.

This is all the theory necessary to derive additional properties of *S*'s behavior during insoluble and unsolved problems. The prediction was already stated that during both types of problems, the protocols should match each other. Further predictions come from applying the theory to the sequence of stimuli employed. Within a problem, the stimuli, it will be recalled, were selected not completely randomly, but to fit stringent counterbalancing requirements. Because this counterbalancing held for every problem, it is possible to derive a predicted performance curve when the response rules described in the theory are applied to these stimulus sequences. In general, the predicted performance curve depends on the memory assumption held for a resampling *S* (i.e., upon variants *a-d* of Assumption 5). The family of memory assumptions generates a corresponding family of predicted curves. Figure 2 shows the curves predicted using each of the four variants. The most striking feature of the predictions is that for all the variants of the memory assumption, the theory predicts that during both insoluble and unsolved problems, performance will be below chance. The theory, then, predicts that not only will the curves from both types of problems be the same, but that for both, fewer than half of the responses will be correct. Furthermore, correct responding will decrease during the first four trials and will then show an upswing. Again, these predictions hold regardless of *S*'s memory, that is, they hold for all the curves in Figure 2. The details of performance following Trial 4 is currently a matter for some speculation and will be discussed later.

The data comparing 12-trial insoluble and unsolved problems are shown in Figure 3. It is seen there that the predictions are verified precisely. The curves show below-chance responding and the initial decrease. Most importantly, the

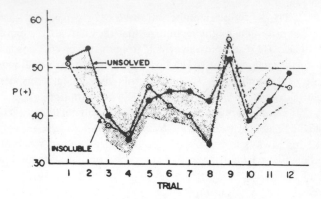

F<small>IG</small>. 3. The trial-by-trial proportion correct during unsolved and insoluble problems (the shaded band shows the .05 confidence interval around the pair of points at each trial).

curves are closely matched: At no trial do the pairs of points differ at the .01 level; at only one trial do they differ at the .05 level. This similarity holds despite the fact that the .05 confidence interval (indicated by the shaded band in Figure 3) is fairly narrow. The conclusion is compelling, therefore, that the relevant dimension is not being sampled by an S when he is faced with a soluble problem which he is not solving.

THE EMPTY SET

The S who does not solve a soluble problem was described above with a general conception: He samples from a finite set of Hs (14, in the particular case considered), and the correct H is outside this set. A basic question for the learning process concerns how S might eventually abandon this incorrect set and turn, at some later point, to sample the correct H. This question is intertwined with a question raised earlier. It was noted above that if S's memory for disqualified Hs is good enough, his set, which contains only incorrect Hs, will soon become empty. What alternatives are open to an S when this happens, when the last remaining H proves to be wrong? Consider a homey example—a person is looking for his car keys. He thinks, "Perhaps I left them in one of my jacket pockets." He opens his closet and checks the pockets of the jackets hanging there (the pockets constitute his H set). Suppose a rapid check of all the pockets reveals no clinking sound of keys (the set goes to zero). One possibility is that he thinks "Did I skip some pockets? Perhaps I should have checked each pocket more carefully." That is, one possibility is that he goes through the set again. A hint that this is happening in the experiment just reported (see Figure 3) is in the cyclic pattern during the insoluble problems. A perfect processor starts with the full set of Hs at the first trial and reduces the set until, by the third trial, he has eliminated everything but the one H correlated with the (absent) correct H for the first three trials. By the nature of the stimulus constraints, the probability that this *H* will lead to a correct choice on Trial 4 is zero. The perfect processor selects this *H* after Trial 3, is told ''wrong'' at Trial 4, and then has an empty set. If *S* checks again through the set at this point, one should see a rise in the proportion correct at Trial 5 followed by another minimum a few trials later. The cyclic character of the curves in Figure 3 suggests that this resurvey of the set might be occasionally occurring.

Another hint that *S*s review the *H* set after it becomes empty comes from an experiment by Erickson (1968), who used four-dimensional stimuli. Erickson presented blocks of three blank trials before each feedback trial as a technique for probing for *S*'s *H*. He disconfirmed the first *H* by indicating that the response to the first feedback trial was wrong. Both Erickson (1968) and Levine (1966, 1969b) (also cf. Assumption 5, above) showed that *S*s do not immediately return this *H* to the set, where it may be resampled. The *H*, then, is out of the set. The twist in Erickson's experiment was that this *H*, for all remaining trials, was made the correct *H*. Thus, an *S* might select the large stimulus for the first four trials. After the fourth trial (i.e., the first feedback trial) the *E* says ''wrong.'' Choice of the large stimulus is then the correct response for all remaining trials.[3] Conditions of the experiment facilitated information processing: not only was there a small number of dimensions, but the stimulus stayed on when feedback was presented, and there was a long intertrial interval (cf. Bourne, Guy, Dodd, & Justesen, 1965, for the effectiveness of these variables). In fact, in a standard control condition, in which feedback was consistent throughout the whole problem, the mean number of feedback trials to criterion was 4.1. In the experimental condition (with the first-trial reversal), 48 of 50 *S*s solved the problem. They required on the average only 2.3 feedback trials more than the control condition, approximately the result one might expect if *S*s typically reviewed the *H* set a second time. One reaction, then, when a set goes to zero is to go through it again.

For another reaction let us return to our friend bereft of his car keys. Suppose that he again goes through his jacket pockets for the keys, this time more systematically (i.e., in such a way as to retain in memory that every *H* was tried and rejected). The set is again empty. What other alternative is open to him? He can leave this set of *H*s and look for a new one. He can do this by scanning his memory (''What was I doing the last time I saw those keys?'') or the present situation (''Could they be among that clutter of things on my desk?''). That new set may be fairly large (''Maybe they're in one of my pants pockets'') or be very small consisting of virtually only the correct *H* (Of course! I was wearing my raincoat yesterday; they must be in my raincoat pocket''). A parallel within the experimental situation would occur if *S*, convinced that he is overlooking something, thinks back to *E*'s instructions, in an effort to retrieve some possibly forgotten dimensions.

[3]This is a loose parallel to Erickson's procedure. He, in fact, used a successive discrimination procedure. The description correctly conveys the relevant features, however, without laboring over the irrelevant differences.

Another reaction, then, when a set goes to zero is to abandon this set and to look for a new one. It is proposed that this is one important process underlying the shift from nonsolution to solution behavior. The description, while it is probably in keeping with everyday experience, is frankly speculative. Nevertheless, it is sufficiently important to the learning process that it warrants the status of an assumption, along with the five assumptions presented above.

6. Changing of sets (or subsets): The reduction of a set to zero Hs serves as a signal to select a new set. As indicated above, this search for a new set may follow one or more reviews of the old set.

THE INFINITE SET

A mechanism was just provided permitting an S who starts a problem with the wrong H set to eventually solve the problem. That set will go to zero and S, perhaps after one or more reviews of the set, will look for a new one. Suppose the initial incorrect set can never go to zero? Suppose, that is, that S is sampling from a set which is infinitely large yet which does not contain the correct H? According to the theory above, S will never abandon that incorrect set. Only Assumption 6 allows for a change of H set, but it requires that the incorrect set become empty. An S, therefore, sampling from an incorrect but infinite set, will never solve the problem no matter how easy it is, that is, no matter how obvious the S-R and feedback contingencies are.

This implication was first explored by Ress (1965; for a summary see Ress & Levine, 1966). To realize the simplicity of the task employed, consider first the control group: Thirty Ss each received a two-dimensional simultaneous discrimination. They went through a deck containing 115 cards, each card showing one large (2.5 centimeter) and one small (1.3 centimeter) circle. In typical fashion, for half of the cards, the large circle was (randomly) located on the right (or left) side. The S was instructed that he should touch the center of one of the two circles on each card, that E would say "right" or "wrong" after each response, and that he (S) was to try to be right as often as possible. The E said "right" whenever S touched the large circle, "wrong" whenever the small. In short, it was formally identical to the discrimination problem one gives to monkeys in the Wisconsin General Test Apparatus or to rats in the Lashley jumping stand. It is not surprising that these adult humans solved the problem in a mean of three trials.

The experimental Ss received the same task. This was preceded, however, by a series of experiences intended to start the Ss sampling from an infinite and incorrect H set. Sixty Ss each received a series of preliminary problems using decks identical (except for shuffling) to the one for the main problem. The solution to these preliminary problems was always a position sequence. The sequences 2L-2R (two left-side responses followed by two right-side responses), 3L-2R,

1L-4R, 5L-1R, 2L-4R, and 3L-3R were presented.[4] The E announced the correct solution after each of these problems. It was assumed that this series of preliminary problems would fulfill the composition assumption that S was sampling from an infinite set containing Hs dealing only with position sequences.

After the preliminary problems, E announced, as he had prior to each of the preliminaries, "Here is another problem" and presented S the reshuffled deck. This time, of course, the correct H was "touch 'large,' " an H not in the set of position sequences. The Ss were run until they either gave 15 consecutive correct responses or made an error after Trial 100. The results were that these Ss required a mean of 62 trials to solve this problem. Twenty-eight of the 60 Ss did not solve it in 115 trials.

The Ss, incidentally, were clearly motivated to solve these problems, and the feedback ("right" and "wrong") qualified as effective reinforcers. The preceding six sequence problems showed a typical learning-set effect. The mean trials to solution went from 65 trials on the first problem to 16 trials on the sixth.

At first glance it appears that the theory is strongly confirmed. The operations employed (i.e., the preliminary problems) for fulfilling the composition assumption that S is sampling from an infinite and incorrect set seemed clearly effective: The Ss required an average of 62 trials to learn a discrimination any self-respecting monkey learns in a few trials. Corroborating testimony comes from postexperimental comments by Ss. Virtually all acknowledged starting the final problem searching for sequence solutions. The results, however, do contain a puzzle for the theory. According to the theory, Ss should not solve at all. If they are sampling from an infinite (and incorrect) set, from a set which does not become empty, then they should never select a new set. Yet more than half of the Ss (32/60) solved the problem, that is, somehow selected a new set containing the correct H.

The puzzle can be resolved in one of two ways: (a) One may look for an additional assumption, postulating some other process by which an H outside the set can be sampled; or (b) one may question whether the composition assumption was fulfilled, whether the preliminary problems really did orient Ss to sample from an *infinite* set of position sequences. A resolution to this puzzle, favoring the second alternative, was suggested in an analysis of sequence structures by Restle (1967). He noted that binary sequence cycles consisting of a single change (true of all the sequence solutions employed by Ress & Levine—cf. above) formed a particular subset of all sequences. The S could code these by what Restle called mandatory rules. More complex sequences, involving several changes in (binary) state within a cycle, required what he called optional rules. His analysis suggested that Ress and Levine trained the Ss with only a subset of sequences, those having short cycles with a single shift within the cycle. This implies that at the final

[4]Two other variables were manipulated: The Ss had either three or six preliminary problems; the sizes of the circles differed (2.5 vs. 1.3 centimeters and 2.5 vs. 2.0 centimeters). These variables had no significant effects. The data are combined here.

problem the Ss might have held not an infinite set of all possible position sequences, but a finite set of similar and simple sequences. This set, of course, could go to zero. Some Ss might then try a different incorrect H set (e.g., "Maybe it's a more complicated sequence") whereas others might come up with the set containing the correct H (e.g., "Maybe it has something to do with the circle").

The best hunch, then, was that Ress and Levine failed to obtain ideal results because the composition assumption had not been fulfilled. The obvious next step was to repeat the experiment employing more complex sequences. This, accordingly, was done. Two groups of 20 Ss each received six preliminary sequence problems followed by the final test problem. The simple group received the same sequences as those employed by Ress and Levine; the complex group had sequences of varying complexity, the most complex sequence consisting of a cycle of 10 trials with five shifts during the cycle (e.g., LLRLLLRLRR). Except for this variation between the two groups, the task was identical to that employed by Ress and Levine.

Thirteen of 20 Ss in the simple group solved the final problem, thereby replicating the earlier results; in the complex group, however, only 3 of the 20 Ss solved the problem. The difference is significant ($\chi^2 = 8.44$, $p < .01$). This experiment, then, suggests that the complex sequences produce more successful fulfillment of the composition assumption. Also, this dramatic demonstration of Ss failing to learn the most obvious associations, further validates the H model described above as a description of the learning (and nonlearning) process.

Before considering the results of the complex group in greater detail, an additional experimental variation will be described. In the experiments above, S touched one of two circles. One of these circles (e.g., the larger) was the stimulus entering into the contingencies. One might propose an exceedingly simple reason why S failed to learn: he did not look at these circles. The S might, by this line of reasoning, touch the right or left side of the card without seeing the circles. To put it another way, Spence's (1945) criterion, that an observing response must occur before the data can be considered relevant to any learning theory, may not have been met.

Another experiment, therefore, was undertaken. The primary change from the preceding experiments was the replacement of the two circles on each card by two letters, A and B. Also, every S received the six complex sequences employed with the complex group, above. Two groups of 16 Ss each were run. The touching group, as before, was told to touch one of the two letters; the speaking group was told to indicate each choice by saying one of the two letters. Note two features about the speaking group during the final problem: First, there is no way that they can avoid seeing the stimuli; second, the contingencies are even more simplified. Instead of discrimination learning, this is now the reinforcement paradigm in its simplest form: Whenever S says "A" E says "right"; whenever S says "B" E says "wrong."

There was essentially no difference between the two groups. Four Ss in the touching group and three Ss in the speaking group solved the problem. This result, along with the observation that Ss in the touching group virtually always directed their gaze toward the letters, eliminates any concern that the nonlearning was an artifact of nonstimulation.

Three groups, then (the complex, touching, and speaking), were run in which the composition assumption appeared to be fulfilled. Of a total of 52 Ss, 81% (42 out of 52) did not reach the criterion of 15 successive correct responses within 115 trials. It is possible, of course, that these 42 Ss, though they failed this fairly extreme criterion, may nevertheless have shown some response strengthening. There is, however, no indication of anything but chance occurrence of the correct response during the 100 trials of the problem. On Trials 91-100, for example, 53% of the responses were correct. Despite a large N (42 Ss $\times$ 10 responses per S), this is not significantly different from 50%. It appears clear that these Ss had not switched to the set containing the correct H.

The remaining 10 Ss did solve the problem. Why these Ss might have been exceptional is suggested by comments made by two of them. One said that the whole experiment had reminded her of Luchins' water-jug experiment, which had recently been reviewed in her course; the other said that he had been looking for a trick—"psychologists always trick you." These comments imply that the preliminary problems did not always succeed in restricting S's H set to position-sequence Hs.

DISCUSSION

Two types of experiments have been presented demonstrating nonlearning. The first experiment showed that an S who had not learned behaved as though the relevant stimuli were literally absent. The second set of experiments, by reducing stimulus complexity to a minimum and by guaranteeing that S observed the relevant stimuli, demonstrated nonlearning in a more dramatic form. Nonlearning was shown also to be not a sporadic occurrence by an occasional S, but rather an outcome of definite problem-solving processes, susceptible to theoretical analysis and to manipulation. According to the analysis, nonlearning can be produced—despite a well-motivated S and consistent S-R feedback contingencies—by making S sample from an H set which does not contain the correct H.

It should be stressed that the theory employed was not ad hoc. A "theory of nonlearning" was not improvised to account for the data. Rather the data conformed to predictions derived from a general theory of hypothesis-testing behavior. The theory had already been employed to account for behavior during blank trials, for the discontinuity in the percentage of correct responses during simple learning, for cue redundancy and cue reversal, etc. The theory was here enlarged to include the concepts of empty and infinite sets, but this broadening followed plausible lines.

This expanded theory and the experimental results have relevance to three other research topics: the effects of random feedback on subsequent discrimination learning, the awareness controversy, and the Einstellung effect.

Random feedback.   Levine (1962) demonstrated that the learning of very simple discriminations was clearly retarded if E said "right" or "wrong" randomly for the first few trials. This result was also shown to hold for concept learning by Mandler, Cowan, and Gold (1964) and for complex (6-D) discrimination learning by Holstein and Premack (1965). Levine suggested that some Ss rejected the simple Hs (including the solution) during the random feedback phase and were sampling from another subset (e.g., sequence Hs) well into the discrimination phase. Holstein and Premack made a similar suggestion. Behind these suggestions was the tacit assumption that if Ss were testing Hs from an incorrect set, then they would not learn the correct contingencies. No attempt was made to demonstrate either that random feedback caused S to sample from an incorrect H set or that such a sampling would hinder the subsequent simple learning. The second type of experiment presented above, however, relates directly to the latter assumption. It demonstrated that by setting S to sample Hs from an incorrect set, the learning of a simple contingency was indeed delayed. The operation of random feedback is well viewed, then, as a gross technique for manipulating the sets from which S samples. The resulting retardation in simple learning follows from H theory as outlined above.

The awareness controversy.   In recent years several hundreds of Es have challenged or defended the reinforcement principle under the banners of the awareness controversy. Two extreme partisan positions in this controversy may be discerned. One (Dulaney, 1968; Spielberger & DeNike, 1966) is that the reinforcement principle is irrelevant, that only when S becomes "aware" of the contingencies will performance increase. The other (Dixon & Oakes, 1965; Verplank 1962) holds that the response strengthening occurs automatically, that awareness is an irrelevant or, at best, an independent process. Postman and Sassenrath (1961) took up a middle position, as have recently several other theorists (Bandura, 1969; Kanfer, 1968; Krasner, 1967). The view of Postman and Sassenrath is that both reinforcement and awareness contribute to the response-strengthening process, the former weakly but persistently, the latter strongly but rapidly, that is, in a discontinuous way. The results presented above are relevant not only to the extreme views but to this last moderate statement as well. These results demonstrated unequivocally that the reinforcement principle can be completely nullified. Establishing effective contingencies is not a sufficient condition for producing learning, that is, for increasing the probability of the contingent response.

The principle, so long a bastion of learning theory, may be defended in two ways. Silver, Saltz, and Modigliani (1970) suggest that learning via H testing and learning automatically via reinforcement may both occur but are mutually exclusive processes. According to this view, the procedures of the present experiments evoke the H-testing mechanism and thereby switch off automatic strengthening. These experiments, of course, cannot negate this possibility. Nor can any laboratory experiments which S might interpret as a problem-solving task. It may be, however, that the Silver et al. formulation will provide the ultimate resolution of the controversy.

The second defense of the principle comes through redefining the response. This is most easily seen in the second set of experiments. One may argue that because of the preliminary problems, saying ''A'' was no longer the functional response. Rather, the functional response, that is, that which was affected by the reinforcement, was S's covert formulation of a position sequence. These covert formulations were so strengthened in the preliminary problems that they did not extinguish over the 100 trials of the test problem. Far from rebutting this defense, one need only note that it is a major conversion to H theory. Indeed, H theory may be regarded as the theory of these covert forumulations. In the early stages of the development of H theory, Levine (1959b, 1963b) suggested that its most important feature was the redefinition of the response—''The H, rather than the specific choice response on a particular trial, is regarded as the dependent variable, i.e., as the unit of behavior affected by the reinforcements [Levine, 1963b, p. 270].'' Subsequently, H theory has had considerable refinement (e.g., the all-or-none character of H strengthening and weakening, the changes in strength of several Hs simultaneously, the encoding mode—visual and verbal—of information, etc.), but the redefinition of the response remains the foundation on which the theory has been built.

Einstellung. The reader, like one S mentioned above, has undoubtedly noticed the similarity of the second set of experiments to the Einstellung experiment (cf. Luchins, 1942). In this experiment also, S has preliminary experiences which render him functionally blind to a subsequent simple solution. For example, Luchins presented Ss with a series of paper-and-pencil maze problems. For the first nine problems, S was given a picture of a maze consisting of both a direct straight path leading from the start toward the goal box and other long circuitous paths. During these problems, the straight path always was blocked, that is, visibly ended as a cul-de-sac just before the goal box. One of the circuitous paths leading off from the right of the start box always eventually led to the goal. On the tenth problem, the direct path was connected to the goal. Nevertheless, the Ss typically chose the round-about alley leading off from the right. In H terms, the analysis is clear: the preliminary problems led S to sample Hs dealing with alleys off to the right. Until this set is exhausted, the S is insensitive to direct central alleys. This theory, incidentally, has an obvious implication not yet tested within the older Einstellung tradition. The theory implies that the larger the incorrect H set, the longer it takes that set to become empty, and the more durably is S functionally blind to the simple solution. This, in turn, implies that for the critical (tenth) maze, the larger the number of incorrect right-hand circuitous paths, the longer will S fail to see the correct direct path.

For decades the Einstellung effect has been treated in isolation from learning theory, primarily because that theory was based on conditioning principles. This deficiency vanishes when the effect is viewed from the perspective of H theory. The Einstellung-like results in the second set of experiments were predicted from the basic principles of H testing. By the straightforward development of H theory, one suddenly realized that the theory encompassed one form, at least, of the Einstellung effect: The S appears functionally blind as long as he is sampling from an incorrect H set. This easy, natural treatment of a hitherto isolated phenomenon further attests, along with the confirmed predictions, to the validity of the H model described above.

ADDENDUM TO CHAPTER 10

A few colleagues and students greeted the nonlearning of the A-B discrimination with some concern. The result, after all, violates not only the reinforcement rule, but also the venerable associative laws of contiguity and frequency. The characteristic comment was that there must be some learning of the A-"correct" relationship. Perhaps the percent-correct measure was too insensitive to detect this learning. I, myself, had some suspicion that this might be the case. The S, though he could not formulate the correct H, might recognize it if it were stated for him.

Accordingly, one of my students and I (Fingerman & Levine, 1974) replicated the A-B discrimination experiment, concluding it this time with a recognition test. Immediately after the critical problem, E remarked to S that he, like previous Ss, seemed to be having trouble with this last problem. The E then requested S to help him understand why this problem was difficult. He asked S to see if he could select the solution from a multiple-choice item, and then presented a card containing six possible solutions. Three of these described position-sequence solutions. Another described the A-"correct" contingency. A fifth was completely irrelevant, to the effect that S had to respond in less than two seconds in order to be told "correct." The final alternative was "none-of-the-above."

None of the 32 Ss selected the A-"correct" alternative as the solution. Fingerman then had each S rank-order the remaining alternatives. The A-"correct" alternative tied for last place with the least appropriate (the respond-in-less-than-two-seconds) alternative.

The conclusion, then, is strengthened. The S who fails to solve this simple discrimination learns *nothing* about the contingency.

11
THE TRANSFER HYPOTHESIS*

INTRODUCTION

The preceding chapter led from the precriterion suppression to the phenomenon of nonlearning. In the process, the concept of the universe of Hs was further developed. Sets of similar Hs, or *domains*, within the universe were considered. Thus, S was presumed to be sampling from the domain of position-sequence Hs when the solution (choose the letter "A") came from some other domain. The present chapter continues this analysis of the H universe.

The applications of the theory will differ, however, from the preceding treatment. Throughout this book H theory has been applied to performance within discrimination-learning problems. In this chapter there will be a shift of emphasis which may be characterized in two ways: (1) The focus will be not upon within-problem dynamics, but upon changes occurring from problem to problem during a series (at least two) of problems. In a word, *transfer* will be the concern of this theoretical development. (2) A variety of phenomena, all from adult humans, will be treated. These include Learning-to-Learn, Einstellung, the Partial Reinforcement Extinction Effect (PREE), and Reversal-Nonreversal Shift effects. The argument will be made that a relatively simple transfer process, labeled the Transfer Hypothesis, is important for elucidating these various phenomena.

Let us begin with the H universe as we might conceptualize it for a 4-D concept-identification (i.e., successive discrimination) problem. Figure 4 provides a schematic representation. It portrays a model of the H universe, subdivided into a variety of domains. In the standard concept-identification task, the S, instructed to say "alpha" or "beta" to each of a series of stimuli, may guess that the solution will be simple (e.g., "red forms are 'alpha,' green forms are 'beta' "). That is, he might sample from the domain of simple Hs (domain A, in Fig. 4). Or, he might think that the solution has a conjunctive form (e.g., "forms both large and red are 'alpha'; anything else is 'beta' "), sampling, that is, from the domain of conjunctive Hs (domain B). He might think it is some other logical

*An expanded version of this chapter will be found in Solso (1974).

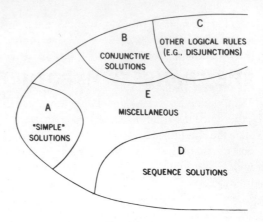

Fig. 4. A schematic representation of the *H* universe, showing some of the possible domains.

rule (domain C). He might think the solution is some sequence (e.g., "it goes, 'alpha,' 'alpha,' 'beta,' repeatedly"). Note that the domain of sequences (D) is open-ended, reflecting the fact that there is an infinite number of sequence *H*s. Finally, the *S* might hold idiosyncratic *H*s (e.g., "if *E* scratches his head say 'alpha'; otherwise, say 'beta' "; or " 'alpha' is called 'correct' only if I respond quickly"). These are included in the "miscellaneous" domain (E). These domains are to be thought of as *H* sets within which *S* is restricting his sampling. At the start of some problem the *S* may think, "It will be some sequence solution." He would then be thought of as sampling within the domain of sequence *H*s.

It can be acknowledged at the outset that this conception is severely oversimplified. No attempt has yet been made to define the term "domain." For a tentative working definition we may take as domains those sets of *H*s which have relatively simple category labels, thus, the *S* may think the solution will be "simple," "a complicated sequence," "has something to do with colors," etc. Each of these thoughts or states of the *S* would specify a different *H* set in which he was searching for the solution.

The Transfer Hypothesis will be clearer if seen in the context of the pretraining procedures employed in contemporary research. One type of pretraining, which had been widely used in earlier concept-identification research (and is still used in some experiments today), entails minimal instructions. The *S* is told merely that he would see cards, that he is to make one of two responses (e.g., "say 'alpha' or 'beta' to each card"), that he would be told "right" or "wrong," and that he is to be "right" as often as possible. This procedure, which will be referred to as minimal pretraining, instructs *S* only in the mechanics of the task. Sampling of *H*s within the universe is, presumably, unaffected.

When first exploring techniques to probe for *H*s, I saw that it would be valuable, if not necessary, to know the domain from which *S* was sampling. To put this another way, it would be virtually impossible to detect *S*'s *H* from response sequences of moderate length if he could try anything in the universe. I, therefore, decided to restrict S's sampling to the domain of simple Hs. This could be accomplished, I hoped, by extensive pretraining. For this pretraining, S was presented with a series of problems, each of which had a different simple solution (See Reading No. 14). These problems were reasonably long, affording S the opportunity to attain the solution. Furthermore, when S did not solve the problem, E announced the solution. Thus, there were these two modes whereby S could experience the solution: by having a long run of correct responses or by hearing E state the solution. I assumed that these two experiences were roughly equivalent in communicating to S a sample solution. This procedure—preliminary problems, with S receiving examples of the solutions—will be referred to as extended pretraining.

Just what did extended pretraining accomplish? My intuition was that the successive problems were changing S from one who might sample any place in the universe to one who sampled only from the domain of simple Hs. We were in effect saying, "Look here. The solutions are not complex sequences. They are not conjunctives, etc. They are '*simple*.' " Furthermore, I felt that the primary information packet was the solution-knowledge, gained either from solving the problem directly or from E's statement at the end of the problem. This, then, was my interpretation of extended pretraining, that the experience of the series of solutions caused S to ignore all but the critical domain.

THE TRANSFER HYPOTHESIS

The pretraining just described presumes some sort of transfer from early problems to later problems. The critical features inherent in this transfer may be described formally as follows:

The transfer hypothesis.   When S receives a series of problems, he infers from the first n solutions the domain within the universe from which the $(n + 1)$th solution will be taken. He will start the $(n + 1)$th problem by sampling Hs from this domain.

This hypothesis merely sounds like an articulation of my feelings about extended pretraining. We will see, however, that it has general significance. Let us, first, consider one detail of this hypothesis. A new concept is introduced—that S makes an inference. We will generally assume that the S who receives minimal instructions (i.e., at the outset of the very first problem—pretraining or otherwise) will sample from the entire universe and that successive solutions will cause a narrowing with greater and greater precision toward the domain from which E selects the solutions. If, for example, E presents a series of problems with simple (or sequential, or conjunctive, etc.) solutions, S will soon start looking for simple (or sequential, or conjunctive, etc.) solutions. Since all the phenomena discussed below deal with grouped data, the precise process operating within an individual S needn't be delineated. Thus, inferences may proceed in step-wise fashion (i.e., be made suddenly) or be gradual; they may lead to the identical domain from which E

has, in fact, selected solutions, or to a larger or smaller domain. Strong assumptions need not be made at this time about these alternatives.

A qualification: The Transfer Hypothesis and the general cognitive machinery will be applied to experiments in which the college student has been the subject. Application is, for the present, intended only for the behavior of this S. Experiments similar to some of those discussed below have also been performed with children and with subhuman animals. I am ignoring these experiments, no matter what their results. For example, learning-to-learn by the college student will be considered. That a monkey does or does not show a similar result is, for now, irrelevant.

APPLICATIONS

Learning-set. Problem-to-problem improvement in the concept-identification experiment has been demonstrated by Paul Fingerman in my laboratory, and by a number of other investigators (e.g., Grant & Cost, 1954; Wickens & Millward, 1971). Typically, in these experiments the S is given minimal instructions. In Fingerman's experiment, for example, S was seated before the stimulus window, was told that pictures would appear in the window, that he should choose one of the two pictures, that he would be told "correct" or "wrong" for each response, and that he was to be "correct" as often as possible. Nothing was said about the stimulus dimensions, the stimulus values, or the possible solutions to these problems. No pretraining problems were presented.

Certain procedural details of the learning-to-learn experiments make it extremely likely that S will experience the solution to each problem. He receives a large number of trials in which to discover the solution, and he must manifest a long criterion run before the problem is ended. Fingerman, who employed a fixed number of trials per problem, announced the solution to all Ss at the end of each problem. In each of the three experiments mentioned above the solutions always came from the domain of simple solutions. According to the Transfer Hypothesis, therefore, with each successive problem the S is more and more likely to sample only from the simple domain. It follows that the group of Ss, because they are going from sampling in the universe at large to sampling in a limited domain, should solve the problems faster and faster—and, as is well-known, they do.

There is another, more direct, implication of the Transfer Hypothesis. If we probed for S's H at the outset of each of several problems, we should find that these Hs come more and more from the simple set. Fingerman probed for the initial H in each problem by inserting a series of six blank trials immediately after the first feedback trial. According to the Transfer Hypothesis, the S's H on the early problems and, therefore, his response patterns, should be of all varieties. As the problems proceed, however, the patterns denoting simple Hs should appear more and more. This, indeed, was obtained. Initially, about half of the patterns were simple Hs; the number increased over the problems toward an asymptote of about 90%.

The technique of probing for the initial H may also be used to investigate the character of S's inference about the domain. Fingerman's result, that initial Hs tend more and more to come from the simple domain, might occur either because S merely repeats experienced solutions or because S is searching within the domain of simple solutions. The latter would occur if S infers that the solutions are keyed to the attributes of the stimuli in the window. According to this interpretation there should be an increase in the frequency of simple Hs, even for attributes that had not yet served as the solution. Fingerman, Taddonio, and I performed the following experiment.

A series of problems were presented with blank-trial probes at the outset of each. The stimuli were constructed from four dimensions. Solutions, however, came from only three of these. Color, for example, never contributed a solution. We then looked at the series of initial Hs to see how often a color H appeared. In three replications, simple Hs from the excluded dimension increased in frequency over the first few problems. The Ss, therefore, were not merely repeating experienced solutions but were more and more sampling from the domain of simple Hs.

One might conclude that the Transfer Hypothesis definitively accounts for the phenomena of learning-to-learn. This conclusion, however, is a bit strong, even for the basic experiment. The hypothesis describes a necessary and important process, but there are undoubtedly other processes. For example, once the S has narrowed down the likely solutions to the correct domain, he can still improve his strategy (see Reading No. 18) for dealing with the Hs within that domain. The Transfer Hypothesis then describes an important transfer process, but not necessarily the only process. In general, i.e., for all the phenomena discussed below, the hypothesis will elucidate rather than explain.

Einstellung. It was demonstrated in the preceding chapter (see Reading No. 20) that S could be so "set" that he would fail to solve a simple concept-problem. The theory was that if S began a problem by sampling in an incorrect domain he would fail to solve that problem. He would fail, that is, until he abandoned that incorrect domain for one containing the solution. It was postulated that S abandoned an incorrect domain after trying all its Hs: An empty domain was said to serve as a signal to try a new domain. This implied that if S were in an incorrect domain that was infinite, i.e., that could never become empty, he would never solve even the simplest problem. If, for example, S were searching within the infinite domain of position-sequence solutions, he would never solve so trivial a problem as choose "A" of the letter-pair A, B.

The Transfer Hypothesis describes the mechanics for bringing S into such a state. According to the hypothesis, S will sample from an incorrect domain if he is first presented with a series of problems whose solutions come from that incorrect domain. Accordingly, Ss were given a series of problems whose solutions were position sequences. Following this series they were given the choose-"A" problem. The results, as we saw, were decisive. Almost all failed to choose "A" consistently in 100 trials. These results confirm not only the general theory but also the validity of the Transfer Hypothesis.

An important by-product of this analysis is that it interrelates learning-set and Einstellung. The two phenomena are complementary aspects of the same process. In both experiments S receives n similar problems whose function, according to the Transfer Hypothesis, is to cause S to sample from a particular domain. In the learning-set experiment the $(n + 1)$th problem comes from the same domain; in Einstellung, the $(n + 1)$th problem comes from a new domain.

The partial-reinforcement extinction effect. The PREE goes back to an experiment by Humphreys (1939) in which one of two events can occur and S makes one of two responses, predicting one of the two events. In a contemporary form of the experiment, S predicts which of two lights will come on, by pushing one of two corresponding buttons. The S receives a long series of prediction trials under one of two conditions: In the 100% condition, the same light flashes at every trial; in the 50% condition, the two lights come on randomly from trial to trial. In conditioning terms (circa the 1930's), the 100% condition yields a response that is strongly conditioned and that should, therefore, be difficult to extinguish; the 50% group has a response that is only moderately conditioned and that should, therefore, be relatively easy to extinguish.

Extinction is begun for both groups by presenting on every trial the light that, for the 100% group, had never appeared during conditioning. Contrary to the prediction from the simplistic conditioning theory, the 100% group extinguishes faster, i.e., consistently makes the correct prediction-response in Phase 2 in fewer trials. An alternative and popular explanation is the Discrimination Hypothesis. According to this, the 100% group extinguishes faster because they receive a clear signal that the situation has changed, i.e., the continual appearance of one light is suddenly replaced by the continual appearance of the other light. The 50% group, on the other hand, lacks a comparable clear signal. This signal facilitates the change in behavior by the 100% group. It is, incidentally, possible to make the two groups more similar with respect to such a signal. At the end of Phase 1, Ss in both groups may be told, "This ends the first problem. We will now start a new problem."

From the framework of H theory the 100% group should extinguish faster than the 50% group, even if both groups receive this "new problem" signal. The reason is straightforward. Before it is elaborated, however, a subtle shift in the view of this experiment should be noted. The S is traditionally thought of as receiving one *experience*, divided into two phases, conditioning and extinction. I would propose, rather, that S be viewed as having two *problems*. Thus, on this latter view, there is nothing conceptually different about the two phases. They are simply two problems with two different solutions. According to the Transfer Hypothesis, then, Ss in the 100% group have just experienced a problem with an extremely simple solution. It is plausible to expect some number of Ss to infer that the E is presenting "baby problems" to them. At the start of Problem (or Phase) 2, they, therefore, tend to look within the domain of easy solutions. The 50% group, on the other hand, has no basis for a similar conclusion. Their experience with

Problem 1 was that the solution was not obvious. Simple solutions hadn't worked. Thus, at the outset of Problem 2, there would be some tendency for these Ss to be searching for solutions that are quite complex, or that come from some obscure domain. According to the Transfer Hypothesis, therefore, even with a special signal that a change in the situation is occurring, the 50% group should "extinguish" more slowly than the 100% group.

If, as just suggested, the second part of the procedure is thought of not as extinction, but as a new problem, then any new problem, if it is relatively simple, should be learned faster by the 100% group. This conclusion is supported by a variant of the Humphreys experiment. Meyers, Driessen, and Halpern (1972), who also interpret the PREE in H-theory terms, ran two groups of 15 Ss each, varying in Problem-1 treatment. One group received a simple single-alternation (LR) problem; the second group received random outcomes. Phase (or Problem) 2 was not extinction, but a new problem: For all Ss the LLR pattern was correct. Two results are pertinent: (1) Whereas all the Ss in the single-alternation group learned the LLR pattern, only four of the Ss in the random group learned the pattern in 90 trials. Thus, even though Phase 2 is now unambiguously new learning, Ss who had first learned a simple sequence (LR) learned a new simple sequence (LLR) faster than Ss who previously had an infinitely complex sequence. That the experience with the first solution had directed the single-alternation S to search the set of simple sequence solutions is borne out by the next result. (2) A third group was run that received the LLR pattern as the initial task. The single-alternation Ss learned the LLR pattern faster than these Ss. The latter required more than twice the number of trials. The S for whom LLR is an initial problem starts out facing a relatively large universe of Hs; the S who receives this problem after single-alternation tends to start within the subdomain of simple sequence solutions.

Reversal-nonreversal shifts. This experimental paradigm was described in Chapter 4 (see Reading No. 6). The pertinent essentials will be reviewed here. Like the PREE experiment, the procedure is traditionally regarded as consisting of two phases. Two groups of Ss, after minimal instructions, receive a multidimensional (ideally, a two-dimensional) simple discrimination problem as Phase 1. When S reaches some clear criterion (e.g., 10 errorless trials) the solution is changed. For the Reversal-Shift Group, the new solution is the reverse of the Phase 1 solution; for the Nonreversal-Shift Group, the new solution comes from a previously irrelevant dimension. When the Ss are adult humans, a reliable finding (with one regular exception to be noted below) is that the Reversal-Shift Group learns the new problem faster than the Nonreversal-Shift Group.

What has the Transfer Hypothesis to say about this result? Again, assume that the procedure consists not of two phases but of two problems, and that the first problem provides S with a sample solution. According to the Transfer Hypothesis, sample solutions permit S to eliminate wrong or unlikely domains and to reduce the size of the universe to a section, some fraction of the starting universe. For the previous topics, S's domain could be thought of as homogeneous. It was not necessary to analyze a domain. For the present topic, however, such analysis is necessary. Specifically, I suggest that the domain of simple Hs is divided into subdomains, each containing the Hs associated with a dimension. Thus, for a four-dimensional problem the domain of simple Hs would consist in four subdomains. There is a tendency, furthermore, for Ss to sample Hs within a subdomain before exploring other subdomains. That is, the probability of sampling Hs within a dimension is greater than across dimensions.

The foregoing may be summarized by two assertions: (1) Dimensions tend to produce groupings, or subdomains, of related Hs, and (2) when only one simple H is salient for S he is likely first to test Hs within the corresponding dimension-subdomain. These assertions sound like crude bending of the theory to the new topic. They would be outrageously *ad hoc* were it not for independent supporting evidence. Two types of data support the assertion that dimension-related Hs tend to cohere. The first is seen in Reading No. 15, in which H probes were applied at each trial within a problem. It was demonstrated that prior to the last error both the solution H (e.g., "large") and the other H on the same dimension ("small") were absent. It was as though the entire dimension was overlooked during the precriterion phase of the problem. The other evidence was presented by Andrews, Levinthal, and Fishbein (1969), and was replicated by Gumer and Levine (1971). These authors probed for the H before and immediately after the first feedback trial. When E said "wrong" at this trial the second H tended to come from the same dimension as the first. If, for example, the H at the outset of the problem was "black," then the next H was "white" more than half the time (chance, in both studies, was .25). It is clear, then, that Hs within dimensions cohere for Ss and that this coherence can influence the sequence in which S tests Hs.

Application of this refined conception to the Reversal-Nonreversal Experiment is straightforward. The S receives minimal instructions. The first problem provides a solution example (e.g., "large") to S.[1] At the start of the next problem, which is signaled by "wrongs" after a long string of "rights," "small" will be sampled with higher probability than Hs in the other subdomains. Thus, a Reversal Shift is learned faster than a Nonreversal Shift.

Since this result had already been nicely explained by neoconditioning ideas, one justifiably wonders whether it was worth invoking the Transfer Hypothesis and complicating the universe conception just to treat this same result. There is, however, another set of results more readily handled by the Transfer Hypothesis. Suppose, instead of minimal instructions one gives elaborate instructions about the stimulus dimensions and about the solutions. A few such experiments (Erickson,

---

[1]Note that typically in this research Ss who fail to attain criterion on Problem 1 are dismissed from the experiment. This procedure is followed even though the results are traditionally related to conditioning theory. The dynamics specified by conditioning theory should operate whether S reaches criterion or not, i.e., the solution experience is of no special importance within that theory.

1971; Johnson, Fishkin, & Bourne, 1966; Neumann, 1972) have been performed in which E tells S that the solutions will be simple, and *enumerates the possible solutions*. According to the foregoing theory, E is now providing S with sample solutions. These should direct S's search for solutions within the domain of simple Hs. Furthermore, for these Ss after Problem 1 the various Hs should have more nearly equal sampling probabilities than they do for Ss who have experienced only a single solution. For the extensively instructed Ss, therefore, the various solutions should tend to be equally easy. That is the standard finding. The Reversal-Shift Ss lose their advantage.

DISCUSSION

Hypothesis Theory has long held, as an approximation to the learning process, that S is in one of two states: the precriterion state, when he samples only incorrect Hs, and the criterion state, when he holds only the solution H. The Transfer Hypothesis supplements this by stressing that the solution experience determines transfer. According to this Hypothesis, Ss who do not manifest the criterion run should show very different transfer effects from those who do manifest it. The definitive test of this implication has not yet been made. Hints that it is correct, however, come from two sources.

Grant and Berg (1948) presented a series of six card-sorting concept problems to several groups, two of which are of interest here. For one group, each problem ended after a criterion run of 10 successively correct trials; for the other group only a 3-trial criterion run was required. Interproblem performance improved for the 10-trial group but not for the 3-trial group. The former Ss are experiencing the solutions and thereby inferring the correct domain. The latter do not have this advantage. Similar results were obtained recently by Sweller (1973) in a parallel experiment employing number concepts.

A second hint comes from an unpublished variant of the Humphreys experiment in which one group received a simple alternation problem for the first phase.[2] A few of these Ss failed to learn this alternation rule. During the "extinction" phase, in which only one of the two responses was always correct, these Ss performed like Ss who had previously received random feedback. The implication is that not the consistent trial-by-trial feedback contingencies, but the solution experience dictates the transfer.

A concomitant of this emphasis upon the solution experience is the question of how the solution is conveyed to S. Three modes were mentioned. (1) The S may discover the solution, as revealed by a criterion run of reasonable length. (2) The E may announce the solution after some number of trials. There are no data on the relative effectiveness of these two methods for subsequent transfer performance. My impression, from experience with both methods during pretraining, is that

[2]F. Irwin, Personal communication.

they are roughly equivalent. (3) The E may present instructions, i.e., before any problems are presented E may announce the various solutions. That this has some effect is suggested in the discussion above of Reversal-Nonreversal Shift problems. D. M. Johnson (1972) has also noted comparable effects: "Telling a college student . . . the relevant attributes in a concept problem or the class of words that are solutions to anagrams reduces the solution time drastically. One sentence of instructions might be equated with twenty minutes of practice [p. 162 ff]." Johnson proceeds to criticize theories of human learning for neglecting these instruction effects. The Transfer Hypothesis points to one function of the instructions. They provide solution experiences (or examples) to the S, leading him, thereby, to sample from a restricted domain. Within concept learning, extensive instructions have included recitation of the individual solutions. Johnson's examples suggest that simply stating the name of the domain might be adequate. There are no systematic data on the effectiveness of such procedures within the field of concept learning. My own experience, however, suggests that verbal instructions abstractly presented, i.e., before an actual problem is given, are less effective than the other two modes.

The Transfer Hypothesis, then, not only points up an important process common to a variety of research topics, but interrelates instructions, pretraining, and criterion attainment. Along with these virtues one residual problem should be noted. The hypothesis deals primarily with S's mode of definition of the appropriate domain. This, clearly, is not the only process important in transfer. In learning-to-learn, for example, Ss may improve, not only by discovering the proper domain, but by learning to search efficiently within that domain for the solution. In the PREE the 100% group is undoubtedly facilitated by the presence of a signal of a new problem (the shift from one consistent outcome event to the other). Furthermore, S's experience with the sequence of solutions over a series of problems may influence the probability distribution of the Hs within a given domain. In particular, the S may become sensitive to sequential regularities within the solution series. The most general conclusion, then, is that H theory provides a plausible framework for viewing transfer. The applications described above testify to its plausibility.

12
THE SUMMING UP

The preceding chapters in this secti~n presented H theory in chronological sequence. The evolution · the theory was outlined. Because the experimental series was closely interconnected the tale was coherent. Nevertheless, theoretical statements appeared episodically. Thus, the conception of subset sampling appeared in one place, the Systems analysis in another, etc. This chapter, therefore, will be devoted to a summing up, to a review of the overall structure of the theory. This characterization will be intended for the adult human subject. Where appropriate, however, the special assumptions needed for children's behavior will be noted.

The fundamental conception, stated now many times, is that in the course of solving a problem, the subject samples Hs from some universe of Hs. This universe has been viewed most recently as consisting of a variety of domains, that is, of groups of similar Hs. Starting with this conception we may distinguish three levels of theory. First, there is the theory of the universe itself. This has been treated in the preceding chapter and has been developed primarily to account for interproblem transfer effects. Second, there is the theory of H sampling from the domain of simple Hs during concept learning. Almost all analyses—by me as well as by others—have been performed at this level of the theory. The third level of theorizing concerns component processes. This type of theory is more molecular in form than the other two. It seeks to establish the details, that is, imagery, verbal coding, rehearsal, etc. that "underly" or correspond to sampling processes characterized at the other levels. These three levels of the theory will be elaborated in this chapter.

LEVEL I: THE THEORY OF THE UNIVERSE

This deals with S's mode of sampling within the universe of Hs as he solves a problem. First, however, a digression should be made. The universe cannot always be postulated. It is conceivable that S may not have such a universe available. Two examples will suffice to make this point. A few years ago, one of my Ss was presented with a simple task in which stimulus cards either contained a black triangle or were blank. The S was given minimal instructions: he was to say "positive" or "negative" to each card, he would be told "right" or "wrong," and he was to try to be "right" all the time. The rule was that blank cards were positive and triangles were negative. Virtually all the Ss solved this problem in a few trials. This particular S, however, was told "wrong" on every trial (he consistently called triangles "positive" and blank cards "negative") for a series of 50 trials. When afterwards asked his interpretation of the experiment, he remarked something like the following: "This was an experiment on frustration. You told me 'wrong' all the time to see if I would become frustrated. I didn't let myself get upset." Thus, the H-universe construct does not seem appropriate to this S's behavior. Another example is the S who, after minimal instructions, believes that he is in an ESP experiment. Rather than search for Hs, he tries to commune silently with E before each response.

It is clear in these examples that the S may confront a soluble concept problem in a way that does not entail sampling Hs from the universe. In order for the H-universe conception to be applicable, we must first make an initial assumption that S regards this task as a problem to be solved. When theorists stipulate the H universe, they tacitly assume this problem-solving orientation. In the initial example, that of the S who, despite disconfirmation, persisted in calling triangles "positive," the absence of such orientation was revealed by S's comment. Another indication exists, however, that he did not have this problem-solving orientation: S manifested a *Response-set H*. That is, he showed a systematic pattern that persisted despite "disconfirmation" (i.e., "wrong"—see Chapter 6 for the contrast between Response-set and Prediction Hs). This example suggests a useful generalization, that the universe construct may not be appropriate to Ss who manifest Response-sets. Thus, a model of sampling from a universe of Hs, a model that presupposes that S has a problem-solving orientation, is probably not the proper conception for Krechevsky's rats, for the monkey data of Harlow and Levine, or for some of the five-year-old children studied by Gholson, Levine, and Phillips (see Readings 1, 7, 8 and 18, respectively). A different model seems more appropriate for these data. The form of such a model is a problem for the future. For now, we end this digression by noting that the theory of the universe presented below is intended only for Ss with the aforementioned problem-solving orientation. Since this orientation leads to Prediction Hs and concomitant strategies, its presence may be inferred from data. Several experiments (Levine 1963, 1969; Gholson, Levine, & Phillips, 1972) indicate that in the standard concept-learning experiments, virtually all older children and adult humans have this problem-solving orientation.

The theory of the universe is intended, then, for such Ss. This universe consists of a variety of domains. The S will be in one of two mutually exclusive states. He may be sampling within the domain containing the solution (the correct domain), or within an incorrect domain. If S is in the correct domain, his behavior will be described by the second level of theory discussed below. Here, therefore, we will consider Ss who begin a problem by sampling in an incorrect domain. For such Ss two separate sets of processes are to be considered: (A) those functioning within a problem and (B) those relating to interproblem transfer.

A. Within-Problem Dynamics

Two assumptions have been made for this case.

ASSUMPTION 1.   *An* S *who is sampling within an incorrect domain learns nothing about the solution.* He will be insensitive to feedback contingencies that mark out the solution, no matter how simple and obvious those contingencies may be. This assumption is the basis for the Einstellung effect demonstrated above and for the similarity between unsolved- and insoluble-problem behavior (Chapter 10).

Since some Ss who begin a problem by sampling from an incorrect domain do eventually solve the problem (see Ress & Levine, 1965, described in Reading No. 20), a dynamic must be postulated which permits S to "break out" of the incorrect domain. This leads to the next assumption, concerning the changing of domains.

ASSUMPTION 2.   *The reduction of a domain to zero* Hs *serves as a signal to select a new domain.* This assumption suggested the form of the experiment demonstrating the Einstellung effect. The implication of this assumption in conjunction with the preceding was that if S could be made to sample from an infinitely large, but incorrect, domain he would never solve even the simplest problem.

Two other considerations relate to S changing domains. The first is the relatively minor detail that when S tests all the Hs within a domain, that is, when the domain becomes empty, the S may first review those Hs before shifting to a new domain. Some indirect evidence was adduced for this process, in Chapter 10. Its ultimate validity does not, however, affect the rest of the theory. The second consideration has greater significance but lacks any data. This aspect of the theory concerns the source of these H domains. Whereas S's past experience clearly produces domains (e.g., S may have served in a previous problem-solving experiment utilizing sequence solutions), it is unrealistic to assume that S has an *a priori* universe of Hs that he carries with him into the experimental setting. Rather, it is plausible that the experimental situation itself suggests sets of Hs. Thus, in the standard concept-identification experiment, the complex pictures changing from trial to trial tend to direct S toward corresponding sets of Hs. In the Humphreys' guessing task (described in Chapter 11) the stark absence of stimulus variation probably evokes sets of sequence Hs. A related idea appeared in Reading No. 20, where it was suggested that when S's set becomes empty he may seek a new domain by scanning the environment more closely for other sources of solutions.

B. Between-Problem Dynamics

When E presents a series of similar problems, a new mechanism comes into play, leading S to change from one domain to another. This mechanism is the experience of the solution. This experience, it was noted, may come about in two ways. The S may have his H about the solution confirmed in a long criterion run, or, should S fail to sample the correct H by the problem's end, the E may announce the solution. Since we are dealing here with S sampling within an incorrect domain, only the latter method is relevant. One or more such solution announcements permit S to make inferences concerning the domain from which E is taking the solutions. This mechanism, solution experience, was formally described as the *transfer hypothesis:*

S *infers from the first* n *solutions the domain from which the* (n + *1*)*th solution will be taken. He will start the* (n + *1*)*st problem by samping* Hs *from this domain.*

It was demonstrated in the preceding chapter that this hypothesis not only accounted for the main effects of learning to learn, Einstellung, the PREE, and reversal-nonreversal shift effects, but clarified novel and puzzling results within those areas.

The universe, then, is seen as consisting of sets of domains. The nature of these domains depends upon both the environment and S's problem-solving history. As long as S is sampling from an incorrect domain he learns nothing about the solution. Two general determinants tend to move him from an incorrect domain. Either that domain can become empty, or S can experience a typical solution.

LEVEL II: THE THEORY OF THE CORRECT DOMAIN

In contrast to the preceding section, this describes the dynamics of sampling within that domain containing the solution. Virtually all of the theorizing has been concerned not only with this situation but, specifically, with the domain of simple concept Hs. While H-theory analyses of sequence learning have been initiated (Lordahl, 1970) it is not yet clear that the following assumptions would apply to this domain.

The theory may be divided into three sets of assumptions. These deal, respectively, with S's mode of sampling Hs, with the determinants of his response, and with the effects of feedback.

A. The Sampling Assumption

Perhaps the most prevalent sampling assumption is this: *The* S *selects a subset of the* Hs *from the domain.* The number of Hs selected can vary from one to all of the Hs in the domain. The exact number is a parameter varying with the S, the type of problem, etc. Support for this assumption, relative to the assumption that S chooses only a single H, was demonstrated with a variety of data in Reading No. 17. Examples included Bower and Trabasso's (1968) finding that some Ss learned both of two correct Hs, Richter's (1965) result that Ss chose correctly in excess of predictions from single-H sampling, and my (Levine, 1969a) demonstration that subset sampling accounted for the latency functions. Other authors have regarded the subset-sampling assumption of sufficient importance to attempt to probe for the subset directly. Thus Kornreich (1968), using the 4-D simultaneous-discrimination procedure described above, had S indicate at each trial all the Hs that might be tenable. Using an 8-D concept-identification task, Millward and Spoehr (1973) also externalized the H-sampling process by having S select on each trial the dimensions he wished to observe.

An analogous form of the subset-sampling assumption is expressed in terms of S's memory. The parameter that specifies the number of Hs in S's sample here becomes the number of Hs that S recalls as being valid. Gregg and Simon (1967) found it convenient to treat subset sampling in this way, as did I in the discussion of nonlearning (Chapter 10).

The parameter defining the number of Hs in the subset can take on the value of 1.0, that is, the subset-sampling assumption does not exclude single-H sampling. Our research with children (Chapter 9) has indicated that young Ss are likely to sample one H at a time. In doing so, furthermore, they sample the individual Hs in definite sequences. From these sequences we inferred systematic processes, or Systems. We tended to treat subset sampling as part of the more sophisticated Systems. By this approach, the two views, subset sampling and the Systems analysis, may be made compatible. A comprehensive theoretical framework, however, which elegantly interrelates Systems and subset sampling, has yet to be developed.

B. The Response Rule

According to the subset-sampling assumption S may be considering several Hs simultaneously. Since each individual H may lead to a different response, on what basis does S behave? The most salient fact bearing on this question is that during a series of blank trials S manifests a single H (see, especially, Reading No. 16). Based upon this fact, the following Working-H Response Rule was proposed (Reading No. 17):

The S chooses from his subset one H—labeled the working H—as the basis for his response.

Other data suggested that an additional rule, the Majority Rule, was occasionally employed. An S responding according to this rule, will make that response dictated by the majority of Hs in his subset.

C.   The Feedback Assumptions

The effects of the absence of feedback. When S receives no feedback following his response, he keeps the same (working) H for the next trial. The consistency during blank trials seen throughout several chapters attests to the validity of this assumption. This assumption served as the basis of the *H* probe. The remaining feedback assumptions are really empirical generalizations resulting from application of this probe.

The effects of confirmation (e.g., "right"). When *S* responds and is told "right," two effects hold: First, the working *H* is always repeated. This statement is a close approximation to the results observed by probing: $P(H_i = H_{i-1} \mid F_i = +)$ = .95. I have argued (Levine, 1969b) that the small deviation is produced by noise in the probing system, that the probability that *S* retains his true (i.e., underlying, as opposed to manifest) *H* is 1.0. Such a strong assumption, of course, requires that *S* remembers the *H* just confirmed. In straightforward simultaneous-discrimination learning this appears to be the case even with 8-D problems. By impairing *S*'s memory, one could undoubtedly cause the probability of repeating an *H* to be considerably less than one. Thus, by interleaving problems (Restle & Emmerich, 1966)—a procedure in which two normally successive trials of a problem are separated by trials of several other similar problems—one can readily demonstrate changes in *H*s after a confirmation. I would suggest, however, that this is a process extraneous to the ordinary problem-solving routine. If not interfered with, *S* will always retain his *H* after confirmation.

The foregoing concerned the working *H*. The second effect of "right" is upon the other *H*s in the sample. It is consistent with the subset-sampling conception to assume that *S* is monitoring these other *H*s as well. The suggestion here is that *S* eliminates from the subset those *H*s that, by implication, were disconfirmed. This process, again, is subject to memory limitations.

The effects of disconfirmation (e.g., "wrong").   As with confirmation, there are two effects of a "wrong." First, the working *H* is never repeated. The same qualification discussed above concerning *S*'s memory applies here. After a clear disconfirmation, changing *H*s is a fundamental dynamic of the *H*-testing procedure. This routine can be disrupted, however, by procedures (cf. the Restle & Emmerich experiment) that produce forgetting.

As with "right," the second effect of "wrong" is on the other *H*s in the subset. The *S*s tend to eliminate other disconfirmed *H*s. It appears, however, that the additional processing required by the disconfirmation (e.g., *S* must search for a new working *H*) imposes sufficient demand on *S* that he is less efficient in this process. Thus, it was seen in Reading No. 14 that *S* was less likely to manifest the solution *H* following a sequence of "wrong" than following a sequence containing some "rights."

A summary of the foregoing theory of the correct domain is that *S* samples a subset of *H*s to monitor. He (most often) selects one of these *H*s as his working *H*, i.e., as his basis for response, or he (infrequently) makes the response dictated by the majority of *H*s in his subset. The working *H* is unaffected by either a blank trial or a confirmation, but the latter is used to evaluate other *H*s in the subset. The working *H* is always changed by a disconfirmation, which is also used to evaluate other *H*s in the subset.

One other point is important. There are hints that a process described for the universe is appropriate for the correct domain as well. It was remarked above that the experimental situation defines domains of *H*s for *S*. The situation may also define subdomains of *H*s within a particular domain. One example was described in the preceding Chapter: *H*s within the same dimension tend to cohere. Another example was shown by Nelson (1971) who performed an 8-D experiment in which the stimuli were divided into two 4-D clusters. By probing for *H*s before each feedback trial, Nelson demonstrated that *S*s tended to sample *H*s first within one cluster, then within the other. A similar tendency was observed by Troyer and Millward (1970).

LEVEL III: THE THEORY OF COMPONENT PROCESSES

This aspect of the theory is concerned with *S*'s mode of coding, storing, and retrieving the information from each trial in the specific task under study. What, for example, happens when *S*"selects a subset"? How does *S* remove disconfirmed *H*s from the set? The answers to these questions consist of a detailed description of covert processes expressed in phenomenological language. Thus, such considerations as *S*'s use of imagery, his translation of the stimuli into words, and his rehearsal of the information are among the processes of concern.

The theory was sketched in Reading No. 14. According to the theory the *S* verbally codes the feedback-trial stimuli. More specifically, in simultaneous discrimination, *S* codes aspects only of the stimulus chosen. Suppose, for example, that on the first trial of a 4-D problem a large black X is presented on the left side with a small white T on the right. Suppose, further, that *S*s initial set consists of all eight simple *H*s and that "large" is the working *H*. According to the process just postulated, *S* repeats to himself words like "large, black X, on the left," responds to the left side, and continues rehearsing these words until the feedback appears. If *E* says "right," *S* will have memorized a subset that contains the solution. If *E* says "wrong," all the verbalized *H*s are disconfirmed. The *S* in this latter circumstance can arrive at a subset containing the correct *H* by finding the complement of the just-disconfirmed *H*s. He can now, that is, say something similar to the following: "Large, black, X, and left are wrong. Then small, white, T, and right-side must be correct." Note the differential effects of right and wrong. After a "right" the coded subset is retained without further activity; after a "wrong" *S* must first recode before he can have a comparable subset of acceptable *H*s. This recoding requires extra time and incurs the risk that an incorrect transformation will occur.

To continue with the example, suppose *E* says "right" and *S* retains the presumed working *H* "large." The next feedback trial is presented which, let us assume, shows a large black T on the right. The *S*, whose subset now contains large, black, X, and left-side, would choose the stimulus dictated by his working *H* ("large") and would code those aspects of the selected stimulus that are in his subset. He would choose, that is, the right-hand stimulus and would verbally code "large and black." Again, a "right" produces the proper subset effortlessly. A "wrong" requires rejecting "large" and "black," returning to the subset of four held at the outset of the second feedback trial, and recovering the remainder of that subset. Again, a "wrong" requires more processing and greater possibility of error than a "right."

This scheme accounts for the decrease in set size shown by adult humans and for the differential effects of "right" and "wrong" (see Figs. 4 and 5, respectively, in Reading No. 14). It has other implications that mesh nicely with experimental results. The coding, since it is verbal, is readily rehearsable. The S, therefore, should have little difficulty in maintaining the subset during any delays of feedback. On the other hand, since the processing of information occurs after feedback, a long intertrial interval (ITI) should result in faster learning than a brief ITI. These results have been demonstrated by Bourne and his associates (Bourne & Bunderson 1963; Bourne, Guy, Dodd & Justesen, 1965).

That more information-processing is required after wrongs than rights has two related implications. First, it implies that S needs more time to process the information after a "wrong" than after a "right." This prediction has been confirmed a few times. The characteristic finding (e.g., Erickson, Zajkowsky, & Ehmann, 1966) is that S's latency is longer on trials following a "wrong." Second, it implies an asymmetry in the effects of ITI. White (1972) compared a group receiving a long ITI after "wrong" and a short ITI after "right" with a group receiving the reverse ITI contingencies. The former group (long ITI after "wrong," etc.) learned more quickly than the latter (short ITI after "wrong," etc.). In addition to these confirmations, Chumley (1969) adapted a mathematical model to the theory. He demonstrated that this model better accounted for his data than more conventional models.

Although the theory, as outlined, has relied heavily on verbal coding, it is reasonable to expect that Ss may use imagery. Upon informal questioning Ss in the standard experiment typically report that they verbally code the stimulus. This implies that one might impair concept-learning performance by having S speak extraneous material. An S required to repeat a stream of irrelevant sentences, for example, should perform relatively poorly in the learning task. It would not be surprising, however, if in this circumstance S shifted to an imagery code to maintain the stimulus information. This possibility suggests that S may have flexibility in his selection of these covert processes.

This concludes the description of the three levels of theory. It is clear that H theory is a complex cognitive system, well elaborated beyond the mere suggestion that S's test Hs. Indeed, this extended statement of theory warrants a final reminder of the experimental counterpart. The reader with lingering behavioristic twinges may be dismayed by the array of insubstantial mental processes described in this chapter. Presented in this outline form, the theory seems to lack any concreteness. It is well to recall, therefore, that some of the fundamental theoretical processes (e.g., that S retains a confirmed H) were, in fact, empirical generalizations. Furthermore, a variety of experimental phenomena were clearly derived from the theory. These included such dramatic effects as the all-or-none backwards learning curve, the Blank-trials Law, the precriterion suppression, and nonlearning. While it is true, then, that H theory is a richly cognitive system, this book is offered in evidence that it rests upon a solid base of data.

EPILOGUE

This book contains a cheerful, optimistic tale: after two decades of subterranean existence H-theory reemerges victoriously, solving old problems with new insights and new techniques. It now dominates the areas of discrimination and concept learning, and shows signs of incorporating neighboring topics. Those of us associated with the theory can feel satisfied at having accomplished a durable piece of work.

Any decent theory, however, not only resolves problems but raises new ones. This theory is no exception. As the final chapters were written some difficulties nagged at the corner of my thoughts. I would like, then, as a way of completing the theoretical statement, to communicate what I feel are the most fundamental problems. Problems, of course, are numerous, and they range from highly specific questions (e.g., what strategies do children employ in 8-D concept tasks) to general issues. I will describe here two problems whose solution should enhance considerably our understanding of man as a learner and problem solver.

Both problems are intimately related, but the first is more restricted. It is seen within the standard concept-learning task. An obvious goal of H theory is the description of the processes underlying problem solution. The characterization of S as a focuser is one such description. The comment has been made that the particular description seems to vary with the task. For example, S may be a focuser (i.e., begin by sampling the entire domain) in a 4-D problem but may sample only part of the domain in an 8-D problem. Furthermore, his strategy may change completely if stimuli from previous trials are left available. Thus, S's underlying process, the description which the theorist is trying to distil, may be different for different situations. A particularly pessimistic presentation of this circumstance has recently been put forth by Dominowski (1974).

To understand the theoretical challenge that these variations pose, consider the third level of theory described at the end of the final chapter. The theory was intended for the S facing a 4-D simultaneous-discrimination problem in which the stimulus terminated with the response, that is, before feedback was given. In order to account for the data it was proposed that S codes (translates into words) the stimulus chosen, and that this verbal form is rehearsed until the feedback is received. If S is told "right," he then has in working memory a subset of Hs containing the solution. If, on the other hand, he is told "wrong," then he must "recode," that is, construct from the (now disconfirmed) Hs in working memory the description of the unchosen stimulus. I have performed some pilot work with Ss who were instructed to think aloud. In this task they tend to conform nicely to the stipulated process: they describe the chosen stimulus as (or before) they choose.

If a small change is made in the experiment, however, a change in speech pattern occurs. The procedure is the same as before, except for one detail: the two stimuli stay available to S for three seconds after the feedback appears. After a few such problems the S's verbal behavior changes: First, he is silent as he chooses, but does his coding *after* the feedback appears; second, he verbally codes the appropriate stimulus (instead of the one chosen). He thus eliminates the disadvantage after "wrong" produced by the former procedure. A seemingly minor change in the experimental procedure, therefore, produces a sensible change in the underlying process.

Consider another, but more hypothetical, example. The reports of most Ss confirm that they remember the stimulus information via this verbal transformation. Suppose, now, that the verbal system were preempted. Suppose, that is, that S had to speak aloud (e.g., count backwards) during the concept problem. Would he now be unable to solve the problem? I would hazard that this would not be the case. The S could, and very well might, resort to an imagery system (i.e., he would try to visualize the stimuli) to retain the information.

The examples suggest not merely that S's processes will differ for different situations. They also suggest that the processes will differ in a manner *appropriate* to the variations of the experimental procedure. The underlying processes may vary from one task to another, but these variations seem to "fit" the structure of the task. The picture that emerges of the S is that he has available varying routines which he can call for according to the demands of the situation.

There is not, then, a unique universal process to be determined. Each task, with its special restrictions may yield a special pattern of process. The description of the underlying process within any one task, therefore, while it is valuable and even necessary, is not the final goal of our science. The various descriptions must be related to the corresponding task structures in order to solve the more ultimate questions: What are the routines (such as verbal coding and imaging) that S has available? What are the experimental and environmental determinants that produce the specific configuration of processing? What are the laws of adjustment producing the neat fit between the process configuration and the task structure?

The second problem is a generalization of the first, taking us beyond the concept-learning and discrimination-learning tasks described in these pages. In these tasks, as we have seen, the stimuli consist of a form with attributes which vary independently of each other. In any stimulus, therefore, an arbitrary relationship exists among the levels of the different dimensions. Furthermore, E can arbitrarily select any of these components to serve as the solution. The stimulus situation facing S, therefore, has a relatively simple, easily specifiable structure. Contrast this type of problem with the other extreme, that in which spatial structure defines the problem and the solution. In the latter category would fall detour problems, the various construction problems studied by Maier, the tool-using problems by Kohler, and the problems of spatial inference employed by Tolman. There are, in short, the vast class of problem tasks in which solution depends not upon some arbitrarily selected stimulus component, but upon the structure of both the situation and the materials that S must work with. For these tasks of object-and-space negotiation, the prevalent psychological notions have to do with S's corresponding knowledge structure: "cognitive map" and "schema" are the central theoretical concepts. Such concepts imply that S may make inferences about (i.e., may be directed toward) the solution, from his knowledge of the structure. Furthermore, solution behavior is said to follow from "insight," a concept suggesting that S's perception of critical details of the structure directs him to the solution. Clearly hypotheses and hypothesis testing play a part in solution to these problems, but no attempt has yet been made to relate the current theory to this conception of knowledge structures.

A more general theory, then, of learning and problem solving must deal with S's interaction with the structure of his environment. Currently, H theory provides only some terminology in which to state the issues: What is the role of the environment in defining the domains of Hs that S will consider? When a domain becomes empty what processes direct S toward a particular new domain? Do special perceptual, that is, environmental, determinants exist directing Ss toward the correct domain? The questions raised in connection with the first problem may also be added to this list. In general, what are the laws relating environmental structure to underlying process?

With this statement of the problems the description of H theory is concluded. It is fitting that the book end with a statement of such perplexing problems. The reader is thereby reminded that the theory is not so much an edifice as a signpost pointing toward future work.

APPENDIX

A system (Sy) analysis was introduced in Chapter 9, as part of the discussion of the child data. The technique for analyzing a set of protocols into the various *Sy*s is demonstrated here. This presentation covers both the assumptions necessary to the analysis and the details of the procedures employed with the data of Experiment I in Reading No. 18.

THE GENERAL CONCEPTION

It is assumed that S begins a problem with some Sy, that is, with some system that dictates his mode of sampling Hs. Each Sy is manifested in one of a small subset of H sequences. For example, the Sy Stimulus Preference is manifested when the same H is continually repeated after each of a series of disconfirmations. Since the particular H is not specified, there is a small subset of these H sequences — S might perseverate on "large size," or on "black," etc.

A second assumption is that this Sy is maintained at least until the fourth feedback trial, that is, the Hs observed after each of the first three feedback trials are dictated by a single Sy.

The third assumption concerns S's manner of resampling for Hs after a disconfirmation. The Hs are divided into two classes. Response-set Hs (defined as S's preference, or bias, causing him to produce long strings of stereotypic responses) and Prediction Hs (defined as S's prediction concerning the solution). Correspondingly, the Sys are divided into two classes: *stereotypes* (e.g., stimulus preference), in which S persists in the same H despite repeated disconfirmations, and *strategies*, in which S follows some plan which, in principle, leads to solution. During strategies an H is genuinely tested, that is, it is retained following a confirmation and is rejected following a disconfirmation. The third assumption is that when S rejects an H and resamples (i.e., during strategies) he always selects a locally consistent H. The procedures of the experiment in Reading No. 18 made this a plausible assumption, since the feedback was given by having a light appear just above the correct stimulus pattern, and both the light and this pattern stayed on for three seconds.

Finally, the set of Sys is specified *a priori*. In Experiment I the following set was considered:

Stimulus preference (abbreviated S-P). *S* selects an *H* and persists with it for the three feedback trials.

Hypothesis checking (abbreviated H-Ch). The eight *H*s are ordered by *S* into the pairs of *H*s from each of the four dimensions, as though *S* imagines a list of four pairs of *H*s. He goes through this list, testing each *H* in turn, one dimension at a time. Thus, he tries an *H*, then, if it is disconfirmed, he tries its complement (the opposite *H*, abbreviated op*H*). If that is disconfirmed, he tries an *H* from another dimension, then its complement, etc.

Dimension checking (abbreviated D). As with *H*-Ch the *H*s are ordered by the four dimensions. In this case, *S* recognizes that, after the first trial, disconfirmation of an *H* also logically disconfirms the entire dimension. (This is logically correct since the just-disconfirmed *H* was, when it had been sampled, locally consistent. Its complement, therefore, of necessity had at that time been locally inconsistent.) After each disconfirmation, therefore, the *H* comes from a different dimension.

Focusing (abbreviated Fo). With each feedback *S* eliminates all disconfirmed *H*s, whether explicitly manifested or not. Thus, each *H* manifested is consistent with all the preceding feedback-trial information. The *H* after the third feedback trial is, of necessity, the solution.

THE ANALYSIS

In principle, *E*'s decision about the *Sy* employed by a particular *S* on a particular problem is simple. He inspects the first three *H*s and, on the basis of the particular *H* sequence, decides which *Sy* is being manifested. However, a more detailed treatment of the general analytical technique is required because there are certain minor complications. First, not all feedback sequences during the first three feedback trials may be used. To take the most extreme example, if *S* makes the correct response for the three feedback trials, according to every *Sy, S* will show the same *H* repeatedly. The *Sy*s may be distinguished only by *S*s mode of resampling following a disconfirmation. In general, sequences in which *S* was correct on the third feedback trial were not used.

A second consideration is that there is occasional overlap in the manifestation of two *Sy*s. For example, an *S* who is following the D *Sy* may, when resampling after the third feedback trial, select the correct dimension and, perforce, the solution *H*. The resulting *H* sequence might be identical to that of an *S* following the Fo *Sy*. Such confounding requires special techniques for arriving at valid estimates of the frequency with which the various *Sy*s occur. These techniques vary somewhat with each type of confounding and with the feedback sequence.

Because of these complications the categorizing of protocols will be described separately for each sequence of feedback trials. Problems with confounding will be discussed as they arise. Before proceeding, however, a few definitions will be helpful:

1. The feedback, "right" or "wrong" will be symbolized by + or -, respectively. A subscript (e.g., $+_2$) will indicate the trial on which the feedback occurred.

2. The subscripts i, j, k, and l will refer to the four dimensions. Thus, the symbol H_j will refer to the first H seen from the jth dimension. If the jth dimension is color and "black" is the first H observed from this dimension, then H_j = black. The complementary, or opposite, H will be indicated by the prefix "op." Thus, if H_j = black, then opH_j = white. In general, the subscripts $i, \ldots, l$ will be used in chronological sequence, so that i will be employed for the first dimension manifested in a problem, j for the second, etc.

3. The correct H, that is, the solution, will be symbolized as H^+.

4. Corresponding to the Sy labels, S-P, H-Ch, D, and Fo, will be the frequencies of these Sys: f(S-P), $f(H$-Ch), etc.

A. Sequence $+_1 -_2 -_3$

Each experimental problem is tentatively catalogued as one of the four Sys according to the manifestation indicated:

Stimulus preference (S-P) manifestation: $+_1 H_i -_2 H_i -_3 H_i$.

Hypothesis checking (H-Ch) manifestation: $+_1 H_i -_2 \text{op} H_i -_3 H_j$.

Dimension checking (tentative cataloguing, indicated by priming the symbol, D′) manifestation: $+_1 H_i -_2 H_j -_3 (H_k \neq H^+)$.

Focusing (tentative cataloguing, indicated by priming the symbol, Fo′) manifestation: $+_1 H_i -_2 H_j -_3 (H_k = H^+)$. Also, H_j must be not only locally consistent (see Assumption 3, above) but consistent with the first feedback trial as well. If this criterion is not met then the sequence is interpreted as a manifestation of D′.

Corrections required. After cataloguing the problems according to the sets of manifestations noted above, a correction is required. An S following the D Sy may choose an H_j consistent with the first feedback trial and an $H_k = H^+$. The resulting H sequence would (mistakenly) be catalogued as Fo, thereby inflating its frequency estimate, f(Fo), and correspondingly decreasing f(D). The relative frequency with which this particular H sequence occurs (given that S holds D and responds so as to receive the feedback sequence $+_1 -_2 -_3$) may be estimated from the following considerations: The corrected D value contains two components, those sequences which cannot be confused with the Fo sequence (labeled D′) and those sequences which resemble the Fo sequence (labeled D′*).

The frequency of D is the sum of the two frequencies, i.e.,

$$f(D) = f(D') + f(D^*),$$

where $f(D')$ is obtained directly from the data. Similarly, the sequences in the category labeled Fo' contain two different sets of sequences: those which are actually the result of the Fo Sy (labeled Fo) and those which are from the D Sy(D*). These two frequencies combine giving

$$f(Fo') = f(Fo) + f(D^*),$$

where $f(Fo')$ is obtained directly from the data.

These two equations contain three unknowns. A third equation is obtained from these considerations: With orthogonal stimulus sequences an S who is holding the D Sy and who will receive $+_1$ and $-_2$ may start the problem with one of only two Hs (there are four Hs which lead to a correct response on trial 1; two of these lead to an error on Trial 2). Starting with one of these two Hs, D*, the sequence resembling the Fo sequence, will occur one-fourth of the time; starting with the other H that Fo-resembling sequence will occur one-half the time. Since the probability that this S (holding the D Sy) will start the problem with each of these two Hs is one-half, the probability of D* occurring is given by

$$\frac{1}{2}\left(\frac{1}{4}\right) + \frac{1}{2}\left(\frac{1}{2}\right) = \frac{3}{8}.$$

Similarly, D' will occur $\frac{5}{8}$ of the time. Therefore, the required third equation is

$$f(D^*) = \frac{3}{5}f(D').$$

Solving the three equations yields

$$f(D) = f(D') + \frac{3}{5}f(D') \text{ and } f(Fo) = f(Fo') - \frac{3}{5}f(D').$$

Thus, the value $\frac{3}{5}f(D')$ must be added to and subtracted from, respectively, the initial, tentative frequency assignments for the D Sy and the Fo Sy.

B. Sequence $-_1-_2-_3$

S-P manifestation: $-_1H_i -_2H_i -_3H_i$.

H-Ch manifestation: This Sy has two sets of sequences depending upon whether one assumes that S holds an H before the problem starts or whether one assumes that S receives information from the first trial before applying his Sy. Each procedure yields its own unique sequence. Either sequence, therefore, was regarded as an instance of H-Ch.

These sequences are

$$-_1H_i -_2H_j -_3\text{op}H_j \qquad \text{or} \qquad -_1H_i -_2\text{op}H_i -_3H_j$$

D' manifestation: $-_1H_i -_2H_j -_3(H_k \neq H^+)$

Fo' manifestation: $-_1H_i -_2H_j -_3(H_k = H^+)$

The same confounding between D and Fo exists with this feedback sequence as with the preceding. Also, the same correction procedure is appropriate:

$$f(\mathrm{D}) = f(\mathrm{D}') + \tfrac{3}{5} f(\mathrm{D}') \qquad \text{and} \qquad f(\mathrm{Fo}) = f(\mathrm{Fo}') - \tfrac{3}{5} f(\mathrm{D}'),$$

where $f(\mathrm{D}')$ and $f(\mathrm{Fo}')$ are frequencies obtained from the initial cataloguing.

C. Sequence $+_1 +_2 -_3$

S-P manifestation: $+_1H_i +_2H_i -_3H_i.$

H-Ch manifestations: $+_1H_i + _2H_i -_3\mathrm{op}H_i.$

D' manifestation: $+_1H_i +_2H_i -_3(H_j \neq H^+).$

Fo' manifestation: $+_1H_i +_2H_i -_3(H_j = H^+).$

Here, again, an S holding the D Sy would, if the correct dimension were second on his list, produce a sequence resembling focusing. Since the correct dimension cannot be first on this S's list (the given feedback sequence has an error on trial 3, an impossible event if S started out holding H^+) it may be either second, third, or fourth. One-third of the time it will be second and a Fo sequence will result, i.e.,

$$P(\mathrm{D}^* | \mathrm{D}) = \tfrac{1}{3} \text{ and } P(\mathrm{D}'|\mathrm{D}) = \tfrac{2}{3}.$$

Therefore $f(\mathrm{D}^*) = \tfrac{1}{2} f(\mathrm{D}')$, and

$$f(\mathrm{D}) = f(\mathrm{D}') + \tfrac{1}{2} f(\mathrm{D}'), \quad f(\mathrm{Fo}) = f(\mathrm{Fo}') - \tfrac{1}{2} f(\mathrm{D}').$$

D. Sequence $-_1 +_2 -_3$

S-P manifestation: $-_1H_i +_2H_i -_3H_i.$

H-Ch' manifestation: As with the sequence $-_1 -_2 -_3$, it is necessary to recognize that H-Ch can have one of two forms: the S may hold an H before the first feedback trial or he may start through his list after receiving information from the first feedback trial. In the latter case no difficulties arise. The manifestation is $-_1H_i +_2H_i -_3\mathrm{op}H_i.$ If, however, S uses the initial feedback trial to reject the first H from the first dimension on his list, then the disconfirmation at Trial 3 causes a shift to a new dimension, yielding the sequence $-_1H_i +_2H_i -_3H_j.$ It should be obvious that this sequence is identical to that produced by D and, if $H_j = H^+$, by Fo. The confounding with D will be treated here; the confounding with Fo will be treated subsequently.

If $H_j \neq H^+$ then the sequence could be the result of H-Ch or of D. A simple way to deconfound is to view the next H S employs. If his Sy is H-Ch, then he will show $-_1H_i +_2H_i -_3H_j -_4\mathrm{op}H_j.$ This clearly is not a product of D. If, on the other hand, S is holding the D Sy, then he will show $-_1H_i +_2H_i -_3H_j -_4H_k$. In summary, $(H\text{-Ch}')$ manifestation:

$(H\text{-Ch})_1$: $-_1H_i +_2H_i -_3\text{op}H_i$, or

$(H\text{-Ch}')_2$: $-_1H_i +_2H_i -_3(H_j \neq H^+) -_4\text{op}H_j$

D$'$ manifestation: $-_1H_i +_2H_i -_3(H_j \neq H^+) -_4H_k$

Fo$'$ manifestation: $-_1H_i +_2H_i -_3(H_j = H^+)$

Correction required. Whereas with previous feedback sequences only the D and Fo Sys yielded the same H sequence, here three Sys, $(H\text{-Ch})_2$ as well as D and Fo, can yield the same H sequence. The derivation of the correction here, however, parallels the derivation in the previous cases.

Thus, the corrected frequency for $(H\text{-Ch})_2$ contains two components, those sequences, here labeled $(H\text{-Ch}')_2$, not confusable with the other two Sy patterns, and the sequence which resembles that from the Fo Sy, labeled $(H\text{-Ch}^*)_2$. The frequency of $(H\text{-Ch})_2$ is the sum of the two frequencies, i.e.,

$$f(H\text{-Ch})_2 = f(H\text{-Ch}')_2 + f(H\text{-Ch}^*)_2.$$

Similarly,

$$f(\text{D}) = f(\text{D}') + f(\text{D}^*).$$

Also,

$$f(\text{Fo}) = f(\text{Fo}') - f(H\text{-Ch}^*)_2 - f(\text{D}^*).$$

Values for the primed variables are obtained directly from the data. In order to determine the corrected values of the Sys, that is, $f(H\text{-Ch})_2, f(\text{D})$, and $f(\text{Fo})$, it is necessary first to determine the values of $f(H\text{-Ch}^*)_2$ and $f(\text{D}^*)$. These may be obtained from the following considerations:

For $(H\text{-Ch})_2$. An S's H sequence will resemble the Fo Sy only if the correct dimension is second on his list. Since it cannot be first on the list (H_i cannot be H^+ because of the error given at the third feedback trial), it will be second one-third of the time. Therefore

$$P[(H\text{-Ch}^*)_2 | (H\text{-Ch})_2] = \tfrac{1}{3} \quad \text{and} \quad P[(H\text{-Ch}')_2 | (H\text{-Ch})_2] = \tfrac{2}{3}.$$

From this we obtain

$$f(H\text{-Ch}^*)_2 = \tfrac{1}{2} f(H\text{-Ch}')_2.$$

For D. The consideration which applies to $(H\text{-Ch})_2$ applies here. One-third of the time an S who holds the D Sy and who receives the feedback sequence $-_1+_2-_3$ will have the correct dimension second on his list. Therefore,

$$P(\text{D}^*|\text{D}) = \tfrac{1}{3}, \quad P(\text{D}'|\text{D}) = \tfrac{2}{3}, \quad f(\text{D}^*) = \tfrac{1}{2} f(\text{D}').$$

The appropriate corrected equations are

$$f(H\text{-}Ch)_2 = f(H\text{-}Ch')_2 + \frac{1}{2} f(H\text{-}Ch')_2,$$
$$f(D) = f(D') + \frac{1}{2} f(D'),$$
$$f(Fo) = f(Fo') - [\frac{1}{2} f(H\text{-}Ch')_2 + \frac{1}{2} f(D')].$$

The foregoing describes the technique of determining the corrected frequency of each Sy for each of the four feedback sequences. The overall frequency distribution, plotted in Fig. 2 of Reading No. 18, was produced by simply adding the four frequency estimates for each Sy, and by then transforming these totals to relative frequencies.

REFERENCES*

Amsel, A. Rate of learning a visual brightness discrimination as a function of discriminanda durations. *Journal of Comparative & Physiological Psychology,* 1952, **45**, 341–346.

Andrews, O. E., Levinthal, C. F., & Fishbein, H. D. The organization of hypothesis-testing behavior in concept-identification tasks. *American Journal of Psychology,* 1969, **82**, 523-530.

Archer, E. J., Bourne, L. E., Jr., & Brown, F. G. Concept identification as a function of irrelevant information and instructions. *Journal of Experimental Psychology,* 1955, **49**, 153–164.

Atkinson, R. C. The observing response in discrimination learning. Technical Report No. 4, 1959, University of California, Los Angeles, Contract Nonr 233 (59). (a)

Atkinson, R. C. A theory of stimulus discrimination learning. Technical Report No. 1, 1959, University of California, Los Angeles, Contract Nonr 233 (58). (b)

Austin, G. A., Bruner, J. S., & Seymour, R. V. Fixed-choice strategies in concept attainment. *American Psychologist,* 1953, **8**, 314. (Abstract.)

Bandura, A. *Principles of behavior modification.* New York: Holt, Rhinehart & Winston, 1969.

Behar, L. Analysis of object-alternation learning by rhesus monkeys. *Journal of Comparative & Physiological Psychology,* 1961, **54**, 539–542.

Bendig, A. W. The effect of reinforcement on the alternation of guesses. *Journal of Experimental Psychology,* 1951, **41**, 105–107.

Binder, A. Further considerations on testing the null hypothesis and the strategy and tactics of investigating theoretical models. *Psychological Review,* 1963, **70**, 107–115.

Blum, R. A., & Blum, J. S. Factual issues in the "continuity controversy". *Psychological Review,* 1949, **56**, 33–50.

Bollinger, P. An experimental study of the pre-solution period of discrimination learning in the white rat. Unpublished master's thesis, State University of Iowa, 1940.

Bourne, L. E., Jr. Effects of delay of information feedback and task complexity on the identification of concepts. *Journal of Experimental Psychology,* 1957, **54**, 201–207.

Bourne, L. E., Jr., & Bunderson, C. V. Effects of delay of informative feedback and length of postfeedback interval on concept identification. *Journal of Experimental Psychology,* 1963, **65**, 1–5.

Bourne, L. E., Jr., Guy, D. E., Dodd, D. H., & Justesen, D. R. Concept identification: The effects of varying length and informational components of the intertrial interval. *Journal of Experimental Psychology,* 1965, **69**, 624–629.

Bourne, L. E., Jr., & Haygood, R. C. The role of stimulus redundancy in concept identification. *Journal of Experimental Psychology,* 1959, **58**, 232–238.

Bourne, L. E., Jr., & Restle, F. A mathematical theory of concept identification. *Psychological Review,* 1959, **66**, 278–296.

Bower, G. H. Properties of the one-element model as applied to paired associate learning, Technical Report No. 31, 1960, Stanford University, Contract Nonr 225(17).

Bower, G. H. An associational model for response and training variables in paired-associate learning. *Psychological Review,* 1962, **69**, 34–53.

*References that have been adapted as Readings in this volume are asterisked.

*Bower, G. H., & Trabasso, T. Reversals prior to solution in concept identification. *Journal of Experimental Psychology*, 1963, **66**, 409–418.

Bower, G. H., & Trabasso, T. Concept identification. In R. C. Atkinson (Ed.), *Studies in mathematical psychology*. Stanford, California: Stanford University Press, 1964.

Broadbent, D. E. *Perception and communication*. New York: Pergamon, 1958.

Brown, F. G., & Archer, E. J. Concept identification as a function of task complexity and distribution of practice. *Journal of Experimental Psychology*, 1956, **52**, 316–321.

Bruner, J. S. Personality dynamics and the process of perceiving. In R. R. Blake & G. V. Ramsey (Eds.), *Perception: An approach to personality*. New York: Ronald Press, 1951.

*Bruner, J. S., Goodnow, J. J., & Austin, G. A. *A Study of thinking*. New York: Wiley, 1956.

Bruner, J. S., Miller, G. A., & Zimmerman, C. Discriminative skill and discriminative matching in perceptual recognition. *Journal of Experimental Psychology*, 1955, **49**, 187–192.

Buchwald, A. M. Experimental alterations in the effectiveness of verbal reinforcement combinations. *Journal of Experimental Psychology*, 1959, **57**, 351–361.   (a)

Buchwald, A. M. Extinction after acquisition under different verbal reinforcement combinations. *Journal of Experimental Psychology*, 1959, **57**, 43–48.   (b)

Burke, C. J., Estes, W. K., & Hellyer, S. Rate of verbal conditioning in relation to stimulus variability. *Journal of Experimental Psychology*, 1954, **48**, 153–161.

Bush, R. R., & Mosteller, F. A model for stimulus generalization and discrimination. *Psychological Review*, 1951, **58**, 413–423.

Bush, R. R., & Mosteller, F. *Stochastic Models for Learning*. New York: Wiley, 1955.

Buss, A. H. Rigidity as a function of reversal and nonreversal shifts in the learning of successive discriminations. *Journal of Experimental Psychology*, 1953, **45**, 75–81.

Buss, A. H. Reversal and nonreversal shifts in concept formation with partial reinforcement eliminated. *Journal of Experimental Psychology*, 1956, **52**, 162–166.

Buss, A. H., Braden, W., Orfel, A., & Buss, E. H. Acquisition and extinction with different verbal reinforcement combinations. *Journal of Experimental Psychology*, 1956, **52**, 288–295.

Buss, A. H., & Buss, E. H. The effect of verbal reinforcement combinations on conceptual learning. *Journal of Experimental Psychology*, 1956, **52**, 283–287.

Cairns, R. B. Informational properties of verbal and nonverbal events. *Journal of Personality and Social Psychology*, 1967, **5**, 353–357.

Chumbley, J. Hypothesis memory in concept learning. *Journal of Mathematical Psychology*, 1969, **6**, 528–540.

Dennis, W. Spontaneous alternation in rats as an indicator of the persistence of stimulus effects. *Journal of Comparative Psychology*, 1939, **28**, 305–312.

Dickerson, D. J. Irrelevant stimulus dimensions and dimensional transfer in the discrimination learning of children. *Journal of Experimental Child Psychology*, 1967, **5**, 228–236.

Dixon, P. W., & Oakes, S. F. Effects of intertrial activity on the relationship between awareness and verbal operant conditioning. *Journal of Experimental Psychology*, 1965, **69**, 152–157.

Dollard, J., & Miller, N. E. *Personality and psychotherapy*. New York: McGraw-Hill, 1950.

Dominowski, R. L. How do people discover concepts? In R. L. Solso (Ed.) *Theories in cognitive psychology: The Loyola Symposium*. Potomac, Md.: Lawrence Erlbaum Associates, 1974.

Dulaney, D. E., Jr. Hypotheses and habits in verbal "operant conditioning." *Journal of Abnormal & Social Psychology*, 1961, **63**, 251–263.

Dulaney, D. E., Jr. Awareness, rules, and propositional control: A confrontation with S–R behavior and general behavior theory. Englewood Cliffs, New Jersey: Prentice-Hall, 1968.

Ehrenfreund, D. An experimental test of the continuity theory of discrimination learning with pattern vision. *Journal of Comparative & Physiological Psychology*, 1948, **41**, 408–422.

Eimas, P. D. Optional shift behavior in children as a function of over training, irrelevant stimuli, and age. *Journal of Experimental Child Psychology*, 1967, **5**, 332–340.

Eimas, P. D. A developmental study of hypothesis behavior and focusing. *Journal of Experimental Child Psychology*, 1969, **8**, 160–172.

Eninger, M. U. Habit summation in a selective learning problem. *Journal of Comparative & Physiological Psychology*, 1952, **45**, 511–516.

Erickson, J. R. Hypothesis sampling in concept identification. *Journal of Experimental Psychology*, 1968, **76**, 12–18.

Erickson, J. R. Problem shifts and hypothesis behavior in concept identification. *American Journal of Psychology*, 1971, **84**, 100–111.

Erickson, J. R., Zajkowski, M. M., & Ehmann, E. D. All-or-none assumptions in concept identification. *Journal of Experimental Psychology*, 1966, **72**, 690–697.

Estes, W. K. Toward a statistical theory of learning. *Psychological Review*, 1950, **57**, 94–107.

Estes, W. K. The statistical approach to learning theory. In S. Koch (Ed.), *Psychology: A Study of a science*. Vol. 2. New York: McGraw-Hill, 1959.

*Estes, W. K. Learning theory and the new "mental chemistry." *Psychological Review*, 1960, **67**, 207–223.

Estes, W. K. Probability learning. In A. W. Melton (Ed.), *Categories of human learning*. New York: Academic Press, 1964.

Estes, W. K., and Burke, C. J. A theory of stimulus variability in learning. *Psychological Review*, 1953, **60**, 276–286.

*Estes, W. K., & Burke, C. J. Application of a statistical model to simple discrimination learning in human subjects. *Journal of Experimental Psychology*, 1955, **50**, 81–88.

Estes, W. K., Hopkins, B. L., & Crothers, E. J. All-or-none and conservation effects in the learning and retention of paired associates. *Journal of Experimental Psychology*, 1960, **60**, 329–339.

Estes, W. K., & Straughan, J. H. Analysis of a verbal conditioning situation in terms of statistical learning theory. *Journal of Experimental Psychology*, 1954, **47**, 255–234.

Falmagne, R. Construction of a hypothesis model for concept identification. *Journal of Mathematical Psychology*, 1970, **7**, 60–96.

Feller, W. *An introduction to probability theory and its applications*. New York: Wiley, 1950.

Fellows, B. J. *The discrimination process and development*. New York: Pergamon Press, 1968.

Fingerman, P., & Levine, M. Nonlearning: the completeness of the blindness. *Journal of Experimental Psychology* 1974, **102**, 720–721.

Fisher, S. C. An analysis of a phase of the process of classifying. *American Journal of Psychology*, 1917, **28**, 57–116.

*Frankel, F., Levine, M., & Karpf, D. Human discrimination learning: A test of the blank-trials assumption. *Journal of Experimental Psychology*, 1970, **83**, 342–348.

Friedman, S. R. Developmental level and concept-learning: Confirmation of an inverse relationship. *Psychonomic Science*, 1965, **2**, 3–4.

Gellermann, L. W. Chance orders of alternating stimuli in visual discrimination experiments. *Journal of Genetic Psychology*, 1933, **42**, 207–208.

*Gholson, B., Levine, M., & Phillips, S. Hypotheses, strategies, and stereotypes in discrimination learning. *Journal of Experimental Child Psychology*, 1972, **13**, 423–446.

Glanzer, M., & Clark, W. H. The verbal loop hypothesis: Conventional figures. *American Journal of Psychology*, 1964, **77**, 621–626.

Glanzer, M., & Cunitz, A. R. Two storage mechanisms in free recall. *Journal of Verbal Learning & Verbal Behavior*, 1966, **5**, 351–360.

Glanzer, M., Huttenlocher, J., & Clark, W. H. Systematic operations in solving concept problems: A parametric study of a class of problems. *Psychological Monographs*, 1963, **77**(1, Whole No. 564).

Glassman, W. E., & Levine, M. Unsolved- and insoluble-problem behavior. *Journal of Experimental Psychology*, 1972, **92**, 146-148.

Glaze, J. A. The association value of nonsense syllables. *Journal of Genetic Psychology*, 1928, **35**, 255–267.

Goodnow, J. J., & Pettigrew, T. F. Effect of prior patterns of experience upon strategies and learning sets. *Journal of Experimental Psychology*, 1955, **49**, 381–389.

Goodnow, J. J., & Postman, L. Probability learning in a problem-solving situation. *Journal of*

Experimental Psychology, 1955, **49**, 16–22.

Goodnow, J. J., Shanks, Betty, Rubinstein, I., & Lubin, A. What is the human subject responding to in a two-choice task? WRAIR Problem-Solving Proj. Memo., 1957, No. 3.

Grant, D. A. Testing the null hypothesis and the strategy and tactics of investigating theoretical models. *Psychological Review*, 1962, **69**, 54–61.

Grant, D. A., & Berg, E. A. A behavioral analysis of degree of reinforcement and ease of shifting to new responses in a Weigl-type card-sorting problem. *Journal of Experimental Psychology*, 1948, **38**, 404–411.

Grant, D. A., & Cost, J. R. Continuities and discontinuities in conceptual behavior in a card-sorting problem. *Journal of Genetic Psychology*, 1954, **50**, 237–244.

Grant, D. A., & Curran, J. F. Relative difficulty of number, form, and color concepts of a Weigl-type problem using unsystematic number cards. *Journal of Experimental Psychology*, 1952, **43**, 408–413.

Grant, D. A., Hake, H. W., & Hornseth, J. P. Acquisition and extinction of a verbal conditioned response with differing percentages of reinforcement. *Journal of Experimental Psychology*, 1951, **42**, 1–5.

Greenspoon, J. The reinforcing effect of two spoken sounds on the frequency of two responses. *American Journal of Psychology*, 1955, **68**, 409–416.

Gregg, L. W., & Simon, H. A. Process models and stochastic theories of simple concept formation. *Journal of Mathematical Psychology*, 1967, **4**, 246–276.

Gumer, E., & Levine, M. The missing dimension in concept learning. *Journal of Experimental Psychology*, 1971, **90**, 39–44.

Haber, R. N. Effects of coding strategy on perceptual memory. *Journal of Experimental Psychology*, 1964, **68**, 357–362.

Haire, M. A note concerning McCullock's discussion of discrimination habits. *Psychological Review*, 1939, **46**, 298–303.

Hamilton, G. V. A study of trial and error reactions in mammals. *Journal of Animal Behavior Monographs*, 1911, **1**, 33–66.

Harlow, H. F. The formation of learning sets. *Psychological Review*, 1949, **56**, 51–65.

*Harlow, H. F. Analysis of discrimination learning by monkeys. *Journal of Experimental Psychology*, 1950, **40**, 26–39.

Harlow, H. F., Harlow, M. K., Rueping, R. R. & Mason, W. A. Performance of infant rhesus monkeys on discrimination learning, delayed response, and discrimination learning set. *Journal of Comparative & Physiological Psychology*, 1960, **53**, 113–121.

Harlow, H. F., & Hicks, L. H. Discrimination learning theory; Uniprocess vs. duoprocess. *Psychological Review*, 1957, **64**, 104–109.

Harlow, H. F., & Poch, S. Discrimination generalization by macaque monkeys to unidimensional and multidimensional stimuli. *Journal of comparative Psychology*, 1945, **38**, 353–365.

Harter, S. Mental age, IQ, and motivational factors in the discrimination learning-set performance of normal and retarded children. *Journal of Experimental Child Psychology*, 1967, **5**, 123–141.

Hayes, K. J. The backward curve: A method for the study of learning. *Psychological Review*, 1953, **60**, 269–275.

Heidbreder, E. An experimental study of thinking. *Archives of Psychology, New York*, 1924, **11**, No. 73.

Hernandez-Peon, R., Scherrer, H., & Jouvet, M. Modification of electric activity in the cochlear nucleus during 'attention' in unanesthetized rats. *Science*, 1956, **123**, 331–332.

Hilgard, E. R. *Theories of learning*. (Rev. ed.) New York: Appleton-Century-Crofts, 1956.

Holstein, S. B., & Premack, D. On the different effects of random reinforcement and presolution reversal on human concept identification *Journal of Experimental Psychology*, 1965, **70**, 335–337.

Hovland, C. I. A "communication analysis" of concept learning. *Psychological Review*, 1952, **59**, 461–472.

Hovland, C. I., & Weiss, W. Transmission of information concerning concepts through positive and negative instances. *Journal of Experimental Psychology*, 1953, **45**, 175 182.

Hull, C. L. *Principles of behavior*. New York: Appleton, 1943.

Humphreys, L. G. Acquisition and extinction of verbal expectation in a situation analogous to conditioning. *Journal of Experimental Psychology*, 1939, **25**, 294–301.

Hunt, E. B. *Concept learning*. New York: Wiley, 1962.

Hunter, W. S. The temporal maze and kinaesthetic sensory processes in the white rat. *Psychobiology*, 1920, **2**, 1–17.

Ingalls, R. P., & Dickerson, D. J. Development of hypothesis behavior in human concept identification. *Developmental Psychology*, 1969, **1**, 707–716.

Jarvik, M. E. Probability learning and a negative recency effect in the serieal anticipation of alternative symbols. *Journal of Experimental Psychology*, 1951, **41**, 291–297.

Johnson, D. M. *A systematic introduction to the psychology of thinking. New York: Harper & Row, 1972.*

Johnson, P. J., Fishkin, A., & Bourne, L. E., Jr. *Effects of procedural variables upon reversal and interdimensional shift performance: II. Psychonomic Science*, 1966, **4**, 69–70.

Kanfer, F. H. Verbal conditioning: A review of its current status. In T. R. Dixon & D. L. Horton (Eds.), *Verbal behavior and general behavior theory*. Englewood Cliffs, New Jersey: Prentice-Hall, 1968.

Karpf, D. and Levine, M. Blank-trial probes and introtacts in human discrimination learning. *Journal of Experimental Psychology*, 1971, **90**, 51–55.

Kelleher, R. T. Discrimination learning as a function of reversal and nonreversal shifts *Journal of Experimental Psychology*, 1956, **51**, 379–384.

Kellogg, W. N. & Wolf, I. S. "Hypotheses" and "random activity" during the conditioning of dogs. *Journal of Experimental Psychology*, 1940, **26**, 588–601.

*Kendler, T. S. Learning, development, and thinking. *Annals of the New York Academy of Sciences*, 1960, **91**, 52–63.

Kendler, H. H., & D'Amato, M. F. A comparison of reversal and nonreversal shifts in human concept formation behavior. *Journal of Experimental Psychology*, 1955, **49**, 165–174.

Kendler, H. H., Glucksberg, S., & Keston, R. Perception and mediation in concept learning. *Journal of Experimental Psychology*, 1961, **61**, 1–16.

Kendler, H. H., & Kendler, T. S. Vertical and horizontal processes in problem solving. *Psychological Review*, 1962, **69**, 1–16.

Kendler, H. H., & Kendler, T. S. Mediation and conceptual behavior. In K. W. Spence & J. T. Spence (Eds.), *The psychology of learning and motivation*. Vol. 2. New York: Academic Press, 1968.

Kendeler, H. H., & Kendler, T. S. Reversal shift behavior: Some basic issues. *Psychological Bulletin*, 1969, **72**, 229–232.

Kimble, G. A. *Hilgard and Marquis' conditioning and learning*. New York: Appleton, 1961.

Koehler, J. Role of instructions in two choice verbal conditioning with contingent partial reinforcement. *Journal of Experimental Psychology*, 1961, **62**, 122–125.

Kohler, W. Intelligence in apes. In C. Murchison (Ed.), *Psychologies of 1925*. Worcester, Massachusetts: Clark University Press, 1926.

Kornreich, L. B. Strategy selection and information processing in human discrimination learning. *Journal of Educational Psychology*, 1968, **59**, 438–448.

Krasner, L. Studies of the conditioning of verbal behavior. *Psychological Bulletin*, 1958, **55**, 148–170.

Krasner, L. Verbal operant conditioning and awareness. In K. Salzinger & S. Salzinger (Eds.), *Research in verbal behavior and some neurophysiological implications*. New York: Academic Press, 1967.

Krechevsky, I., "Hypotheses" in rats. *Psychological Review*, 1932, **39**, 516–532.   (a)

*Krechevsky, I. "Hypothesis" versus "chance" in the pre-solution period in sensory discrimination learning. *University of California Publications in Psychology*, 1932, **6**, 27–44. (b)

Krechevsky, I. The docile nature of hypotheses. *Journal of Comparative Psychology*, 1933, **15**, 429–443. (a)

Krechevsky, I. Hereditary nature of "hypotheses". *Journal of Comparative Psychology*, 1933, **16**, 99–116. (b)

Krechevsky, I. A note concerning "the nature of discrimination learning in animals." *Psychological Review*, 1937, **44**, 97–103.

Krechevsky, I. A study of the continuity of the problem-solving process. *Psychological Review*, 1938, **45**, 107–133.

Lashley, K. S., *Brain mechanisms and intelligence*. Chicago, Illinois: University of Chicago Press, 1929.

Lawrence, D. H. Acquired distinctiveness of cues: II. Selective association in a constant stimulus situation. *Journal of Experimental Psychology*, 1950, **40**, 175–188.

Levine, M. A model of hypothesis behavior in discrimination learning set. Unpublished doctoral dissertation, University of Wisconsin, 1959. (a)

*Levine, M. A model of hypothesis behavior in discrimination learning set. *Psychological Review*, 1959, **66**, 353–366. (b)

Levine, M. Cue neutralization: The effects of random reinforcements upon discrimination learning. *Journal of Experimental Psychology*, 1962, **63**, 438–443.

Levine, M. The assumption concerning "wrong" in Restle's model of strategies in cue learning. *Psychological Review*, 1963, **70**, 559–561. (a)

*Levine, M. Mediating processes in humans at the outset of discrimination learning. *Psychological Review*, 1963, **70**, 254–276. (b)

*Levine, M. Hypothesis behavior by humans during discrimination learning. *Journal of Experimental Psychology*, 1966, **71**, 331–338.

Levine, M. The size of the hypothesis set during discrimination learning. *Psychological Review*, 1967, **74**, 428–430.

Levine, M. The Latency-choice discrepancy in concept learning. *Journal of Experimental Psychology*, 1969, **82**, 1–3. (b)

Levine, M. Neo-Noncontinuity theory. In G. Bower & Spence, J. T. (Eds.). *The psychology of learning and motivation*. Vol. 3. New York: Academic Press, 1969. Pp. 101–134. (b)

*Levine, M. Human discrimination learning: The Subset sampling assumption. *Psychological Bulletin*, 1970, **74**, 397–404.

*Levine, M. Hypothesis theory and nonlearning despite ideal S–R-reinforcement contingencies. *Psychological Review*, 1971, **78**, 130–140.

*Levine, M., Leitenberg, H., & Richter, M. The blank trials law: The equivalence of positive reinforcement and nonreinforcement. *Psychological Review*, 1964, **71**, 94–103.

Levine, M., Levinson, Billey, & Harlow, H. F. Trials per problem as a variable in the acquisition of discrimination learning set. *Journal of Comparative & Physiological Psychology*, 1959, **52**, 396–398.

*Levine, M., Miller, P., & Steinmeyer, C. H. The none-to-all theorem of human discrimination learning. *Journal of Experimental Psychology*, 1967, **73**, 568–573.

*Levine, M., Yoder, R., Klineberg, J., Rosenberg, J. The presolution paradox in discrimination learning. *Journal of Experimental Psychology*, 1968, **77**, 602–608.

Lordahl, D. S. An hypothesis approach to sequential predictions of binary events. *Journal of Mathematical Psychology*, 1970, **7**, 339–361.

Luchins, A. A. Mechanization in problem solving: The effect of *Einstellung*. *Psychological Monographs*, 1942, **54** (6, Whole No. 248).

Mandler, G., Cowan, P. A., & Gold, C. Concept learning and probability matching. *Journal of Experimental Psychology*, 1964, **67**, 514–522.

McCulloch, T. L. Comment on the formation of discrimination habits. *Psychological Review*, 1939, **46**, 75–85.

McCulloch, T. L. & Pratt, J. G. A study of the pre-solution period in weight discrimination by white rats. *Journal of Comparative Psychology*, 1934, **18**, 271–290.

Meyers, L. S., Driessen, E., & Halpern, J. Transfer following regular and irregular sequences of events in a guessing situation. *Journal of Experimental Psychology*, 1972, **92**, 182–190.

Millward, R. B. & Spoehr, K. T. The direct measurement of hypothesis-sampling strategies. *Cognitive Psychology*, 1973, **4**, 1–38.

Moore, J. W., & Halpern, J. Three-stimulus two-choice auditory discrimination learning with blank trials. *Journal of Experimental Psychology*, 1967, **73**, 241–246.

Moss, E. M., & Harlow, H. F. The role of reward in discrimination learning in monkeys. *Journal of Comparative Psychology*, 1947, **40**, 333–342.

Neimark, E. D. Effects of type of nonreinforcement and number of alternative responses in two verbal conditioning situations. Unpublished doctoral dissertation, Indiana University, 1953.

Nelson, J. L. Perceptual influences in concept identification. Unpublished doctoral dissertation. State University of New York at Stony Brook, 1971.

Neumann, P. G. Transfer effects of simple and detailed instructions in the presence and absence of pretraining in reversal and nonreversal shifts. *Psychonomic Science*, 1972, **29**, 233–237.

Neussle, W. P. The influence of conceptual tempo on the hypothesis testing behavior of children. Unpublished doctoral dissertation, University of Pittsburgh, 1971.

Oseas, L., & Underwood, B. J. Studies of distributed practice: V. Learning and retention of concepts. *Journal of Experimental Psychology*, 1952, **43**, 143–148.

Osler, S. F., & Kofsky, E. Stimulus uncertainty as a variable in the development of conceptual ability. *Journal of Experimental Child Psychology*, 1965, **2**, 264–279.

Penfield, W. The interpretive cortex. *Science*, 1959, **129**, 1719–1725.

Postman, L., & Bruner, J. S. Perception under stress. *Psychological Review*, 1948, **55**, 314–323.

Postman, L., & Bruner, J. S. Hypothesis and the principle of closure. *Journal of Psychology*, 1952, **33**, 113–125.

Postman, L., & Sassenrath, J. The automatic action of verbal rewards and punishments. *Journal of Genetic Psychology*, 1961, **65**, 109–136.

Reese, H. W. Discrimination learning set in children. In L. P. Lipsitt & C. C. Spiker (Eds), *Advances in child development and behavior*. Vol. I. New York: Academic Press, 1963.

Ress, F. C. The effect of previous sequence problems on simple discrimination learning. Unpublished master's thesis, Indiana University, 1965.

Ress, F. C., & Levine, M. Einstellung during simple discrimination learning. *Psychonomic Science*, 1966, **4**, 77–78.

*Restle, F. A theory of discrimination learning. *Psychological Review*, 1955, **62**, 11–19.

Restle, F. Discrimination of cues in mazes: A resolution of the "place-vs.-response" question. *Psychological Review*, 1957, **64**, 217–228.

Restle, F. Toward a quantitative description of learning set data. *Psychological Review*, 1958, **65**, 77–91.

Restle, F. Additivity of cues and transfer in discrimination of consonant clusters. *Journal of Experimental Psychology*, 1959, **57**, 9–14.   (a)

Restle, F. A survey and classification of learning models. In R. R. Bush & W. K. Estes (Eds), *Studies in mathematical learning theory*. Stanford, California: Stanford University Press, 1959.   (b)

Restle, F. A note on the "hypothesis" theory of discrimination learning. *Psychological Reports*, 1960, **7**, 194.

Restle, F. Statistical methods for a theory of cue learning. *Psychometrika*, 1961, **26**, 291–306.

*Restle, F. The selection of strategies in cue learning. *Psychological Review*, 1962, **69**, 329–343.

Restle, F. Significance of all-or-none learning, *Psychological Bulletin*, 1965, **64**, 313–325.

Restle, F. Grammatical analysis of the prediction of binary events. *Journal of Verbal Learning & Verbal Behavior*, 1967, **6**, 17–25.

Restle, F., & Emmerich, D. Memory in concept identification: Effects of giving several problems concurrently. *Journal of Experimental Psychology*, 1966, **71**, 794–799.

Richard, J-F., Lépine, D., & Rounet, H. Première étude d'un modèle général d'identification de concepts unidimensionnels. Paper presented at the International Congress of Psychology, London, July 1969.

Richter, M. L. Memory, choice, and stimulus sequence in human discrimination learning. Unpublished doctoral dissertation, Indiana University, 1965.

Richter, M. L., & Levine, M. Probability learning and the blank-trials law. *Psychonomic Science*, 1965, **2**, 379–370.

Riopelle, A. J. Transfer suppression and learning sets. *Journal of Comparative & Physiological Psychology*, 1953, **56**, 108–114.

Rock, I. The role of repetition in associative learning. *American Journal of Psychology*, 1957, **70**, 186–193.

Scharlock, D. P. The role of extramaze cues in place and response learning. *Journal of Experimental Psychology*, 1955, **50**, 249–254.

Schrier, A. M. Comparison of two methods of investigating the effect of amount of incentive on performance by monkeys. *Journal of Comparative & Physiological Psychology*, 1958, **51**, 725–731.

Schusterman, R. J. The use of strategies in the decision behavior of children and chimpanzees. *American Psychologist*, 1961, **16**, 424. (Abstract).

Silver, D. S., Saltz, E., & Modigliani, V. Awareness and hypothesis testing in concept and operant learning. *Journal of Experimental Psychology*, 1970, **84**, 198–203.

Skinner, B. F. *The behavior of organisms*. New York: Appleton, 1938.

Skinner, B. F. *Science and human behavior*. New York: Macmillan, 1953.

Skinner, B. F. *Verbal behavior*. New York: Appleton, 1957.

Skinner, B. F. Teaching machines. *Science*, 1958, **128**, 969–977.

Solso, R. L. (Ed.) *Theories in cognitive psychology: The Loyola Symposium*. Potomac, Maryland: Lawrence Erlbaum Associates, 1974.

Spence, J. T. Verbal reinforcement combinations and concept-identification learning: The role of nonreinforcement. *Journal of Experimental Psychology*, 1970, **85**, 321–329.

Spence, K. W. The nature of discrimination learning in animals. *Psychological Review*, 1936, **43**, 427–449.

Spence, K. W. The differential response in animals to stimuli varying within a single dimension. *Psychological Review*, 1937, **44**, 430–444.

Spence, K. W. Solution of multiple choice problems by chimpanzees. *Comparative Psychological Monographs*, 1939, **15**, No. 3, serial no. 75.

Spence, K. W. Continuous versus noncontinuous interpretations of discrimination learning. *Psychological Review*, 1940, **47**, 271–288.

*Spence, K. W. An experimental test of the continuity and non-continuity theories of discrimination learning. *Journal of Experimental Psychology*, 1945, **35**, 253–266.

Spence, K. W. *Behavior theory and conditioning*. New Haven, Connecticut: Yale University Press, 1956.

Spielberger, C. D., & DeNike, L. D. Descriptive behaviorism versus cognitive theory in verbal operant conditioning. *Psychological Review*, 1966, **73**, 306–326.

Spiker, C. C. An extension of Hull-Space discrimination learning theory. *Psychological Review*, 1970, **77**, 495–515.

Stone, C. P. multiple discrimination box and its uses in studying the learning ability of white rats. *Journal of Genetic Psychology*, 1928, **35**, 557–573.

Straughan, J. H. An application of statistical learning theory to an escape learning situation using human subjects. Unpublished doctoral dissertation, Indiana University, 1953.

Sweller, J. Effect of amount of initial training on concept shift problems. *Journal of Experimental Psychology*, 1973, **99**, 134–136.

Tolman, E. C. Purpose and cognition: the determiners of animal learning. *Psychological Review*, 1925, **32**, 285–297.

Trabasso, T. R. Additivity of cues in discrimination learning of letter patterns. *Journal of Experimental Psychology*, 1960, **60**, 83–88.

Trabasso, T. R. Stimulus emphasis and all-or-none learning in concept identification *Journal of Experimental Psychology*, 1963, **65**, 398–406.

Trabasso, T., & Bower, G. H. Presolution dimensional shifts in concept identification: A test of the sampling with replacement axiom in all-or-none models. *Journal of Mathematical Psychology*, 1966, **3**, 163–173.

Trabasso, T., & Bower, G. H. *Attention in learning*. New York: Wiley, 1968.

Troyer, K. & Millward, R. Direct observation of hypothesis-sampling strategies. In Studies in Human Learning, Tech. Rept. No. 6. Brown University.

Underwood, B. J., & Richardson, J. Verbal concept learning as a function of instructions and dominance level. *Journal of Experimental Psychology*, 1956, **51**, 229–238.

Verplanck, W. S. Unaware of where's awareness: Some verbal operants—notates, monents, and notants. *Journal of Personality*, 1962, **30**, 130–158.

Warren, J. M. Additivity of cues in visual pattern discriminations by monkeys. *Journal of Comparative & Physiological Psychology*, 1953, **46**, 484–486.

Warren J. M. Solution of object and positional discriminations by monkeys. *Journal of Comparative & Physiological Psychology*, 1959, **52**, 92–93.

Weir, M. W., & Stevenson, H. W. The effect of verbalization in children's learning as a funtion of chronological age. *Child Development*, 1959, **30**, 173–178.

White, R. M., Jr. Relationship of performance in concept identification problems to type of pretraining problem and response-contingent post-feedback intervals. *Journal of Experimental Psychology*, 1972, **94**, 132–140.

Wickens, T. D. & Millward, R. B. Attribute elimination strategies for concept identification with practiced subjects. *Journal of Mathematical Psychology*, 1971, **8**, 453–480.

Wyckoff, L. B. The role of observing responses in discrimination learning. Part 1. *Psychological Review*, 1952, **59**, 431–442.

Yerkes, R. M. The mental life of monkeys and apes: a study of ideational behavior in man and other animals. *Proceedings of the National Academy of Sciences*, 1916, **2**, 631–633.

Zeaman, D., & House, B. J. An attention theory of retardate discrimination learning. In N. R. Ellis (Ed.), *Handbook of mental deficiency*. New York: McGraw-Hill, 1963.

SUBJECT INDEX

A

Adaptation of cues, *see* Conditioning models
Additivity of cues, 52–53, 127–129
All-or-none learning, 3, 5–15, 103–119,
    131–141, 191–198
  concept tasks, 107, 131–141
  discrimination tasks, 3, 5–15, 191–198
    humans and, 191–198
    rats and, 3, 5–15
  cyclid conditioning, 115 117
  performance functions
    hypothesis sequence, 193, 196
    learning curve, 107, 193, 196
  verbal learning, 103–106, 112–115, 118–119
Attention, 19, 24, 58, 60
  mediating response, 58
  physiological mechanism, 60
  receptor adjustments, 19, 24
Awareness controversy, 60, 255, 266–267

B

Backwards learning curve, *see* Presolution
  performance
Blank-trials probe
  with children, 222, 226–231
  data, 185–186, 192, 195, 199–202, 228–229
  inconsistent patterns, 159, 164–166,
    183–185, 192, 219, 239
    accidental (oops) errors, 183, 185, 192
    null hypothesis, 179, 192
    as residual H, 159, 164–166
    stereotypes, 239
  method, 146–147, 158–161, 182–185, 222,
    226

C

Coding of stimuli
  with imagery, 286, 290
  verbal, 189–190, 285–286, 290
Concept identification, 37–39, 55–57, 61–74,
  76, 106, 121, 130–132, 141, 158–161,
  217, 266, 269–273, 277–278
  tasks
    reception, 56, 63
    selection, 56
    two-vs.-four responses, 38
  types
    conjunctive, 56–57, 61–74, 141, 269–270
    disjunctive, 141, 270
    redundant, 37–39, 217
    simple, 37, 141, 269–271
Conditioning models, 17–19, 33–53, 129
  and adaptation, 37–39, 49–53, 129
  for rats in T-maze, 17–19
  stimulus-sampling theory, 33–43
    matching law, 34
    stimulus variability, 43–47
Continuity-noncontinuity controversy, 19,
  21–31, 104, 108, 140

D

Discrimination tasks
  contingent discrimination, 174–175
  discrimination box, 3, 5–7, 26–27
  eight dimensions, 199–200
  four dimensions, 158, 182–185, 226–228
  learning-set procedure, 80–81
    alternation learning set, 155
    two-trial problems, 154–155

311